GYPSY JAZZ

MICHAEL DREGNI

GYPSY JAZZ

*In Search of Django Reinhardt
and the Soul of Gypsy Swing*

OXFORD
UNIVERSITY PRESS

2008

OXFORD
UNIVERSITY PRESS

Oxford University Press, Inc., publishes works that further
Oxford University's objective of excellence
in research, scholarship, and education.

Oxford   New York
Auckland   Cape Town   Dar es Salaam   Hong Kong   Karachi
Kuala Lumpur   Madrid   Melbourne   Mexico City   Nairobi
New Delhi   Shanghai   Taipei   Toronto

With offices in
Argentina   Austria   Brazil   Chile   Czech Republic   France   Greece
Guatemala   Hungary   Italy   Japan   Poland   Portugal   Singapore
South Korea   Switzerland   Thailand   Turkey   Ukraine   Vietnam

Copyright © 2008 by Oxford University Press, Inc.

Published by Oxford University Press, Inc.
198 Madison Avenue, New York, NY 10016

www.oup.com

Library of Congress Cataloging-in-Publication Data
Dregni, Michael, 1961–
Gypsy jazz : in search of Django Reinhardt and the soul of gypsy swing / Michael Dregni.
p.   cm.
Includes bibliographical references (p.   ), discography (p.   ), and index.
ISBN 978-0-19-531192-1
1. Jazz—France—History and criticism.   2. Romanies—Music—History and criticism.
3. Reinhardt, Django, 1910–1953.   4. Jazz musicians—France.   I. Title.
ML3509.F7D74 2008   781.65089'91497—dc22   2007038061

Lyrics to "Gens du Voyage" copyright © 2004 by Syntax (Christian Windrestein). Reprinted courtesy of
Syntax, with thanks to Laurent Soullier at L'Ouïe Fine Productions. Translation by Michael Dregni as
approved by Syntax.

All interview and text translations throughout this book are by the author, unless otherwise noted.

Portions of Chapter 9 "Dynasty" and Chapter 12 "The Unsung Master of the Gypsy Waltz" previously appeared in *Vintage Guitar* magazine in dramatically different forms. My thanks to Editor Ward
Meeker and *Vintage Guitar* for permission to use them here.

9 8 7 6 5 4 3 2 1
Printed in the United States of America
on acid-free paper

To Tigra

CONTENTS

GYPSY JAZZ FAMILY TREE

THIS BY NO MEANS PURPORTS TO BE a complete list of Gypsy jazz musicians. It's simply a sort of dramatis personæ, an aid to tracing the history of the music. The generations are loosely formed at best, based on when musicians were or are making their strongest statements. I have added musicians' dates of birth and death when known.

Founding Generation 1920s–1950s

Jean "Poulette" Castro
Mattéo Garcia
Auguste "Gusti" Malha
Vétese Guérino (accordionist)
Jean "Django" Reinhardt (1910–1953)
Stéphane Grappelli (violinist) (1908–1997)
Joseph "Nin-Nin" Reinhardt (1912–1982)
Jean-Joseph (aka Pierre) "Baro" Ferret (1908–1976)
Étienne "Sarane" Ferret (1912–1970)
Jean (aka Pierre) "Matelo" Ferret (1918–1989)
Charles-Allain (aka René and Auguste) "Challain" Ferret (1914–1996)
Eugène Vées (1915–1977)
Louis "Vivian" Villerstein (violinist)
Henri Crolla (1920–1960)
Marcel Bianchi (1911–1997)
Joseph Sollero
Joseph Gustave "Tatave" Viseur (accordionist)

Georges "Jo" Privat (accordionist)

Jacques "Montagne" Mailhes (?–1942)

Léo Slab (née Slabiak) (violinist)

Antonio "Tony" Muréna (accordionist)

René "Didi" Duprat

Jacques "Piton" Reinhardt

Henri "Piotto" Limberger (violinist)

Alfred "Latcheben" Grünholz

Eddie "Bamboula" Ferret

Second Generation 1950s–1970s

Jacques "Montagne" Mala (1926–?)

Schnuckenack Reinhardt (violinist) (1921–2006)

Savé Schumacher-Racine

Étienne "Patotte" Bousquet (1925–1998)

Gérard Cardi

Paul "Tchan Tchou" Vidal (1923–1999)

Henri "Lousson" Baumgartner-Reinhardt (1929–1992)

Paul Pata

Maurice "Gros Chien" Ferret (1928–1999)

Joseph "Babagne" Pouville

René "Néné" Mailhes (1935–)

Laro Sollero (1937–2002)

Jean-Jacques "Babik" Reinhardt (1944–2001)

Christian Escoudé (1947–)

Jacquet Mailhes

Jean "Cérani" Mailhes

Chatou Garcia

Mondine Garcia (1926–)

Spatzo Adel

Jozef "Wasso" Grünholz

Francis-Alfred Moerman (1937–)

Third Generation 1970s–1990s

Fapy Lafertin (1950–)

Koen De Cauter (1950–)

Hans'Che Weiss

Louis Faÿs

Titi Winterstein (violinist)

Lulu Reinhardt

Michel "Sarane" Ferret (1948–)
Jean-Jacques "Boulou" Ferré (1951–)
Élié "Élios" Ferré (1956–)
Paul "Challain" Ferret
Jeannot "Titote" Malla
Coco Reinhardt
Samson Reinhardt
Marcel Loeffler (accordionist)
Tchavolo Schmitt (1954–)
Mandino Reinhardt (1955–)
Dorado Schmitt (1957–)
Titi Bamberger
Mito Loeffler
Martin Weiss (violinist)
Zipflo Reinhardt (violinist)
Mike Reinhardt
Didier Roussin (1949–1996)
Dominique Cravic
Patrick Saussois (1954–)

Fourth Generation 1990s–Today

Raphaël Faÿs (1959–)
Biréli Lagrène (1966–)
Isaak "Stochelo" Rosenberg (1968–)
Jacques "Ninine" Garcia (1956–)
Angelo Debarre (1962–)
Rodolphe Raffalli (1959–)
Patrick "Romane" Leguidecoq (1959–)
Moréno Winterstein (1963–)
Macho Winterstein
Stéphane "Tchocolo" Winterstein
Serge Krief (1962–)
Christophe Lartilleux
Florin Nicolescu (violinist)
Lollo Meier
Paulus Shäfer
Jean-Yves Dubanton
Jean-Claude Laudet (accordionist)
Jean-Philippe Watremez (1961–)
Jimmy Rosenberg (1980–)

Sammy Daussat (1972–)

Pierre "Kamlo" Barré

Samson Schmitt (1979–)

Ritary Gaguenetti (1978–)

Joscho Stephan (1979–)

Titi Demeter

Yorgui Loeffler

Dino Mehrstein

Eddy Waeldo

Wawau Adler

Frédéric Belinsky (1974–)

Noé Reinhardt (1979–)

Steeve Laffont

Christian "Syntax" Windrestein

Dallas Baumgartner (1981–)

David Reinhardt (1986–)

Richard Manetti (1986–)

Rocky "Falone" Gresset

Mundine Garcia

Rocky Garcia

Simba Baumgartner

Lévis Adel (1997–)

People say we Gypsies are robbers and thieves—and I agree. We steal everyone's music, and make it Gypsy music!

—Danny Fender, 2007

Music is essential. It's a history, it's a tradition. Music is like a voyage. It's our past, our present, our future, our destiny. We might not have written texts of our history, but it's all in the music. C'est une patromonie.

—Syntax, 2007

GYPSY JAZZ

Music in the Shadows

The Imperfect History of Gypsy Jazz

IDNIGHT, PIGALLE. The red-light district of Paris glows in a nocturnal carnival of neon and incandescent color. It spreads out from place Blanche along rue Fontaine and boulevard de Clichy, the lights a lure to the infamous nightspots down through history— *bals musette* to brothels, Russian cabarets to jazz joints, La Grand Guignol to *centime* peep shows. Pigalle is where Django Reinhardt played his music, known today as Gypsy jazz. From the early 1930s, when the then-unnamed Quintette du Hot Club de France gathered for some of its first jam sessions at the brasserie L'Alsace à Montmartre to Django's own louche nightclub La Roulotte of the World War II years, Pigalle was his base. Then as now, when the clock here strikes twelve, the night has only begun. Drag queens tuck themselves into sequined gowns for the evening's song and dance at Madame Arthur; oystermen shuck shells at Charlot on place de Clichy; B-girls and prostitutes await under halos of red light; the streets and sidewalks are an everlasting parade of hucksters, shell-game artists, bums, lovers, and wandering strangers. And above it all, the neon-lit windmill of the Moulin Rouge never stops turning.

I'm descending La Butte de Montmartre, drawn from the charm of place du Tertre to the glorified grime of Pigalle. Once a rebellious bohemian *ville* on the edge of Paris, Montmartre is now alternately *trop* chic in its penthouse apartments and too quaint in its cute bistros with plastered-on atmosphere. Yet at a typical tourist café atop La Butte, Au Clarion des Chasseurs, today's generation of Gypsies are still playing Django's jazz. The music is good—guitarist Ninine

Garcia, accompanied by Jeannot "Titote" Malla of the venerable Malha clan. But the *bière blanche* is too expensive and too watery. I've come now to Pigalle in search of more music and a late-night *steak au poivre*.

As I drift through the crowd around place de Clichy, I spy the sign. For some reason, it catches my eye down an adjoining street—surprising, as the main *place* is a kaleidoscope of light, whereas this side street stretches away into nothing but darkness. Just a hundred paces into the shadows sits a lone wooden sandwich board on the edge of the sidewalk. No spotlights, no ballyhoo. Just paint on wood, brushed on in the curlicued hyperbole of a lost era: "Cirque Tsigane." An arrow points off down an even murkier, even smaller alley.

There's no reason to follow that arrow. All of the thrills of the modern world are alive around place de Clichy—and who knows what waits down the alley. Still, something in the promise of a Gypsy circus at midnight allures.

I turn off the *place* and walk up the street under the boulevard trees. Away from the hubbub of Pigalle, the world is suddenly silent: You can hear the midnight wind through the branches, and it's dark—too dark. I imagine the metallic click of a switchblade opening in a doorway, my imagination primed from reading too many Simenon *série noire* tales.

Halting in front of the sign, I follow the arrow's direction and look with distrust up the street. Passage Lathuille appears to be one of those French village *rues* transported into the midst of Paris. I've found them in most every arrondissement, forgotten and overlooked. They're cobbled with all the elegance of a drunkard's stumble between buildings lurching and leaning overhead as if they're holding each other upright. Yet there's a light at the end of this passage.

I almost tiptoe up the cobbles, not wanting to disturb the night—or let anyone know I'm approaching. I reach an elbow in the street, and suddenly there's nothing there. The buildings end in a crumble of walls and spilled bricks, a gapped-tooth space in the urban grimace. Where a large corner building once stood there is just a hole in the city. The surrounding edifices reveal their embarrassed backsides, blank walls with neither paint nor windows, all surrounded by a jumbled silhouette of those far-sung Parisian rooftops crowned with chimneys and insectlike television antennae.

Within this hole in the city are parked six Gypsy caravans and their modern-day horses—road-weary, low-riding automobiles. The caravans are not the glorious old wooden *verdines*, as they were affectionately known in Romanès. These are contemporary camper trailers lacking any romance and called simply *campines*. They're all metal and plastic, assembly-line prodigies, yet tired and dusty as well from many miles of travel.

In the center of this Gypsy encampment stands the tent of the Cirque Tsigane. Far from the grand multicolored, multistoried tents of a three-ring circus, this tent is some twenty meters across, made of green, or gray, or black canvas—the night, and time, hides its true colors. The tent is held aloft by wooden poles. A wire of flickering yellow lightbulbs is strung across the facade like a string of pearls dressing up the drabness. The lights sway in the wind to an unheard melody.

I stand as if in an enchantment. Here is a world of wonders hidden within the heart of one of the great modern capitals.

Gypsies throughout the world long survived and thrived as showmen and women. They were known for their trained bears dancing for flea-market crowds, feats of legerdemain in cup-and-ball games, magic shows, circus acts. Others carried movie projectors and a caravan stocked with old, taped-together films that they screened for a few *centimes* in the open-air night on a suitable blank wall in country towns. And Django's parents themselves traveled Europe with the tailgate of their *verdine* converted into a small stage on which his father played music while his mother danced for spare coins in village squares and for market-day *fêtes*. Whether it was making music for eleventh-century Persian princes or Django playing jazz for modern-day kings and queens, many of the Romani became a caste of entertainers. And passage Lathuille is a passage into that world.

Sadly, the show here is over for the night. The string of light bulbs still glows feebly, but the tent is dark, lit only by starshine. There are just a few last lights on in the *campines*, the sound of accordions and guitars and the ringmaster's shrill being recharged for tomorrow.

I hoped to return the next night to see the circus in its glory but instead am forced to catch an airplane and leave Paris behind.

Back in the city six months later, I hurry to passage Lathuille as soon as evening comes. I have money at the ready for a seat under the Cirque Tsigane tent. But turning up avenue de Clichy on this autumn night, I can't seem to find the alleyway. I remembered it being just paces away, and now I wonder if it was off a different street radiating from place de Clichy. Perhaps my sense of direction was skewed. Or maybe I was dreaming it all.

When I finally find passage Lathuille, it doesn't seem nearly as mysterious or dangerous. There's no sign for a Cirque Tsigane, and I have a sad premonition of what I will find. The street now just looks empty and gray. The hole in the city is still there, but it's deserted.

I return to the circus site again a year later, still hoping. The vision of the caravans, the tent, and the string of golden lightbulbs shines brightly in my memory. This time, I find the street, but the hole in the city has been filled.

A new apartment building stands now tall and proud, white and antiseptic, a symptom of the contagious ugliness worming through modern Paris. Not even a hint remains of what once briefly graced this lot.

Gypsy jazz too lives in the holes in history. Like a Romani circus, it's as likely to depart silently for destinations unknown as it is to be documented and recorded. This is a music of joy and sadness and fire that burns brilliantly for a brief moment, and then is gone.

While the genre of Gypsy jazz is enduring, the musicians and their music are evanescent. From the beginning, it was a vagabond music. Gypsy jazz was born on the move, whether it was with Django and his contemporaries such as his brother Joseph Reinhardt, the Ferret dynasty, the Malha and Garcia clans, or the Romani musicians of today. And most of the music is lost forever as soon as the last notes fade away.

Similarly, the history of the earliest days of jazz in New Orleans is largely documented only in salacious rumors and aggrandizing tall tales. Storyville maestros such as Charles "Buddy" Bolden and Freddie Keppard—men who truly *made* the music—never recorded. In the realm of Gypsy jazz, too many musicians were never or rarely recorded either: pioneers such as Jean "Poulette" Castro, Mattéo Garcia, and Auguste "Gusti" Malha; Jacques "Montagne" Mailhes, Jacques "Piton" Reinhardt, Eddie "Bamboula" Ferret, Jean "Memette" Ferret, and probably the sole woman among them, Mano Rena. Even musicians like Pierre Joseph "Baro" Ferret, Étienne "Patotte" Bousquet, and Paul "Tchan Tchou" Vidal, who were all relatively well recorded, left behind just a small trace of their musical abilities considering the grand impact they had on others. And this is music made largely within our lifetimes.

To many who heard this Gypsy jazz as it was first being played, it was merely charming ambience—Gypsy muzak or Romani elevator music. In Pigalle, Montmartre, Montparnasse, and in the *quartiers chaud* of other French cities, Gypsy jazz provided the rhythm to the bump and grind of strippers, softened the rough edges of a squalid nightclub, or at best, was a swinging tune for dancing. In the circuses, music played by Gypsy bands—including Django's—was the dramatic buildup before a trapeze artist swung through the heavens or a clown fell flat on his *derrière*. As that ultimate French snob, Jean-Paul Sartre, infamously decried all jazz, it was throw-away music made to be consumed on the spot, like a lowly banana.

In the early years, only a few bothered to take this outsider jazz seriously. In Paris, their names were Pierre Nourry, Hugues Panassié, and especially Charles

Delaunay, three Frenchman—non-Gypsies—who simply loved jazz. It was Delaunay who largely made Django and kept his career and legacy alive, even after the guitarist's death. And it was Delaunay who recorded everyone from Baro Ferret, Jean "Matelo" Ferret, and Tchan Tchou to Django's second son Babik Reinhardt, as well as providing numerous sessions for numerous Romani jazzmen to earn livings as accompanists. Without Delaunay, who can guess how little of this music would have survived.

There was also the curious effect of Django's star power, which eclipsed the brilliance of too many of his own contemporaries. Django won the press accolades and received the recording contracts; his fellow Gypsy jazzmen often played their music in his shadow. And sometimes, they even aped the master, playing not only his compositions but even growing moustaches and fretting their instruments with just two fingers to mimic Django himself. In the end, their legacy was missed by the spotlight as well.

All of this is a roundabout way of stating that this isn't your typical book of music history as this is not your typical music. Gypsy jazz is still very much alive. Its story lives in today's Romani encampments, flea-market bars, backstreet cafés, and jam sessions at religious pilgrimages, from Paris to Les Saintes-Maries-de-la-Mer, on back roads throughout France and Europe, and even hidden in plain sight in the United States. This book is an account of my own travels in search of this music, and as such, it's pure detective story. Yet I am ultimately and rightly just a bit player; the musicians and the music are the heroes.

Thus, my footnotes rarely follow the status quo of historiography. I cite documents and printed works where they're available. But more often I tell firsthand of campfire conversations, card game chatter, and barroom bull sessions, wild one-upmanship jams and gigs at both Pigalle dives and tony concert halls—as well as a couple of switchblade duels, a fortune-telling and its subsequent fleecing (the only bit of the future I can now guess at for certain), numerous culs-de-sac, a couple of discoveries, and too many *noisettes* and too much *pastis* along the road.

As with the history of the pioneers of mainstream jazz, the Gypsy jazzmen's stories may at times be bloated with bombast and braggadocio, or, on the other hand, half-truth cover-ups to protect the not-so-innocent from the long arm of the gendarmes. There's a French Romanès saying, *Si khohaimo may patshivalo sar o tshatshimo*—There are lies more believable than truth. And there's another Romani saying that's a twist on this: A good tale is truer than the truth. Both of these sayings are especially true when told to a *gadjo*, or non-Gypsy, such as myself. I have done my best to weigh various accounts and separate the legends from the legendary, the lies from the alibis. It's the job of journalists or readers or jazz fans to do their own best to listen closely for the true story or the honest solo.

This may make for imperfect history, but it's all part of the nature—and soul—of Gypsy jazz.

ONE

The Guitar with a Human Voice

In Search of Django Reinhardt

NE MAN, ONE GUITAR, two fingers, six strings, an infinity of notes. This jazz is joy made song. Alive and iridescent, it swings with effortless intensity, transcending the everyday world. Yet it's also infused with a bittersweet spirit, nostalgic, melancholic, something nameless and impossible to articulate in anything but music. Within the melodies and strophes of improvisations resound an emblem of a people. An emblem, and a mystery. Here is the legend of the Romani in music, leading back a millennium, stretching across continents. These melodies are fully modern, yet ancient and ageless.

I don't remember when I first heard of Django Reinhardt, but it seems as though his name at least was always in my musical consciousness. This is of course not true. But on the other hand, I can't remember when I *didn't* know of him. We each discover a music through different routes, sometimes a direct path, sometimes a wandering road. And that same music speaks to each of us with a meaning fresh and new and unique, yet still universal. Every guitarist or fan of guitar music—whether it's country or rock'n'roll, bluegrass or jazz—comes across Django at some early point, often in company with his violinist foil, Stéphane Grappelli. We all may not be able to whistle one of Django's melodies, but we know of him as the Gypsy guitarist of jazz. Django was the Big Bang in the universe of the guitar, one of the pioneers of the guitar as a solo instrument. His story is a musical fairy tale, and who wouldn't be entranced?

Oddly enough, it was the influence of B. B. King that pushed me finally to seek out Django's music. Without question, B. B. seems an unlikely ambassador.

Here was a sharecropper from the Mississippi Delta turned Memphis bluesman, and he was sharing with the world his own fascination for a French-born Gypsy.

B. B. was still Riley King when he first made his own discovery. Even though a handful of Django's recordings were available in the United States on licensed discs, the Quintette du Hot Club de France hadn't hit it big in rural Mississippi. A friend from B. B.'s hometown of Indianola, a fellow music fan and guitar player named Willie Dotson, had been drafted into the U. S. Army during World War II. On leave in liberated Paris, Dotson heard Django play and was fired by his find. As B. B. recounted in his autobiography, "My friend bought some records—those big ol' easy-to-break 78 rpm shellacs—wrapped them up in tissue paper and cloth like they were precious jewels (which they were), and presented them to me when he came home to Mississippi. I couldn't believe what I heard."

What B. B. King heard deserves to be recounted in its entirety. He describes listening to Django's jazz as a musical epiphany. It made clear to him aspects of music theory that had been like foreign words—aspects such as Django's deep appreciation of harmony, a unique and personal sense of phrasing, and a fluency of scales that B. B. now strived to learn from a musical illiterate. And there were technical innovations, things like bent and smeared notes, the full use of the complete twelve-note scale, and a free interchange of modes of the scale, shotgun marriages of the apparently disparate Mixolydian to Phrygian modes that resulted in harmony. Yet beyond all the technicalities, it was the spirit that moved him most. As B. B. remembered with enthusiasm:

> Django was a new world. Him and Grappelli swung like demons. The syncopation got me going, but the beat was just the beginning. It was Django's ideas that lit up my brain. He was light and free and fast as the fastest trumpet, slick as the slickest clarinet, running through chord changes with the skill of a sprinter and the imagination of a poet. He was nimble like a cat. Songs like "Nuages" and "Nocturne" took me far away from my little place in Indianola, transporting me over the ocean to Paris, where people sipped wine in outdoor cafes and soaked in the most romantic jazz the world has ever known. I loved Django because of the joy in his music, the light-hearted feeling and freedom to do whatever he felt. Even if I hadn't been told he was a Gypsy, I might have guessed it. There's wanderlust in Django's guitar, a you-can't-fence-me-in attitude that inspired me. It didn't matter that he was technically a million times better than me. His music fortified an idea I held close to my heart—that the guitar is a voice unlike any other. The guitar is a miracle. Out of the strings and the frets comes this personality—whether a blind black man from Texas or a Gypsy from Belgium—of a unique human being.

When I ran across B. B.'s epistle on Django, I was in turn besotted by Mississippi Delta blues, working to decipher the playing of old-time maestros like Son House and capture at least a faint echo of their intensity with a bottleneck slide on my own suitably battered National Duolian steel-bodied guitar. B. B. King was about as far from Son House or Robert Johnson as the blues could get; while he was raised on the same down-and-dirty juke joint blues, he took the music uptown, at least as far as Beale Street in Memphis, and injected it with a newfound elegance. Yet as B. B. was never too proud to tell the world, much of that beauty he added to the blues was inspired by a French Gypsy's guitar.

It was the late 1980s when B. B. opened my eyes again to Django, but opening my ears to him was to prove more difficult. In those days, simply finding Django's music was a trial of its own. Compact discs had arrived in 1983 in the United States but reissues of classic music lagged behind, and it would still be a decade before I bowed to buying my first CD. LPs by Django were hard to come by: Few labels were bothering to reissue his music on vinyl any more. And collectors fought over his LPs at premium prices in rare record stores—when, that is, another collector was foolish enough to sell off an old Django Reinhardt album in the first place. Many of the vinyl reissues of Django's music were less than perfect. Some producers had notoriously speeded up the already quick-paced music until the band sounded frenetic and the keys shifted tonalities. On other records, song titles were confused. It was tough to find what you wanted, hard to know what you were getting, and difficult to determine if what you got was the real deal.

And so the first time I heard Django play was the old-fashioned way—via an original 78 rpm recording. I remember setting the needle down on a tired platter and then waiting in anticipation. The label stated that this was Django and Stéphane's version of "Limehouse Blues." Recorded on September 30, 1935, Django's Quintette du Hot Club de France included Stéphane's violin backed by bassist Louis Vola and a rhythm guitar section comprising Django's best friend, fellow Gypsy Pierre "Baro" Ferret, and Django's younger brother, Joseph, better known by the affectionate Romani diminutive nickname of Nin-Nin. The tune was a novelty number, although in just over a decade since its composition in 1922 by English songwriter Philip Braham, it had already become a jazz standard. The fast-paced foxtrot evoked London's notorious Limehouse Chinatown in its mock Oriental melody. The song emerged through an opium-hazed ambience, Hollywood stereotypes of mysterious Chinamen and sultry dragon ladies; as the lyrics bemoaned, "Rings on your fingers and tears for your crown, that is the story of old Chinatown." This tidbit of chinoiserie had been a hit for American bandleader Paul Whiteman and His Orchestra, rising to number four on the pop charts. And so now here was a French Gypsy with his guitar imitating American hornmen playing faux Chinese jazz. It was all musical chop suey.

But it wasn't the ethnomusicology that grabbed me. It was simply the music.

As the needle rode the grooves, the Quintette struck up the theme. The *boom-chick boom-chick* of the beat was pounded out by three acoustic guitars, the violin soaring angelically above, the heartbeat of the string bass below. Then Django's guitar impatiently cuts through the theme into a first solo chorus. And the music blossoms. He takes the lead as the rhythm guitars fall back into the famous stride of *la pompe*—that rock-steady Gypsy jazz rhythm known descriptively as "the pump." Django's guitar is sublime and pure, dashing through cascades of elegant arpeggios, playing at once with style and sheer aleatoric abandon. Never before at that time had so much guitar been played by one man for so many. Even now, half a century later and on the other side of the globe, my wife sways to the music as we cook dinner. My teenaged son, the budding punk guitarist, whistles along with the melody. And I never want the song to end. The sheer exuberance of the band often pushes the sonic limits of the era's single-mic monaural recording technology. Django's sound carries echoes of his Romani background in its virtuosity. But there's also something else, something foreign: He has drunk in jazz—a music from another, far-off world—assimilated it wholly, and is now giving it back, glistening with a new, unique brilliance.

As many people during the day swore, Django's guitar speaks with a human voice.

When Django was at his zenith in the 1930s and 1940s, no one termed the music he played "Gypsy jazz." It was simply jazz, played by a Gypsy with a guitar. He learned the music primarily from recordings and only later by playing with many of the early greats—Louis Armstrong, Coleman Hawkins, Duke Ellington, Eddie South. And with the music from those foreign 78s still reverberating in his ears, he was trying to sound as American as he possibly could. Combining his influences, his pioneering use of the guitar, and his individual sensibility, Django created a music of his own. There are few others who single-handedly gave birth to a whole musical genre. And it's a genre that is today continually *recreated*.

Django's first instrument was the violin. He learned the instrument from his father, fingering classic Hungarian, Romanian, and Russian Tziganes tunes, songs like the campfire lament "Les yeux noirs" with its dark, minor-key melody, likely played in a waltz's three-four time as they did in those days. He also learned popular songs of the era, barrel-organ turns, simple one-step dance tunes, and light-opera overtures—anything people at small-town markets, country fairs, or city flea markets might pay to hear.

By the time Django was twelve, he was a professional musician. He was now playing a *banjo-guitare*, a bizarre bastard of a diminutive banjo resonator mated with a dwarf six-string guitar neck. Hired by another Gypsy, Italian Zingaro accordionist Vétese Guérino, their band performed in the underworld dance halls in the backstreets of Paris. The music they played was known as musette, a music as distinctly Parisian as the tango was native to Buenos Aires and jazz, at least at the start, was indigenous to New Orleans. Musette was good-times music, un-reeled for factory workers and shopgirls in the Eldorado of the weekend nights, the low-class ballrooms known as *bals musette*. This was the pop music of the day, most of it composed in cheerful major keys and timed in dancing tempos. Alongside the waltzes, other music was also adopted, but only if it was dance-able: tangos, mazurkas, paso dobles, early cakewalks, and a quick-paced romp known as *la java*.

During the years Django performed in the *bals*, he came upon another new music—American jazz, played across town in the fancy *boîtes du nuit* of Pigalle, Montparnasse, and along Les Champs-Élysées. This early jazz was not particu-larly jazzy, but it was wild and raucous and free, all enlivened by a heartbeat of drums. To Django, it was an awakening.

By the dawn of the 1930s, he was playing his own interpretations of Louis Armstrong's cornet solos on his guitar. On Django's first jazz recording—an August 1934 audition acetate cut at Paris's amateur Publicis Studios—he and his brother Nin-Nin jammed on the Dixieland classic that Dippermouth made famous, "Tiger Rag." Django's guitar playing was alive with dizzying melodic improvisations. Here was a young Romani man—just twenty-four at the time—who had barely been able to scrape together the money to buy a guitar, per-forming a music of a different culture from another world, and playing it in his own campfire style, reborn, recreated, renewed. And so Gypsy jazz was born a wanderer's music, blending influences from a Romani violin and a flamenco gui-tar, the Parisian underworld's accordion, and Louis Armstrong's horn.

From the beginning, Gypsy jazz was a pariah's music. Just as the blues and jazz gave voice to African Americans, this bastardized string jazz allowed another dispossessed people to speak. When Django picked his guitar, his fellow Romani listened. And over the years, his music became a symbol of Gypsy identity.

Django's jazz was a pariah music even within the world of jazz, simply for the instrument on which he performed. Jazz to most musicians and aficionados alike was horn music, piano music. In the 1930s, guitars were rhythm instruments, part of the percussion section plonking out a four-to-the-floor beat; guitars were better suited for parlor-song sing-alongs than for improvising jazz solos. Even finding a guitar suitable for playing jazz was nearly impossible—an instrument loud enough to be heard through the sound and fury of the horns and yet lucid and sonorous in tone. There were certainly others playing jazz on guitar at the time—in particular, Lonnie Johnson and Eddie Lang. But no one took the guitar as far as Django. Thus, he was not only pioneering the music but also pioneering the use of the guitar as a solo instrument. In the Parisian galaxy of artistes and philosophes, of impressionists, Dadaists, surrealists, cubists, existentialists, Django created a completely new being—a guitarist.

While most of Django's sidemen in his Quintette du Hot Club de France were Romani cousins, his soloist foils were all *gadjé*—non-Gypsies. First and foremost, there was the dapper and sophisticated Parisian Stéphane Grappelli, whom Django chose as his duet partner because he played jazz on the Romani's signature instrument, the violin. Then, in Django's Nouveau Quintette during the World War II years, came clarinetists Hubert Rostaing and Gérard Lévêque, doubling during the hot days of swing as Gaul's answer to Benny Goodman. Finally, fired by bebop, Django played alongside saxmen André Ekyan and Hubert Fol, standing in as French Charlie Parkers.

Even in the early years before Gypsy jazz bore its name, Django was not the sole Gypsy guitarist playing jazz. There were the famous *frères* Ferret—Baro, Étienne "Sarane," Jean "Matelo," and their cousin and honorary "fourth brother" Charles-Alain "Challain." The Ferret brothers all accompanied Django in his Quintette at various times, led their own jazz groups, and recorded stunning music in their own images. Django's brother, Nin-Nin, was in demand in Parisian jazz bands, waxing stellar sides with several ensembles. Django was but the brightest star in the heavens of Jazz Age Paris, his brilliance outshining the others in his orbit.

Matelo Ferret once proclaimed that this jazz genre should rightfully be called simply "Django's music," as Django was so instrumental in its creation. Yet Matelo also believed—as he often told his follower, guitarist Francis-Alfred Moerman—that Gypsy jazz would have been born even if Django had never played a note; the elements were all there and waiting, and the other Gypsy jazz guitarists of the 1930s were all similarly inspired. If it hadn't been Django, there was Baro, Sarane, Nin-Nin, Matelo himself.

And yet, the music would never have been the same without Django. Gypsy jazz is largely the legacy of one man.

This music was not christened "Gypsy jazz" until some two decades after Django's death in 1953. In attempting in the 1970s to describe the music's uniqueness, its history and its heritage, Francis-Alfred Moerman first termed it *jazz tsigane*—French for "Gypsy jazz." In later years in France, it also won the misnomers *jazz manouche* (as Django was a Manouche, although many of the other players were Gitan Gypsies) and *jazz gitan* (which, in turn, leaves out its creator). In English, its broad moniker of Gypsy jazz conveniently leaves behind any clan identity.

Today, Gypsy jazz is more popular than ever—among Gypsies and *gadjé* alike. European Romani teach their children to play as soon as they can grip guitars. It's not uncommon at the annual Gypsy pilgrimage to Les Saintes-Maries-de-la-Mer in France's Camargue or the tribute concerts to Django at Samois-sur-Seine to see teenaged Gypsy boys picking their guitars in blurs of virtuosity. Among Romani in the United States, Django's music also inspires generations of guitarists proud of their heritage, from John Adomono to Johnny Guitar to Danny Fender and a new era of young American Gypsies. Django has become a hero for a people with few heroes.

In recent decades, Gypsy jazz has again found fans beyond encampments of Romani caravans. People of all nations listen and hear that human voice within Django's guitar. Here is music with real emotion in a modern age when so much electronic pop music wears a false heart on its sleeve. While today's priapic hits are often not even played on true instruments, in Gypsy jazz the soul of the music can be heard in the wood of the guitars and steel voice of the strings. This is music honest and *real*. Musicians adopt and adapt Django's melodies, copping his licks off CDs just as he himself first learned jazz from Louis Armstrong's 78s. There are now Hot Club bands formed in Django's image in most major cities around the globe, from Parisian cafés to American and Japanese nightclubs to international festivals. Gypsy jazz remains a music born of many roots and a rootlessness. It is music personal to one culture and yet universal to all.

When I heard Django's music, I had to play it, to feel the guitar strings and the notes and the melodies under my own fingers, to make that music myself. Unfortunately, I was in the wrong place at the wrong time. Minneapolis, Minnesota, in the early 1990s was not the epicenter of Gypsy jazz. In fact, at the time Gypsy jazz itself was a little-known commodity anywhere beyond the confines of French Romani encampments. Transcriptions of Django's compositions, let alone insight into his technique, did not exist. And I didn't know anyone playing the music from whom I could crib lessons. So I struck out on my own.

Armed with my elderly blues guitar—a World War II–era Gibson Southerner Jumbo—and a Fender Model 351 medium-weight pick, I sat down next to my turntable and lowered the needle onto a 1937 recording of Django and Stéphane playing "Minor Swing." In the pantheon of Django's tunes, it's a relatively easy song head. Yet when I first attempted to decipher the notes and where and how he played them, it could have been written in Sanskrit. Whistling the melody over and over in my head to lock in on the notes, the music at least transformed itself into French, which I could begin to understand from my elementary school lessons.

Little did I know, however, but I had one of the American LP reissues of Django's greatest hits speeded up to increase the impression of guitar wizardry. The band played "Minor Swing" at a pace few mortals could attain—and especially not this mortal. After hours of playing and re-playing those first two bars, I finally could pick out the melody and translate the simple three-chord structure of the song itself. I've since heard that song played by Django and his Quintette hundreds of times and covered by other bands thousands of times, but I still remember the simple happiness I found in first playing it myself. Of course, due to the speeded-up recording, I had it all wrong. Still, here I was, playing Django with an American guitar using blues barre chords and a regimented down-up picking style all with a rock'n'roll touch. Yet recreating the music with my own fingers was a key to unlocking a first door into Django's world.

Then, on another day, I listen again to Django's original recording, and realize there is an element absent in my playing. Django's jazz has something I can't touch, something I can't even put my finger on. American jazz boasts otherworldly players like Satchmo, rhapsodic ones like Lester Young, and demonic, sold-my-soul musicians like Charlie Parker. Yet their music has at heart a happiness, or at least a faith in the pursuit of happiness. Even when Coleman Hawkins sings a sad song through his sax, his blues is a stoic stance. American blues and jazz exorcised its demons.

Django played jazz as joyful as any. Yet underlying his music, there's an inconsolable Romani sadness in its heart. I can almost hear the voices of all the Gypsies of all the years: those conscripted from their homes in India a century ago to fight the Moslem horde, those left to wander the Gypsy diaspora along the Romani Trail over a millennium, those enslaved in the Balkans by the original Dracula, those exterminated by the SS during *O Porrajmos*—the Great Devouring, as the Romani term their own, near-forgotten Holocaust—and those still today living in hiding on the edges of society, ever-present pariahs. Django could play with virtuosity and make it soulful, jump a swing tune to a racing tempo and fill it with emotion. Listen to his "Swing 42." He composed the song during World War II even while the Nazis were rounding up and exterminating his fellow Romani; the melody came to him one night after dinner as he was playfully scat-singing in his best Dippermouth impression. The song as Django recorded it with his Nouveau Quintette du Hot Club de France in September 1941 may just be the happiest, most transcendent tune ever. But when I play it slow on my guitar, the melody line is transformed like a miracle of legerdemain. The music reveals a secret soul, and I hear all the beautiful sadness deep within.

How did a twelve-year-old Gypsy waif from the slums of Paris, who had to hustle and steal to get his first instrument, inspire the world with the possibilities of the guitar? How did this outsider create the soundtrack to the city of Paris? Why do today's European Gypsies still find meaning in this music almost a century old and teach it to their children when they are first capable of grasping an instrument? Who are these master musicians behind this music, from Django's day to the current worldwide renaissance? And how did Gypsy jazz become *the* cultural emblem—even a religious rite—for a whole people?

There is something enigmatic, something ineffable within this apparently simple and joyful jazz. And so I decide there is nothing else to do but pack up my guitar and set off to Paris in search of clues to the mystery.

TWO | # The Boy with the Banjo
Into a Zigzag Paradise

GYPSY JAZZ WAS BORN in the flea markets of Paris, and it's here that much of the history is found today. Arriving in Paris, I skirt La Tour Eiffel and L'Arc de Triomphe, skip Notre-Dame-de-Paris and the Louvre, and make my way straight for *le marché aux puces*—the market of the fleas—at the Porte de Clignancourt in grimey Saint-Ouen. This is my first destination in seeking traces of the music's history. Here, Django lived much of his life in a caravan, from his childhood on, even during the years when his star ascended. Here, he played his violin and *banjo-guitare*, whether it was around a campfire, in the lost dance halls of the back alleys, or on the streets and café *terrasses* for tossed coins. And here, in 1928 when he was just eighteen, his caravan burned, leaving him near dead. His left, fretting hand was almost destroyed by the flames, forcing him to recreate how he played guitar and setting the stage for his rebirth from the ashes as the world's most famous jazz guitarist.

Coming up out of the darkness of the Porte de Clignancourt *métro* station, this other side of Paris opens before me. At first, I'm blinded by the light. Then the cacophony of sights and rainbow of noises takes shape and form. All around me is the glorious anarchy of *les puces*. This is no longer Paris, no longer even France: It's at once a Moroccan souk, an Arab casbah, a Gambian bazaar, an Eastern European thieves' market, a Gypsy horsetrading fair. And more. The center of Paris is today gentrified and stylish—*bon chic, bon genre*, as the French say—but it's at the expense of the suburbs outside Le Périph, the city's encircling ring road. This is where Paris becomes a Third World realm.

Once upon a time, in Django's day, it was all different, and yet all still the same. The roots of *le marché aux puces de Saint-Ouen* date back to the mid 1800s and the era of Napoléon III, although the wares for sale were, then as now, timeless and ageless. The market blossomed out of the mud each weekend and was named in honor of the fleas that inhabited the upholstery of the old furniture and clothing for sale. There were scores of ragpickers and junksellers— Les Ministres à la Mort, as they were known: the Ministers of the Dead—with wagonloads of bric-à-brac, farmers with fruits and vegetables still breathing the scent of the earth, Gypsies with dancing bears pirouetting to tambourines, costumed monkeys demanding coins for organ grinders, belches of flames from fire-eaters, and the song of a street singer such as that quintessential *parigote*, Edith Piaf, who got her start here as well.

Somehow, little has changed. I smell the wondrous scent of Middle Eastern gyros cooking on spits amid the shill of Africans selling black statues of their gods for mere *centimes*; Romani fortune-tellers read palms while boomboxes cry out like muezzins' calls to prayer translated into voluptuous rai and rap. I uncover paintings by lost masters and the thrones of guillotined monarchs. I pass a stall like a religious shrine devoted to Steve McQueen; another stand full of nothing but buttons in all their myriad varieties like stars and galaxies without end. Pickpockets and prostitutes are on the prowl. I'm offered Marlon Brando's leather jacket and Bob Marley's pirated reggae and Michael Jordan's trainers as well as Corsican switchblades, herbs for sexual prowess, and curses for all purposes. Not even Sacré Cœur is visible from here; the Champs Élysées could be on another planet.

This is where the glories of Paris came to a dead end, today as yesterday. Medieval ramparts once girded the city, and in those times, entrance was through a grand *porte* in one of the ancient *octroi*—the customs barriers—guarded by soldiers. Within lived the good citizens of Paris. Without was a vast nether region known with a hint of menace as *La Zone*. Outside the City of Light, this was a city of blight. It was in *La Zone* that Paris's cesspool cleaners dumped their waste each night, and where the human refuse of the city found refuge. This was not the Paris of boulevards, monuments, and cathedrals. Instead, *bidonvilles*— shantytowns—crowded the city's entrances like beggars holding out their hands for offerings. And this was a true Court of Miracles as well, where the robbers and their fences reveled in their wealth, where *les pilons*—the "wooden-legged" beggars—were tranformed back to health under cover of darkness. The inhabitants of *La Zone* were cursed with spite by Parisians as *les zonards*. And many feared the Gypsies as the worst vermin among them.

Django's family lived here on the doorsteps of Paris. The Manouche and Gitans parked their caravans in *La Zone* where they could find streamwater along the lost second river of Paris, La Bièvre. Django grew up amongst his clan at favored campsites in *La Zone* near their livelihoods in the flea markets. They moved between encampments outside the Porte de Choisy or Porte d'Italie on the southeastern side of the capital neighboring the Kremlin-Bicêtre flea market and the horse-trading market in the Vaugirard galleries. Porte de Montreuil and its never-ending thieves' market was to the east, Porte de Clignancourt to the north.

In Django's day, the unsung poet of this unsung world was Serge, the *nom de plume* of Maurice de Féaudierre. Serge was a *gadjo* who traveled France and Spain with Django's people—the Gypsy circuses and vagabond flamenco fandangos. He celebrated *La Zone* and *les marchés aux puces* in his 1963 remembrance of things past, *La grande histoire des bohémiens*:

> *La Zone* is a zigzag paradise on wheels of lace-curtained Gypsy caravans filled with hidden treasures of gold and silver. . . . In the center is the flea market, downtrodden in the rain, a marketplace selling past wreckage and miseries. . . . Then, brutal and sordid and yet enchanting, bursts forth the plaintive song of *La Zone* where enchantement is alive in the rot: "La valse des puces"—the waltz of the flea markets—offers up its heavy heart. At night, five hundred *roulottes* glow like oriental palaces and the Gypsies gather around immense blazing infernos and dance alongside the flames while the music of several bands rings out. . . . Between the interplay of the shadows and the fires, everything takes on fantastic proportions. . . . It is the camp of a thousand and one surprises. . . . Mustachioed musicians attack a plaintive air with their guitars while a nightingale sings on a nest of brambles. Where are we? . . . Far, far away, on a lost road of another world.

Even today this other world endures. I make may way through the Clignan-court markets to the north where Romani encampments hang on. Near the Stade de France—that modernistic soccer stadium like a behemoth from outer space—a pathetic handful of Gypsy caravans huddle in a triangle of unused land beneath a highway and the shaking embankment of the railroad tracks. Roofs and walls of discarded plywood connect the trailers like expansion rooms; scraps of rugs carpet the mud pathways. A bonfire of burning junk emits a noxious black cloud in the center of this little *ville*, a scrum of Romani standing around it, joking and laughing. A little further on, in Le Bourget, a vast no-man's land has become a nomads' land. This is a giant's step in upward mobility. Modern campers are scattered over the hard-packed dirt field, a satellite dish crowning each rooftop. Around the edges of the lot, rags and junk that even the scavengers don't want litter the ditches that double as latrines. *La Zone* lives on in scars and scabs that refuse to heal.

Back in the heart of *le marché aux puces* there remains a venerable Gypsy bar, La Chope des Puces—the Beer Mug of the Flea Market. I come down rue des

Rosiers—the main street of *les puces*—and find the bar just around the corner and mere footsteps away from where Django parked his caravan, back in 1928. La Chope is an oasis of peace amidst the markets. It's also an oasis against time: Opening the door and walking inside, I could just as easily be stepping back into a bar in the 1920s, so little has changed. The glass door with its creaking doorhandle still needing oiling, the lace curtains allowing in a lazy afternoon sun, the black-and-white tiled floor, the menu written on a scarred chalkboard, a *café* machine and beer tap that are always flowing, even the tin signs for Byrrh are all remnants of old Paris. And inside, during every afternoon of every weekend of every year for as long as anyone can remember, two Romani guitarists have been pounding out the rhythm to Django's melodies. They play on old jazz guitars that look like the short end of a long-ago horse trade in the flea market. The two Gypsy musicians are a father-and-son duet. Mondine Garcia is the elder, always wearing a brimmed cap and flannel shirt, rarely smiling: he takes this music seriously as he's played it his whole life. His fingers move across the pitted fretboard of his Favino "Enrico Macias" guitar with its equally archaic Stimer pickup held in place by swathes of packing tape. These days, his son, Ninine, has taken over playing the solos. Ninine's jovial, always grinning, his smile re-sounding in his improvisations. He began playing on an elderly Busato jazz guitar from the 1950s, the top scratched and caved in, the bridge held up by a broken-off matchstick. But these days, with a CD to his name and his growing renown bringing him concert offers on the other side of Paris, he plays a new archtop American Epiphone electric guitar, its gleaming lacquered finish and nickel-plated pickups a modern anomaly in La Chope. Yet the song remains the same—the jangling guitar chords, the minor-key tune at once happy and heart-broken, the toasts of beer glasses when the song ends from the bar's Romani regulars as well as tourists now from around the globe.

Django was born in a caravan at a crossroads in the dead of winter. His family traveled with the seasons, steering their horse to the Midi in springtime for the lucrative tourist season. When the lavender fields faded in autumn, they packed up and headed north to weather the winter in Belgium. Their habitual ren-dezvous was alongside the Flache ôs Coûrbôs, a pond (*flache* in the local dialect) haunted by a coven of ravens (*coûrbôs*). This pond awaited them outside the *ville* of Liberchies in the southwestern Hainaut region. Here, the family made camp. And here, on the frigid night of January 23, 1910, Django came into the world.

He was christened Jean Reinhardt, a proper surname and family name as required by law. This was the name by which the police, small-town bureaucrats, and border officials would know him, the name he was baptized with three days later in the church of Saint-Pierre-de-Liberchies. But among his fellow Romani he would never be called Jean. His mother and father also gave him a Gypsy name—Django—and it was by this name alone that he was known throughout life. Most Romani children were named after animal totems, such as Bero (bear) or Niglo (hedgehog) for boys; or flowers, like Fayola (Violet), for girls. "Django" was an extraordinary name even within the Romani encampments. It was Romanès for "I awake," a direct and strong statement. And it was a name of which Django grew proud as it bore a sense of destiny and fate.

Django's father was Jean-Eugène Weiss, a man of many skills, all necessary for survival on the road. Basket maker, horse trader, repairman, juggler, *prestidigitateur*, and above all, musician adept with violin, cymbalom, guitar. At times he carried an upright piano in his family's caravan on their travels. He sawed off the caravan's rear roof and covered it in canvas like a traveling theater stage in miniature. Rolling back the curtain, he played his music at country fairs, small-town market days, and big-city flea markets for the spare coins of the crowds.

Django's mother was Laurence Reinhardt. She was better known among the Romani as Négros—Spanish for "black," in honor of her dark, ravishing beauty. And she was introduced to *gadjé* audiences as *La Belle* Laurence when she danced to her husband's music.

The family's home was their caravan, a box on wheels pulled along by a single horse. Caravans were called in the Romanès of the time a *vurdon* or *verdine*, and known in French as *une roulotte*. Within, a caravan measured some seven feet wide by fourteen feet long and just seven feet high. The family carried everything they needed wherever they traveled—clothes and quilts; pots, pans, and food; tackle and feed for their horse; musical instruments; and their own religious effigies and devotions.

I too lived in Belgium for several years when I was a child, and can't begin to imagine how Django's family survived winters there camped in caravans. We had the benefit of a house, but even then, from autumn until spring, there was always a deep, wet chill seeping into our world. The sun was just a distant memory from summer months past. In its place came pure, undiluted, absolute gray. Rain blew down on icy winds from the Atlantic, picking up speed across the flat plains of France and Belgium, blowing at a slant to soak you to the bone, or in a slow, steady drizzle, waterlogging your soul. And on those rare days when it wasn't raining, the world was veiled in fog that often lasted from dawn to dusk. And when it was nighttime, the fog probably stayed on—who could know?

Looking back at my own childhood, I seem always to have known something of Gypsies. And yet most all of this knowledge was a farce. Romani haunted fairy tales read at bedtime, nefarious "others" plotting your demise, leading good children astray or stealing them away from their happy homes. Later, there was Caravaggio's Gypsy fortune-teller, reading your palm while picking your pocket. The romantic Carmen of Bizet and the silly rock'n'roll romanticism of Jimi Hendrix's Band of Gypsies. Then came movies. As a youth, the most memorable "Gypsy" to me was Bela Lugosi bringing the maleficent curse of the werewolf to the innocent in *The Wolfman*. And finally, literature. The evil heart of Victor Hugo's hunchback of Notre Dame, Quasimodo, being explained by his being a Gypsy while the purity of the perceived Romani girl Esmeralda is unveiled as she was a French child stolen by Gypsies and brought up to do bad. And whereas Virginia Woolf turned up her Bloomsbury nose at the Romani as savages, D. H. Lawrence saw them instead as *noble* savages. Throughout, Gypsies have been held up by *gadjé* as metaphors for freedom, thievery, or mysticism: they're cast as free spirits, happy wanderers, children of the wind; chicken-stealers and boogiemen; soothsayers and thaumaturges. It's easy to romanticize, easier still to vilify. But it's vastly more difficult to understand. Spanish poet Federico García Lorca wisely summed up Gypsies in both fact and fiction, describing them as half bronze, half dream. Most any mention of the Romani came with a stern warning.

And what better way to instill curiousity.

While living in London as a child, I remember a scrum of Gypsies ringing our doorbell one day in 1971. They were ragpickers, seeking donations. My mother let them in. One of them requested to use the bathroom and another asked for a glass of water. While my mother's back was turned, the Romani spread out through our house. My mother tried to round them up and direct them to the water closet while also shooing us kids upstairs and out of their way. Still, we listened from the stairway. When they were finally ushered back out the door, I was left at home, wondering what journeys they might have taken me on.

During my family's own travels—family vacations in station wagons—we often came across Romani parked alongside the road. Antiquated wooden caravans in Portugal; modern camping trailers in Italy, the Netherlands, or Wisconsin. These encampments were alive with color and excitement, cook-fires and clotheslines and foraging horses, while we rode by enclosed in our automobile.

Even in the 1980s while I was working for a newspaper in small-town Minnesota, I remember a somnolent Saturday afternoon in the newsroom listening in with one ear to our police-radio scanner, the one-stop source of all "news." Through the static, the police dispatcher from the neighboring county warned in a rare worried voice that a convoy of Gypsies was rolling by. He advised his fellow officers in our good county to meet them at the border and chauffeur them along, making certain they didn't stop for anything. Anti-Semitism and racism in general is despised today, but hatred of Gypsies is still in vogue the world over.

The history of such fear is as ancient as the Romani themselves.

While non-Gypsies have their fairy tales telling of Gypsy legend, there are few histories of the Romani written by Romani. One of the best is Ian Hancock's *We Are the Romani People*. Hancock is a busy man, harried almost. Born in England, he's part of the Benczi Imre Romani family. His ancestors escaped Hungary in the late nineteenth century, eventually moving on to the British Isles. Hancock earned a Ph.D. at the University of London. These days, when I speak with him, he's a professor of Romani studies at the University of Texas in Austin and director of the Romani Archives and Documentation Center. In 1998, President Bill Clinton appointed him to represent the Romani on the United States Holocaust Memorial Council. Throughout, in his prolific output of journal articles and books as well as in news interviews and everyday conversation, he focuses as much of his energy on dispelling myths as on telling the Romani's side of the story.

The Romani's journey is a long one, counted in centuries and countless miles. The Romani Trail began in India, where an army of lower-caste people was conscripted in A.D. 1001 to battle Muslim invaders. The wars lasted three decades, after which many of these Indians migrated on to the west: They knew what was to the east, so why not strike out for the unknown? From Byzantium, the trail diverged. Some moved south through Egypt and eventually across North Africa. Others continued north into Russia and Eastern Europe; they were first chronicled in Germany in the year 1407, in France by 1418, and as far as Spain by 1425.

Proclaiming themselves Egyptian royalty to assuage the Europeans, these dark-skinned wanderers became known by the bastardized variation of "Egyptians" as "Gypsies." Some were also variously called "Tziganes," a Byzantine term for animal trainers and traders, one of their common livelihoods; as "Sinti" since they believed themselves to have begun their journey from along the Indian Sind River; or as "Manouche" from the Romanès *manus* and the Sanskrit *manusa*, meaning "true man." And they've also been kown as Cigani, Cingano, Cikan, Cingene, Tsingani, Zigeuner, Sipsiwn, Yiftos, and more. Many today prefer "Romani" or "Roma," a name derived from their own word for "human," and adopted as the offical form of reference at the First World Romani Congress, held in London in 1971. Yet most Romani I know still call themselves simply "Gypsies." And proudly so.

Gypsies did not travel of their own will. Forced into an army, they left any homeland far behind. As they wandered from Persia to Africa to Europe, they were viewed as scourge. Arriving in the Balkans, they were enslaved or expelled.

The first recorded sales of Romani slaves in Romania was chronicled in 1385. By 1445, Prince Vlad Tepes III of Wallachia—inspiration for the legendary vampire Dracula—enslaved some 12,000 persons from Bulgaria "who looked like Egyptians." Gypsy slavery in the Balkans continued over the next five centuries.

Popular folklore long held that Gypsies willingly wrought the nails to crucify Jesus on the cross, which was enough to curse them forever. Yet the Romani still today tell their own version of this legend with a twist that casts them as both victims and heroes: Four, not three, nails were originally smithed for the crucifixion. After the first three were pounded through Jesus' feet and hands, a Gypsy stole away the fourth nail destined for his heart. The Gypsy saved Jesus this agony but was forever after labeled a "thief" and kept on the run.

The first Romani likely came to Paris on August 17, 1427; we know the day because their colorful arrival caused such a commotion that it was written about in detail by the anonymous bourgeois who penned the early *Journal d'un bourgeois de Paris*. These Romani gave a convoluted account of their background, but promised that they too were good Christians terrorized, exterminated, and hunted by Moslems and Saracens. Upon visiting the Pope, they were given the penance of traveling the world for seven years without ever sleeping in a bed— while also carrying papal orders that every bishop must pay them ten thousand livres traveling money. Or so they said. They were not allowed within Paris— like Django's family, they were forced to camp outside the fortified walls, then at La Chapelle–Saint-Denis. But they quickly won a spot in the city's dark imagination. The bourgeois described their grip on Paris:

> Almost all of them have both their ears pierced and wear a silver ring or two in each ear, saying that this was a sign of nobility in their country. The men were very dark, with curly hair; the women were the darkest and ugliest you've ever see, with scarred faces and hair as black as a horse's tail. They wore no dresses but ancient, coarse bits of blankets tied around their shoulders by a string; under this they had nothing but a poor smock or shift. Sadly, they were the poorest creatures ever seen in France in all of human history. And yet in spite of their poverty, they had sorceresses amongst them who looked into people's hands and told them of their past or their future. They brought contention into many marriages, because they would say to the husband, "Your wife's cuckolding you," or to the wife, "Your husband's deceiving you." And what's worse, these creatures contrived—either by magical or black arts, or the help of Hell, or their own cunning—to make money flow out of the people's purses and into their own.

In this first description of Gypsies in France, all the superstitions and suppositions of today can be seen in first blush.

Gustave Flaubert delved deeper into this instant fear inspired by Romani. In a letter to fellow writer George Sand, Flaubert mused on his visit to a Gypsy camp outside Rouen: "They excite the *hatred* of the bourgeois even though inoffensive as sheep . . . that hatred is linked to something deep and complex; it is found in all orderly people. It is the hatred that they feel for the bedouin, the heretic, the philosopher, the solitary, the poet, and there is fear in that hatred."

The earliest traces of the Reinhardt clan are also swathed in fear and loathing. Dating back to the 1700s, police records note them traveling the Rhine River valley, through the forests of the duchy of Swabia, and into Switzerland. Three generations of Reinhardts led a dreaded bandit gang terrorizing their namesake Rhineland. Antoine-Alexandre Reinhardt—known and feared as Antoine de la Grave—marauded the region before being captured and executed in Giessen in 1726. His grandson Jacob, better known by his *nom de bandit* as Hannikel, bested even Antoine's reputation. He ruthlessly raided the towns of the law-abiding citizenry before retreating into the shadows of the Black Forest. Yet these Reinhardt outlaws were no saintly Robin Hoods, nor even popular desperados like Billy the Kid or Ivanhoe "Rhyging" Martin—except perhaps among their own clan. Hannikel too ended his days hanged by the neck alongside his brother Wenzel at Sulz in 1787.

Family lore recalled that Django's grandparents fled Bavaria during the Franco-Prussian war of 1870. They wandered westward, eventually ending up near Strasbourg. The regions of Alsace, Lorraine, and the Rhineland with Strasbourg at its center, drew Romani for as long as anyone today can remember. This was a natural passage between the Black Forest and the Alps, Jura, and Vosges mountain ranges. It was suitable as both a marketplace for horse trading and as a hideout.

While Europeans prided themselves on not having India's social castes, they did have a place for Gypsies—outcasts. Laws were passed in most European countries to rid them of the perceived Gypsy menace. Soon after Romani were first chronicled in France, in 1418, expulsion orders followed, in 1427. A 1560 decree bound any remaining Gypsies to a lifetime pulling oars in the French Navy's galleys. In 1682, Louis XIV sentenced Romani men rounded up to serve as slaves in perpetuity; the women were to be flogged, then banished from the kingdom. France later deported Gypsies to Africa's Mahgreb, Senegal, and Gambia as well as to Louisiana in the New World. Enslaved, expelled, or chased from city to city, the Romani became nomadic of necessity rather than desire. And they were forced to keep on the move to retain their freedom and their way of life, traveling onward in an exodus with no destination and no end. Wherever they traveled, they carried what mattered with them: Always ready for the road, their whole lives were portable—their customs, trades, dance, wealth, music, even a purely verbal language. Thus, their footsteps and their caravans' tracks were blown over as soon as they passed by, leaving their history unwritten and much of their music unrecorded.

By the time of Django's birth in 1910, his people had been on the road for almost a millennium.

A great journey to new horizons. An uncountable fortune in silver and gold. A soulmate to mend a broken heart. A great destiny. Health. Happiness. All of this and more I am promised.

It is there in the palm of my hand, the Romani woman tells me. I am sitting innocently enough having lunch on the *terrasse* of a café in Paris's place du Marché Sainte-Catherine when she descends on me and makes her pitch: "*Lire les lignes de la main?* Read the lines in your hand?" And, little did I know, I am soon to discover firsthand the magical Romani art of making money flow out of people's purses, as the long-ago bourgeois of Paris described it.

The Romani fortuneteller's *nom de la rue* is Poupée—Doll—as I later learn after seeing her all about the city, a fixture of Paris. A tall, slender, stately Gypsy woman of maybe fifty, she wears a dress printed with a glorious summer day's worth of flower blossoms. Over this, she has a full fur coat of some unknown pelt, her feet teetering in tall and extremely red high heels. A rainbow of a scarf covers her head. From her ears, wrists, and neck hang rings and bangles of gold. Her smile is warm and her face kindly, although a bit weary: Walking the *pavé* of Paris all day in heels, tirelessly catching the sleeves of passersby on the sidewalks, and looking into a hundred futures, good and bad, happy and painful, who wouldn't be tired?

So of course I give in. She pulls a chair away from a neighboring table and sits down knee to knee with me. Her hand on mine is dry and coarse. She follows the lines across my palm with her index finger as if reading an ancient and wondrous road map, then gasps a perfect, "*Aaah!*"

And naturally, now I need to know all.

Chiromancy—the art of reading palms—is older than the ages. Originating in India, it spread with Islam to China, to Egypt, to Europe. Aristotle studied it, Julius Caesar swore by it, Napoléon believed in it. Even Hitler is said to have listened. People's horoscopes lie in their hands, each finger representing a god—Mercury, Apollo, Saturn, Jupiter. There is the fate line, heart line, head line, and life line; their length, width, depth, and number of branches tell everything. The medieval Church, worried that it was losing its control over its followers' futures, warned against the Romani fortune-tellers: Gypsies were agents of the great Prince of Darkness. The Gypsy fortune-tellers foresaw this too. *The Devil fears the sign of the cross and the power of silver,* they whispered conspiratorily. *Cross my palm with silver and you will be safe from him.* The fortune-teller kept the silver in trade for telling the fortune.

Everyone is of course curious about what the future holds. And although it might or might not be just a masquerade, many feel Gypsies are innately intuitive in telling their fortunes. Through time, their powers of augury have been deemed magical and mysterious. Some *gadjé* trusted in it with all their hearts. Other scoffed. Among the Romani themselves, people may or may not believe—but one thing they could foresee is the money to be earned from telling fortunes.

The Romani also quickly came to understand the art of mystery. Whether it was tarot cards, crystal balls, or palmistry, Gypsies were alchemists turning the lead of life into the gold of promise. A Romani fortune-teller held a man's hand, hinted of great wealth, and felt his pulse. She studied the lines in a woman's palm, spoke of romance, and looked her in the eye. The fortune-teller gauged the reaction to the bits of information offered like a carrot on a stick before a donkey. The twitch of an eye, the arch of an eyebrow, the twist of the corner of lips into a smile or a frown told her what the *gadjé* wanted their future to hold. And so the fortune-tellers cast their spells, all with a hint of mystery that kept customers coming back for more. As the master French magician Robert-Houdin swore, it's easier to dupe a clever person than an ignorant one.

Now, Poupée is determining my fate. In the creases created by the anatomical formation of my metacarpal bones, ligamentum carpi, volar arches, and adductor pollicis, she sees my rise—or demise. Following the line from the thenar eminence to the metacarpophalangeal joint, she reads my future:

"You have a long life line and you will live to be 112," she begins.

That sounds okay, although 112 is longer than I wish to live.

"You are *très artistique.*"

Well, I suppose I like to think so.

"There is turmoil in your life now . . ." she says, and pauses with an eyebrow arched in drama: "but everything will work out for you in the next three months just the way you want."

No particular turmoil, but having everything work out just right—and on such a quick schedule—is fine by me.

"Great happiness in love will come to you soon."

Too late; love has already arrived.

"Many travels. Much happiness."

I can live with all that. Although I bet she tells it to everyone.

"And you have a great heart!"

Well, perhaps she *is* clairvoyant.

Then she reaches inside her fur coat and takes something between her thumb and index finger with great and fine theater. She places it in my palm, closing my hand over it. I can feel it there, small yet warm, though she won't let me look at it.

"This is a special bead, from Les Saintes-Maries-de-la-Mer, from our pilgrimage. It is a gift that will bring you good fortune."

And then she demands one hundred euros.

I now look at that bead: Good fortune it may hold, but it appears like your typical Made-in-China plastic bead, albeit with pretty blue and white stripes. I think I know who has the good fortune here—and where I fall in Robert-Houdin's dictum.

When I hesitate concerning the hundred euros, the warmth in her smile disappears and her eyes go hard. And yes, superstition or not, I fear some sort of Gypsy curse, which she's no doubt also banking on.

We barter and bargain over my future. When I finally escape, I'm twenty euros poorer, but the owner of a magical plastic bead.

In Paris, on any given day, yesterday as today, a Gypsy somewhere is making music.

It's a sun-drenched Sunday in a glorious March, and I'm on my way via the *métro* to the down-and-dirty *marché aux puces* at Montreuil—half flea circus, half thieves' market, here one can buy anything and everything from vermin-chewed rags to primped and pimped automobiles. Awaiting the next train going the opposite direction are members of a Romani *orkestar*, the style of Eastern European brass band that once led the charge into battle. They're dressed in Hungarian field clothes—baggy slacks and small-brimmed fedoras—and their farming hands hold tubas and clarinets and trombones that are impossibly battered. Jumping into a train headed west, I pass in front of the Musée d'Orsay where two Gypsy youths bearing the first hints of Djangoesque moustaches strum their well-traveled jazz guitars with vigor and flair to win the tourists' hearts and spare change. At the next subway stop, a Romani—likely one of the new wave of immigrants escaping Eastern Europe—enters the car carrying an East German accordion. His squeezebox lacks a multitude of buttons like a gapemouthed smile. He pumps and saws away at a musette waltz, playing by rote and passing a cup for coins with equal emotion.

The scene was likely similar in Django's day.

It's of course ridiculous to think the Romani as a people are inherently more musical than the rest of us. And yet many Gypsies seem to bear a deeper appreciation—and belief in the importance—of music. Bolstered by tradition, the elders have a willingness and patience to teach their children to play. The children, not pushed to attend the outside world's idea of schooling, often have endless hours to practice. To many Romani, music is their history, their legends, their culture.

Django's father played music with his seven brothers in a loose-knit band. They often performed in a Clignancourt dance hall called Chez Clodoche bordering the flea market, as well as at stylish hotels in Paris and along the Côte d'Azur, in open-air dancing *guinguettes* on the banks of the River Marne outside the capital at La Varenne–Saint-Hilaire, and anywhere else there were a few *sous* to pay for music—weddings for the rich and famous, birth celebrations or funerals for the poor and nameless. Romani such as Django's family were a caste of entertainers. Like human jukeboxes, they knew snatches of every song for every audience. Django's sister Sara "Tsanga" Reinhardt remembered their father's repertoire including good-time drinking sing-alongs, light opera airs, popular tunes, barrel-organ grinds, early one-steps, Chopin waltzes, and melancholy Eastern European Tziganes melodies. For virtuosic showpieces, they performed the dazzling *Czardas* of Vittorio Monti and *Sérènade* of Frantisek Drdla.

Django too began on violin. The Romani were enamored with the instrument: The violin was ideal for their music due to its portability—and it was blessed with a dark voice that spoke to the Gypsies. In the 1910s and 1920s, Romani violinists were at a peak of fame throughout Europe. Jean Goulesco was the celebrated violinist of the Russian Tsar, his virtuosic violin trickery of dizzying pizzicati evoking the calls of cuckoos and nightingales that even charmed the Tsar's éminence gris, Rasputin. Georges Boulanger, the French stage name of Romanian Ghita Bulencea, was renowned for his rapturous tone. His 1910s version of "Les yeux noirs" was likely the earliest recording of the Russian Romani anthem, played like an epic narrative telling the joys and woes of all Gypsy history.

Django was probably six or seven when he began, learning from his father as well as his uncle Guiligou, a star on violin, banjo, and guitar. I can imagine Django learning violin around his family's campfire somewhere on the road, picking up the instrument in the call-and-response teaching style common among Romani. His father played the tune on his own violin, painstakingly displaying the fingerings and patiently playing the song over until Django knew it by heart. Django's sister remembered him first performing with his father's ensemble when he was between the ages of seven and twelve.

By then, a new, modern musical instrument caught Django's fancy. The banjo arrived in France from the United States in the hands of African-American minstrels and soon was providing a raucous rhythm to *les années folles*—the Crazy

Years of the Jazz Age. Django learned to play from a cousin, Gabriel, and his mother soon bought him his own banjo after selling some homemade jewelery in *les puces*. Now, Django and his younger brother Joseph "Nin-Nin" Reinhardt, born on March 1, 1912, set forth each morning from their caravan into the city. They played melodies for laborers on lunch break in Ménilmontant as well as serenading the prodigal expatriates on the café *terrasses* of chic Montparnasse. And on the weekends, Django and Joseph were back home performing amid the chaos of the flea markets.

There were other Gypsy musicians whom the young Django strived to emulate. Jean "Poulette" Castro was revered as *Le Grand Gitan* among his fellow Romani. His surname denotes a Spanish Gitan lineage, and in the few surviving photographs, Poulette is swarthy and handsome, the ideal of a Gypsy musican for Paris audiences of the day. And he was indeed a wizard of the strings. Poulette was a rarity among the Romani: he could read musical notation, earning him a vaunted seat in the established pit orchestra at the city's Théâtre du Châtelet accompanying theatrical presentations and opera divas alike. Among the Romani, he was renowned as an encyclopedia of Gypsy music. Having traveled the continent as well as to England, he boasted a vast repertoire of Tziganes melodies, flamenco songs, dance tunes, and waltzes of all nations under his fingers.

Poulette was a teacher of a fast-developing new style of guitar playing blending flamenco influences with a more-modern fashion of holding and picking the instrument. He taught young Gypsy players like Django to use banjos and steel-string guitars plucked with plectrums, their picking hands kept off the soundboard, loose and free for fast playing action. Poulette favored a then-popular style of Italian guitar featuring fifteen strings. He also used a large-bodied guitar crafted by luthier Julián Gómez Rámirez, a Spanish guitar maker who immigrated from Madrid to found an *atelier* in Paris. This Rámirez guitar featured six standard strings supplemented by three sympathetic bass strings tuned *à l'italienne* to E, A, and D, ideal for playing the *valses* in vogue. It was Poulette's style that Django would take into the future.

For all his influence, however, recordings of Poulette remain rarities. Along with his brother Laro Castro and two other Gitan musicians, Coco and Serrani Garcia, Poulette formed the quaintly named Quatuor à Plectre—the Plectrum Quartet, the moniker displaying the novelty of their style. Together, they backed *chanteuse* Rosita Barrios, who sang a variety of gay Spanish songs then popular in Paris with romantic and evocative titles such as "Tierra de España" and "Araga Corazon." The all-string ensemble featured guitars, banjos, mandolins, and bandurias doubling up on the melody lines to create a multilayered sound highlighted by trills and tremolos. Yet the import of Poulette's influence comes through best on another 78 disc of his namesake melody, "Valse Poulette."

This record exists today thanks to those same flea markets where Gypsy jazz was born. The disc's survival and discovery were pure serendipity. English expatriate jazz fan Tony Baldwin stumbled across the only known copy of "Valse Poulette" in a *marché aux puces* in Nîmes recently. Yet the 78 was barely playable. The disc was both cracked and warped—a double strike that would discourage most aficionados from even bothering to read the label. But Baldwin took the recording back to his studio and patiently and exactingly restored the track. "I managed to get a successful trace by slowing it down to around half speed, repairing the cracks, and then speeding it back up to pitch digitally," he explains to me.

The recording was issued on the obscure French Sonnabel label, and mistitled "Valse Paulette." Castro is credited as the composer—noted as "Jean Castres," likely a French transliteration of his surname—and the band is listed as Orchestre Guitares et Banduria des Frères Castro, likely including Poulette on guitare, Laro Castro on banduria, and perhaps the young Baro Ferret on second guitar, as he often accompanied Poulette in these years. Happily, Sonnabel was one of the few French labels that bothered to date its releases, and along with the catalog number (12042) and matrix number (50.032), the date is encoded as 15531, denoting 15 May 1931. As Baldwin says, "I suspect it's a release date rather than a recording date, but the studio session was probably only a month or so earlier."

The flip side is a paso doble, "Tierra Hispana," credited to José Sentis, where the Castros are almost mechanical in their playing; as Baldwin notes, "The Castros sound as if they're either highly rehearsed or they're reading a chart—possibly both."

But on "Valse Poulette" the sound of the stringed instruments is enchanting in their interplay and layering of timbres. The song is a simple waltz, yet the melody is alluring, composed in ascending and descending lines. Poulette was indeed *Le Grand Gitan*, and in his playing on this single signature *valse* I hear the genesis of Gypsy jazz.

Amid this new and thriving Gypsy banjo and guitar tradition, Django was taking it all in. Paris was the epicenter. There were the Gypsy encampments in *La Zone*, the city's innumerable rowdy dance halls, even the *cabarets russe*—the blossoming Russian nightclubs—where Romani violin and cymbalom orchestras and vocal choirs took the stage each night. And there were also Romani pilgrimages where music accompanied religious devotion, serving as a crossroads for pollinating the music. Through the grace of his parents' and relatives' tutelage and travels, the music they heard and played coalesced under Django's fingers.

He was just twelve in 1922 when he and Nin-Nin were busking in a café near Paris's southeastern Porte d'Italie. They were overheard by another Gypsy, the Italian Zingaro named Vétese Guérino. Known among his fellow Romani as "Tête de mouton"—Sheepshead—for his unruly fleece of curly black hair, Guérino was also famous for his accordion and the musette band he led. Now, he heard something special in Django's banjowork and offered to hire him as an accompanist for the princely sum of ten *francs* a night. Django accepted the offer, impatient to become a professional musician and descend into the underworld of the *bals musette*.

THREE | *Bals Musette*
♪ *Music from the Dark Side of the City of Light*

I SENSE EVEN NOW the spirit of Django alive in the crumbling old *bal musette* known as La Java. The venerable dance hall stands still, a rare survivor among the hundreds of *bals*, *guingettes*, and *guinches* that once were the nighttime paradises of Paris. La Java was one of Django's favored haunts. It was here in the mid to late 1920s that Django often strummed his *banjo-guitare* alongside star accordionists such as Vétese Guérino and Maurice Alexander. And it was here, as the legend goes, that Django played on the eve of October 26, 1928, before the caravan fire almost took his life.

I've come to La Java seeking a sense of the world of the dance halls and their influence on Django. Almost all of the old-time Gypsy jazzmen got their start playing the *bals musette* and accompanying accordionists. Poulette Castro, Mattéo Garcia and others of the Garcia clan, Gusti Malha, Baro Ferret and his brothers and many cousins, Patotte Bousquet, Tchan Tchou, Louis Faÿs—the list goes on. And there were no doubt further Romani banjomen in the *bals* whose names have been lost to history.

La Java at 105 rue du Faubourg du Temple is on the borderline between the 10th, 11th, and 19th Arrondissements—the red-scarf working-class *quartiers* of rough Temple and tough Belleville. This neighborhood is today a havoc of Tunisian *patisseries*, Halal *boucheries*, and Chinese noodle factories. In Django's day it too was an immigrant's *faubourg*, but home to Auvergnats coming to the capital for work. The building housing the *bal* is a crumbling *galerie*, towering three stories above the street, regal in its sooty grandeur. The arched roof façade proudly bears the inscription in stone, "Palais du Commerce": this *galerie* once housed all sorts of small shops and was the heart of the neighborhood, day or night. A large entry lobby is open to the roof, airy and breezy, lined with balconies where the storefronts once looked out. I stroll straight on through, all the way to the back, and there between two Ionic—or better in this case, ironic—pillars stands a stout double door. Gates of faux art nouveau ironwork still protect the doorway. Once upon a time, as evidenced in photos of the day, a neon sign crowned this entryway, spelling out "La Java" in jazzy cursive letters. Today, a backlit sign stolidly announces the venue, the romance long since departed.

It's early evening and La Java appears deserted before the nighttime rush. I slip in uninvited. Descending a wide, curving stairway, the passage leads me down into the depths. Fittingly, perhaps, the decor here is all red. In the half-light, the curtains covering the walls look like satin and velvet, but the *bals* were the make-believe world of the weekends, so the fabrics too are likely false in their glamor. The stairway swings around, bringing me back 180 degrees and under the floor of the main lobby. Here, the dance hall opens out before me. A long, wide dance floor of dark wood runs the length of the room. It is bordered by red vinyl-covered *banquettes* and tables, a bar awaiting at the end. I have an old, browned photo that shows the *bal* in full swing, grim-looking couples gripping each other with a weekend-night intensity, banishing the grit of work and forgetting it all as they danced to the accordion and banjo. In Django's day, a treacherously narrow balcony, known as a *surplomb*, was cantilevered out over that dance floor.

Standing now in the center of La Java, empty and silent, I feel that aura of Django. These days, the dance hall no longer resonates to the sound of an accordion and banjo; instead, the ancient *bal* is now a salsa disco. But beyond the music and the crowd it draws, so little has changed it's almost eerie, a step back in time. The inside of the *bal* looks just as it did in the photographs from the 1920s. I can picture and almost hear the twelve-year-old Django strumming out his first rhythm lines from the band's balcony on his diminutive *banjo-guitare*. Above the choking clouds of cigarette smoke, the musicians played their songs like a heavenly entourage.

In Buenos Aires, they danced to the tango. In Sevilla, flamenco. In New Orleans, jazz. In Paris, it was musette that set their feet alight and helped them forget their worries on a Saturday night.

The lustiest descriptions I have found of this long-lost world come from the pen of Françis Carco, the poet laureate who sang the *bals* electric. Carco celebrated Paris's lowdown dance halls and the city's trademark music, and his 1922 prose-poem elegy *Panam* was one of his earliest portraits of this world. I hold a fragile copy of this minute booklet, a leftover from another era, which I discovered in a Seine-side *bouquiniste* stall. The book measures a mere four by five inches and runs just fifty-four pages, printed by Paris's Librairie Stock and once selling for a paltry single *franc*. "Panam" was the underworld's nickname for Paris, a slang contraction of "Paris Madam," as in the "grand old dame." And as Carco reminisced about Panam, "Of all the pleasures, it is those of the night that I prefer, when the street glitters in the fog and around the corner in a cul-de-sac glows the red light with the three letters of that magnetic word: *Bal*."

These gas lamps advertising the *bals* burned in the darkness along rue Monge and rue de Lappe, around place Pigalle, and up the climbing rue de la Montagne Sainte-Geneviève. Befitting the magical escape the dance halls promised, Django, Guérino, and the other *balochards* often dressed in costumes provided by the owners. Some nights, they were Argentine gauchos. Other evenings, they portrayed *matelots*—sailors—dressed in the signature white-and-blue-striped jerseys of the French maritime. Or they wore the blouses and red scarves—*foulards rouge*—of the Auvergne. At still another *bal*, they might button themselves up in black evening dress—which, in the world of the *bals*, may have been the most fantastical garb of all.

The dance halls also had their fashions and codes of behavior among *les mulots*, the "mice," slang for the dance hall habitués. The women dressed up for the night out in skirts held aloft by suspenders over bright-colored blouses. On their foreheads, they fashioned the cheap and simple hallmark of *bal* beauty—*coques poisseuses*, spit curls. The men's dress was based on Auvergnat work clothes. They wore black trousers—once known as *sans culottes*, or "without breeches," a style of working-class pantaloons that lent their name to the revolutionaries of the *faubourg* in times past. On their backs were blue work shirts, set off by their beloved red scarves tied around their necks in a fashion that made them look, in Carco's words, "as though they were grimacing as they were being strangled." Their hair was shorn short and rounded in the back, a style they requested from barbers as *en boule*, "like a ball," or *en paquet de tabac*, "like a pack of tobacco." Their necks were shaved raw with a razor, a style Carco described as "a flash of gray skin running from one ear to the other, cynically evoking the cut of a guillotine—like the *toilette* of the condemned." Snap-brim caps invariably topped their heads. And as Carco noted, they removed their hats in deference to nothing and no one.

Carco was not the only artist enamored by the mysteries of the City of Lights' dark side. Hungarian photographer Brassaï wandered the nighttime underworld of the *bals* as well as the Gypsies' *fêtes foraines* and Paris's world-famous brothels. Brassaï's images and reminiscences of the dance halls were published in his portfolio, *Le Paris secret des années 30*:

The *bals musette* had their fashion, their music, their code, and also their typical, unvarying decor: red imitation-leather banquettes, tables solidly nailed to the floor—against possible fights—large mirrors, lamps with Venetian-glass globes, multicolored paper streamers festooned from the four corners of the ceiling to the center of the room, where a prismed, multifaceted ball was hung, casting a confetti of light over the walls and the dancing couples, wafting them into a starry sky. The dancehalls were full of poetry and dreams, but they were also full of pitfalls: true love came close to prostitution. In these dancehalls, young pimps seduced girls and recruited the labor force for the streets and the whorehouses. . . .

Every band had its accordion player, who was the "One and Only," its "World Famous" singer who crooned languorous tangos, rowdy waltzes, and the latest java into a megaphone. Need I say that the immodest, provocative, and vulgar sound of the java was, at least before the last war, the only typically French popular music, the only living, animated music that originated in the Parisian dancehalls.

Some of the customers sat at tables; others stood around the bar, where the drinks were half price. Their caps either pulled down over their eyes or pushed back from their foreheads, they sipped colored drinks—green, red, violet, orange—through straws. Because of the constant threat of brawls, it was forbidden to serve drinks by the bottle—that would have furnished dangerous ammunition.

An invitation to dance was made at long distance. In places like this, no man got up and bowed to a woman. He gave her a hard stare from across the room and emitted a loud, sonorous *psst!* The sounds—*Psst! Psst!*—shot from table to table in every direction before every dance, like an orchestra of crickets. Yet, no sooner did these couples take a few turns on the floor, bouncing around, the men's hands around the small of the girls' backs, than the band ground to a halt and the owner's voice rang forth: "*Passez la monnaie! Passez la monnaie!*" And each dancer would dig into his pocket and pull out twenty-five *centimes*, five *sous*, the price per dance. Only the men paid. And the band would strike up again.

According to the strict etiquette that prevailed, no woman had the right to turn down a stranger's invitation to dance, even if she was with an escort, even if she was new to the place. Also, a girl who accepted an invitation to have a drink with one of the regulars was tacitly agreeing to go to bed with him. A refusal could cause a brawl. Other pretexts for a fight were: a mistress's infidelity or betrayal or a girl's changing neighborhoods to escape from her pimp. These brawls, these "settlings of account," usually didn't occur inside the *bal musette*, but in the street outside, after closing time. A dreadful and dreaded moment! Knives flashed from pockets, and out of the women's corsets and garters. There were real pitched battles between rival gangs, between the clients of different dancehalls or from different neighborhoods. So that the police wouldn't interfere, some *bals musette* were located at the ends of private alleys, where no *gendarmes* dared go.

Francis Carco summed this whole world up succinctly. In his 1922 prose poem "Au Bal-Musette," he wrote, "*Ici, la danse n'est pas un art*—Here, dancing is not an art." Rather, it was a joyous nighttime release from the daytime grind, a dance of freedom to the music that became known as musette.

The history of musette could be composed as a Symphony for Bagpipes, Accordion, and Banjo. The first movement was played out on rue de Lappe, where I've come at dusk just as the neon lights are charged, spreading their promise. This is the heart of *La Bastoche*—Auvergnat slang for La Bastille, the frayed fringe of Paris spreading northeast through the old Faubourg Saint-Antoine. It was here that immigrants from the Auvergne staked their claim on a new life in the capital in the mid 1800s, and here where they opened their *bals*. The northern edge of the *quartier* is bordered by rue de la Roquette. Most Parisians in the 1800s only ventured down this street when dressed in black as they followed a funeral cart to the Cimetière du Père-Lachaise, or in chains as they were carted to the city's main prisons, Petite-Roquette for women, Grande-Roquette for men. The southern edge of *La Bastoche* was the site of the prison-fortress of the Bastille, the flashpoint for the many insurrections that rose out of the Faubourg Saint-Antoine's working-class streets in the century before. Between these inspiring landmarks, the Auvergnat made a new life.

They came to Paris dressed in their regional finery: flowing blue or black blouses known as *biaudes*, broad-brimmed black felt hats, and those red scarves knotted at the neck, their arrival in the city's streets heralded by the clack of their wooden *sabot* clogs on the *pavé*. The even-then-sophisticated Parisians sneered at these country cousins. Yet the Auvergnats were nothing if not resourceful and driven; as Honoré de Balzac caricatured them in his 1848 novel *Le Cousin Pons*, they "thirsted for gold like the devils in hell thirst for the dew of paradise." The Auvergnats worked hard during the day—carrying and selling fresh water on the streets, an oxen yoke over their shoulders; laboring in factories and as coppersmiths and boilermakers, the dirty jobs no one else wanted; and running cafés and restaurants that soon became *bals*. And they danced hard through the night, on the street that was their nocturnal paradise.

Rue de Lappe is a bastard of a Parisian boulevard. Narrow and straight, it lacks any hope of being picturesque. During the day it is grim and gray; the immigrants had traded the glories of their grand Auvergne alps for a horizon of rooftops and chimneys. But at night, the street comes alive. Auvergnat factory workers, boilermakers, and craftsmen arrived in droves with the darkness. They pushed their way into the numerous *bals* that lined rue de Lappe, spinning around the dance floor with *les grisettes*—the shopgirls—to the sound of musette, and settling grievances with stilettos out on the cobblestones. Les Champs-Élysées may have suited the gentlepeople of Paris, but rue de Lappe was the nighttime Elysian Fields of the working class.

In the beginning, musette was played on bagpipes. Known as *un musette*, the bagpipes gave their name to the music they made. In the Auvergne, the *musette* was more commonly called a *cabréta* from its airbag made of goat skin, or *cabra*. And it was the music of a certain former Auvernat goatherd that formed the basis for musette now in Paris.

Antoine "Bousca" Bouscatel was born March 9, 1867, in Cornézières in the Cantal region of the Auvergne, and began playing bagpipes when he was just eight tending his family's goats and cows high in the mountains. He arrived wide-eyed in the capital in 1890 when he was twenty-three to find work. But factory hands like him were everywhere; what was needed instead was a good Auvergnat musician to play their native *bourrée* dances and help them forget the agony of the laboring day. Bousca and his bagpipes were first hired to play in the *cafés-charbons*, the bars that also sold reliable Auvergnat coal to heat homes. His fame spread, and soon he had his own namesake *bal musette* on rue de Lappe, Chez Bousca. Later photographs show Bouscatel a proud, dignified gent with grand flowing moustachios and cheeks creased into a permanent smile alive with music. And in every picture I've found, he holds his bagpipes, as if they were an inseparable part of him. In 1906, the French newspaper *La Haute Loire* published a colorful report on his *bal*, entitled, "Chez Bouscatel, Un Soir":

> In a corner, Bouscatel, the legendary *cabretaire* himself, is enthroned on a dais. His *musette* is covered in red velvet, and he has fastened *grelotières* [bracelets of bells] to his ankles. His red shirt sleeves are rolled up due to the heat.... He calls out, *"Hé les enfants!"* And here is where the *bourrée* begins. Bouscatel, the *cabretaire*, pumps the airbag with his right arm while his left arm controls the wind at the exit; the *musette* is inflated like an enormous, full cheek. His two knees jump to make the *grelotières* sound in time to his music and his nimble fingers dance over the pipe holes.

To spread the sound of their musette to the faithful, an Auvergnat record label was soon started in Paris, operated by *cabretaire* Martin Cayla. Entitled Disques le Soleil, the name itself was an evocation of halcyon days back in their beloved Cantal. Listening today to these old 78s of Bouscatel in his prime, they too evoke gilded images, but of wild nights on rue de Lappe. I'm awed by the virtuosity of Bousca's bagpipery and the soul he breathes into his quaint old dance tunes. Bouscatel honed his crude country style and no longer sounded like a pastoral goatherd playing for only his hoofed audience. Even though his musette emits a sound as primal as the mountains, his music is somehow modern in its dynamics and movement—a sense and sensibility, perhaps, now infused with a big-city energy. He coaxes sounds of enchantment from his crude instrument, playing those rousing *bourrées* and other folk dances that kept the good times alive.

The site of Chez Bousca survives still on rue de Lappe. Next door is the century-old grocery Aux Produits d'Auvergne, pungent with country *saucisses* hanging from the ceiling, glass cases overflowing with *tripoux* and rich yellow rounds of the famous Cantal cheese. Today, Chez Bousca is itself gone. It has been replaced by a modern sports bar, complete with the usual electronic music and big-screen televisions, which in its own way still provides its customers with much needed nighttime solace. Bouscatel had foreseen such changes coming, as well as the enduring need for a rue de Lappe. Before he died in his adopted Paris on February 16, 1945, he had a premonition of time passing, and yet some things staying true. Over a late-night *verre* after the music had ended and his *bal* was silent, he told his bandmates, "The days of my *cabrette* are numbered.... *Et moi mort, on dansera encore rue de Lappe*—And yet when I am dead, people will still be dancing on rue de Lappe."

On the other side of Paris there's another warren of ancient streets that have also somehow survived time. I'm scaling the heights of La Montagne Sainte-Geneviève, climbing from the Seine's *Rive Gauche* through the Latin Quarter to the peak at the Panthéon. Following the southwestern approach from the countryside into the old city, these torturous medieval passages in the neighborhood known as La Mouffe are paved-over horse and oxen pathways. The buildings here are low and rambling, canted inward over the streets and rue de Mouffetard's long-running food markets. Rue de la Montagne Sainte-Geneviève wanders like a drunkard's stagger, ever higher. And it climbs past the site of what was once one of the most famous dance halls in all Paris, the humble pantheon of accordionist Émile "Mimile" Vacher. It's here that the second movement of the musette story was in part played out.

An accordionist first joined Bouscatel on stage at Chez Bousca in 1905 or 1906, the newfangled accordion and the ancient bagpipes playing a musette waltz in harmony. The accordion was a recent immigrant to Paris, arriving in the baggage of Italians seeking a better life. This musical instrument was the apex of modernity compared to the bagpipes, a sort of futuristic band in a box, capable of playing complex melodies and harmonies all by itself. Auvergnat *cabrettaires* at first fought against the accordion, rightly sensing it would replace their hallowed instrument—"Death to these foreign squeezeboxes that are good only to make bears dance, but absolutely unworthy to start the legs of our charming women of Cantal in to dancing!" read the screed of a *cabrettaire* named Meyniel in an Auvergnat newspaper. Bouscatel resisted the accordion, but he soon realized he'd better join forces than be forgotten himself. "*Ça tourne!*" the dancers at Chez Bousca cheered the new sound. It was the end of the war between *cabrettaires* and accordionists. It was also the beginning of a new music.

In the hands of accordionist Émile Vacher, musette evolved in breadth and sophistication in the 1910s and 1920s. There were other accomplished accordionists during this formative era—Louis, Charles, and Michel Péguri, Émile Prud'homme, Joseph Colombo, Adolphe DePrince, Medard Ferrero, Marceau Verschueren, Jean Vaissade, and Fredo Gardoni. But it was Vacher who adopted and adapted the traditions of Bouscatel and the Auvergnat *cabrettaires* to pioneer almost single-handedly the music of musette.

Naturally, many of the most famous accordionists in Paris were Italians—"Rituals" in Panam slang. Yet this amazing new squeezebox was quickly picked up by French musicians as well. Vacher was born in Tours on May 7, 1883, before being carried to Paris by his mother. Settling in the 20th Arrondissement, Émile soon had a new stepfather, Louis-Paul Vacher, who played accordion and began tutoring his new son. Young Émile was a quick learner, and by the time he was fifteen in 1898, he was accompanying his adoptive father at Bal Delpech, a Montreuil dance hall presided over by the ferocious, 265-pound *taulier*, Madame Delpech. Émile later graduated to a one-of-a-kind, custom-built *accordéon mixte*—a Frankenstein's monster with diatonic buttons for the melody on the right and chromatic bass buttons for the left that must have been fiendishly difficult to play. In 1910, the Vacher family purchased the Bal de la Montagne Sainte-Geneviève at 46 rue de la Montagne Sainte-Geneviève. The dance hall soon became legendary for wild nights and wild times.

The *bal* also became famous for the music Vacher played. Alongside the ancient Auvergnat *bourrées*, his fingers danced over his accordion unreeling quadrilles, polkas, mazurkas, Spanish paso dobles, and maxixes from Rio de Janeiro; the tango, foxtrot, cakewalk, biguine, rumba, and *le shimmy* were fashionably late arrivals on the scene. Vacher also composed numerous accordion waltzes that became known as *valses musette*. These waltzes were joyful dance tunes that enveloped the *bal* crowds in their gay sound. Their mechanics were standardized: an A section theme followed by a B section *duet* that lead inevitably back to the melody to start the crowd dancing around once again.

In addition, Vacher played the java, a dance that became the pride of musette. Legend held that the java got its name at Le Rat Mort, a grand *bal* reigning over place Pigalle. Here, the women were infatuated with the three-four-time Italian mazurka "Rosina" that they pranced to in quick, minced steps with their hands planted on their partners' *derrières*. Throughout the nights, dancers demanded the *orchestre* play "Rosina," calling for encores of the song, "*Ça va?*," which in the Auvergnat accent came across as "*Cha va?*" And so a new dance was born. The java was a quick-pulsed *valse* that lured all onto the dancefloor. Yet old traditions died hard, and the debut of a new dance was contentious. Some staunchly Auvergnat *bals* bore signs proclaiming "*La java est interdite*—the java is forbidden." Embraced or cursed, dancers continued to call for encores, and Vacher hurried to write fast-paced javas for his customers.

Along with modernizing the music, Vacher also modernized his band. The Auvergnat's quaint old *grelotières* were forgotten, and *père* Vacher appeared behind his stepson playing a simple drum kit to power along the rhythm. On a different eve, Émile counted out a melody with another new instrument at his side—*un banjo*.

The union of accordion and banjo, with their disparate backgrounds, was a marriage of convenience. And yet they proved they belonged together in the *bals* like Romeo and Juliet. Arriving with the drum kit in France via America in the hands of minstrel-show and jazz-band musicians, banjos proved an ideal accompaniment to accordions. They were blessed with the percussive sound of a drum, harmonic chords of a harp, or bass lines of a string bass. And banjos boasted a trebly tone that cut through the accordion's powerful voice. Three different types of banjos came into vogue: the elfin banjo-mandolin, four-string tenor, and six-string *banjo-guitare*. Vacher played with numerous banjoists over the years, including the solemn, unsmiling Lucien "Lulu" Bélliard, whose banjo solos erupted with vigor and virtuosity. Yet Vacher's favorite banjomen were Gypsies, who appeared out of *La Zone* with their banjos under their arms to add new spice and flavor to musette.

Place de Clichy on the border of Pigalle and Montmartre was home to a *bal musette* where even the tough *mecs* of Belleville and Ménilmontant would have paused before entering. Quaintly named Le Petit Jardin—The Small Garden— the title belied this dance hall's true character; it would have been better named for a cemetery plot. The *bal* was frequented by Corsicans and Gypsies, and native French accordionists spoke of it with trepidation. It was here that the Romani honed their skills with their banjos, playing out the third movement in the musette symphony.

I hold in my hands a creased, age-browned photograph of Auguste "Gusti" Malha. Alongside Poulette Castro, Gusti was one of the greatest of all Gitan banjomen. He was a dance hall star, but in this photo he appears short and stout, his hair receding, his features undistinguished; he looks like the sort of unremarkable man one passes on a Parisian street without noticing as he picks your pocket. Yet Gusti put his deft fingers to legal—if less-profitable—use. As one of his musical partners-in-crime, accordionist René "Charley" Bazin remembered decades later with awe still in his voice, Gusti was a banjo virtuoso who plucked the strings "as if he had six fingers on each hand."

Gusti learned his banjo skills from another Gitan, Mattéo Garcia. Little is known of this Garcia: no photos remain of the man, no recordings survive. He was likely related to Coco and Serrani Garcia, the bandmates of Poulette. And yet, as with much early Gypsy jazz history, Garcia remains but a shadow, his story lost to the wastelands of *La Zone*. He strummed his banjo alongside Vacher in the 1920s, likely at the Bal de la Montagne Sainte-Geneviève as well as Le Petit Jardin, playing an unsung part in the creation of the music.

Garcia's legacy lives on in one song, "La minch valse," still proudly played today by Romani guitarists throughout France. The melody of "La minch valse" was borne on rippling arpeggios running in ascending lines. The title of this rhapsody, however, had a jocular, base background straight off the dirty floors of the *bals*. *Minch* was vulgar Romani slang for "slut." Or worse.

Gusti inherited his mentor Garcia's chair alongside Vacher. The accordionist was the first to hire Romani banjomen, but his lead was soon followed by most every *bal* band. The Gypsies provided what was termed *une passion rabouine*—a Romani passion. Early musette waltzes were often cheerful dance ditties, composed in sunny major keys and without any surprises. The Romani added nuance and character, even menace. The result was a beautiful music. Garcia and Malha's musical styling was due not to sophisticated training, but rather to playing what pleased and provoked their untutored ears. The Gypsies had not set out from their caravans in *La Zone* with their banjos in hand to change the musette world; they simply found an avenue to translate their talents of playing around their campfires into a way of making a living.

Gusti's influence endures today in both musette and Gypsy jazz. While Garcia's legacy was sadly muted, Gusti won several opportunities to record. Solo sessions by musette banjomen were rarer than stardust—the stellar accordionists often eclipsed even mention of the banjo players on the record labels—and so the existence of these recordings, even on small, obscure labels, were testaments to the quality of Gusti's music. A session for the Javo-Disque label by "Les Frères Gusti banjoïstes" featured Gusti on banjo-guitar and his brother Joseph Malha on something called a banjo-luth performing "Souvenir de Montreuil" and "La vraie musette." Two records released on the forgotten Lutin label dating from about 1925 listed them as "Les Frères Gousti." Playing a banjo duet, Malha and his brother blazed through "Paris-Rome," "Ca c'est Paris," "La vraie valse musette," and "La Montmartroise."

Whereas Garcia's legacy rests on just his one surviving *valse* that became by forfeit his masterpiece, Gusti was prolific. Yet after writing many *valses*, including the now-standard "Reine de musette," he sold the publication rights to bandmates, principally pianist Jean Peyronnin, who played alongside Gusti in Vacher's *orchestre*. Gusti could have become a member of the vaunted Société des Auteurs, Compositeurs et Éditeurs de Musique (SACEM), but instead of earning publishing and recording royalties, he preferred his payment up front in money he could count. It was all part of the Gypsies' outsider existence.

Gusti's highly evolved waltzes became known as *valses manouche*. Gusti and the other pioneering Romani banjomen introduced minor-key melodies, adding deeper flavor to their compositions. These Romani themes were then often further spiced by passing seventh chords and even diminished chords, all building tension within the harmony. And their melody lines often added flamenco-inspired sixth, ninth, and even thirteenth notes to the stew.

Gusti's "Reine de musette"—"Queen of the musette"—became his most famous composition, a Parisian classic. The song shows the hand of a banjo player as composer rather than an accordionist with melody lines that fall readily under the fingers on a banjo-guitar neck. Lacking the accordionists' ability to sustain notes, Romani banjomen instead filled the air with furious flurries of notes, ornamenting melodic lines with triplets and tremolos, virtuosity impressive to the Gypsies. Gusti incorporated elements of the accordionists' playing into his waltzes, especially in the roller-coaster melodies of ascending and descending arpeggios and chromatic runs of "Reine de musette." This character of musette melody came from the right-hand button "keyboard" favored by accordionists of the day: The sensible layout made rapid two- or three-octave arpeggios a simple dash for the fingers across the buttons. Vacher and others used these arpeggios liberally in composition and ornamentation, and Garcia and his fellow Romani wholeheartedly adopted this style to their banjos.

Gusti and the other Gypsies also added a third section—akin to a bridge—to the suddenly old-fashioned two-part *valse musette* compositions. In "Reine de musette," Gusti's A section theme is followed by a B section with a quick-moving melody line of near-nonstop triplets. The waltz reaches its crescendo of emotion here, and dancers spun in a frenzy to the B section in a move known as *la toupie*, named for a child's spinning top. The waltz then returns to the theme before transitioning into the C section, which leaps to a major key. Gusti's C section was a relaxed melody giving dancers a chance to catch their breath before launching back into the theme. "Reine de musette" was a romance in musical miniature. The melodic theme was sweetly nostalgic like the remembrance of an old love. Then the *duet* arrived on a note of trepidation like a lovers' spat, before the song resolved itself in the crescendo of a warm embrace.

Gusti's "Reine de musette" and his other numerous compositions—"La valse des niglos," "Carmette," "Brise napolitaine," which he likely co-authored with Guérino, and probably more whose true authorships have been lost to time—set a standard for musette that inspired the coming generation of Romani banjo-men. For Django, watching the elder's fleet fingers with their many jeweled rings aflash in the dance hall spotlight, Gusti was a lure to the success promised a musician.

Django was just twelve years of age when he entered the *bals* at the side of Guérino. He served his apprenticeship playing alongside his father and uncles as well as with Poulette and Gusti. Now, this slight Romani youth armed with his banjo was himself a professional musician.

Django grew up in the underworld dance halls over the next six years. He moved between *bals* and accordionists like a true vagabond. He played La Java, Bal de la Montagne Sainte-Geneviève, Chez Marteau off place d'Italie, Chez Berlot, La Rose Blanche and La Chaumière near the Porte de Clignancourt, Bal Ça Gaze—even Chez Bousca on rue de Lappe. And he accompanied Guérino, Alexander, Gardoni, Marceau, Vaissade, and likely others. It was Vaissade who recalled Django's fantastical feats on the banjo best: "Already everyone admired him, for if he didn't yet have the mastery he was eventually to display, he was already carving out a style that was different from anyone else's. I remember thinking how fantastic he was when I heard him play. He stuck his fingers to his nose and played incredible, complicated things the other banjomen that worked with us could not have even imagined. Although he was our accompanist, it was we who were unable to follow him! He played almost too strongly and, deep down, we were always afraid that he would overshadow our accordions!"

Django owed his first opportunity to record to Vaissade. In spring 1928, Django cut four sides with the accordionist at the Compagnie Gramophone du Française studio in Cité Chaptal in Pigalle. Along with the accordion and banjo, the band included an unidentified musician playing *jazzflûte*, a sort of slide whistle that was the *bal* version of a horn section on the cheap; its soothing sound smoothed out the harsh treble of the lead instruments. The four songs they recorded were characteristic of repertoires of the day. A mix of *chansons, valses,* and light opera airs, they were jolly, upbeat tunes tailored to dancing: popular composer Charles Borel-Clerc's "Ma Régulière," a *chansonette* that was later a hit for Maurice Chevalier; Frank Wolter and *chanteuse* Mistinguett's "Parisette"; Auguste Bosc's street-organ *valse* "Griserie"; and "La Caravane," better known as "La Fille de Bédouin," an air from Raoul Moretti's 1927 operette *Le Comte Obligado*, then the rage in Paris.

I'm listening now to "Ma Régulière," a recording of such immense charm that it calls forth the whole era of musette in its simple melody. There were many better recordings made and much more beautiful songs composed, but this early 78 is alive with infinite energy. Django played here with a power and assurance beyond his eighteen years of age. He starts out hitting straight, on-the-beat rhythmic chords that buttress the accordion's melody. But he did not seem content with this role for long; such playing appeared to bore his youthful impetuousness and dreams of dance hall grandeur. Playing behind Vaissade, Django seemed to be throwing down the gauntlet, challenging the accordionist to a duel over the song. Soon, he adds a strummed half-note accent after the beat, and then, in a sleight of hand, triple-time chords, bringing the song to full gallop. With just his banjo, he creates an undercurrent of swinging electricity within the trio's limited sound. In the next chorus, he pattern-picked a harmony line behind the accordion's melody, dropping effortlessly into tremolos on the secondary chords that built tension to deliver the song to its dénouement.

Django recorded musette in several more sessions during 1928, his banjo ringing out though the concatenation of the accordion bands. His name appeared on record labels transliterated variously and carelessly from Romanès into French as "Jiango Renard" or just "Jeangot." Yet however they spelled his name, Django's banjo playing too was direct and strong.

At some point during his dance hall career, the young Django's ambitions shone on another front as well: He worked to compose a small handful of waltzes of his own. I imagine him during the afternoon hours after waking late from his night in a *bal*, practicing his banjo on the steps of his caravan in *La Zone*. He crafted four or five *valses*, all following the newly established tradition of the *valses manouche* of Mattéo Garcia and Gusti. And sadly, like his predecessors, Django did not record his waltzes at the time.

Django's *valses manouche* might never have survived if it hadn't been for his fellow Gypsy jazzmen who remembered and recorded them in later years. Baro and Matelo Ferret and Patotte Bousquet saved Django's earliest compositions, recreating them on later recordings. Django may not have even named his waltzes: Bousquet called his version of one of Django's tunes simply "Valse à Django"—"Waltz by Django." Matelo, who recorded four of them in 1960, visited Django's widow, Naguine, to ask her to bestow names on the compositions:

she christened them for two of Django's grandchildren—"Gagoug" and "Choti"—as well as for the old *bals* Django once played—"Chez Jacquet: À la Petite Chaumière," named for a café near the Porte de Clingnacourt, and "Montagne Sainte-Geneviève" in honor of Django's days playing with Guérino in La Mouffe.

"Montagne Sainte-Geneviève" is a jewel of a waltz. Its melody was not just for dancing, as with most other *valses musette* of the old school. Instead, it bore a sentimental tone, even a bittersweet longing—deep emotions for a young man of just eighteen years. The mood came through in cascades of arpeggiated minor-key runs accentuated by a major-key *duet*.

Due to its stunning beauty and virtouosic guitar, many budding Gypsy jazz guitarists instantly select this song as the first waltz to decipher. And unwisely so, as I myself learned. Those alluring arpeggios in the A section fall under my fingers with elegance. The notes run in a graceful strophe from the bass registers on the guitar's sixth string in a diagonal dash down the neck to the first string. This melody is a pleasure for the ears *and* the fingers.

Yet the waltz is a siren's song. As I learn the melody, my confidence grows and I strive to play it at a pace that's quick yet still danceable, just as Django likely did from the balcony of La Java. And that's when I discover the snare hidden in the B section.

The melody of the *duet* is made up of breathless tirades of triplets, and for lesser banjoists or guitarists than Django, it's a trap, pure and simple. Charging into the B section, my fingers become twisted in those quick triplets until I fall off the tempo I had foolishly set. I have to start all over, playing the song at a slower pace. And this is perhaps just what Django wanted: a bravura showpiece, demonstrating his own fleet-fingered prowess.

It may also have been something more. Django didn't read or write music, and as an eighteen-year-old Romani he also did not have a way to publish, and thus copyright and protect, his composition. Most of the accordionists were members of SACEM, and were diligent in copyrighting their songs to stake their claim—and earn royalties from them. Django was an outsider; he wouldn't become a SACEM member until years later. So instead, as a young *bal* banjoman, he made his song almost unplayable in order to protect it. The key to unlock his *valse* was in his own fingers alone.

Never again would Django compose such a complicated melody as "Montagne Sainte-Geneviève"—or at least one with so many *notes*. This *valse* was likely designed to impress, displaying Django's youthful fervor and putting his ambitions to music. He probably performed the song in a *bal* on the rue de la Montagne Sainte-Geneviève, his fingers a blur from one end of the banjo fretboard to the other, crisscrossing the neck in a dance of virtuosity that dazzled crowds and sent them spinning like tops across the floor. Meanwhile, accordionists such as

Vaissade, with a false smile glued to their lips and droplets of sweat itching at their brow, struggled to keep up.

I hold in my hand *un jeton de bal*—a small token—minted by the *bal musette* La Java. Most dance halls did not charge an admittance fee. Instead, men paid by the dance, purchasing *jetons* at each *bal* and good only within that establishment. A *jeton* cost twenty-five *centimes* or five *sous*, the price of a dance. It weighs next to nothing in my palm, as it was stamped out of cheap brass. On one side, it bears the *bal*'s name and address; on the other, the legend *Bon pour une danse*. This jeton is a stylized octagon, but others from the *bals* across Paris were made of poor aluminum in an array of shapes from diamonds to hexagons, triangles to ovals; some featured squares or stars punched out of the center; others had scalloped edges—perhaps to make them easily identifiable from true French coins in the darkness of a dance hall. Holding this *jeton*, even now I can feel the promise of the night, as these false coins were a fitting currency for the make-believe world of the *bals*.

I found the *jeton* that I hold in *les puces*, of course. It was good for one dance at La Java in the 1920s, during the years when Django was becoming a banjo star. But these years gave rise as well to several events that changed his life forever.

In about 1925 when he was fifteen and flush with his *bal musette* success, Django met a Manouche girl named Sophie Irma Ziegler. At fourteen, she was a dark beauty, her black hair and olive skin highlighted by warm, rosy cheeks. For her complexion, she was known among the Romani as Naguine or La Guigne after the red cherries that grew in the wild. Django was enchanted.

Then one day in 1927, he left Naguine for another Manouche woman. Florine Mayer was seventeen and, in honor of her charms, called simply—and truthfully, as the sole surviving photograph shows—"Bella." Django and Bella stole away from their families for several days. Upon their return, their union was received as a marriage. This "run-away marriage" was a common and honorable form of marriage among the Manouche, although not among other French Romani, including the Gitans and Kalderash. Nor was it recognized by French bureaucrats, a fact that would resonate through the family's—and Gypsy jazz—history. In the Manouche tradition, Bella's parents made the newlyweds the present of a *roulotte*, a helping hand on the road of their married life—as the Romani saying went, *Das dab ka i roata le never vurondeski*, To give a push to the wheel of the new caravan. They parked alongside their families' *roulottes* near the Porte de Clignancourt. Within a short time, Bella was pregnant.

At the same time, another event was occurring that awakened new vistas to Django. Jazz had arrived in France from the other side of the world, and in 1924,

Django discovered this exotic music in a nightclub on place Pigalle suitably named L'Abbaye de Thélème. The music was hot, strange, wild, alive with howling clarinets and screaming cornets, all propelled by a racing heartbeat of drums. The musicians were Billy Arnold's Novelty Jazz Band, five Americans creating the most amazing music Django had ever heard. Each afternoon, he made a pilgrimage from his caravan to this musical mecca, sitting outside on the pavement with only a breadcrust to eat, straining to hear this jazz through the windows.

As a child around the caravan campfires, Django listened to the Gypsy violinists and banjomen and resurrected their melodies on his instrument. Now, he tried to do the same with the songs by Billy Arnold. It marked the beginning of a new epoch in Django's music, and he never looked back. From listening to Arnold and hearing recordings of early jazz, Django was absorbing and assimilating American jazz, striving to master the harmonies they played, their scales and arpeggios, their phrasing, the bent notes and smears, and most of all, that sense of rhythmic movement inspired from black dance that infused the music, the swagger known as swing. He no longer wanted to sound like a Gypsy or play Gypsy music; throughout the rest of his life, he rarely ever recorded Romani tunes. From the far side of the Atlantic Ocean, through the fleeting sound of jazz bands on a Pigalle stage and the more enduring magic of records played in his caravan in Paris' *La Zone*, he sought now to play his guitar like an African American hornman.

Yet jazz was not as simple as it sounded. To start with, the time structure heralded a rebellion against much European classical and popular music. Most of the French popular music that Django performed in the *bals* was to a marching two-four time or the loping three-four of the *valse*, both time signatures that stressed the first beat in the bar. Jazz was typically played in four-four time, providing a suprising freedom within its greater number of beats to the bar. To swing it, the second and fourth downbeats were stressed. This bizarre concept of swing was nearly incomprehensible to the Europeans who tried to play jazz. It was also nearly impossible; much of the early jazz played by French musicians boasted all the swing of a starched Viennese waltz.

And then there was the not-so-simple art of improvisation. Improvising was a concept that went against centuries of European musical training. European musicians—as well as many white *and* black American musicians striving to play jazz—were so used to reading the notes they were to play that improvising was like learning the language of music anew. But for Django, music *was* improvisation. He learned by listening and improvising—and then improvising upon his improvising. Romani musical tradition was erected on improvisation, whether it was adding flowery embellishments to a violin song in a *brasserie*, *duende* flourishes to a flamenco *buleria*, or composing "original" pieces based on existing melodies, as with many Balkan Tziganes songs. Django bore none of the dogma of a *conservatoire* training nor even the dictates of reading music to slow him down in playing what he wanted to play. And he saw no reason to conform to the strict dictates of the melody; it was simply a starting point to playing *music*.

Returning to his nightly chair in the *bals*, Django tried to play some of this foreign jazz. The music now filled his imagination. From the *surplomb* of the dance halls, he added new spark to the old repertoire, sometimes playing and improvising on a tame American foxtrot when the bandleader agreed to showcase Django's virtuosity to play *un hot*—a solo—improvising choruses, reworking the melodies, adding to them. Like his father before him, the caravan musician and *prestigitadeur*, Django was pulling notes out of thin air. Yet accordionist Maurice Alexander led Django aside to offer him some paternal advice: Beware this new music.

Django was accompanying Alexander at La Java one night in late October 1928 when a gentleman in tailored black evening dress and smoking a large cigar entered the *bal*. To the dance hall *mulots*, this interloper had strayed into the wrong part of Paris. He had a beautiful woman on each arm, one dressed in lustrous mink, the other in a jacket of Tuscan lamb, their Chanel *le numero cinq* overpowering the sweaty scent of the dancers. He made his way through the crowd of *apaches* to ask to speak to *Monsieur* Reinhardt. He had a deal to offer.

This interloper was Englishman Jack Hylton, a name that even many of the *mulots* would have recognized. He was the impresario of the most famous symphonic jazz orchestra in all Europe—a show band, replete with singers, dancers, and comedians. In 1929 alone, his orchestra performed 700 concerts while traveling 63,000 miles and selling 3,180,000 records—one record every seven seconds.

Now, Hylton had come in search of Django. Somehow he had heard of Django's skill as a banjoman in the *bals* and his renown at improvising American jazz. Hylton offered him a chair in his orchestra.

Hylton looked nothing like a Mephistophelian character, yet he offered Django a pact for which most would have sold their souls. Django likely examined Hylton and liked what he saw: rewards of the jazz life beyond just playing the music—tuxedos, cigars, and a woman on each arm. And so of course he accepted.

Dreams for his new future likely in his head, Django returned to his and Bella's caravan outside the Porte de Clignancourt in the early morning hours of October 26, 1928, after playing La Java. Entering, he found his *roulotte* in bloom. Bella had crafted bouquets of celluloid flowers for the burial later that day of a

Manouche boy; dozens of plastic chrysanthamums, dahlias, and roses now blossomed in the dark interior of the caravan.

Romani legend tells the next part of the story in several variations. Some claim that the pregnant Bella was already asleep. Hearing Django enter, she awoke and reached for a match and the stub of a candle near the bed. She lit the candle, but in her sleepy state, fumbled, and the candle fell to the floor and rolled into a bouquet of plastic petals. Others tell that Django himself dropped the candle. Either way, those celluloid flowers instantly turned into flames. In a heartbeat, the caravan was an inferno.

Django pulled Bella from the bed. Her hair afire, he pushed her out into the night. Then, he tried to fight back against the blaze. He beat at the flames with a blanket, but the heat and smoke overwhelmed him. Outside, Bella was screaming to wake the surrounding caravans: *"Django est dedans! Django est dedans!"* The other Manouche rushed from their own *verdines* to see the caravan burning like a pyre.

Finally, when they thought all was lost, Django stumbled out of the burning caravan, he himself embroiled in flames.

The other Romani rolled him to the ground and smothered the fire. Then they rushed Django and Bella to the Hôpital Lariboisière, the sprawling public "hospital of the poor" near the Gare du Nord. The doctors discovered that Django's whole right side was scorched and his left hand was horribly charred. Fearful gangrene would set in, a doctor prescribed his right leg be amputated to save his life. Not trusting the doctors and their unnatural ways, Négros commanded the other Romani about her and they spirited Django away

The Manouche carried him back to their encampment in *La Zone*. The old women of the camp descended on Django, packing his burns with secret ages-old concoctions of *drab*—homemade poultices of wild herbs. Medicinally or magically, the *drab* would bring him back to life. Or so they hoped.

Yet in the coming weeks, Django did not recover. Négros brought Django now to the Hôpital Saint-Louis, and humbly asked for aid. Under the new doctors' care, Django's suppurating burns finally began to heal. His leg was saved.

His left hand was another matter. It was semi-paralyzed by the flames that ate away the skin and consumed the muscles, tendons, and nerves, and the doctors held little hope Django would ever recover its use. It seemed Django had played his last music.

Négros and Bella's family hawked everything they could, selling off their belongings in *les puces* to pay a private clinic to operate on Django's hand. On January 23, 1929—Django's nineteenth birthday—his wounds were suppurated of pus, washed clean, then burned for a second time with silver nitrate to shut them. The doctors believed this would give them a new chance to heal.

As Django convalesced back in the Hôpital Saint-Louis, his brother Nin-Nin brought a new guitar and laid it in the bed beside him. The doctors were emphatic: Django would never play again. Yet his family prayed this guitar might serve as a talisman to aid Django in recovering.

In January 1930 as he turned twenty years old in the hospital ward, a French military agent came to track Django down for military service. He found him bedridden, bound in bandages. The agent crossed Django's name from the list: The military had no use for a cripple.

Bella too left Django behind. Just weeks after the fire and while Django was still confined in the hospital, their child was born. Bella gave birth to a boy christened Henri in honor of her father. This *petit* Henri was called *l'Ourson*, or "bear cub." Over time, the nickname transformed into Lousson. Yet during the months following the fire, something changed in Django and Bella's marriage. Perhaps it was the trauma of the fire and the shock of his wounds; maybe it was simple differences between two young people. Perhaps Bella turned her back on Django, believing him a cripple who could now only make a living as a beggar, *un pilon*—one of those who displayed his handicap to make passersby pay for their pity. Either way, Django and Bella parted. She soon married another Romani named "Niglo" Baumgartner.

In Django's hospital bed lay the guitar Nin-Nin brought him. Now, within the ward, he tried to play again. His left hand was but a claw; the hand's back, a scarred knot. The tendons and nerves of his two little fingers were damaged, leaving the digits paralyzed. He could still move his index and middle fingers, though, and so during the eighteen long months of his convalescence, he forced them into motion, limbering the muscles, retraining them to his command. Limited in the number of fingers he could use to fret the guitar, he now had to rethink his approach to the fretboard. Instead of playing scales horizontally across the fretboard as was the norm, he sought fingerings running vertically down the frets as they were simpler to play with just two fingers. He fashioned new chord forms with a bare minimum of notes—often just triads made with his two fingers and his thumb reaching around the neck to the bass string. He then slid his hand up and down the neck, employing these chord forms to speak a fluent vocabulary. As he played in his hospital bed, the old melodies were reborn—a *valse* reviving memories of nights at La Java, an American jazz theme from Billy Arnold.

On the spring day in 1930 when Django finally left the hospital for good, there was a surprise awaiting him. In front of Hôpital Saint-Louis stood Naguine. She had recently returned from Italy, and when she heard word of Django's tragedy, she set out for the hospital to wait patiently for his release. She now handed Django a bouquet of tulips, saying simply, *"Tiens!* These ones are real. They won't start on fire." They would live the rest of their lives together.

As summer came, Django and Naguine set off on foot for the Midi. It was a 1,000-kilometer trek from Paris to Nice, and they hiked it all, sleeping in haystacks, stealing chickens, and surviving by Naguine's palm-reading and fortune-telling. In Toulon, they met up with Nin-Nin, and the musical duet formed again to busk in cafés, passing their borsalinos for change.

In July 1931, they ran across a bohemian artist named Émile Savitry in Toulon, who was charmed by the jazz they performed on their guitars. Savitry now invited Django and Joseph to his apartment to play them his collection of records from the United States—new 78s by Duke Ellington and His Cotton Club Orchestra, swinging string jazz by Joe Venuti's Blue Four with Venuti's violin backed by Eddie Lang's guitar, and Louis Armstrong leading his big band on "Indian Cradle Song," among others.

Django had heard jazz before, from the live music of Billy Arnold to recordings of Jack Hylton and others. But jazz had jumped ahead in the past years during his convalescence. Now, listening to Armstrong's joyous trumpet, Django was transformed. He put his head in his hands, unashamedly starting to cry. *"Ach moune! Ach moune!"* he repeated over and over again—a Romanès expression of stupefaction and admiration, meaning, coincidentally, "My brother! My brother!"

FOUR | *Jazz Modernistique*
𝄞 *Revisiting the Babylon of Gypsy Jazz*

I F YOU'RE SEEKING SIN IN PARIS, simply catch a number 67 bus or
the number 2 or 12 *métro* and get off at place Pigalle. Then help yourself.
Pigalle is the Storyville of Paris. Today as yesterday, it makes that better-
advertised Sin City, Las Vegas, look like a one-horse town out in some desert
somewhere. It casts Soho into quaintness, forces Buenos Aires's Palermo district
to blush.

Seeking clues to Django's life, Pigalle is the place to be. In Django's era, jazz
made the night bright here in the *quartier chaud*—the "hot" quarter, Paris's un-
chastity belt. The music sent the can-can dancers kicking their gams ever higher,
sparked the strippers' bump and grind, serenaded gangsters and tourists, prostitutes and addicts, the slumming rich on their way down and the poor on the
make. Pigalle is where Django won his fame.

I'm walking from place Pigalle past Django's haunts—the former site of
L'Abbaye de Thélème, the Moulin Rouge where he jammed nightly, his own club
La Roulotte, and Baro Ferret's sinister Baro Bar. The vestiges of old Pigalle await
the unwary on every street. Dubious hotels lurk up side streets; raffish bars offer
an innocent guise to the crooked sidewalks; broken pipes of neon signage leak out
their gases like a glass-plumber's nightmare; the chasms of buildings loom in
the dark like gargoyles stalking their prey. This is the sad fate of the past in the
modern city: monuments become exhaust-pitted traffic islands; fountains, once
the source of fresh water and life in a neighborhood, are now deserted and dry,
used as *pissoirs*; and the former palaces of deposed despots are museums. High
above all in Pigalle, the cornice of the old Élysées Montmartre show hall survives

as well. Django played here once upon a time. Now, the street level of the building is gussied up in a modern façade while the stonework at the top is covered in chicken wire, presumably so the past doesn't collapse on today's passersby.

I turn the corner to rue Lepic and almost step into the sharp end of a stiletto. On the street in front of me are two men dancing a ballet around the blades of knives. One has blood splashed over him from a gash running the length of his forearm. The other has a jacket wrapped around his other hand to fend off the switchblade in the time-tested manner of the duelist. A crowd hasn't so much formed as been stopped in its tracks on boulevard de Clichy in between yet another red-lit *théâtre du sex* and an ice-cream stand. The crowd moves like an amoeba as the knifemen spar: People jump backward with a joust, rush forward with the riposte. The fighters make no noise, but the crowd *oohs* and *aahs* in perfect Grand Guignol fashion. The knifemen are both dark of skin and moustachioed; they could as easily be Romani as French or North African. The one soaked in blood now starts screaming with atavistic terror. His guard down, the other lunges and slices him again along the arm, and then it's all over in maybe five or ten seconds, the two knife fighters running off shrieking curses back at each other, heading in separate directions before *les flics* arrive. It's just seven in the evening, and the crowd moves off now in search of an *apéritif*. There's nothing new on these streets.

I retreat into the Café-Tabac des Deux Moulins and order the largest *bière blanche* imaginable.

The first time Stéphane Grappelli met Django, the French violinist thought the Gypsy was going to knife him.

It was the autumn of 1931, and Stéphane was on stage at the *boîte* Le Croix du Sud improvising jazz on his violin when he found himself being stared down by an unsavory character in the audience. "This young man with the very hostile look resembled none of the other guests who came regularly to that place," Stéphane recalled in his 1992 autobiography *Mon violon pour tout bagage*. "You would rather have said he was a gangster straight out of an American film. He had skin the color of *café au lait* and greasy hair, black as coal. His upper lip was topped by a thin black moustache in the shape of a circumflex. He really didn't inspire confidence." And this audience member did not appear to appreciate his playing; as Stéphane remembered, he looked as though he preferred to see the violinist in the back alley at knifepoint.

"All at once, he started to move in the direction of the *orchestre*. I had a bad premonition and instinctively took a step backward—I came within a whisker of falling off the bandstand.

"The young man came toward me and, awkwardly, proceeded to speak to me in the most extraordinarily strange-sounding French: 'Monsieur *D*rappelli, I believe?' he began, standing before me. It was only later that I realized it was difficult for him to say his Gs.

"'Yes,' I answered, and asked what I could do for him.

"Then he told me—with his left hand hidden as deep as possible in the pocket of his baggy, over-large trousers while his right held a cigarette butt— that he was a musician too, and was looking for a violinist who played like me."

Django invited Stéphane *chez lui* to play, and one afternoon the violinist journeyed to the Porte de Montreuil and the *verdine* Django then called home. "We jammed—*faite la bombe*—all afternoon," Stéphane remembered. "We played 'hot' purely for pleasure." Django was intrigued by Stéphane's jazzy violin playing, but both were booked in other bands and they went their separate ways. For the time being.

Born January 26, 1908, at Paris's Hôpital Lariboisière, Stéphane grew up an orphan—an orphan living with his father. His mother had died when Stéphane was just four, leaving him in his father's care. Yet Stéphane's Italian father instead spent his days in the Bibliothèque Nationale translating obscure Latin or Greek texts, and Stéphane was on his own in the Paris streets. When Grappelli *père* was drafted into the Italian Army during World War I, Stéphane was left behind in a true orphanage.

He learned to play violin from street musicians and was soon busking himself. When his father returned from the war, he enrolled Stéphane in a three-year course at the Paris Conservatoire National Supérieur de Musique et Danse; from sawing away on his violin in the streets, Stéphane was now studying harmony, ear-training, and solfège, the traditional European system of learning music by ear. He soon found work playing in a theater pit orchestra providing music for the early silent films. But during breaks, Stéphane ducked around the corner into the musicians' favored brasserie, Le Boudon, to listen to the latest American jazz on the jukebox—Louis Mitchell's Jazz Kings playing "Stumbling," George Gershwin's "Lady Be Good," and soon, Louis Armstrong. As Stéphane remembered, hearing Armstrong "changed my destiny." By the late 1920s, when Django was convalescing from the caravan fire, Stéphane was playing and recording on piano and violin in France's most famous jazz orchestra, Grégor et Son Grégoriens.

After their encounter at Le Croix du Sud in 1931, it was not until three years later in 1934 that Django and Stéphane crossed paths again. This time, they were both hired into the same band. Their music now, however, was stolid waltzes— tunes that wouldn't ruffle the crinoline gowns or tuxedos at tea dances in the regal Hôtel Claridge at 74 avenue des Champs-Élysées. Their fourteen-piece orchestra kept the music tame, but backstage things were different. "One day, just before we were due to go on, a string broke on my violin," Stéphane recalled. He put on a new string, then improvised a quick jazz riff to check that he was in tune. That theme caught Django's attention, and he repeated the phrase. The next they knew, they were jamming on it, improvising choruses, throwing in licks copped from American jazz 78s they both knew. The following day they did the same, and soon other band members joined in—fellow *bal* guitarist Roger Chaput, *boulanger*-turned-bandleader Louis Vola on bass.

It all began with a broken string. And in keeping with the band's personality, it was only fitting that the genesis of the Quintette du Hot Club de France took place behind the bandstand rather than on it. As Stéphane wrote some five decades later near the end of his days, "My life started when I met Django. Because at that time, before him, I was a musician, playing here, playing there; but I realized when I was with Django, we can produce something not ordinary."

I hold in my hand a well-worn yet proud membership card in the world's first jazz fan club. Printed with number 228 and hand-dated July 1, 1933, this two-by-three-inch card was issued to one Charles Delaunay, conferring on him acceptance into the Hot Club. I can only imagine the musky cellar jam sessions and smoky café discussions to which this card gained admittance. The card itself is simple, straight to the point: these jazz aficionados had no time for frills. There was music to be heard, concerts to be organized, jazz to be bureaucratized, and a world of heathens to be converted.

As soon as there was jazz, there were jazz fans, attracted like instant disciples to an upstart religion. Django and Stéphane's backstage jam sessions were discovered and then seized upon by a rabid group of young French aficionados. There was Pierre Nourry, a teenager who should have been studying instead of haunting Pigalle jazz *boîtes*. Jacques Bureau, a budding radio builder who tuned in to nocturnal jazz broadcasts across the Atlantic and could hum every Bix Beiderbecke solo from memory. Hugues Panassié, their king and in fact, dictator, who wrote a monthly jazz column in the world's first jazz magazine, *Jazz-Tango-Dancing* (soon to become *Jazz Hot*). And there was Delaunay, the forgotten scion of artists Robert Delaunay and Sonja Delaunay-Terk, who turned to jazz seeking a family of his own. Together—and at times, *not* together, as they'd incessantly and inexorably excommunicate each other for various fine points of ideological heresy—they erected the world's first jazz club. Upon its founding in autumn 1931, it was baptized the Jazz Club Universitaire, as they were all still students. Already in 1932, it was reborn—with a sexier name and without several ousted adherents—as the Hot Club de France.

The Hot Club of course now needed a manifesto. In the November 1932 *Jazz-Tango-Dancing*, they published their new creed's screed in a curious *ménage* of Trotskyite and Bourbonist rhetoric underlined by an evangelical tone—which was only right, considering the members' wide-ranging political leanings and their beatification of jazz. They vowed to spread their self-proclaimed "jazz propaganda" far and wide, organize concerts, and "help jazz conquer the place it merits among the movements of artistic expression of our times." In magazine rants and radio raves, these jazz acolytes began worshipping music from a country they'd never seen sung in a language they didn't speak. Along the way, through meticulous volumes of codified accountancy, they studiously notated the art into detailed discographies. The Hot Club viewed jazz as a faith. Now, discovering Django and Stéphane, the true believers found their crusade.

Here were Frenchmen—conferring on Django honorary Frenchness whether he wished it or not—who played jazz as if they had the Mississippi River in their blood. Hearing Django and Stéphane jam for the first time was nothing less than a religious experience for Delaunay, who described the event in his autobiography fifty years later as though he and his club buddies were magi at the holy birth:

> At the Claridge, we walked across the dancefloor . . . to access an unused backroom that served as a lounge or dressing room for the musicians during their break. There, in a corner, four men were playing a music suffused with a melodic verve, refined improvisations, and efficient rhythms. Our ears were used to the aggressive sounds of brass horns and the rudeness of drums, and this music gave us the impression of returning in a dream through many centuries of history to the court of some distinguished nobleman. Louis Vola dominated the situation from the height of his string bass. Around him were two guitarists: Django Reinhardt (a Gypsy practically unknown outside of the world of professional musicians) and Roger Chaput. Stéphane Grappelli had left the piano and taken his violin from its case. They repeated their minor arrangements that served as intros or codas to standard songs or their own compositions. They played truly for fun, without any thought of creating a band. Several other musicians had come by to hear them play and they too could not resist the charm of the music. Django and Stéphane swapped choruses with each other, each of them visibly happy to discover the inventions of their partner.

The Hot Club immediately set out to organize this band that wasn't a band, record their find, and bring fans to the fold.

Before the Hot Club could come to agreement and mobilize, however, Django and Stéphane were already forming their own band. The backstage jams at the Claridge were becoming a rite. During that summer of 1934, the quartet was also jamming after hours at L'Alsace à Montmartre, a Pigalle brasserie where Parisian musicians often met for a last swan song before heading home for the night. One evening, Stéphane sensed reticence in Django's playing: "I could see something was worrying Django. And when I asked him what the trouble was one day, he replied: 'It doesn't matter all that much. It's just that when you're playing, Stéphane, you've got both Chaput and me backing you, but when I'm soloing I've only got one guitar behind me!'" Stéphane acquiesced, and Django's brother Nin-Nin was brought on as second rhythm guitarist. The four were now five.

Their hot jazz was still just an after-hours diversion, however. Django and Stéphane were not seeking gigs—their quintet did not even have a name. Each one of them was playing in other bands, making music that made money—dance tunes, tangos, sweet songs known among the musicians as "*soupe*" that went down easy and at a tempo that wouldn't cause anyone indigestion. None of the members yet believed they could make a living from the music they loved; as Vola stated bluntly, "Nobody had confidence that the band could go anywhere."

Nobody was asking for a jazz band playing all string instruments, either. Jazz was trumpets, clarinets, and pianos, with drums essential for making it move. Violins were for Mozart; playing jazz on a violin was practically sacrilege. Guitars were for wooing maidens on balconies, or at best, mere rhythm makers for serious instruments. Nobody was requesting *jazz à cordes*, string jazz.

And nobody was looking for a jazz band composed of Gypsies and Frenchmen. To most fans, jazz was black. In Paris, it was the imported African-American bands and their otherworldly music that the people came to hear. The French—if not the rest of the world as well—seemed to believe that all blacks had jazz in their blood. In the 1920s and 1930s, Paris was crazed for all things black, from the African art mimicked by Picasso and Modigliani to the semi-comic tribal jazz boogies performed by Josephine Baker wearing naught but a tutu of bananas. This *Négromanie* spun so far out of control that white French jazzmen sometimes had to play wearing blackface. By 1922, French musicians were complaining of *le péril noir*—the Black Peril—robbing them of their gigs. The Assemblée Nationale responded, passing a law limiting the number of foreign musicians in an *orchestre* to 10 percent of the French musicians.

For Django, the story was worse yet. Many African Americans came to Paris to revel in France's freedom from racism. But while there were no color barriers for blacks, there were entrenched barricades erected against the Romani. Django and his people were the untouchables of France, and cabaret owners were dubious of hiring him as a soloist or bandleader based as much on the fact that he wasn't black as that he was a Gypsy.

To their credit, the Hot Club believers overlooked all this; they were simply besotted by the jazz Django and Stéphane made. Club members organized jam sessions with Django in the basement of their favorite record store, La Boîte à Musique at 135 boulevard Raspail in Montparnasse. Here, Django jammed with African-American stalwarts like saxman Frank "Big Boy" Goodie and pianists Freddy Johnson and Garland Wilson. He also played solo guitar pieces that were part jazz, part flamenco improvisations. And the club organized concerts for Django and Stéphane's group—although the band still lacked a name by which to advertise them. Commercialism was not yet on Django's mind.

And yet there were dissenters among the Hot Club. While no one doubted Django could play guitar, several were unsure whether this Gypsy could really play *jazz*. After a jam session on February 4, 1934 featuring Django, Jacques Bureau lauded the club's "own" jazzman in *Jazz Hot*, writing that "the lightness and freshness of Rheinart's playing was delightful. We now know that Paris has a great improviser!" Yet privately, his doubts tested his belief, as he told me sixty years later: "I was hesitant about [Django and Stéphane's string jazz] because it was so shrill and had a Viennese sound. If there's one thing jazz detests, it's Central Europe, *ça c'est sûr*. Jazz isn't Gypsy music; it's different. Jazz is a stronger music, and Django didn't know much about jazz at this time." One of the club founders was American expatriate Elwyn Dirats. Like the other faithful, he too marveled at what Django did with a guitar, but was hesitant to pronounce it jazz. As Dirats explained to me, "At that time, the guitar was only a rhythm instrument and there were few soloists. Django's style was brilliant for the day, but hadn't reached his full sophistication. There was virtuosity, but I don't believe at that time there was that kind of depth of feeling of a black musician. Going up and down the scales with no feeling behind it was not the jazz I loved. Django developed this feeling later. I was impressed by Django only because of his novelty: He was pioneering something, and *that* was of great interest."

Nourry, however, was convinced. In August 1934, he led Django and Nin-Nin into the Publicis Studios, a small recording studio for amateur musicians. Nourry paid for the brief session out of his own pocket, gambling eighty *francs* on Django's talent. To back the two guitarists, Nourry tracked down Juan Fernandez of Martinique, a bassist who played at several Hot Club jams as well as with Freddy Johnson and His Harlemites. Together, the trio waxed test acetates of the Dixieland classic "Tiger Rag," the lovestruck American ballad "Confessin'," and Henry Creamer-Turner Layton's confection "After You've Gone." In addition, Django and Joseph alone recorded a take of "Tiger Rag." Their performances on Nourry's test acetates were pure youthful ebullience. Nin-Nin's bouncing rhythm was as impressive as Django's improvising. His vagabond chording urges Django on, and he responds with flowing melodic strophes, bedazzling coloratura, and even quotes from classical music that resonate with irreverent humor within the jazz themes. These tests showcase better than any later commercial recordings the rapport the two brothers built in a decade of playing together around the campfires of *La Zone* and busking on Parisian streets. Nourry was overjoyed with the results, and he sent copies to several of the world's great jazz critics. And yet, the response was cool at best.

Nourry never faltered. He now sought a true recording session to launch and validate his full band. He and Delaunay approached the established Odéon label, famed for its recordings of musette and popular French *chanson*, and won the still-unnamed group an audition. On October 9, 1934, the quintet arrived at the Odéon studio. With them they brought African-American singer Bert Marshall from the Hôtel Claridge band; Django told the others that vocals—by a true black jazzman—would make for a more "commercial" recording.

Delaunay remembered the session: "Once in the studio, the musicians grouped themselves round the microphone and began to play—to the astonishment of the engineers, who asked discreetly what kind of music it was they were making. Django, unfortunately, overhead this remark and decided to leave the studio on the spot. Only with the greatest difficulty was he persuaded to stay until the two test sides ["I Saw Stars" and "Confessin'"] had been recorded—the two wax platters on which the fate of the quintet seemed to hang. Impatiently, they waited for them to arrive. When they did, the musicians were delighted; they were hearing themselves play for the first time."

Their delight was soon dispelled. Several days later, the band received a letter from Odéon ruling on the band's audition: "After deliberation, our administrative committee has found that your band is far too *modernistique* for our firm."

Modernistique was the perfect description of the band—yet it was also their undoing. "No recording label wanted us," Stéphane remembered. "The formula was new: a jazz band 'without drums nor trumpet,' as we said. It was completely original." And completely unsellable, in the minds of record-label directors.

Nourry now changed his tack. He organized a premiere concert for the band, unveiling them on a Sunday morning, December 2, 1934, at Paris's École Normale de Musique at 78 rue Cardinet. Yet the ensemble was still so new they lacked even a name: Concert flyers announced them simply as *un orchestre d'un genre nouveau de Jazz Hot*, led by "Jungo" Reinhardt.

When the concert was set to begin, however, Django was nowhere to be found. Seized by stage fright, he stayed behind in his caravan in *La Zone*. Nourry went to find him. At the *verdine*, Nourry discovered a discouraged Django who refused to play. Nourry first tried encouraging Django with soft words. Failing, he switched to a military manner, ordering Django to the show. As Delaunay recalled, "We did not yet know Django's shadowy and unforeseeable character..." They were soon to learn.

Django was hustled on stage, and the nervous band shakily launched into their first song. In the end, Django and the ensemble hit all the right notes with the audience. As Panassié pronounced, "It was a grand success."

This success helped Nourry convince the Hot Club to sponsor his band. The club disciples had long dreamed of an all-French jazz ensemble; as Delaunay later remembered, "The Hot Club of France, whose actions were beginning to make themselves felt, was seeking to form a French orchestra which could adequately symbolise the jazz of France and serve to represent that organization." Now, Nourry won permission from Panassié to brand the Hot Club's name and stamp its seal of approval on his new ensemble. "I was a little dubious about giving the name of the Hot Club de France to the group," Nourry recalled. "Stéphane was none too keen on it; Django, on the other hand, was agreeable." Thus, for its second concert, on February 16, 1935, again at the École Normale de Musique, the ensemble finally had a name: "Django Reinhardt et le Quintette du Hot Club de France avec Stéphane Grappelly."

I'm listening to a 78 rpm test pressing of recording matrix number 77161. Naturally, I found this test in yet another *puces*—this time, that grand flea market to all the world, eBay. Typical of such test pressings, the back side is flat and smooth, untouched by the stylus's carved grooves. Only the front holds the music, in this case the December 27, 1934, recording of the Dixieland warhorse "Dinah." The band is notated here by an unknown hand writing with an old-fashioned fountain pen on a fill-in-the-blank label: they're listed simply as "Hot Club." This is in fact the first commercial recording by Django and Stéphane's Quintette du Hot Club de France, soon to be issued on the Ultraphone label under the near-hieroglyphic coding "Ultr AP 1422." On a line on this test acetate with the key query "Result," the engineer's all-important verdict is noted: "OK."

The record needle lowered, the music almost immediately bursts forth as if the grooves cannot contain all the joy in this song. The music's not loud, the song being led off by Django's acoustic guitar. Nor is the tempo all that fast-paced. But there's a boundless *joie de vivre* alive in these notes. Like a magician, Django pulls from his hat every trick he knows. Yes, he's showing off here, but he has much to show: As with a peacock's plumage, the wonders make the pride forgivable. Django's two fingers charge across the fretboard, proudly unreeling his trademark riffs. His solo may have relied too much on hocus-pocus, but it was fresh and it was stylish. He no longer wanted to play Gypsy music, yet his jazz bore his Gypsy signature. It could be heard in the glitter of the glissandos, the colorful hues of the chromaticism, the glamor of the diminished flourishes with their odd intervals adding rhythmic punctuation, and above all in the virtuoso display of improvisation. He proved he had assimilated the music of Louis Armstrong and was now playing it his own way, returning it enriched. The genius of all his future music was in embryo in that one solo. Gypsy jazz begins with this recording of "Dinah."

Behind Django, Nin-Nin and Chaput pump out *la pompe*, the fierce *boom-chik, boom-chik* rhythm that would become the trademark of Gypsy jazz. Their chording was based on Balkan Tziganes music, striking each beat with a percussive strum, any sustain choked off by dampening the strings instantly after the downward stroke. Django and the other Gypsy guitarists hit the first and third beats with bass notes—often alternating notes—then accentuated the second and fourth beats with chords. Each beat was quick and crisp, a combination of a guitar's chords, a bass's walking line, and a drum's beat, creating a full band's sound with a minimum of instrumentation. The *pompeurs* adopted this Tziganes rhythm to accompany *valses* and javas in the *bals*, as well as four-four-time foxtrots. The sound of *la pompe* was best when it was *"leger et sec"*—light and dry—making an ideal rhythmic accompaniment to a violin, accordion, or, as the music developed, a solo guitar. This basic *pompe* could then be accented by syncopated half-note fills and quick rhythmic triplets, such as strummed adaptions of the Gypsy flamenco *rasqueado*, which *flamencos* played with a quick unfurling of their fingernails across the strings. Among the Gypsy jazz players, this device became known as *les trousseaux de clés*—a shaking of a bunch of keys. To drive the harmonic chords, Django, Nin-Nin, and the other *pompeurs* added tremolo chords, echoing the sound of balalaïkas from the *cabaret russe* orchestras. While the rhythmic *pompe* was based in the banjo playing of the *bals*, it flourished in the Quintette into a complex rhythmic style that was unique—swinging and hot and charged.

Above it all soars Stéphane's violin, the Romani's favored instrument turned now to jazz. Stéphane plays with phrasing that can only be described as perfect. His sense of swing is sure, as if he's proving that the fiddle was made for jazz.

Yet it's the interplay between Django and Stéphane that astounds. Fighting for the spotlight, the duo had become best of friends—and worst of enemies. Apart, they were excellent musicians. Together, they dueled to outdo each other, pushing their creativity beyond what either might have achieved alone. The result here on "Dinah" is a sense of happy rivalry, a tension let loose in the thrill of playing jazz. As Stéphane repeated in characteristic understatement, together he and Django were "producing something not ordinary."

It was the indefatigable, undeterrable Pierre Nourry who convinced Ultra-phone's young chief, Raoul Caldairou, to record their *modernistique* music. But before the session could start, Nourry and Caldairou got entangled in an argument over pay for the band. This battle was initiated by Django's preposterous demands, based on an exalted sense of self-worth—even though his name and music were unknown. Finally, Caldairou laid down the law in a letter: "I shall not attempt to conceal that I am somewhat taken aback by the astronomical pretensions of the musicians in your Quintette.... I rely on you to give your artists a more realistic vision of the fees they can expect to receive."

Humbled for the moment, the band now had to work in harmony to get Django to the studio. Ultraphone scheduled the session for nine in the morning; the studio was reserved for the label's stars in the prime time of the afternoon. With a loan from Delaunay to buy gas for Vola's car, the bandmates set off in search of Django. Finding his *roulotte* parked in *La Zone* beyond the southern Porte de Choisy, they roused Django and collected his guitar. As Stéphane was quickly learning, working with Django meant accepting his wiles: "For Django, it was always an act of pure martyrdom to get out of bed in the morning. Each time that we were going to record, I would go at seven in the morning to his bedside, where I truly had to drag him out of bed—along with many promises and, if necessary, threats—and I had to make him understand that without his presence the rendezvous would be cancelled. Each time it was an incredible drama." And this was only the beginning.

At Ultraphone's Montparnasse studio, the band circled around the single recording microphone to best capture their sound. Django and Stéphane were close in—and when possible, standing—to elicit their solos while the rhythm section sat down a step back to balance the tone. They recorded directly onto a wax-acetate matrix—quaintly known as *une galette* after a Breton buckwheat *crêpe*—which the engineers retrieved from a refrigerator when they were ready to record. As the needle carved its groove into the *galette*, an engineer carefully swiped away the swarf. "The recording sessions of this time appear prehistoric today," Stéphane remembered. "We played in a circle around only one microphone. There were only eight matrixes, so there was thus no question of starting a song again as many times as we wanted. We had to play two *morceaux* of three minutes each for each 78-rpm record. Everything was incredibly simple.... We prepared arrangements of the song heads right before playing them. It was incredible! When I think that these discs became so famous!"

Along with their rhythm section, Django and Stéphane had several other accompanists in the studio that day. Nourry, Delaunay, and Panassié also stood by. But they were not simply observers; they viewed themselves as *auteurs*, on hand to direct the musicians in making music. In one of his several memoirs, Panassié remembered the session—also detailing his essential role in the recording: "After several wax tests, they wanted to record the final version. The musicians played excellently but one of them made a mistake and it was necessary to start again. As Django and Grappelly were completely improvising, the new version was very different. I was pleased with this take, because Grappelly appeared to me even more inspired. As soon as he had played the last chord, Django bumped his guitar against a chair, which produced a small, ugly noise. The engineers came out of their sound booth and said that it was necessary to start again because of this inopportune noise. But I feared that the musicians had run out of inspiration and insisted that they keep the last take, assuring the engineers that this noise would hardly be noticed." To his everlasting credit, Panassié coerced Caldairou and engineer Willy Kuhn to use this take, choosing hot improvisation over cold precision.

In two and a half hours, the Quintette recorded four songs: Louis Armstrong's hits, "Dinah" and the ubiquitous "Tiger Rag"; Stéphane's favorite tune by George and Ira Gershwin, "Lady Be Good"; and the current American hit "I Saw Stars." The four sides would be released on two Ultraphone 78 rpm discs in limited pressings of just five hundred units each.

Django was paid on the spot fifty *francs* royalty advance for each side. Now, with his fame and future assured, Django, his band, and its impresarios left the Ultraphone session and strolled up boulevard Saint-Germain in fine spirits. Suddenly, Django disappeared. Moments later, he was back—now sporting a brand-new broad-brimmed American fedora. The hat cost every *centime* he had just earned, but Django could care less: He expected soon to be earning a fortune. With his swarthy complexion and his trademark Romani moustache set off by this ivory-white fedora cocked just right over one eye, he was Louis Armstrong. Duke Ellington. Django Reinhardt.

Once Django started, the music poured from his guitar without end. Acceptance was slow at first, but soon the Quintette's star was on the rise every night in Pigalle. Between cutting "Dinah" on December 27, 1934, and the Quintette du Hot Club de France's last prewar recording session in August 1939 in London, the band waxed some 140 sides. And that's not including some hundred more they played on, backing French *chansonniers* as well as *la crème* of the visiting American jazzmen—Coleman Hawkins, Eddie South, Bill Coleman, Benny Carter, Arthur Briggs, Rex Stewart, and others.

Django played his unique Romani-influenced string jazz on covers of American jazz melodies already established as standards and then-new tunes on their way to becoming classics. He cut versions of everything he could by his hero Louis Armstrong. And he recorded a broad range of other melodies, from Fletcher Allen's reefer song "Viper's Dream" to Duke's "It Don't Mean a Thing (If It Ain't Got That Swing)."

The band also cut jazzed versions of classical music. As classical music was still a popular music of the day, making it swing on their strings was not so silly an idea as it seemed. The Quintette adapted Franz Liszt's composition, "Liebstraum No. 3," which Django re-harmonized using the chord progression from "Basin Street Blues," the New Orleans jazz classic penned by Spencer Williams and made immortal by Satchmo. Later, Django recorded selections of Edvard Grieg's *Norwegian Dances* as "Fantaisie sur une Danse Norvégienne." With classically trained African-American jazz violinist Eddie South, Django and Stéphane recorded two takes of Johann Sebastian Bach's *Concerto in D Minor*, released in 1937 as "Interprétation Swing du 1er Mouvement du Concerto en Ré Mineur de J.S. Bach" and as an "Improvisation" on the same theme.

What Django rarely recorded was Romani music. The sole exception in these early years was a version of the lachrymose Gypsy lullaby "Muri wachsella an u sennelo weesch," retitled as "Tears." Cut on April 3, 1937, for the British label His Master's Voice, Django fingerpicked the song, creating a mournful minor-major melody against a backdrop of descending harmonic chords that shuffled along like a New Orleans funeral parade. Django and Stéphane's interpretation was unique in jazz—a Gypsy song harmonized with jazzy diminished, minor sixth, and minor seventh chords, casting a wistful spell.

More and more, Django was turning to composing. Early on, the Quintette recorded its own "originals" such as "Oriental Shuffle," cut on May 4, 1936, for Gramophone. Yet this was a thinly veiled recasting of Armstrong's own "Oriental Strut." Better was to come.

Django's first true original tunes were likely band jam riffs built into song heads. Stéphane often served as musical transcriber and thus earned co-songwriter credits. Among the best of Django's early compositions was his eponymous "Djangology," first recorded in September 1935 for Ultraphone. It began with a baroque intro, Stéphane's violin matching Django's guitar note for note in a teaser, building tension before leaping double time into the melody. Django's theme was a repeated riff in descending arpeggios on a circle of fourths, the lines rhyming in poetic form. With "Djangology," Django and the Quintette created a catchy melody with all the simple grace of Fats Waller's "Honeysuckle Rose."

And yet to get Django to make music was sometimes a near-insurmountable task. There were card games to play, Gypsy weddings to attend, or the open road called. As Stéphane later famously stated, "What troubles he gave me. I think now I would rather play with lesser musicians and have a peaceable time than with Django and his monkey business."

The first problem was simply getting Django to show up. Panassié listed the hurdles in overcoming this deceptively easy stage: "It was never possible to assure that we'd have Django's services. He always agreed to come, but it was folly to hope he'd arrive at the studio on time. Most of our sessions were in the morning between nine o'clock and noon. Django didn't go to bed until six or seven in the morning, and there was always the question of awakening him and then if he'd have the strength to quit his bed. I had to send someone to awaken him, but never before eight in the morning. He had to be awakened as gently as possible, and then Django would not want to budge. *Alors*, my envoy then went to the nearest café to fetch him a *café crème* and croissants. Django could then be enticed to sit up in bed to eat breakfast. This was the first step down the road to success. Then Django would ask for some music on the radio, and my friend would play with the tuning dial to try and find music to please Django. *Enfin*, after many yawns and every delay or excuse possible, he'd accept his fate and get up to *faire le toilette* and dress. There was no question of hurrying him; everything was a compromise to his mood. *Finalement*, he'd arrive at the studio at 10:15, and we'd have lost forty-five precious minutes—yet Django's playing was so good that he compensated for any time we lost."

Once finally in the studio, Django needed to determine *what* to record. Whether the songlist was set by the label, producer, or, more rarely, left open to the musicians, one or another band member often needed to be taught the tune, especially if it was one of Django's new compositions. Then, an arrangement had to be crafted. Django often jumped into a song on the spur of the moment, directing each musician in that player's role. He illustrated the harmonies for his accompanists by performing his pieces on guitar and simply whistling or humming the accompaniment for the band to learn their parts.

Stéphane's approach to recording, on the other hand, was much more serious—sometimes too serious, requiring a bit of artificial inspiration to oil his playing. As Panassié recalled, "During the sessions, Stéphane was 'supported' by frequent absorption of glasses of Cinzano, one of his preferred aperitifs. There was a bistro next door to the studio, and one of his friends marched back and forth unceasingly, carrying fresh glasses of Cinzano. *Finalement*, it appeared more convenient to buy a bottle. It was set on the piano and Stéphane could serve himself his frequent glassfuls. While he had a good many glasses, he was never drunk and I never saw him lose control of himself. At most, he was a little merry toward the end of the last session, when he said to me with his Parisian street accent: 'I must send a letter of thanks to Monsieur Cinzano.'"

For Django, recording was like painting, the studio his *atelier* and the wax discs blank canvases upon which to create. Panassié described this artistic process with disbelief: "Django recorded with great *esprit*. He dashed off the most daring improvisations and completely modified his solos from one test to another. You had to see him listening to the wax tests: When he heard one of his own lightning-like phrases, he leaped up, stupefied, crying with joy—a child astonished at his own brilliant exploits. Grappelli and the other guitarists also expressed their satisfaction in a resounding fashion. The engineers were amazed at all this joy: '*Eh bien*, they are happy with what they do!' one of them said to me. *Evidemment*, this attitude was in contrast with that of most artists who recorded: They listened to their wax tests with a concerned air, endeavoring to tighten their interpretation more and more until they considered it to be ideal, fixed once and for all. *Ici*, there was none of that. Each wax test represented a fresh creative effort, completed in joy and enthusiasm; the musicians intensely lived each phrase, each note—it thrilled and excited them all. Moreover, Django's joyous outbursts after hearing some of his phrases were not of pride or conceit: Django listened as though it was another musician—he didn't know that he was capable of this, he was sincerely amazed when he heard the phrases that he had played. He played them without planning them; they had come from some unknowable region of his subconscious. Listening, he laughed and repeated his favorite expressions: '*Oh, ma mère!*' or '*C'est n'est pas possible!*' "

I am listening now to Django's composition "Boléro." The song runs almost four minutes, and thus did not fit on a conventional 78. Instead, Gramophone was forced to release it on a twenty-five-centimeter 78 rpm record, the large, expensive platters usually reserved for serious classical music. This was only fitting. With "Boléro," Django proved for all time he was serious as a composer. He cut the song on December 14, 1937, almost three years to the day after he recorded his opening jazz salvo with "Dinah." But oh how far he had come.

Django here melded flamenco with jazz, but he was inspired as well by classical music. He composed and arranged "Boléro" as an orchestral piece, and carefully conducted the recording to paint a picture in music. The Quintette was joined by a small orchestra of three trumpets, two trombones, a flute, and three violins—yet not Stéphane. The song began with Django quoting the Spanish Gitanos rhythmic dance figure of Maurice Ravel's *Boléro*. A horn section then made its entrance, softly sounding a mournful obbligato modulating in ascending half-steps, building anticipation. When the tension's almost too much to bear, the song suddenly breaks wide open in an exaltive flurry of Django's majestic flamenco guitar riffs.

Listening to this recording today, seventy years later, I'm amazed by how modern it sounds. Here was an homage to the Gitan music of Django's childhood blended with the impressionist modal music of Ravel and Debussy, all arranged and conducted with the sophistication of Duke Ellington. And yet despite the multiple and varied influences, in the end, this "Boléro" was all Django.

I'm sitting in a cozy apartment in Montparnasse in 2003 talking with Emmanuel Soudieux, reminiscing about his days as bass player with the Quintette du Hot Club de France. Stuffed armchairs are protected by antimacassars, family photographs populate the walls, fresh flowers cast their scent from a vase. Monsieur Emmanuel is a classic gentleman as they only come from France: suit-coated and dapper even in retirement, silvery hair still combed back stylishly from his brow, a smile made of warmth. After a lifetime playing bass in most every great French jazz ensemble, he now spends his days tinkering with radios, a fascination left over from his youth when radios were as new as swing. The fact that I'm sitting is important simply because Monsieur Emmanuel is not: He's prancing and dancing around the living room, belying his eighty-four years, acting out with a spry step and twinkle and great laughs incidents of Django's shenanigans as bandleader, drinking companion, travel compatriot, and all-around character.

No one, not even Stéphane Grappelli, played alongside Django longer than Emmanuel—no one except Django's brother Joseph, that is, but then he got a head start as they began busking together with their banjos when they were just boys. Emmanuel joined Django when the bassist was nineteen. And in photographs from those days, Emannuel indeed looks fresh-faced, a happy-go-lucky kid lost behind the bulk of his string bass. In those band pictures, he also appears starry eyed, perhaps not quite believing that he had won a berth in the hottest band in all Europe. Now, he's a jazz pensioner, living off his memories of wild nights in those Pigalle clubs—and he still has stars in his eyes as he talks about the old days.

The jazz life did not pay well enough to keep many musicians afloat, and even with its success, the Quintette was not a lucrative venture for the sidemen. Roger Chaput was the first of the original members to go. Believing Stéphane pocketed more than his share of the take after a 1938 English concert, Chaput demanded a fairer split. Stéphane refused, so Chaput wound up and punched him in the nose. He then turned on his heel and said goodbye to the Quintette forever. Vola was next. Offered better pay in Ray Ventura's big band, Les Collégiens, he quit in late 1938. Stéphane too left in 1939, partly to stay behind in England as World War II began, partly to start his own solo career—and partly because he was weary of Django's wiles. And then there was Nin-Nin, who probably quit—and then rejoined—the Quintette on a weekly basis when he was on the outs with his lordly big brother.

Through the years, Django went through bandmates like he went through guitar strings. But the pace was the quickest with bassists, who were paid the least and treated the worst. That game of musical chairs finally ended in 1938 with the arrival of Emmanuel. Born July 30, 1919, he played in musette and tango bands, but dreamed only of jazz. Django heard him one night, and then during the band's break, asked, "What are you doing tomorrow?" As Emmanuel now acts out for me in his Montparnasse apartment, he replied, *"Rien."* To which Django stated simply, *"Eh bien!* You'll come play with us." Emmanuel would play his basslines with Django for the next eleven years.

Yet behind the music, all was not always harmonious within the Quintette. While seeking Django's musical approval, Emmanuel fended off Stéphane's intimate advances. And there was also an impenetrable cultural divide between the band's Gypsies and *gadjé*. During their second trip to England, Baro Ferret taught the naïve Emmanuel to play poker and in the process, emptied most of Emmanuel's wallet. Soon after, Emmanuel realized the rest of his tour earnings were missing as well: He always eyed Baro as the slick pickpocket. "Baro was a great guitarist," Emmanuel tells me, with an evil glint, "but he was also *un gangster*."

Emmanuel quickly proved himself indispensable to Django. Performing one night in the 1940s, the band was jamming on Django's thoroughly modern reworking of the classic "Dinah," which he titled "Dînette." In the midst of Django's solo, Emmanuel struck a stylish counterpoint bass line to Django's guitar. The bass obbligato caught Django's ear, and he spun around mid-solo to regale Emmanuel with a rare, beaming smile of appreciation, as Emmanuel too now demonstrates for me. That smile has burned bright with him through all these years.

Now, retired from jazz, Monsieur Emmanuel lives here with his woman friend of many years in an apartment alive with memories. He played with jazz greats from Henri Crolla to Martial Solal, Yves Montand to Miles Davis. But in his mind, none of them matched Django. Monsieur Emmanuel leans over, resting his hand on my arm and looking me straight in the eye; he wants to be sure I am listening as he sums up all of his nights and jams and love for Django: "*Django, c'était la musique fait l'homme,*" he tells me. "Django was music made man."

Everyone who played alongside Django remembers that incredible musicality. I'm backstage in the dressing room of Beryl Davis, the English singer who sang with the Quintette starting in 1937. It's now February 2004, and she's just about to go on stage again. To calm herself from an uncharacteristic attack of the butterflies, she's reminiscing with me about her days with Django.

Beryl was a mere twelve years old when she was hooked up with the band. Twelve, perhaps, but experienced. She was the daughter of guitarist Harry Davis and performed regularly on the bandstand alongside her father as well as over BBC radio. In a surviving photo of Beryl with the Quintette, she looks impossibly young and innocent, especially when surrounded by Django's cabal of swarthy and mustachioed Gypsies.

Beryl met the Quintette via impresario Lew Grade, a former Cossack dancer turned agent. He was half of Will Collins & Lew Grade Theatrical & Vaudeville Exchange, and was booking the Quintette for its premiere tour of Great Britain in 1938. Grade was setting up the band to perform on the English vaudeville circuit, where he believed they'd reach a broader audience than just playing to jazz fans in traditional concert halls. Yet the plan had risks. The Quintette was unknown to the British public, and there was no telling how their new music would resonate. So, Grade sought to educate his audience. He hired a movie crew to film a six-minute-plus promotional short entitled *Jazz "Hot"* to be shown in British theaters providing a lesson in jazz appreciation to warm up the crowds. The film opened with a classical orchestra playing Handel's *Largo* with all of the energy and charm of a dirge. Then the narrator explained the differences in jazz interpretation and improvisation so no one would be offended as Django and the Quintette swung with all their might through "J'attendrai." If the British harbored any questions about the Quintette, Django and Stéphane's jam on the silver screen answered them.

Part of Grade's plan, as Beryl is telling me, was to add her vocals to the shows to further broaden their appeal. She arrived in Paris complete with chaperone, which must have perplexed Django and band. Beryl was booed by her first French audiences for singing in English, but then there weren't many jazz tunes in French. In the end, however, her swing singing won over both the crowds and band. She would sing with Django on and off for the next three years.

Beryl was young, but she lacked nothing in sophistication. She was born to show business, and wore off-the-shoulder evening gowns with a style beyond her age. And she belted out torch songs of love lost and broken hearts as if her own tears would never dry and her heart was cleft right down the center.

Impresario Grade's scheme proved a success. Playing Great Britain's vaudeville circuit in 1938, Django and the Quintette became overnight stars. And with Beryl in tow, they set off on tours through Belgium, the Netherlands, and Scandinavia. Grade then booked them for a return tour to England in 1939, plotting to enlarge it into a world tour, venturing next to India, and perhaps even the United States. Straightaway, Beryl and the Quintette scored a hit with their version of the swinging lament over indecision, "Undecided."

And tonight, on stage again almost seven decades later, Beryl is going to sing "Undecided" once more.

Now in her eighties, Beryl lives in Southern California, where she ended up after playing with the Quintette and then moving on to the United States to sing with the likes of Louis Armstrong and Frank Sinatra. She's about to take the stage again to reprise her hit, singing now with multitalented multi-instrumentalist John Jorgenson and his band at a Django tribute concert in Laguna Beach. In her dressing room, she's just finished putting on her makeup, a glorious lacy white gown, and high heels. She's more than a bit nervous; talking about the old days seems to quell some of this rare stage fright.

"On stage, Django showed little emotion as he played," Beryl remembers. "I would sit on a chair next to the band, then get up and act as the emcee. I learned just enough French to introduce the band at shows at Paris's ABC Théâtre and the Olympia and sing a few songs in French as well as English." She often sang slow tunes such as "Wishing," "Don't Worry about Me," and a plaintive "The Man I Love" before launching into "Undecided." As *Melody Maker* magazine reported on one of their English concerts, the song would be greeted with much "palm-pelting."

Beryl's on a roll herself now as she reminisces: "Django would never open his mouth on stage—he was very lovely, very handsome, and very shy. He was like Harpo Marx in front of an audience. He never spoke to them. He said everything in his music."

When she is chaperoned now into the spotlights, Beryl is just the opposite. Effusive and warm, she herself lights up the stage. After a shaky start, she and Jorgenson's band nail "Undecided"—and with panache. And just as it was all those years ago, the audience is on its feet with enthusiastic and sincere applause. Enough so that Beryl is ready to sing another song—or three—unrehearsed.

For Django, life—like music—was all one grand improvisation.

With concert tours across Europe and his records being released in France, England, and even as far afield as Czechoslovakia, Japan, and the homeland of jazz, the United States, Django made fortunes. And he spent them just as easily and quickly. The Rothschilds paid him to perform at their Paris *soirées*, movie stars danced to his guitar in Pigalle, and royalty lined up to shake his magical hand. Django believed in enjoying his success—fancy fedoras, feasts for family and friends that cost him every *centime* he earned, impossible bets on billiards, *belote*, and *boules*. He earned money as fast as he could pick his guitar.

When times were good, Django and Naguine camped out in a glorious apartment on Les Champs-Élysées. More often, he and Naguine lived in hotel rooms or small apartments in Pigalle or Montmartre—temporary caravanserais along the way. Still, Django never grew used to living indoors. He preferred skies to ceilings. Indoor silence disturbed him, so he left the faucet running all night to mimic the lullaby of an outdoor stream. He never liked sleeping under sheets, which were better used for covering dead bodies; he preferred the down quilts of his traveling youth. And he could not bear the harshness of electric lights, so he struck a match to candles or kerosene lanterns that lit their rooms with a more hospitable glow recreating the ambiance of a *roulotte*. As Naguine explained, "For us, houses are like prisons." And so, even when he was living in style in *haute* Paris, Django still also always kept his true home—a caravan in *La Zone*—ready for the road.

Growing up, a horse always pulled the family's caravan, but now Django, the modern Gypsy, had a modern steed—an automobile. Throughout his life he was besotted by cars. He never earned a driver's license, but he owned many auto-mobiles, and usually the fastest or most luxurious possible. When he first made money playing jazz in the early 1930s, he immediately bought a car, a 1926 Dodge convertible, the pinnacle of American glamor. This Dodge, dusty and decrepit, had traveled far past its glory days, yet in his eyes it glittered and gleamed. A photo taken by Louis Vola shows Django with his new steel horse, leaning against the engine cowling, his hand jauntily on his hip and a brilliant white snap-brim cap cocked over one eye, the sheik of Araby in person. Django often bought new cars, paid for them in handfuls of cash, and drove them to an early grave—one into the Mediterranean, others into poorly sited trees. As Emmanuel Soudieux described, "Whenever Django had money, he bought him-self a car. He loved cars! And when he was broke, he smoked *mégots*—cigarette butts—but he was never unhappy. When he was broke, he simply stayed *chez lui* and Naguine went on the scrounge for money. And when he had money again, he bought champagne—he was the *grand seigneur!*" But the freedom of an auto-mobile was a thrill that never faded. Again Naguine explained: "I would rather have an automobile than the most beautiful *château*."

As a child, Django was impatient to experience life and could not be bothered with the confines of sitting at a school desk. One result was that he never truly learned to read or write, neither words nor music. And yet as he once told Emmanuel, "With my guitar in my hands, I am not afraid of anyone, neither the Pope nor the President of the United States." Romanès remained his first lan-guage, and he never spoke French perfectly, retaining a Manouche accent as well as a slight lisp. When asked questions by radio interviewers or journalists, he was strictly a yes and no man, rarely explaining himself, never effusive. Yet with his guitar, he was a different man. His guitar joked and jested, moaned and cried. As a Gypsy, he learned to hide his feelings and fears from the *gadjé*, but in his music he was pure eloquence and emotion.

It was Stéphane who taught Django the rudiments of spelling in the long hours between shows and on tours in the mid 1930s. "There was a chink in his armour," Stéphane explained. "Sometimes he was intimidated because of his lack of formal education, though you had to know him well to discern this. As you would expect, he was not keen on people knowing that he could neither read nor write. In the first days of the Quintette he was often shown a contract which he would eye for some time before nodding his acceptance. He was not a man who found it easy to ask advice, and he would sometimes okay an offer without even showing it to me. That was one reason why we had a few catastrophes at the beginning. Later on most of the letters came to me, and I tried to arrange the work for the group. Even so, two signatures were needed, and after a time I said: 'Look, Django, when we sign a contract it is miserable for you having to put a cross.' (It was a funny cross too.) 'I think it will look brighter if you sign your name.' At once he was enthusiastic to learn—so long as we kept it a secret—and I began showing him the letters of the alphabet. As it was a difficult matter for him, I taught him just the capitals. I will not say that I taught him to write; but I certainly showed him how to sign his name. We began, naturally enough, with 'Django,' and took so long on the word that I said: 'Never mind the 'Django'— 'D' will do just as well.' At first he was insistent on the whole name; he really liked the name Django, said it sounded nice (he never liked me to call him Reinhardt, always Django). Finally, he got tired, too, and agreed with me that 'D' would do. That was all right. The great job came when we started on 'Reinhardt.' It is a complicated name and spelling meant nothing to Django anyway. Still, he was a painter who could remember a shape, and at last he got it. Once he had, there was not enough paper in the room to satisfy him. Everywhere I looked I saw 'D. Reinhardt.' It was a relief, because few things were ever more difficult than getting that man to sign his name. And it was worth the effort, because in his face I saw such pleasure."

Even now that he had learned to sign a contract, doing business with Django was still a hazard. Stéphane recalled negotiating a contract to tour England, advising Django to follow his lead: "I said to Django, 'Listen, Django . . . I will show you the paper, and when I'm reading, if I said OK, remember: OK. I'll give you the paper and you say OK. *Bon?*'" Stéphane read the contract, and everything was proper. He signaled Django with a simple, "OK." Django, however, had other plans. He studiously pored over the contract he could not read, then pointed out a paragraph and indignantly stated, "I don't like this!" Turmoil rendered the negotiations, until Stéphane could scan the clause that so upset Django: It promised the band all expenses paid to travel roundtrip via first class. Stéphane quickly told Django to shut his mouth and sign his hard-learned scrawl.

For Django, business deals were always horse trades. And oftentimes, it seemed he was a success in spite of himself. He demanded whatever Benny Goodman or Cary Grant or Tyrone Power were paid on the other side of the world. And even then, he might or might not make his scheduled appearance if a good game of cards was at hand. Or he simply hit the road when the mood struck him. *Jazz Hot* always listed who was appearing where on the French jazz scene; in January 1937, the magazine reported that "Django Reinhardt was seen on Route Nationale number 7, at kilometer post 489, close to Lyon."

I too am lost, but on a backstreet in Paris, when I discover a diminutive bistro known as Le Clown Bar. The *boîte* is about as big as one of those miniature clown cars that pull up and park center ring as clown after clown after clown piles out.

The bar itself is parked at 114 rue Amelot, just a fortunate few footsteps from Le Cirque d'Hiver, the capital's winter circus quarters housed in the magnificent twenty-sided polygonal theater dating to 1852. Le Clown Bar has served the circus clowns since 1902, and likely earlier. Not only did clowns slip out the circus side door for a quick nip *entr'actes*, but the bar was also a makeshift employment agency for impresarios seeking clowns, a clown flophouse with rooms to rent upstairs, and a *poste restante* for clowns traveling with circuses throughout France and Europe. It's also simply a fine place to cool your heels while waiting for your clown shoes to be made or mended down the street at Cordonnerie Amelot, where the cobbler's windows displays big-toed, long-footed shoes in shiny patent-leather reds, yellows, and blues with designs from polka dots to flames to a patriotic *tricoleur*.

Inside, Le Clown Bar is all clown. The décor celebrates "Les Vrais Rois des Rires," as one hoary Ancillotti Plege circus poster announces. The age-old tiled floors feature a fitting star design while the walls are tiled with Art Nouveau bas-relief Sarreguemines faïence depicting clowns at work—or, more properly, at play. A horseshoe-shaped zinc bar is center stage for good luck, while overhead is a backlit painted-glass ceiling with more clowns. Dividing the bar from the *salle* there's a wooden archway inset with circus lightbulbs and a clock in pride of place at center, presumably so the drinking clowns know what time they have to be back on stage. But the crowds would wait for a tardy clown: They were often the stars, and many a circus was named after its clown. Just in case a clown forgot, however, the walls and shelves and even the glistening coffee machine here are hung with clown memorabilia of all sorts: turn-of-the-last-century posters, programs, ads, autographed photographs, teapots, even clocks. There are happy, sad, and devilish clowns; midget clowns and dwarf clowns such as Le Nain Goliath—"The Dwarf Goliath"; jesters and harlequins and merry-andrews; Pulcinella, Arlecchino, Pierrot, Pickelherring, and Auguste; a small statuette of Emmett Kelly as Weary Willie; a still of Lon Chaney in *He Who Gets Slapped*; the *frères* Fratellini, who danced in the 1920 surrealist ballet *Le Bœuf sur le Toit*; and of course, that greatest of the greats, Achille Zavatta. There is a porcelain figurine of Pagliacci pounding on his infamous drum, and other clowns playing accordions, bugles, violins, and, of course, guitars.

Django and most of the Romani musicians of his generation played music for the French and Gypsy circuses at one time or several others. From the family-run *cirque forains* that wandered France in *caravanes* like Django's own mother and father to the majestic tented circuses that set up in vacant lots outside cities, they all needed musical accompaniment. No one understood this better than the Gypsy musicians themselves.

Even at the peak of his career, Django made circus music. During World War II, when both jazz and circuses were in the midst of golden ages, Django played with the Cirque Frattaloni clowns at L'Alhambra music hall in Paris. He led his Nouveau Quintette to perform with the Cirque Médrano in summer 1943 and created the soundtrack for the Cirque Bouglione and Zavatta himself in 1945. There's a photo of Joseph Reinhardt leading his *orchestre*, including Django's second son, Babik Reinhardt, and Dingo Adel, here at Le Cirque d'Hiver in 1967. And they all likely played for more circuses at other times as well.

Bassist Emmanuel Soudieux acted out for me one *soirée* when Django and band were performing with the Cirque Frattaloni at L'Alhambra and someone forgot Django's guitar. Carrying his guitar was never Django's own responsibility; he believed this labor below him, and one of his bandmates—often Nin-Nin—was responsible. Yet without a guitar, there was no music. Happily, the Frattaloni clowns had a guitar—a metal-bodied toy with wire strings they used to hit each other over the head. Django didn't care. He tuned the wires as best he could, and played it as though it were his Selmer. When the evening was done, the calluses on his fretting fingers were sliced through, blood dripping down his digits. But Django had made music on a clown's toy guitar.

Playing music for circuses likely influenced Django's own music, but today I can only speculate on how. No recordings of his circus scores survive, no compositions specially marked for the tent shows remain. Yet whether it was the bombastic soundtrack to an acrobat performing derring-do or the jazz score for dancers to step to in a Pigalle *boîte du nuit*, both musics share elements. There's the drama and dynamics, the build-up, and finally, the release—all elements that Django became adept at in his compositions. And he was long a master of song quotes within jazz improvisations, designed to catch the audience's ear or even provoke a laugh.

Whatever influence the circuses had on Django's music, they certainly fueled his dreams of spectacle. Performing with the Cirque Médrano in 1943, he watched the acrobats and trapeze artists in the heavens of the circus tent. With this inspiration, Django envisioned himself lowered to the stage perched on a luminous star of his own as he played. "It'll be *très américain!*" he pronounced with pride. The circus hands built Django a star, yet when it was ready, one of his bandmates teased him that the rope holding it looked none to strong. Seized by fear of riding a falling star, no amount of reassurance could get him onto the seat. In the end, Django arrived on the circus stage in less stellar style—on a miniature trainlike dolly that rode just centimeters above the safety of the earth on steel rails.

Walking back through Pigalle these nights, it's the same old refrain: much has changed and much is still the same. Street lamps and neon lights glint off the *pavé* under my feet, the moon—and Sacré Cœur—shining above. Gone are most of the illustrious old cabarets where Django played. Bricktop's, La Boîte à Matelots, Les Nuits Bleues, Chez Florence, Swing Time, Chez Jane Stick, La Roulotte, and the glorious Russian cabarets that were the best of the best—the Casanova, Don Juan, and Shéhérazade. All are now just history. But soldiering on night after night in Pigalle is the Moulin Rouge as well as others across the rest of Paris—the Villa d'Este, Montecristo, Cinema Normandie, Le Bœuf sur le Toit, and more. Sometimes, only the names—and the music—have changed.

Ernest Hemingway brashly proclaimed the movable feast that was jazz had already left Pigalle and Montmartre behind by the 1930s. According to Hemingway, the music moved across town to Montparnasse years before, and what he says goes. But F. Scott Fitzgerald—who knew both the high and low life better than Hemingway could ever comprehend—still ventured to Pigalle. Montparnasse might have been chic, but Pigalle was *real*. In Fitzgerald's short story eulogy, "Babylon Revisited," he writes in what was obviously a thinly veiled description of his own travels, "After an hour he left and strolled toward Montmartre, up the rue Pigalle into the place Blanche. The rain had stopped and there were a few people in evening clothes disembarking from taxis in front of cabarets, and *cocottes* prowling singly or in pairs, and many Negroes. He passed a lighted door from which issued music, and stopped with the sense of familiarity; it was Bricktop's, where he had parted with so many hours and so much money."

Django's Quintette was one of the star attractions at Bricktop's. This Pigalle *boîte* was the hottest spot in the *quartier chaud*. African-American hostess and songstress Bricktop was once known back home in West Virginia as Ada Beatrice Queen Victoria Louise Virginia Smith. In Paris, she was reborn as Bricktop in honor of her frazzle of brick-red hair. Each evening throughout the summer of 1937, the Quintette performed several sets of their unique brand of string jazz, then served as the house band, backing Bricktop for her nightly spot in the light. And they accompanied African-American singer Mabel Mercer for her appearance on stage. As Bricktop remembered the wild nights in her eponymous autobiography, "After the sun went down, Paris did become the City of Light, and Montmartre changed from a sleepy little village to a jumpin' hot town." In remembrance of those nights, Django composed his songs "Bricktop" and "Mabel," sultry jazz jumps that captured all the nocturnal allure of Pigalle.

Poet Langston Hughes fell prey to the trap, too. He was dreaming of becoming a writer, while also escaping Jim Crow at home for the apparent racial freedom of this Parisian Harlem where African Americans were accepted—better yet, celebrated—for their jazz. Hughes slaved away nights as a dishwasher in another Pigalle nightclub, Le Grand Duc at 52 rue Pigalle. Here, he scrubbed pots and pans while gazing at American temptress Florence Embry Jones singing out on the stage. To Hughes, Jones was a sepia-pelted tigress dressed in skintight golden gowns with crowns of orchids in her hair—"a brownskin princess, remote as a million dollars." He remembered those nights in his 1940 autobiography, *The Big Sea*: "Blues in the rue Pigalle. Black and laughing, heart-breaking blues in the Paris dawn, pounding like a pulse beat, moving like the Mississippi!" And it was Django's Quintette often pounding out those blues at Le Grand Duc.

The Hot Club itself settled into offices at 14 rue Chaptal in Pigalle in 1939. The nocturnal members spent most of their time here anyway, so they must have figured they should make it their official home. Delaunay celebrated the club's new headquarters with a big night as Django and his Quintette played for special guest Duke Ellington, in Paris during a European tour. The Hot Club's quarters were replete with a library of jazz records and books, a small garden perfect for *plein air* jams, and cellar *cave* ideal for dances. Across the street was a bistro run by *la mère* Berthe Saint-Marie who watched over her young jazz aficionados, keeping the best table reserved for them as they arrived for breakfast on their way homeward after a long night. Django stopped in here for *le petit dejeuner* most days, joining his bandmates and other musicians of Pigalle, his swarthy face needing a shave and wearing just slippers on his feet, settling in to break his baguette and down a *café crème* while discussing the latest records with Delaunay.

These days, rue Chaptal—like much of the rest of Pigalle—is a curious mélange of residential neighborhood and red lights. Schoolchildren's games and laughter fill the air down the street from where the Hot Club's headquarters once were; the old offices were razed in later years, part of some well-meaning city planner's idea of urban renewal. Now, the street's staunch-faced buildings frown down on the surrounding *boîtes* and brothels of Pigalle. As the sun rises, I pass *cocottes* wandering unsteadily home to a well-earned rest just as other residents leave for work. By afternoon, the *putains* and *danseuses* are awake and fresh. They venture out into the sunlight for their breakfast and to walk their poodles, crossing paths with the *faubourg*'s respectable women on their way home with the day's shopping.

Place Blanche remains the heart of Pigalle. The *place* is so named for a historic insane asylum that once housed white-clothed inmates. Today, it's picturesque mostly for the lurid red. And yet still, it gets photographed as much as the Tour Eiffel by tourists—including me. This is the home of the Moulin Rouge, where the neon namesake windmill never stops turning. When Django played Le Bal du Moulin Rouge in the early 1940s, it was just another seedy dance hall. The bandmates remembered lounging around between sets with nothing better to do than throw their knives at a target drawn on their dressing-room door; by the time they moved on two weeks later, the door was nothing but splinters hanging on hinges. These nights, the Moulin Rouge is filled to capacity with Japanese tourists watching the sanitized yet still suitably naughty can-can.

I walk from place Blanche down rue Fontaine to rue de Douai. Here, music stores crowd the streets, selling well-traveled old Gypsy guitars alongside glittery new Stratocasters to today's rock'n'rollers. This is guitar heaven: There are more guitar, bass, amplifier, and effects stores here within six blocks than anywhere on the globe. It's all part of Django's legacy as the one of the first guitarists to show the world of what this strange instrument was truly capable.

Then as now, rue Fontaine is a sideshow of the night. Josephine Baker opened her *haute* Chez Josephine cabaret here in the late 1920s. La Boîte à Matelots, where Django played alongside Guérino and Baro Ferret, was down the street. Bricktop's was at number 42. These famous *boîtes* are long gone, but their former sites are still clubs today—strip joints, B-girl bars, and small-time bordellos brightened by halos of neon and bearing the suggestive names La Bohème, La Nouvelle Eve, Carrousel de Paris, Atomik Bar, Caprice, Le Cancan Club, Lucky Bar, Dirty Dick, Le Jet d'Eau, Kiss Me. Leaning out perfectly sited windows or sitting on stools in doorways, women and men of all shapes and sizes and colors await under the aurora of red light.

In Django's day, the soundtrack here was pure, hot, salacious live jazz. Today, the music's all prerecorded disco and techno. The songs have changed, but the aim remains the same.

And yet, walking Pigalle on a rainy eve in autumn, it's jazz that made these streets. Like Storyville, like Harlem, so with Pigalle. Even today, only jazz seems right, the soundtrack of midnight. Then as now, Django's music is Paris—Paris beautiful, Paris tragic, Paris golden, Paris *noir*.

Songs of One Thousand and One Nights

F I V E *Django Reinhardt, Schnuckenack Reinhardt,*
and Gypsy Jazz under the Nazis

M ORE THAN ANYTHING at the Bergen-Belsen concentration camp I'm struck by the silence. Even on a fine sunny day, it's quiet here. No birdsong, no squirrels, no insects. Not even the wind seems to make a sound.

I've come to Bergen-Belsen in northwestern Germany seeking a sense of Django and his fellow Romani's lives during World War II. This was the most mysterious period of Django's life, and yet ironically, it was also his most successful and prolific. At times, he was fleeing from the Nazis. At others, he was encamped in a luxurious apartment on the Champs-Élysées. And throughout, his muse never left him; he continued to compose and record, crafting some of his most wonderful sides ever.

At Bergen-Belsen, there's little left today. At the start, this was a prisoner-of-war camp, Stalag 311. But the Nazis later converted it into a concentration camp, the first inmates arriving on April 30, 1943. Following them through the camp gates came tens of thousands of Romani, Jews, political prisoners, homosexuals, Russian POWs, forced laborers, and other *Untermenschen*—"undesirables." During the next two years, some 100,000 people died or were exterminated at Bergen-Belsen by the Nazi Schutzstaffel (SS). Yet it was SS-Reichsführer Heinrich Himmler who, foreseeing the end of the Third Reich, handed the camp to the British. Plotting behind Hitler's back to negotiate a secret peace with the Allies to join Germany in a new war against the Communists, Himmler surrendered Bergen-Belsen on April 15, 1945, as an act of goodwill. But when the British Army entered, it filmed the unbelievable sights greeting them at the camp—mounds of some 10,000 rotting corpses and numerous unmarked mass graves, including that of Anne Frank. The film was shown in theater newsreels throughout England and the United States, the rest of the world's first view of Nazi atrocities. And still, even after the camp was liberated, typhus was so rampant that some 13,000 more inmates died. To destroy the typhoid-carrying lice, on May 21, 1945, the last compound at Bergen-Belsen was burned to the ground. So, to accompany the silence today, there's an absence of any camp buildings. Just a flat plain with foundation outlines, grown over now with heather.

During the worst years, there was lots of noise here, from the guards' orders to the inmates' cries. And even music. Most of the Nazi camps boasted orchestras of conscripted musical inmates who played for the officers' and guards' relaxation as well as a death march for prisoners on their way to the gas chambers. Bergen-Belsen's *kommandant*, SS-Sturmhauptführer Josef Kramer, formed an orchestra of inmates to play for him his beloved Viennese waltzes. At Auschwitz, SS-Sonderführer Thies Christophersen, a fan of Romani music, organized a Gypsy orchestra. And there was even jazz. Jewish guitarist Coco Schumann played Django-inspired swing in a conscriptées' band at the Theresienstadt camp christened by the Nazis as the Ghetto Swingers. Transferred to Auschwitz, he was one of the Happy Five jazz quintet. It's almost impossible to even imagine.

Most Romani I meet don't want to talk about the Nazis' war on their people, which is of little surprise. The Gypsies call the Holocaust, *O Porrajmos*, a Romanès word meaning "The Great Devouring." Even before he set out to rid the Third Reich of Jews, Hitler began rounding up, sterilizing, and deporting Romani from across Europe. In the end, hundreds of thousands of Gypsies perished—even the estimates on how many were killed varies dramatically, from 200,000 to 2,000,000. As Romani historian Ian Hancock states, whatever the exact number, the death toll of Romani proportionate to their population exceeded that of Jewish victims. Django's cousin, the legendary violinist Schnuckenack Reinhardt, says more explicitly: "Whole families of Gypsies departed this world in smoke." Yet while the Jews make a point of speaking of the Shoah so the world remembers, the Romani in contrast seem to prefer to forget—or at least to mourn in silence.

When the Gypsies do talk of *O Porrajmos*, their story often begins, "Music saved my life..."

It was true of Django. It was true of Schnuckenack. And it was true of many others. It was all they had to fight back with. They played their music to stay alive.

During the years of the Nazi Occupation of France, between being a Romani and a jazz musician, Django appeared to be doomed.

Even before the Nazis waged war on the Romani, they began a blitzkrieg on jazz. Led by Hitler's propaganda minister, Josef Goebbels, the National Socialist Party worked zealously devising euphemisms to condemn the music—*jazzbazillus, niggerjazz, judenjazz.* In jazz's jungle rhythms and blue notes, Goebbels heard music corrupting German cultural greatness, a conspiracy of American-Judeo-Negro decadence destroying the minds and morals of Germany's youth. Jazz more than any other art form symbolized to the Nazis the evils of depraved races and soulless modernism. Goebbels now added one final label in the hopes of silencing swing—*Entartete Musik,* "degenerate music."

Goebbels's war on jazz began with the unveiling of his *Reichsmusikkammer* on November 15, 1933, a ministry devoted to propagating proper German music and quelling the undesirable. Composer Richard Strauss was named president, and soon began issuing *Reichsmusikprüfstelle* lists of "unwanted" music. Jazz tunes headed the lists. Goebbels meanwhile was usurping control of Germany's airwaves, even before seizing the press: He foresaw the power of the new medium of radio as a propaganda tool and sought to bend it to the Nazi will. Under Goebbels's command, on October 13, 1935, German radio director Eugene Hadamovsky banned the broadcasting of jazz for the nation's own good. The saxophone, that clarion of jazz, was in the spotlight as the culprit. Goebbels's final pincer move on jazz came when the United States entered the war, and he outlawed selling and playing American jazz records. Swing was a force so strong it had to be controlled.

Yet as much as he hated jazz, Goebbels held his hand in banning it outright. Swing was the rage in German homes as well as nightclubs, as popular among the *hausfraus* as with German soldiers and officers. Goebbels understood the insidious art of propaganda like no one else, and he knew he would never win over the masses to the Nazi cause if he deprived them of their favored dance music. Swing was both an enemy of the Reich and at the same time essential to the war effort as it provided escapism from everyday life and wartime worries. Jazz was a useful opiate of the masses.

With this in mind, the *Reichsmusikkammer* gave its grudging nod to select German and European bands to play jazz that was not too American or too hot. Playing concerts in German cabarets and halls as well as entertaining German troops before the war began were Jack Hylton's orchestra, Belgian bandleaders Fud Candrix and Stan Benders's big bands, and numerous native ensembles, including violinist Helmut Zacharias's groups with Django-inspired Italian guitarist Alfio Grasso. It was swing with the Nazi seal of approval.

Once war was declared in 1939 and the Germans overran Paris on June 14, 1940, Django, that doomed man, instead became a star. The Nazi-occupied City of Lights was to be the German Army's brothel. Goebbels planned that as reward, each and every German soldier would have a chance to come to Paris from wherever they were stationed in the Reich's growing realm. His slogan was soon on the lips of all German soldiers—*Jeder Einmal In Paris*, Everybody Once in Paris. And to make their dreams of Paris come true, there had to be wine, women, and song. And no one could play those songs like the Gypsies.

Django—as well as Nin-Nin, Baro, Matelo, and Sarane Ferret, Gusti Malha, and other Romani jazz musicians—were in great demand. Like all French entertainers, they had to have their music approved by the German Propaganda Abteilung. This official censorship bureau sought to stamp out the playing of degenerate music before the first notes were struck. And the ministry had its spies, with the Gestapo and SS to enforce its decrees. Yet banned jazz was what the German soldiers wanted, and so it was what they got. The Pigalle clubs were hopping each night with German soldiers and Parisians who wanted to forget the war. Other *boîtes du nuit* had been appropriated by the German officers as their own: Matelo Ferret's mainstay, Le Shéhérazade, that most elegant Russian cabaret, became the German High Command's after-hours headquarters. In these clubs, the same Germans who were rounding up and sending Gypsies to concentration camps like Bergen-Belsen were throwing reichsmarks like confetti at Django and his fellow Romani musicians to play encores of outlawed American swing.

Django was also inspired anew in his music. Hearing the lighter, fresher sound of Benny Goodman's swing, he launched the Nouveau Quintette du Hot Club de France in October 1940. His old Quintette with Stéphane Grappelli had been influenced first and foremost by Louis Armstrong and his flavor of New Orleans and Chicago jazz. Now, Django sought to swing. He did away with the all-string sound and heavy-handed *pompe* rhythm, seeking now a sonority that was fleet and airy. He added a drummer, Egyptian Pierre Fouad, and enlisted a new second soloist, a young clarinet player named Hubert Rostaing.

With the reichsmarks he was earning, Django and Naguine were supping on steak while the rest of France was rationed to turnips. And at the height of his wartime fame, Django was encamped—with various Gypsy cousins—in a posh apartment on Paris's poshest avenue, Les Champs-Élysées. In spite of the Nazi crusade against jazz—and in part because of it—the war and occupation heralded a golden age of swing in Europe. Yet each night, Django was playing his music simply to survive.

Jazz was dance music and good times music. It was also resistance music and protest music. In Paris—as in other cities occupied by the Nazis and even in the heart of the Third Reich—a new age of jazz fans was emerging with the war. This crowd first materialized in Paris as if out of nowhere, taking seats at one of Django's concerts on December 19, 1940, at the Salle Gaveau. Impresario Charles Delaunay awaited his usual audience of jazz fans, including those wearing German uniforms. But to his amazement, the hall filled to overflowing with fresh-faced French teens hooked on swing. Delaunay could not believe his eyes: "I was witnessing the sudden and extraordinary explosion of popularity of jazz in France." These youthful jazz aficionados were dubbed *les petits swings* by the derisive French press. But these teens soon had a better name for themselves. Enamored with Cab Calloway's scat singing, which they transliterated as "Za-zouzazouzazouhé," they called themselves *les zazous*.

For *les zazous*, jazz was a political stance, a fashion they wore on their cuffs for all the world to see. They copied Calloway's zoot suits, natty American style that stood against the German mode. They wore their hair long in a sort of proto-pompadour, and boys grew moustaches in the style of Django, carefully cut circumflexes accenting their top lip. Even their sunglasses were a sign of protest, the dark-blue lenses reflecting the blue-tinted windows of Paris's blackout in a cynical statement against their parents' generation and all it had wrought on them. And their elders, the collaborationist Vichy government, and the occupying German forces were all suitably outraged. *Les zazous* were a proud flourishing of a rebellious youth culture. To *les zazous*, swing was freedom. And if they couldn't have freedom, they could at least have swing.

Similar circles of swing kids were flaunting their music, joyous dance steps, and lifestyle in other cities under the Third Reich. The most famous were the Swing-Heinis of Hamburg, wealthy and worldly youths who chose jazz over the Hitler Youth—and ended up for the most part in prison or concentration camps. Other swingers were more clandestine. The Harlem Club of Frankfurt and more hot clubs in Berlin, Leipzig, and elsewhere learned to keep their volume and visibility down. Interrogating one of the Hamburg Swing-Heinis in July 1944, Gestapo SS-Sturmbannführer Hans "The Fox" Reinhardt warned the youth, "Anything that starts with Ellington ends with an assassination attempt on the Führer!" He may not have known how true his words were.

In Paris, Goebbels's Propaganda Abteilung was bringing its boot heel down harder on those who flaunted their swing as the war wore on. Delaunay and other jazzmen fashioned their own rules to this game: They cheated. With wit and wile far beyond the comprehension of the blindered fascist bureaucrats, Delaunay simply camouflaged the titles of American jazz tunes to win the Propaganda Abteilung's approval for play. The classic Dixieland jaunt "Tiger Rag" thus became "La rage du tigre," which, Delaunay explained in a century-long stretch of the truth, was based on an ancient French quadrille. Some American songs were simply translated into French, "Sweet Georgia Brown" becoming "Douce Georgette," "Honeysuckle Rose" blooming anew as "La rose de chèvrefeuille," and "Sweet Sue" now "Ma chère Suzanne." Others, meanwhile, were transliterated into jibberish as "I Got Rhythm" became "Agatha Rhythm." Delaunay was not the sole one to use this subterfuge. This same "cheating" was used in Belgium and the Netherlands—and even by some bands in Germany as well. In 1937, the Paul Krender Orchestra recorded its version of Ellington's "Karawane," which was released on that bastion of German music, Deutsche Grammophon. And most famously, "St. Louis Blues," named for the city, was renamed by Delaunay as "La tristesse de Saint Louis" in a beautifully ironic double entendre that summed up the era. In a subtle twist of wording, Delaunay had conferred sainthood on Louis Armstrong—a feat most fans would have applauded. And now, Saint Satchmo was blowing the blues for the fate of jazz under the Occupation.

Whether one was an old-time fan or a newborn *zazou*, the Nazi zeal against jazz grew more cruel as the war reached a turning point in 1943. To swing was to sin. Yet for some, jazz brought salvation.

I'm talking now with Jacques Bureau, one of the founders in 1931 of the Jazz Club Universitaire and then in 1932, the Hot Club de France. Born in 1912, Monsieur Bureau was in his mid-nineties at the time of our meeting, yet he still remembers those days with joy—and sometimes, anger. A compact man with white hair, he's dressed in a suit to greet me on a weekday morning, his lapel bearing a tiny pin with the French *tricoleur*, the symbol of a captain of industry.

Monsieur Bureau lives still in the *ville* where he was born, Meudon, just to the southwest of Paris, on a hillside overlooking the Seine, the capital splendid in the distant sunlight. His home is what the French lovingly term *une vieille pierre*—an old stone. This small *château*, encircled by trimmed hedges and a gravel drive, embodies the enduring France the way the French dream of it. In Monsieur Bureau's living room are vintage radio sets and Modernist paintings by Daudet and others, all symbols of his lifelong love affair with jazz, art, and the avant garde. He can talk from personal experience of everyone from Louis Armstrong to Django, Salvador Dalì to Leon Trotsky.

He starts, however, by telling me of the day when his world was changed forever—by jazz. He was just a thirteen-year-old boy in 1925 when his industrialist father brought home an American record of Paul Whiteman's orchestra, and the whole household—from his mother to the maids—was swept away, dancing to the infectious music. To Bureau, jazz suddenly and totally infused his life: "I viewed jazz as a three-dimensional liberation of music." A youthful enthusiast for the brave new world of radiotelephony, he built his own shortwave radio and lay awake nights in his bedroom in Meudon, tuning in to a jazz radio station in Schenectady, New York. He recalls for me the moment seventy years ago when he first heard Bix Beiderbecke on those nocturnal radio shows: "Beiderbecke, what a revelation! It was music from beyond! I quickly learned the difference between Whiteman and true jazz. Whiteman was a condiment to give taste to the sauce; Armstrong and the others were the red hot peppers!" Bureau's father arranged an interview for his eighteen-year-old son with Lucien Lévy, who in 1917 invented the superheterodyne radio and later started Paris's pioneering Radio L.L. station. Looking for something to fill the empty airwaves, Lévy invited the young Bureau to broadcast a weekly jazz show. Bureau was afraid to lose this opportunity if he admitted that his feeble collection included only thirty hard-won records, so he contacted Hugues Panassié through *Jazz-Tango-Dancing*. Soon, the two fast friends were sharing discs with each other and ultimately all of Paris over the radio. Their friendship would lead to the creation of the Hot Club.

Paris in the 1930s was a fine place to be a jazz fan. Monsieur Bureau talks of nights with Duke Ellington, Coleman Hawkins, Eddie South, and more. And of course, there were many evenings when he shared *un verre* with Django. "Django was totally illiterate. *Il était nul*—he was nil, a blank slate. He was a child. I told him stories about anything in history, and he looked at me saying, 'Oooh!' He loved when somebody told him a story." Spending evenings at Pigalle's Brasserie Boudon, Bureau described dinosaurs from his school studies, leaving Django speechless with amazement and fear. Django leafed through Bureau's textbooks, covering his eyes in horror from paintings of Tyrannosaurus Rex. "He would not believe me when I told him about dinosaurs that were twenty-five meters long. '*Tu me bourres le mou*—you're stuffing my brain with nonsense,' he'd tell me, 'you're making this up!' He was a child, a marvelous child, amazed at everything. He was a virgin spirit: He had only pragmatic things stored in his head—the things of daily life, money, food, all that you would find in a Gypsy encampment."

And then came the war, and the beautiful little world of French jazz was torn apart. Most African-American musicians fled for home on the last boat from Le Havre. Bricktop moved on to Mexico City where she opened a new cabaret.

Charles Delaunay read Hitler's *Mein Kampf* and now feared for the future of all Europe. His mother was Jewish, so he hid his record collection, and then hurried to the U.S. consulate in Marseille and applied to emigrate to the United States. When asked if he was Jewish, he cautiously said no. His visa was refused. Now he—as well as saxman André Ekyan and others—were drafted into the French army. Delaunay served with the 401st *batterie* antiaircraft emplacement, trying in vain to defend Paris. Monsieur Bureau used his childhood radio expertise to fight the Nazis. He served with the British Army in Lebanon, spending long hours with his headset scanning airwaves for German transmissions, then tracing their locations via triangulation to order in bombing runs or commando raids.

From 1943, the Occupation of France worsened as German losses mounted in North Africa and Russia. French resistance also grew, although the Germans were ever more ruthless in reprisal. The Nazi war on the Romani increased in ferocity as well. SS and Vichy police rounded up 30,000 Gypsies throughout France and interned them at camps where they provided slave labor for French farms and factories. France soon had twenty large Romani internment camps and numerous smaller ones, including the major camp at Linas-Monthléry, just outside Paris. On November 5, 1942, SS leader Heinrich Himmler's proposition to exterminate Gypsies, Jews, and others was approved by Hitler, and German Gypsies were first marched to their deaths in the new camp at Auschwitz. An estimated 20,000 French Gypsies soon followed them to camps like Bergen-Belsen and others. Some French Gypsies hid deeper in the forests and mountains. Others fought back. Manouche Jean Beaumarie and his brother served with the *maquis*, only to be captured and hanged. Armand Stenegry—who would become better known as guitarist and singer Archange in the 1960s—led Romani guerillas in partisan raids coinciding with the Normandy invasion. His resistance was rewarded with medals from both the British and Free French forces.

At the same time, Delaunay was using the Hot Club as cover. He toured France organizing concerts—all sanctioned by the Propaganda Abteilung. But in each *ville* he visited, Delaunay made contacts among the growing *résistance* and carried intelligence on German troops and defenses back to Paris to be transmitted to England. Within the British Special Operations Executive, he was coded "Benny" and his network was "Cart"—all in honor of saxophonist Benny Carter. But by 1943, the Germans were on to him. In October, they raided the Hot Club and hauled away Delaunay and his secretary, Madeleine Germaine. Interrogated for five and a half hours, Delaunay held firm, maintaining he knew nothing of the resistance. He was finally freed, but his secretary was not: Germaine and the head of the Marseille Hot Club both perished in German concentration camps. As Monsieur Bureau now tells me, "For all Delaunay did for French jazz, he did even more for the *résistance*."

Bureau himself was also working for the resistance now. With aid from the British SOE, he slipped back into France armed with a radio transmitter in 1944 and joined the *maquis*. Yet he was soon trapped. Tracked down by the Gestapo, he was hauled off to the notorious Fresnes prison outside Paris.

It's at this point in telling his story that Monsieur Bureau's voice turns to anger. After fifty years, he speaks still in a growl.

At Fresnes, the Gestapo dumped him into a cell that was nothing more than a black hole. He spent six months here, locked away from the world. To retain his sanity and dream of better times while surrounded by darkness, brick walls, barbed wire, and watchtowers, Bureau sang to himself over and over again the solos of his favorite Bix Beiderbecke recordings. From his childhood listening in on those American radio broadcasts, he knew Bix's solos by heart. Now, they saved him, allowing him to create a fantasy world that he could travel to in his own mind, far from the Nazi jail cell.

Django, meanwhile, continued to play his guitar. As the most famous jazz musician in Europe, he was trapped in the spotlight. This saved him from the fate facing other Gypsies, but Django was sweating under the glare.

Django had always spoken in music, and during the war, he had much to say. The Occupation inspired him to compose new songs that were some of his finest, richer than ever in elegant melodies and opulent harmonies, but also with depths of meaning like never before.

In the months immediately after the Nazis overran France, Django unveiled two new songs that were counterparts to each other yet spoke of the same fears and tensions of war. When the Germans invaded Paris, Django and Naguine fled the city like hundreds of thousands of others. They walked south toward perceived safety, refugees on a hegira with nowhere to hide. Finally, they returned to the capital, playing German-requisitioned jazz.

Now, in a first recording session under the Occupation on October 1, 1940, he led his Nouveau Quintette in cutting his new "Rythme futur." The song was indeed futuristic, an avant-garde jazz composition unlike anything before. Django translated the terror of the *blitzkrieg* into music: while Nin-Nin played *la pompe* like a panzer rolling over the rhythm, Django's melody line was the staccato stutter of a machine gun. "Rythme futur" was a song of war, a fully human commentary on the terror of the times.

If "Rythme futur" was war made song, Django's next composition from the same session was a melody of peace. He titled the wistful, laconic tune "Nuages"—Clouds. Django's theme was built on a seemingly simple chromatic run with modulations in notes and time structure at each pass. Much like

Debussy's 1897 nocturne *Nuages*, Django's was an impressionistic melody, the chromaticism coloring the song in a rainbow of tones. In a single composition he captured the weariness of war that weighed on people's hearts. And then, like a blue mood, the sadness lifts, overpowered by an indomitable spirit, transcending all in a melody like a benediction of consolation and peace.

"Nuages" struck a chord with the French public. It was an aeriform, floating tune easy to whistle, speaking to Parisians in these gray days of ration cards, curfews, and blackouts. Django debuted the song in concert at the Salle Pleyel, and the crowd's subsequent applause reverberated through the august hall. When he launched into the next song, they forced him to stop and replay his new melody. And then play it again. In all, he performed "Nuages" three times in a row, and still the crowd was not satisfied. Overnight, Django became a French hero. With the swing-crazed public, he was suddenly a household name, a star on the level of Maurice Chevalier or Josephine Baker. Pinup portraits of Django were sold in news kiosks and shops everywhere, replacing the old photographs of Tino Rossi and outselling those of Suzy Solidor. His image appeared throughout Paris on posters pasted to the walls announcing his next concerts, which often sold out within a day. With the release of "Nuages," all of Paris seized upon the melody and more than 100,000 copies of the 78 were sold. It was more than just a hit song: "Nuages" was both a war-lorn orison and an ersatz national anthem.

And yet Django still had more to say.

The flip side of "Nuages" released on Swing No. 88 was "Les yeux noirs"—Dark Eyes—a Russian Gypsy melody played for as long as anyone could remember and tracing the route of the Romani back through time. It was carried westward with the caravans, often the first melody struck up around a campfire anywhere on the road from Poland to France to Spain. The song was likely one of the earliest the young Django ever learned to play on his violin or *banjo-guitare*. Originally known as "Ochi Chernye," it was an unadorned waltz dedicated to a Gypsy woman of legendary beauty and the dark eyes of the song title. Now, Django led his Nouveau Quintette in a bayonet charge through the tune. He picked out fiery runs and ferocious arpeggios, playing with fury, if not outrage. Whether Django meant the song as a protest against the Nazi war on the Romani or not, it was without doubt a powerful jazz statement of Gypsy identity and pride.

With the success of "Nuages," Django now launched a big band, entitled Django's Music. Fronting a true orchestra seemed to be the zenith of every jazzman's ambitions, and Django was never lacking in ego. He arranged several of his older melodies for full orchestration as well as composing new pieces, creating ever more intricate and adventurous music. The symphonic sonorities provided him new powers. Directing thirteen musicians, Django recorded two new tunes on March 31, 1942, "Nymphéas" and "Féerie." Both flowed with the flavor of Debussy, yet were accented by the *wah-wah* horns of Ellington. Ricocheting between classical impressionism and the modernity of jazz, "Féerie" was even highlighted by a drum solo. Back to back, they were minor masterpieces without precedents in Django's work.

Django had a grander vision yet for his orchestra. It was a dream inspired by a dream. As he told his bassist Emmanual Soudieux, the image and theme came to him in his sleep one night. He dreamed he was in a wondrous *château* out of a fairy tale, lost in the midst of a never-ending forest; it was midnight, and he was playing on a grand pipe organ the music he would title *Manoir de mes rêves*— Castle of My Dreams. Now he labored to awaken the music heard in his sleep. With his new clarinetist, Gérard Lévêque, at his side, Django picked out his ideas for the full orchestra on his guitar while Lévêque tirelessly transcribed note after note, page after page. Django's concept was daunting. His admirer, Jean Cocteau, promised to write a libretto for a choir totaling eighty singers as required to fulfill Django's fantasy. It was to be a production beyond anything Django had ever attempted before.

For months, Django and Lévêque worked on the score even as its premiere was being talked about around Paris. They labored throughout the nights, finishing just days before the scheduled concert. But as with many of Django's plans, organization was not part of it—he trusted to fate that things would fall in place. When Django and Lévêque delivered the sole manuscript score to conductor Jo Bouillon at the ABC Théâtre, they were met with disappointment. Bouillon was overwhelmed by the daring music: He paged through the piles of manuscript and declared it impossible to perform. Bouillon may have feared as well that the Propaganda Abteilung would condemn such modernity, costing him his position—if not his life. Cocteau had also not written his libretto as Django had not thought to send him the synopsis. And there may have been technical problems with the score itself as Lévêque confessed he did not possess the musical skill to notate all of Django's complex ideas. In the end, "Manoir de mes rêves" was never performed. And to add to the disappointment, the original score disappeared and was feared lost.

Django did not fret. He instead tuned up his guitar and taught the theme of "Manoir de mes rêves" to his jazz band. He first recorded the melody on February 17, 1943, backed by his guitarist cousin Eugène Vées with a basic bass-and-drum rhythm section. To recreate the strains of an organ by starlight, his Nouveau Quintette featured two clarinets, played by Lévêque and André Lluis, giving a sonorous tone. This distilled jazz version of "Manoir de mes rêves" was sublime—and perhaps more stunning in this simple setting than it ever could have been performed by a full orchestra.

With Django's run of successes, the German *Kommandantur* in Paris now requested that he bring his Nouveau Quintette to perform in Berlin for the Nazi High Command. Django held them off. The request became a demand. Django countered by requiring an impossible fee, which the Germans refused to pay. Yet the exhorbitant fee was pure cover; Django had vowed never to venture into the heart of the Third Reich. When the Nazis grew angry, reminding him it was compulsory to comply, Django simply disappeared. In autumn 1943, he, the pregnant Naguine, and his mother, Négros, vanished from Paris. Django piloted his venerable Buick south toward neutral Switzerland.

They finally made it to the Haute-Savoie spa town of Thonon-les-Bains on Lac Léman. Here, Django hired *un passeur*—a mountain guide—to lead them over the Alps during a night in late October or November 1943. Yet Django's unexplained arrival in Thonon sparked rumors that he sought to flee France, and now German soldiers arrested him before he could act. Hauled into headquarters, Django was searched. Found carrying a membership card from a British musician's union, he was declared a spy and locked away in a cell. Django despaired, believing his end had come.

A miracle appeared in the unlikely uniform of the local German *kommandant*. He was a jazz fan, and when he came to question his new prisoner, he was astonished. "*Mon vieux* Reinhardt," he said, "Whatever are you doing in this fix?" After promising not to try to escape again, Django was freed to play his music once more.

Few Romani were so lucky, as Django knew well. While performing for a *thé dansant* in Paris, a fellow Gypsy arrived at the door and asked the maître d'hôtel for Django. "I want to speak to this so-called Django Reinhardt," the stranger announced.

"Why do you say, 'so-called'?" Django's bandmates queried.

The stranger was indignant: "Don't try to trick me. I've just come back from a prisoner-of-war camp where I stayed six months with Django Reinhardt. The sign here advertises 'Django Reinhardt,' but I came to see the real one. Don't treat me like an imbecile!"

The sad truth was that in an internment camp somewhere in Europe, one of Django's Romani cousins had faked his identity in the desperate hope of saving his own life.

Other such stories also circulated within France's Gypsy community. Hiding their *caravanes* in the woods or scrublands in an attempt to keep out of sight of the Germans, Romani passed along warnings by word of mouth. One such story, remembered today by Mondine Garcia, concerned a family of the Weiss clan, and thus likely relatives of Django. This Weiss family had been musicians for generations: The father was a violinist while his son played guitar. The son learned at age six, and by thirteen now in 1943 was a virtuoso, his idol of course being Django. The father saved his *centimes* to buy a phonograph, and the son taught himself Django's music off 78s found in *les puces*. Now the family was hiding out in the central Limousin region, traveling with fellow Romani in their *caravanes* pulled by horses, hunting and fishing for food or buying potatoes from remote farms. They kept to the countryside to hide from the Germans, but now and then they surreptitiously entered a town where the father and son played their music on café *terrasses* for spare change to purchase needed food. Their *caravanes* were parked in a field early on the dawn of July 7, 1943, when they were awakened by pounding on the door. *Père* Weiss looked out the window to see German soldiers, rifles ready. In front of every *caravane* in the encampment, the situation was the same: Soldiers lined up all the Gypsy families under gunpoint and promised to shoot anyone whose papers were out of order. *Père* Weiss produced his identity papers for a German officer while soldiers ransacked the *caravane*. When this officer spotted their violin and guitar, he asked them, "*Vous êtes musiciens?*" *Père* Weiss was wracked by fear, but was able to respond, "*Oui.*" Then the officer ordered forth chairs and told them to play: "*Jouez*—and don't disappoint me. Or else." Taking their courage in hand, father and son began to perform what they feared would be their final concert. They selected one of Django's tunes, and played with as much swing and fervor as they could muster. The officer told them to continue, and they played song after song by Django, finishing with "Bouncing Around." At the end, *père* Weiss built up the nerve to look over at the German officer—and saw tears in his eyes. The officer stood up and ordered his soldiers back in their trucks. But before leaving, he turned to the father-and-son duo and said, "For me, Django is the undisputed master. Continue to play this music, and God keep you."

Romani throughout the Third Reich were being devoured by the Nazi regime, yet perhaps nowhere with such ruthlessness as in Germany itself. Django's cousin, violinist Schnuckenack Reinhardt, bears testament. His family was deported from Germany and sent into a diaspora of its own. He lost his brother and numerous cousins to Auschwitz. And five times Schnuckenack himself was to be shot by the Nazis, five times he escaped. In one instance, he "played himself free" with his violin.

In his later years, Schnuckenack was a short, compact man. He prided himself on his thick moustache and dressed in spruce style, always sporting a fedora. He was as quick to burst into song as into laughter. Yet, telling his story of the war years, he also fell into long interludes of contemplative silence.

He was born February 17, 1921, in Weinsheim in the Rhineland of Germany; the name "Reinhardt" fit him and his family well. His first name was also well chosen, as he recalled the family legend: "When I was born, my whole family gathered around my crib and an aunt said, 'Listen, he makes such a beautiful noise!' And so they said, 'Fine, we'll named him 'Schnuckenack'— Romanès for 'Beautiful noise.'"

He would continue on to create more beautiful noise. His father was a violinist, and he taught Schnuckenack to play when he was just three years old. By the time he was twelve, he was playing professionally. In the 1930s, the family gave up their nomadic life and moved into an apartment in Mainz. Here, Schnuckenack was enrolled in the Peter-Cornelius-Konservatorium with the dream of joining a classical orchestra.

At 5 A.M. one morning in 1938, the German police knocked on the Reinhardts' door. The family was told to pack its belongings immediately, but no more than forty-five kilograms (a hundred pounds) for the whole family. Then, they were herded to the Mainz train station along with other Romani families and shipped off.

Traveling some thousand miles by train, they were dumped in the town of Częstochowa in south-central Poland. They found new rooms to live in. Claiming to be from Hungary, Schnuckenack got a job in the local Café Europa with a Balkan band. The ensemble dressed up like Gypsies in brocaded vests, billowing blouses, and long bowties. Their music was the Hungarian Romani music Schnuckenack had played since his youth. Each night their audience was German soldiers, who toasted the band after songs with flutes of champagne.

Then, the SS raided the town. They rounded up some fifteen Gypsy youths, including Schnuckenack, and ordered them up against a brick wall. In the confusion, Schnuckenack escaped into the crowd and took refuge in a nearby hairdresser's shop. From his hiding place, he watched as the SS gunned down his compatriots. From that day on, his mother prayed regularly to the Black Madonna of Częstochowa for his safety.

On another day, Schnuckenack and a Romani friend were walking along a country road outside town when a car halted alongside them. Two SS officers demanded to see their identity papers. When they explained they had left them at home, the SS pulled their pistols and aimed at the Gypsies' heads. Schnuckenack said his last prayers and waited. Then one officer jeered at them,

"You're not even *worth* killing." And they screamed with laughter as Schnuckenack and his friend fled.

And still, each evening, he was back in the Café Europa unreeling Romani music for his German fans, playing to buy food for his whole family.

One day in 1943, a German soldier who was an avid fan of Schnuckenack's music came in secret and warned them the SS were returning to round up all remaining Romani. The Reinhardt family ran, traveling on foot some two hundred miles to the city of Kraków. Here it was the collaborationist Polish police who confronted them at gunpoint. Schnuckenack's sister Bischa Winter remembered their fear: "We told ourselves, now this is the end; they will kill us all." Recovering, his father pleaded with Schnuckenack, "Play, play something—play our music!" Schnuckenack extracted his violin and began to play a Romani song. The policemen were at first astonished, then enamored. As Schnuckenack said, "The music charmed the police and they warned us, 'Be careful of the SS. There's a hotel up the road on the left and you can rest there for the night.'"

He continued: "We were always afraid—the police, Gestapo, SS. We were always afraid. . . . In almost every Romani family, there were three or four who were taken and killed. Some families completely disappeared. I lost my brother, my little brother. He stayed one night in a German hotel, then discovered he didn't have enough money to pay the bill. The patron called the Gestapo, and they hauled him away to Auschwitz. Within 15 minutes, it was all over."

In 1944, the Russians liberated Poland, and Schnuckenack and his family traveled behind the army to Prague. Returning eventually to Germany, they met up with the 7th U.S. Army under General Lucius Clay and serenaded the GIs at their bases for two years. "I learned jazz from the Quintette du Hot Club de France," Schnuckenack said. "It was from the American GIs that I now learned all sorts of American melodies."

Schnuckenack went on to assemble a jazz band along the lines of Django's Quintette, performing traditional Hungarian Romani songs intermixed with swing. And yet his style was his own, separate from that of Stéphane Grappelli, who influenced so many Gypsy jazz violinists. Schnuckenack's was a much more classical Tziganes violin; even when playing swing he sounded like the Paginini of jazz. Over the years, his band's roster read like a who's who of German Gypsy jazz: Guitarists Bobby Falta, Häns'che Weiss, Holzmanno and Ziroli Winterstein, Daweli Reinhardt, and child-prodigy violinist Titi Winterstein—most of whom eventually led their own bands.

Schnuckenack, the survivor, died at age eighty-five in 2006 of natural causes.

Before he passed away, this violinist who could charm the hearts of evil with his melodies, was humble yet philosophical in discussing his music: "I am alone, you are alone, we are all alone—but we are all one. Yesterday or today, it doesn't matter. Life goes on.... We Romani make music that brings pleasure to everyone. My violin is my heart. And it remembers everything."

On June 6, 1944, the Allies invaded France at Normandy, and two days later, on June 8 in Paris, Django and Naguine's first son was born. They named him Jean-Jacques, but affectionately called him first Chien-Chien and later Babik. He was a cheerful, plump baby, born to the promise of better times as the Allies fought back the Germans. During the spring nights in 1944, Django was performing at a new Pigalle club christened La Roulotte–Chez Django Reinhardt. Rumors of liberation were everywhere, and the nights at La Roulotte were wild with jazz. Yet now Allied air raids were rocking the city as well, sending Django into the depths of the Pigalle *métro* station, cradling Babik in his arms, trying to comfort him and sing him to sleep. On August 24, the Allies broke into Paris, and the city took up arms to fight off the Germans. Hitler ordered the city to be blown up and burnt to the ground, but instead Wehrmacht General Von Choltiz spared Paris and surrendered. And with the Liberation complete, the city awoke from its nightmare to celebrate. As Naguine remembered in her usual stoic understatement, "When *les américains* arrived, it was craziness—*c'était formidable!*"

On April 30, 1945 as the Russian Army strangled the last defenses of Berlin, Adolf Hitler and Josef Goebbels bit into cyanide ampules in the Führer's bunker below the Reich Chancellery. As the two men who had unwittingly launched the golden age of jazz in Europe committed suicide, swing was on the record player in the Chancellery canteen. German soldiers, drunk with beer and intoxicated with fear of the oncoming Red Army, were having one last party. Annoyed by the music that was interrupting their final moments on earth, Goebbels commanded an SS officer to telephone the canteen and have the record player turned off. Despite his demands, the jazz played on.

Django too had one last song to play. Following the Liberation, he was back in the studio with Delaunay, recording a session on November 3, 1944, for the Swing label. With his twelve-man big band behind him, he cut a new, four-minute opus. In the spirit of Tchaikovsky's *1812 Overture*, Django's theme was a jazz symphony of war and peace. The tune began like a victory parade down Les Champs-Élysées with all the brash swagger of a brass marching band. Over the triumphant bass riffs came the joyous sound of Django's guitar like the delirious cheers of the crowd. The song was released as "Artillerie lourde"—Heavy Artillery. But that's not the title Django wanted. As Delaunay's surviving notes in the archives of the Bibliotheque National de France detail, Django, in a twinkle of humor, originally named it "Panzer Swing." Either way, the song was a celebration of liberation.

SIX

Gypsy Bebop

*From Dizzy and Bird to Django
and the Gibson Generation*

RUE VERCINGÉTORIX, PARIS'S SOUTH SIDE. Named in honor of
the Arverne chieftain who surrendered Gaul to Julius Cesar in 52 B.C. at
the battle of Alésia, this street looks like the site of a war of its own. The
burned-out carapace of a Renault rests curbside—and has been here long
enough that rust is blossoming now across the charred metal. The wrong side
of the street backs onto the RER railroad tracks with all its graffiti-gilt
picturesqueness, cast-off plastic shopping bags and crumpled newspapers
taking wing like forlorn putti as trains pass. The sunny side of the street is
inhabited by 1970s apartment blocks that are the closest things to slums
within Le Périph, the promise of the concrete now gray and tired with age.
Innumerable overflowing trash cans line the pavement, the telltale sign of
another strike—or simply of a neighborhood passed by. African, Romani,
and a mixed team of other immigrant children kick a soccer ball between two
garbage-can goalposts. And yet there's little of the usual joyous sound of kids
at play.

But there is the sound of music.

I'm sitting with Gitan guitarist René Mailhes in his Peugeot parked next to
the carbonized car, listening to an early mix of René's forthcoming album of
Gypsy bebop. He's playing in duet with Django's one-time trumpeter Roger
Guérin. The windows are rolled down, the volume on the car CD player turned
up like a rap dub. René doesn't care who overhears his music.

The sounds of Gyspy jazz—now electrified and hot-rodded, intensified and intellectualized—flow down rue Vercingétorix. These Third-World Parisian street urchins would likely rather be hearing rai, but the beauty of René's music catches their ears, and they pause to listen for at least a moment from the glory of their backstreet World Cup.

The music also stops cold a gang of Romani men. This is truly a gang—all dressed alike in black-leather jackets, stylishly smoking cigarettes (French smoking warnings aren't written in Romanès on their favored Marlboro packages), and every one of them bears a Djangoesque moustache. You may not expect bebop to be a streetwise anthem, but it was in Harlem in the late 1940s and it is here to these Romani in Paris in the 2000s as well. The gang are all old-timers, and all René's friends—and most all of them play some guitar too. They sing out a *Salut!* to René, who then introduces them to me, one by one, making sure I catch their lineages: Gitan guitarist Christian Escoudé's cousin, Joseph Pouville's brother, Jacquet Mailhes's son, and more, all bearing the surnames Ferret, Malha, Reinhardt, and other clans of Romani musicians.

I searched for René for several months to talk of Django's bebop years and its legacy through to Gypsy jazzmen like René himself. It may be an oxymoron to schedule an interview with a Gypsy, but I tried. Even today, Romani live on the fringes of Parisian society, an invisible nation within France. The horrors—as well as grandeurs—of *La Zone* are long gone. Yet old habits—and the residue of generations of ruthless racism—die hard. The Gypsies of Paris live within French society but on the outside edges, safely hidden from sight. They inhabit public-housing apartment blocks like these on rue Vercingétorix or in the drear suburbs of Drancy and Vitry-sur-Seine; others still park their *campines* in generations-old encampments around Le Bourget, Kremlin-Bicêtre, and Montreuil. If you want to track down the address or telephone number of a certain Gypsy guitarist who followed in Django's footsteps, good luck. He's likely unlisted in phone directories, may have an alias, simply not have an address or phone, or be on the road.

Some things haven't changed after all.

I faced all these hurdles when I wished to contact René. At seventy now, he is one of the last of his generation of Gitan guitarists. On his father's side, he is a direct link back to Gusti Malha. On his mother's side, he is of the Ferret clan. His mother was the sister of Challain Ferret and cousin of Baro, Sarane, and Matelo. As René himself bemoans, he never had the opportunity to meet Django, but he took up where the master left off. René was of the Gypsy bebop generation, and he played alongside Baro, Lousson Reinhardt, Laro Sollero, Django's second son Babik, and nearly everyone else.

Trying to track René down, I asked several of my Romani acquaintances if they knew his whereabouts. One responded: He believed René hung out at Café les Boulistes somewhere near the Porte de Vanves *puces*. Finding the address on the Internet from across the Atlantic, I wrote a letter to René in care of the café: I would be in Paris on Saturday, March 15, stopping by the bar for *un café* at 10 A.M. I'd love the opportunity to chat with him.

Then I had to find Café les Boulistes, a single café in a city populated by tens of thousands of cafés. Wandering north from *les puces*, I passed the ancient horse-trading *galéries* on rue de Vaugirard that first drew the Romani to this *quartier*. I turned up the side street honoring Vercingétorix and walked for block after block through this neighborhood wisely skirted by the tour buses. Reaching the northern end of the street, I realized I must have missed the café—or else it too was bygone history. I retraced my steps and only by keeping a careful lookout did I at last stumble upon it.

Café les Boulistes must be the original hole in the wall after which all others are named. Just a small sign, a lamp, and a door marks the spot. Yet inside, the bar is surprisingly cheerful and bright. It's wide enough for a short bar counter and a couple stools, before opening up in the back for several small tables and their accompanying chairs. In the rear, a kitchen does double duty for the bar and the owner's home.

And yet the bar is empty. The barman looks bored, so I ask after Monsieur René Mailhes, only to be greeted with a shrug of the shoulders. He's never heard of him, nor seen sign of any letter. Tired and disappointed after my search, I order *un café* to regain my strength for the hike home.

And then in walks René.

He had indeed miraculously somehow received my letter and is most happy to talk history with *un américain*. In fact, he brought all of his gang in tow. A couple rounds of dark coffee is served for all, *belote* cards are shuffled, and we soon hit the stiffer stuff, building a fine morning buzz. As the French proverb goes, alcohol preserves everything—except secrets. We discuss Gypsy jazz for some three hours, René and his friends dropping famous names—all of which they knew well or are kin of some sort. Next thing I know, we're out in the Peugeot listening to the early mix of the CD, only to be called back to the warmth of Café les Boulistes as lunch is served.

Bebop first arrived in Paris unannounced and unexpected on a fine spring day in 1946. World War II was over, if not yet merely a memory, and Paris was returned to the Parisians who know and love it best. On that springtime day, a nondescript package arrived by post at the Pigalle headquarters of the Hot Club de France. Addressed to Charles Delaunay, the package contained a new batch of jazz recordings from the United States. Such packages of records had fed the Hot Club's growth since the early 1930s. But now, for the long years of the war, Delaunay had heard nothing of the latest American jazz. No music, no rumors, nothing but silence. He anxiously tore open the wrapping.

Inside was a simple 78 that went off like a bomb.

Encoded within the grooves of that record was a sound so novel, so wild, so exciting, it was like an immaculate conception of a new jazz. The blood-red label from the Guild company listed the A-side song as "Salt Peanuts," recorded in New York City on May 11, 1945, by then little-known trumpeter John Birks "Dizzy" Gillespie and his All Star Quintette with alto saxophonist Charlie Parker. When Delaunay played it for the first time, he could not believe what he was hearing. "Salt Peanuts" exploded out of his record player speakers like musical onomatopoeia of an ancient street vendor calling out his fresh-roasted peanuts amid the cacophony of modern Harlem streets. Delaunay hailed Django and all his Hot Club disciples to listen as he spun "Salt Peanuts" and its flip side, "Hot House," over and over. As *Jazz Hot* critic André Hodeir proclaimed, on this 78 was "inscribed the future of African-American music." And the future of Gypsy jazz.

Hearing bebop, Matelo Ferret remarked of Charlie Parker, "He plays so well, he must be a Gypsy." Django too shook his head in admiration and stupefaction, saying over and over, "They play so fast, so fast." Bebop was indeed fast—as well as daring and dazzling with more chromatic coloring to the melody lines, new harmonizations, and off-kilter rhythms. It was a jazz revolution, Dizzy staging a coup d'état on the trumpeter's throne held by Louis Armstrong, Bird over-throwing Lester Young. Their comrades on the barricades—jam sessions at the Harlem nightclubs Minton's Playhouse and Monroe's Uptown House and on-stage at New York's Three Deuces—included guitarist Charlie Christian, pianist Thelonious Monk, drummer Kenny Clarke, trumpeter Howard McGhee, and a handful of others.

For Django, "Salt Peanuts" opened a world of new ideas. Or at least, crys-tallized ideas he had been experimenting with himself and displayed their possibilities.

Far from New York's 52nd Street, Django had moved in the years since 1940 in some of the same directions as bebop with his Nouveau Quintette du Hot Club de France. Without the constraints of formal training or the rigors of music theory, Django had often experimented with melodic extremes. Dizzy's beloved flatted fifth was a recurring tone in Django's playing, and his palette of arpeggios had long included the colorful notes the beboppers were now able to use as they jump-started their own bands away from a big-band leader's dictates. Django's Gypsy sensibility savored minor keys and favored emotional intervals as well as diminished arpeggios played over major chords. Django also was well versed in the use of flatted and natural seconds or ninths from his flamenco influences and employed a variety of minor scales, including the Phrygian mode and deep-toned harmonic minor scale, even in a straightforward riff tune such as "Minor Swing."

Like the Harlem beboppers, Django was also inspired to reharmonize old songs to breathe new life into classic melodies. His evolving approach to harmonization came alive in "Dînette," a resurrection of "Dinah." His new harmonies took two directions. First, he was infatuated by the mood of major and minor sixth and seventh chords, adding dark dissonances to enhance melodies. He was experimenting with further minor-major key shifts within songs and adding passing chords—often intriguing diminished chords—to the harmonization.

Second, his Nouveau Quintette usually featured only his guitar, as in "Dînette"—although he was at other times still backed by his favorite accompanist, Nin-Nin. Django's ensemble sound consciously moved away from the powerful *pompe* and into a looser feel, breaking the rhythm wide open. Accompanying his clarinetist, Django rarely hung on one chord voicing for more than one or two beats. As in the old days behind musette accordionists when his banjo provided rhythm, harmony, and a moving bass line all in one, his rhythm guitarwork now was constantly on the go with ascending and descending chord lines, offbeat and syncopated chordal flourishes, and stabbing accents vamping out the harmony. Django was no longer playing dance music.

Even in "Dînette," his ensemble was still a giant step away from Dizzy and Bird's bebop in velocity and rhythmic inventiveness. But in "Salt Peanuts," Django too heard the sound of the future.

And yet the first among the Paris Gypsy jazz guitarists to compose and record new compositions on the cutting edge of bebop was not Django but Baro Ferret. Django may have been moving in musical directions that would coalesce in bebop, but Baro was already there—even though the music and the term "bebop" were at this point unknown in France.

Baro had come to play in Paris's *bals musette* from his home in Rouen. He soon was jamming alongside Django in dance bands and the *cabarets russe*, and when Django formed the Quintette du Hot Club de France, Baro was often sitting in one of the rhythm chairs. Through all those nights, Django and Baro became best friends—and musical rivals.

During the early years of the Occupation—the same time Dizzy and company were experimenting on stage at Minton's and Monroe's across the ocean—Baro remained in Paris's *bals musette*. But while the music was still made for dancing, Baro and a new comrade-in-arms, accordionist Gus Viseur, were injecting swing into the old musette songs. Their 1940 tune "Swing valse" served as their declaration of independence. Working within the frame of a classic *valse musette*, they spiced up the harmony with jazzy chords and freely improvised and jammed over the melody. The result was a new genre of musette known as swing musette, and the battle was on in the traditional dance halls between the old and new guard.

Baro was likely amused. He had already moved on anyway with ideas more daring, even bizarre. From musette to jazz hot, swing to swing musette, Baro was now hearing a different sound, a music that then had no name.

Baro began composing a series of musette waltzes unlike anything before—or since. They bore elements of the old-guard's *valse musette* as well as the charged *valse manouche*, hints of jazz hot and swing musette, but all set to a distinct sense of rhythm and harmony. Much like the jazz he played, his guitar style was inherited from his Gitan forebears but infused with his own unique sensibilities. When they were finally recorded, likely several years after Baro first composed them, these melodies were termed *valses bebop*. While it was true that they kept a steady three-four and six-eight beat, Baro's tunes certainly stretched the boundaries of the term "waltz." And yet there was no better description for them than *valses bebop*.

When Baro began composing these bebop waltzes is not known for sure. His nephew, René Mailhes, stated over lunch at Café les Boulistes that Baro told him in later decades that he started during the war years, in the days after swing musette was born. And yet they were not recorded until at least 1946, according to Odéon label matrix numbers. And some bear copyright dates as late as 1949, 1951, and 1955 on their sheet-music publication by Éditions Léon Agel. Throughout this time, Baro's *valses bebop* were probably works in perpetual progress, honed on stage and in ballroom gigs.

Among the first of these *valses bebop* to be released was "Panique...!" The title alone hinted of a sense of foreboding, even doom brought on by the modern age. "Panique...!" was in the key of D minor, but the harmony jumped backed and forth from major-seventh to minor keys following the headlong rush of the melody. The melody line seemed to be running from something unknown, fleeing as if it were in a hurry to escape its own being. Led by Baro's virtuosic guitar playing, the tune took surprising turns down dark alleyways and into dangerous back streets. Odd rhythms followed the theme like an ominous shadow, Baro adding stabbing chordal accents and spine-tingling obbligatos behind the accordion—precursors of bebop rhythmic accompaniment. The result was an impressionistic song of a strange, unnerving atmosphere. It was likely a reflection of Baro's own character.

Released under the band name Pierre Ferret et Son Ensemble, Baro's group included his brother Sarane Ferret on rhythm guitar as well as a young Gitan guitar player, Jacques "Montagne" Mala; they were backed by bassist Jeremy Graind'son. Ballroom hero Jo Privat added the inevitable, essential accordion. Yet Privat played at times on Baro's *valses bebop* with a tentative touch, almost as if he was struggling to keep up. Or perhaps to understand this music.

Baro recorded some four or six of his *valses bebop* in the late 1940s. "Panique...!" was backed by "La folle," co-written with Privat. These were followed by "Dinalie mineure" backed by "Turbulente Zoë." Others, such as "Survol de nuit"—copywritten in 1951—may never have been recorded, or at least surviving copies have yet to be discovered in *les puces*.

In 1966, Charles Delaunay lured Baro back into the studio to re-record his near-forgotten *valses bebop*. For a series of recording sessions running from February 28 to May 2, 1966, Baro headed a band including once again Jacques Montagne, Matelo, vibraphonist Géo Daly, and organist Jean-Claude Pelletier. With the addition of vibes and organ, the sound was now more modern, adding texture like a futuristic Romani cymbalom. Various versions of the waltzes were released on LP and EP, both entitled *Swing valses d'hier et d'aujourd'hui*. In the liner notes, Delaunay wrote that Baro's compositions were a "revolution" created twenty years ahead of the three-four-, five-four-, and six-eight-time explorations of American jazzmen Dave Brubeck, Horace Silver, or Cannonball Adderley. And yet still these were timeless pieces—or more properly, compositions out of time.

Baro's *valses bebop* won Django's everlasting admiration. Yet it would be several years after Django heard these *valses bebop* and Harlem bebop in the form of "Salt Peanuts" before he too composed and recorded bebop tunes.

Two interconnected factors held Django back—and eventually freed him. The first was the control exerted by his sometime-manager Delaunay, who continued to play *auteur* behind the recording studio controls. While Delaunay too was smitten by bebop, the sessions he arranged for Django from 1945 through 1947 still resulted in classic swing sides. Perhaps Delaunay believed the French market was not ready for bebop. Or maybe he viewed his greatest star as only a swing player.

The break—both for Django's music and freedom from Delaunay's control—arrived in late 1946 when Django finally realized his long-held dream of traveling to the United States to play his jazz. Ironically, this had also been a wish of

Delaunay, and the impresario labored for years to arrange an American tour for his find. Now, Django was going stateside, but Delaunay was not part of the plans. A representative from New York's prestigious William Morris Agency caught up with Django while he was touring Switzerland in mid 1946; he extended an invitation from Duke Ellington to join a tour running from Cleveland to Minneapolis to Kansas City and then back to the East Coast, highlighted by two nights at Carnegie Hall. At heart, Django was always a horse-trader in his business dealings, and this U.S. tour was no different as he now left Delaunay behind. Django and Delaunay would work together again, but their friendship was never truly the same.

To Django, the United States was the promised land. For decades he dreamed in American jazz, and now he saw those visions coming true: As he was the greatest guitarist who had ever lived, he believed in his innocent hubris the famed American luthiers would hand him their finest instruments like keys to the city. As his records spun magic on turntables across Europe, the renowned American labels would vie with each other for the privilege of recording him. As he was the brightest star in the constellation of European jazz, lucrative concert deals would be waiting with his name on the marquee. And as Dorothy Lamour was rumored to be his greatest fan, Paramount and other movie studios would rush to exalt him on the silver screen.

So Django set off. He overcame his fear of flying and took wing from London to New York on a Pan American Yankee Clipper to land on October 29, 1946. He left Naguine and two-year-old Babik behind amid talk of later bringing them to the United States to settle for good. In his excitement now, he arrived in New York with only the clothes he wore, unburdened by any luggage or even a toothbrush. And he left his famous Selmer modèle Jazz guitar behind. Django was starting a new life.

The music Django created with Duke on their four-week tour wore out the American newspaper and magazine critics' stock of superlatives. They gushed over the shows, lauding Duke but claiming Django—a new discovery for many of them—stole the spotlight. Despite a hiccup in one of the Carnegie Hall shows when Django arrived an hour late for his cue, those two nights were also hailed.

And yet when Django unexpectedly returned to Paris in February 1947, his dreams had faded. While in the United States, Django was not presented with lucrative recording contracts nor a starring role in the Hollywood film of his naïve reveries. The Gypsy had been a stranger in a strange land, cut off by language and culture from his bandmates and fans. Homesick, he hurried back to his family.

Django's U.S. tour of 1946–1947 was a pivotal point in his life. His American sojourn included great successes and cruel disappointments. Many—

including Django himself—later labeled the tour a failure. And, in some aspects, it was. The feeling that he had failed in the United States haunted his final years. He had believed he was starting a new life, and he was—but it was a life even his Gypsy fortune-tellers could not have foreseen. While in the United States—whether it was jamming with Duke and his bandmates like Johnny Hodges, playing jazz in New York City clubs, or venturing to Harlem to hear the latest bebop—Django found something money could not buy: inspiration. He came to America playing swing. He returned to Paris playing modern jazz.

The rift with Delaunay instigated by the U.S tour dealings now showed a bright side. Django had recorded sporadically for others in the past, but in the coming years he broke free from Delaunay and the Hot Club's auteurship. During a May 1947 Belgian tour with his Nouveau Quintette, clarinetist Hubert Rostaing arranged a recording session with the Belgian Decca label. Delaunay was not there to dictate the playlist, and Django cut six new compositions that blazed a novel path.

In just three months since returning to France, Django wrote a trove of new songs. These latest tunes were a step into the future, leaving the golden days of swing behind. The session launched with "Porto Cabello," Django's modernistic melodic structure built on whole-note scales. The song began in a nostalgic preamble, then exploded in fireworks, discarding any sentimentality for the past in a crescendo of choruses of rhapsodic guitar, avant-garde in tone and charge. This song was as a warning: The past was past. Django's jazz was aimed at a new sound.

He first truly tried his hand at crafting a bebop manifesto in "Babik (Bi-Bop)." Named of course for his beloved young son, the music too was fresh. "Babik" built on Dizzy's "Salt Peanuts" with its trademark octave riffs, then modulated those octaves to create an energetic and elegant line. Django proved he learned quickly when it came to bebop rhythm, as *la pompe* was now updated in jarring syncopations. Django's guitar spoke the syntax of bebop, but his was not just the bebop of Dizzy and Bird. Theirs was horn music; his was pure guitar. He could fret their notes, but he created his own new language on six strings.

The electric guitar was a key part of Django's new sound. According to newspaper reports, Django first used an electrified guitar during that 1946 Swiss tour, likely his Selmer with an added Swiss-made Bâle or another early European pickup. American guitarist Charlie Byrd, who was playing in a U.S. Army band, jammed with Django and Nin-Nin in a Parisian nightclub in 1945 or 1946, the brothers both plugged in. But it was on the American tour that Django truly found his electric sound, playing a Gibson hollow-body L5 fitted with a DeArmond pickup and amplified by a small combo amp. Bootlegged recordings from a Chicago concert with Duke reveal Django fully in control of his new guitar. His acoustic playing had been rapturous, but now with electricity, he found new tones, novel textures, and revived power in his music.

Les Paul, one of the fathers of the electric guitar, was there when Django was first going electric. Les has never been too proud to tell the world he himself first learned guitar in far-off Waukeesha, Wisconsin, by copping Django's licks off 78s and playing them on stage and radio note for note. He met his hero during Django's U.S. tour, and well remembered Django's newfound interest in electricity. Forty years later, Les recalled for me with obvious relish their first meeting: "I was performing at New York City's Paramount Theater at the time. One day, the doorman yelled up six floors to my dressing room, 'There's a fellow down here wants to see you. Says his name is Django Reinhardt.' I laughed at the joke and called back, 'Yeah, sure. Send him up with a case of beer and Jesus Christ, and I'll give them both an autographed picture,' because I thought someone was joshing me. So in he walks. Johnny Smith was with him, leading him around New York. I had two Epis laying on the couch. These were blonde 1939 Epi Deluxe Regent hollow-bodies, but I had added all the electronics. I had the pair in case I broke a string on stage. Johnny Smith picked up one guitar and Django picked up the other. He asked me for a pick, and I had a whole pocket full of them; the majority were Les Paul picks, round like a button. Django said that's just what he was looking for, which made me feel good. Django led off and the first number he played was 'Rose Room.' It was just the most awesome thing. Here I was in my dressing room shaving and straightening out my makeup to go on, and Django's playing guitar. It just stunned me.

"Django was very intrigued by my electric guitars. He liked their sound. He was fascinated by that electric sound. In fact, there's that film footage of him back in Paris and he's playing an acoustic blonde Epi just like mine. That guitar could have been the sister to mine.

"I next saw Django in Paris in 1950. We were riding in a cab going to some club and he punches me on the shoulder and says, 'Why don't they like me in the States?' I said, 'It was the background, and they weren't expecting an electric guitar. If you come back, they will surely like you.' He said, 'I don't play that bad, do I?' Well, that surprised me, I can tell you. Then he asked me, 'Do you like bebop?' I said, 'No, not in particular. I'm not too fond of it.' He said, 'That's the way I want to play.'

"He never took my advice. That's my contribution to Django Reinhardt: He never took my advice. From 1946, he went electric and played bebop".

In 1951, Django was playing at a new venue with a new band creating new music for a new crowd. The epicenter of jazz in Paris had migrated from Pigalle and Montparnasse to Saint-Germain-des-Prés. Here, dark and dank cellar *caves* became clubs for a youthful breed of jazz fans, known in jest as *Les Troglodytes*. Besotted by modern American jazz and Existential philosophy both, they dressed *à l'americain* and danced away the night below the city. As *chanteuse* Juliette Gréco, the It Girl of *Les Troglodytes*, said, looking back on these times, *"C'était une période nocturne mais lumineuse."*

Django, now forty-one, was fronting an ensemble of musicians a generation younger than he. Known as the Bebop Minstrels, the group was led by alto sax-man Hubert Fol and his pianist brother Raymond with bassist Pierre Michelot, drummer Pierre Lemarchand, and trumpeters Bernard Hullin or Roger Guérin. Playing at the Club Saint-Germain or across the street at the bar Le Montana, they were truly luminescent nights, broadcast on French radio capturing the band in full flight. As Michelot recalled, "Django was in ecstasy.... The audacity of Bop just took his breath away. This music reached deep down inside him and little by little, his playing evolved, you could hear it, without premeditation. The phrases that belonged to the Hot Club Django were still there of course, but they were transformed."

Now, Django returned to one of the first songs he likely ever played as a child, the Russian Gypsy waltz "Les yeux noirs." He resurrected the tune in bebop, titling his new version "Impromptu." Built on the same harmonic chord structure as the Romani anthem, "Impromptu" also borrowed from Dizzy's proto-bop tune "Be Bop" of the mid-1940s. Django's melody was a breathless rush of notes played in unison on guitar and Hubert Fol's sax in the mode of the best Bird and Dizzy duets. The harmony jumped between minor and major chords, creating a sense of dynamic tension and dramatic movement. Far from the version Django likely played as a youth, "Impromptu" was angular and cubist. It was at once both ages-old and brand new, bebop intensely *modernistique*.

Throughout the late 1940s and into the 1950s, Django was alternately at the forefront of the Paris jazz scene or completely absent from it. At times, he simply took to the road in his *caravane*—even if a gig or recording session was scheduled in his way. Charles Delaunay remembered venturing to a muddy Romani encampment at Le Bourget outside the capital to lure Django to play a concert. Django lazily waved him off, lifting up his mattress to display the bed of banknotes upon which he slept, saying, "There's money here. I don't need any more."

Finally, in 1951, he moved his family to the somnolent town of Samois-sur-Seine south of Paris and rented a simple cottage. Here, he could fish away the days, while Babik evaded school and learned to pocket teaspoons from *cafés*—all part of Django's proud parenting technique.

In Samois, Django was at peace. He had lived the musician's life with burning intensity since he was twelve. Now, it was time for something more. Naguine was philosophical in describing the changes in him: "In Samois, he was no longer the Django of old. He was *un autre homme*—another man, a new man. He was now a poet. He had the time to look at the beauty of the world around him. In the evening, he might remain at the edge of the river until three in the morning. He watched the river, the movement of the trees, the concert made by the water, and he told me that there he saw the true music, he heard it all, he was crazy for it. He said to me, 'Here is the true music!'"

Django was inspired in Samois to compose again, creating one last masterpiece, a melody he labeled "Anouman." Like "Nuages," the theme was built on relatively simple variations of ascending and descending arpeggiated runs. And yet the melody's ictus was constantly on the move, inspired by a sophisticated bebop sensibility worlds beyond "Nuages." The tune was at once nostalgic, even pastoral. It was at the same time world-weary and bittersweet, summing up a life fully lived and capturing a sense of melancholy in a melody so simple yet so profound.

This melody was sung by Hubert Fol's alto sax, his pristine tone giving lyrical voice to the resigned longing of the theme. He played "Anouman" as though he believed in every note. His attack was straight and true, without any of the false emotion of a quavering vibrato. Taking over the lead in the impromptu bridge, Django's guitar contribution was a short solo of just eight measures, gossamer strands of aeriform riffs, brief but brilliant in intensity. Far from the profligate munificence of notes that marked his prime Quintette du Hot Club de France days, "Anouman" was now cool jazz. Django said everything in the simple yet elegiac beauty of the melody.

The source of the song's name was a mystery, however. It may have been in honor of the golden-faced Hindu monkey god Anouman, a legendary trickster whose exploits were regaled in the Sanskrit *Mahabharata* and *Ramayana* holy books. Anouman was also a hero to some Romani, part of the Hindu pantheon that survived through time and assimilation with Catholicism. Or, more simply, I wonder if "Anouman" may have been Django's phonetic spelling of the English-language phrase, "A New Man," symbolizing his own rebirth and deliverance in a new music.

And yet that new life was not to last long. On the morning of May 16, 1953, Django rose early to go fishing. He was just back in Samois from another Swiss tour, with plans for a world tour in a couple of months headlining Norman Granz's Jazz At The Philharmonic extravaganza. But for now, it was a wondrous spring day and Django was happy to be home. He strolled to his favorite café, Chez

Fernand–Auberge de l'Île, for a cup of breakfast tea. He was sitting on the *terrasse* chatting happily with friends when he suddenly collapsed. His compatriots carried him back to his cottage and Naguine. Django regained consciousness just long enough to refuse a doctor one last time. At four o'clock that afternoon, he was dead. The cause was listed as cerebral hemorrhage. Django was just forty-three.

In the old days, the Manouche buried their loved ones by placing them in their *caravanes* and setting it ablaze with all of their worldly goods. It was thus too with Django, but in a fashion keeping with modern times. Django was buried in Samois' cemetery. Then, Naguine and Négros amassed Django's last possessions—his meager wardrobe of clothes, his proud collection of fishing rods and tackle, his tape recorder and a batch of last tapes of compositions and new music recorded in Samois. Naguine piled Django's things in a pyre, placed his guitar on top, struck a match, and set it on fire.

Following Django's death, Joseph Reinhardt put his Selmer Modéle Jazz in its case and locked it tight. Nin-Nin was Django's greatest fan and his longest-running sideman—even considering all the fights sending them on their own ways with vows never to play together again. Joseph had made music with his brother since they were boys, from busking in *les puces* to stardom on tours throughout Europe. In the Romani tradition, Nin-Nin now honored Django's memory with a year of silence.

He then disappeared. Returning into the nether regions of France that the Gypsies inhabit, Nin-Nin lived among his clan, outside the cities and towns, hidden alongside a stream or wood, omnipresent but invisible. He worked with Ninine Vées, who also set aside his guitar in Django's honor. Together, they labored as *casseurs* or *ferrailleurs*—"breakers" or "ironmen," slang for scrap-iron dealers—collecting, sorting, and selling scrap. It was a job Django too loved as a youth. The brothers had often *faisait la ferraille*—literally, "made metal"— gathering scrap in a wheelbarrow to barter back to foundries. Naguine remembered that even when Django and Nin-Nin were at their peak as well-paid professional musicians they became nostalgic for their days dealing scrap. As grown men traveling on a tour in a first-class train coach, they once spotted a scrap-metal heap out the window and began reminiscing of the good old days. Nin-Nin had returned to his roots.

Yet music was like air to Joseph, and by 1955 he tuned up his guitar once again.

Nin-Nin first led his own band and recorded during the World War II years. His guitar was always in great demand: behind Django, he proved himself perhaps Paris's best accompanist. After one grand battle on New Year's Eve 1937 with his brother that ended with him stomping out of the Quintette, he was snatched up to play in Aimé Barelli's big band and Alix Combelle's Jazz de Paris. A follower rather than leader, Nin-Nin finally organized his own ensemble at the dawn of the 1940s. The Orchestre Swing Jo Reinhardt first recorded in March 1942 with accordionist Gus Viseur and clarinetist André Lluis. He returned to the studio in December 1943 with violinist Claude Laurence—the *nom de jazz* of writer-musician André Hodeir—to cut four more sides including two of his own compositions, "Un peu de rêve" and "L'œil noir."He proved himself a confident and stylish soloist, without Django's flash but with a melodic style all his own.

After the Liberation, Nin-Nin had collaborated in 1945 with violinist Léo Slab to launch a quintet. Impressed by Slab's playing and seeking a replacement for Stéphane Grappelli, Django had soon tried to steal Slab away for his own band, as Slab told me. But by then, Nin-Nin was used to standing up to his brother. Now, in 1955, Joseph joined with Slab once again to play Paris's clubs.

In 1959, a group of French jazz aficionados arranged for Nin-Nin to record anew. He played electric guitar and led a band featuring violinist Pierre Ramonet, guitarists Jean "Cérani" Mailhes and Paul Mayer, and bassist Pierre Sim. The LP was filled with his brother's compositions, interspersed with several of Joseph's originals. This limited-edition disc was entitled *Joseph Reinhardt joue Django*, which would become a common tune sung through all of Nin-Nin's later recordings. He was forced by reluctant record companies to ride on Django's coattails—a ride he immediately proved he didn't need. Through the 1960s, he sporadically ventured back into studios, cutting other albums paying homage to Django, each EP and LP buttressed by his covers of Django's songs that were already becoming Gypsy jazz standards.

Hidden between the inevitable tunes by Django, Nin-Nin placed several of his own compositions, pieces uniquely—and exotically—idiosyncratic. Nin-Nin's 1960s LP *A Django* with Manouche violinist Louis "Vivian" Villerstein, included his own "Bric à brac," a strange, upbeat jazz jump set to a haunting minor-key tonality. "Triste mélodie" was a lyrical tune weeping with a dark Gypsy spirit but still bouncing to a jazz beat. The songs he wrote were the most intriguing tunes, their complex melodic lines of dark intervals creating a distinctive blue mood. As Nin-Nin told the Parisian magazine *Combat* in 1967, "I don't want to copy the familiar traits of my brother. I want to create proof of my originality and affirm my personality while conserving the famous Gypsy style. To this end, I have prepared a series of arrangements based on the themes of Django. But my repertoire also includes several of my own new compositions."

Not only did Nin-Nin create his own music, but he made that music on his own homemade electric guitar. While Gypsy beboppers were adopting American Gibsons, Joseph stood alone between the old and new generations. He crafted his guitar's soundboard from an old bistro bartop, mating it to a Selmer neck and tailpiece. Then, he screwed on a microphonic pickup. Those who tried Joseph's guitar remember it being near-impossible to play, but it seemed to suit him perfectly and he used it throughout the late 1950s.

Nin-Nin continued to alternate playing jazz with long stretches of silence, disappearing back on the road. When director Paul Paviot filmed a 1957 biography of Django, Joseph agreed to perform. And in the mid 1960s, he recorded several more sessions released on LPs and EPs. When his fellow Gypsies began to meet for a weekend each summer in the late 1960s in Samois to pay tribute to Django, Nin-Nin played for his people in groups including his old compatriot Léo Slab as well as Django's sons, Lousson and Babik, both of whom were playing now and then in the cafés of Paris. Joseph's own son, Kuick Reinhardt, and in-law Henri "Dingo" Adel also accompanied him.

When Nin-Nin passed away in 1982, he was buried alongside Django in the Cimetière de Samois.

Listening today to Nin-Nin's 1959 album *Joseph Reinhardt joue Django*, the music remains peerless, intriguing. Joseph and Django's sister, Sara "Tsanga" Reinhardt, could only jest when attempting to describe Nin-Nin's eccentric music, *"Mon frère Nin-Nin? C'est un arabe."* Did Nin-Nin copy Django? No. Did he play bop? No. Did he remain true to swing? No. He played in his own voice, making his own music. Which is the best compliment.

I'm back at Le Montana, that Saint-Germain-des-Prés hotel-bar where Django jammed many times in the early 1950s. Tonight in March 2007, more than fifty years later, René Mailhes is making the music. Gypsy bebop is alive and well in the same clubs where it was born.

Le Montana is pure chic, a far step from a *puce* dive. In Django's time, the only things hot in Saint-Germain-des-Prés were the philosophy and the jazz; today, the *quartier* is pure glitz and glamor. The bar is all mirrors and chrome, leather chairs like squat, avant-garde dumplings that you perch on more than sit in, and a bar stocked with fancy drinks for fancy people. When I make the mistake of ordering *une mauresque*, the arch of the bartender's eyebrow tells me I'm on the wrong side of Paris, if not the wrong end of France. Alain Antonietto, Paris's Gypsy jazz historian bar none, is here as well, and he's drinking a regular beer, so I turn my back on the bartender's disdain and look to the music.

Tonight at Le Montana could be a step back in time to 1951, bebop the new music on the block. René is playing with a simple trio—just himself, a drummer, and a bassist with a good old string bass. And René's guitar too is from the day: a well-patinated sunburst Gibson ES-175 with only a sole single-coil P-90 pickup, warm and rich in tone, yet with an angry edge when needed.

René's guitar was itself a statement in its time. Django and his generation played Selmers, hot-rodded with Stimer pickups when bebop first boomed. But René was of a new generation. He arrived on Django's heels, taking Django's bebop inspiration, blending it with new sounds from American guitarmen Barney Kessel, Jimmy Raney, Tal Farlow, and Jim Hall, and creating something novel. They called themselves *Le génération Gibson*—the Gibson Generation: René, his *copaine* Laro Sollero, Jacques "Montagne" Mala, Christian Escoudé, and even Django's son Babik.

Montagne came first. He straddled the two generations, pounding out *la pompe* for Nin-Nin, Baro, Matelo, and others of his elders. He learned to play at the side of his uncle, Gusti Malha. But when Montagne played his own jazz, he played bebop—loud, fast, and furious. Befitting his position between the two eras, he still picked a Selmer, yet mounted with a Stimer S.51 that gave him that modern voice. And he chose to fret his guitar with just two fingers, his smaller two digits curled into his palm. He sought to replicate the master's last music as close as he could.

Christian Escoudé followed. Born September 23, 1947, in Angoulême in the southwestern Charente region, he was raised far from the Paris scene. His father, Serrani Escoudé, was a guitar sideman in the regional *bals*, and his mother's father was Gusti's brother. Serrani taught Christian to play when he was just ten, that Romani rite of passage. The first *morceau* he ever learned was his uncle Gusti Malha's "La valse des niglos." As Christian tells me, "I met Gusti when I was just a young boy and he was an old man, *le professeur* to a whole generation of guitarists. My father took me to a bar in *les puces* at the Porte de Clignancourt, and Gusti was there playing *belote* with other Gypsies. I begged him to play guitar with me, and finally I badgered him enough that he said, '*D'accord!*' and we played one song together. I was so nervous I could hardly play. But he was incredible!"

By age fifteen, Christian too was a professional musician. He performed at American armed forces bases across the Midi. As Christian remembers, "The U.S. Army was still in France at that stage. There was a U.S. base right next to us in Angoulême. I used to play there with an *orchestre*; we'd do all the classics of American popular music, from 'Misty' to 'All the Things You Are.'" With a repertoire ranging from his father's *bal* classics to Django and American standards, he next joined Aimé Barelli's *orchestre* in Monte Carlo.

Arriving in Paris in the late 1970s, Christian was now solidly of the Gibson Generation, his sound modern and smooth. And he had turned his back on Django: "Stupidly, I considered Django as out of style, a jazz musician of the previous generation, and if I ignored his music, it was also a type of rebellion against my father." Yet he soon came around to realize his debt to both his father and the father of Gypsy jazz: "My ability to improvise, that's what I got from Django—and from Charlie Parker too. Django's music is timeless, like Bach or Ravel. He was the precursor, the original genius."

When Christian released his 1980 LP *Gousti*, it was dedicated to the inspiration of Gusti Malha, although the jazz was all new. Throughout his numerous subsequent albums, Christian wanders a long road, from bebop to free jazz and back to tonal jazz. He often plays alongside his *pôte*, Paul "Challain" Ferret, son of Challain. Christian recorded albums as far ranging as 1989's *Gipsy Waltz* and 2005's progressive *Ma Ya Ya*. And still, in his repertoire, he keeps Gusti and Django's memory alive, covering several of Gusti's ancient *valses* and Django's now-standard melodies in between his own original bebop and modern jazz compositions.

At the same time, Babik too was on the road to becoming an adept guitarist. He had a record of numerous run-ins with the *gendarmes* for automobile and other minor theft—all part of Django's legacy in parenting. But Babik soon turned instead to music. Born in 1944, he was just twelve when Django died, and he learned to play guitar later. By the mid 1960s, he was playing a Gibson ES-175 or ES-335 in a more modern style—rock'n'roll. He joined the quaint French *yé-yé* group Glenn Jack et ses Glenners along with René Mailhes and Laro Sollero, appearing on EP covers striking guitar-hero poses.

It was not until 1967 that Babik first recorded his own jazz, following in his father's footsteps in playing for Charles Delaunay's Vogue label. As with Nin-Nin, many of Babik's early recordings were labeled "tributes" or "homages" to Django by uncertain record companies. Yet Babik soon proved he had his own voice. He rarely played an up-tempo tune, perhaps eschewing the rollicking early jazz or swing of his father. Instead, his compositions were ruminative rubato pieces, soulful and stirring, reflective of his own directions. Up until his death in 2001, Babik toured worldwide, cutting a variety of albums of his very personal Gypsy jazz.

Yet it's in René Mailhes' hands that Gypsy bebop became truly lyrical. At Le Montana tonight, he plays tunes by Django, Thelonious Monk, and several American bebop standards, all intermixed with his own compositions.

René was born in 1935. His father was Fillou Mailhes, part of the Malha clan; his mother, Marie Ferret, was Challain's sister and a renowned singer. With this ancestry, there was really only one choice for him—musician. Still, René didn't take up guitar until he was fifteen, an impossibly late age among his fellow

Romani. While he never crossed paths with Django, he watched closely and learned from both Poulette Castro—*"terrible!"*—and Gusti—*"un fou!"*

By the time he was twenty, René was playing rhythm guitar for Sarane Ferret and touring Germany. In 1962, he jammed with Jimmy Raney, cementing his interest in bebop. In between sets at Le Montana, he tells me of how difficult it was to get acceptance for his modern Gypsy jazz among his elders—even from Baro Ferret. "I used to play rhythm for Sarane and Baro, playing bebop single-note and double-stop rhythm lines," René remembers, humming a typical ob-bligato. "Baro would say, 'That sounds *good!*' And then he would plug his nose and laugh."

But René had *un copaine* in his pursuit of bebop, and together they set the nights alight in Saint Germain-des-Prés. Laro Sollero also came from a lineage of Romani musicians stretching back to the creation of Gypsy jazz. The Sollero and Castro clan are one and the same, and many of Laro's family, cousins, and ancestors played the music—Poulette and Laro Castro, of course, but also Joseph Sollero, rhythm guitarist for Orchestre Swing Jo Reinhardt when Nin-Nin first recorded, in 1942. Born in 1937, Laro and his cousin René took the lead of Django's bebop and blended it with American influences, Jim Hall remaining their favorite. The duo jammed through many a night in the late 1950s and early 1960s at the Saint Germain-des-Prés *cave* La Conchée.

Yet Laro never recorded commercially; his playing shines only on private recordings from 1964 saved by Alain Antonietto. Later that year or the next, Laro joined *La Mission évangélique tzigane de France*, the evangelical Christian church run by and devoted to Gypsies. And, as part of his vows, he set aside his guitar. When Laro died in April 2002 and was buried at the special *carré gitan* in the Saint Ouen cemetery, Christian Escoudé eulogized him: "Laro had a great influence on our whole generation."

Fortunately, René did have opportunity to record—but not until 1995, after playing guitar professionally some forty-five years. That year, he released his first album, *Gopaline*, followed by 1998's *Gitrane*. Tours de force of Gypsy bebop, they also pay homage to generations past, with songs dedicated to Gypsy wildman drummer Baptiste "Mac Kak" Reilles, René's cousin Jacquet Mailhes, Nin-Nin, and naturally, Django. Yet it's in the title track "Gitrane" that René's influences merge. Written with both his uncle Challain Ferret and John Coltrane in mind, the song is old and new, both ancient in styling and modern in melody.

René released *Carrément* later in 2003, that duet CD with Roger Guérin that he previewed for me in his Peugeot parked on rue Vercingétorix. With tunes by Charles Trenet, Django's "Manoir de mes rêves," and a variety of originals by both René and Guérin, the album is alive with a glorious tone and a truly *douce ambiance*. Five decades on in his career, René proved he was at the top of his game.

At Le Montana, René simply sits in a corner of the barroom with his old Gibson ES-175, his drummer and bassist, and fills the room with glorious music. He's a man quiet, unprepossessing, and not needing to play to his ego. Between sets, he talks of recording a new album of solo bebop guitar, and then takes up his guitar again to preview for Alain and me a ballad he composed in honor of his late wife. He still picks that same Gibson through all these years, still playing those bebop rhythms that made Baro laugh.

On any given night in Paris, you can hear Gypsy jazz of all sorts, from unbelieveable fretboard pyrotechnics played by young Romani tyros to street-tough rap manouche, stylish swing played at impossibly fast tempos to *valses musette* that leave fretting fingers in a knot. Yet there's nothing to match René Mailhes playing his bebop with the essence of cool. He plays it slow and sweet, no flash, no need for show-off virtuousity; just pure, beautiful bebop lyricism. His fingers move over the frets like he's caressing the melody.

SEVEN | *Les Guitares à Moustache*
Revolutionary Jazz Guitars for a Jazz Revolution

I AM HURRYING ACROSS the ancient place des Vosges on the border of Paris's Marais *quartier*, past the glorious palaces and arched *galeries*, through the sun-filled park of plane trees and on out the other side. Place des Vosges is often considered the most perfect and beautiful of all the world's squares, piazzas, and various other assorted public spaces. The *place* is architecture in harmony.

Yet around the corner from place des Vosges something equally wondrous awaits me. A guitar store.

Wedged in among *patisseries* and *boulangeries* and bistros along the rue du Pas de la Mule—the bygone Passway of the Mule—is Instruments Musicaux Anciens. It's a classic Parisian shop front with grand windows ideal for *lèche-vitrines*—literally "window licking," as the French so descriptively term window shopping. The proprietor's name, André Bissonnet, is painted proudly above in gilt letters. I've come here trying to decipher the mysteries behind Django's guitar sound, a tone and voice unlike any other in guitar music.

Yet this is not your typical guitar store. There are no Fender Stratocasters here, no teens playing "Stairway to Heaven." In truth, guitars are one of the lesser instruments in this musical world of wonders. And they border on being too practical. Monsieur Bissonnet specializes in the bizarre, the unique, the forgotten, and the extinct. I step into his shop and am standing in a living cabinet of curiosities, shelves of memento mori of melodies past. Here are the musical Dodo birds, the instruments that lost out in Darwinian selection: ophicleides and céciliums, hurdy-gurdies and zithers, harps and harmoniums and hunting horns, a cavalryman's *trompette ergonomique* that once wrapped around a hip for leading the charge into battle, musettes and balalaïkas, bugles that have sounded their final reveille and panpipes that have played their last revelry, accordinas and concertinas, snake-shaped woodwind serpents with python heads fashioned from creepy-crawly twisted tubing like a wrong turn down the path of musicality. Some of these instruments appear vaguely menacing, more akin to medieval torture devices designed to flail, to stretch, to batter the air into telling all through music. Others look like escapees from a ten-in-one show on a carnival midway. Step this way to see the two-headed trombone! The freak lute! The fire-breathing cornet! Marvel at the fascinating hybrids of musical species, the dimorphic wonders of the violophone—half violin, half trumpet! The amazing three-necked harp-lyre! The mysterious claviharp, harp-guitar, guitar-lyre, violin-harp, and the strangest of the strange, the mellifluous monochord—part Mozart, part Dalí! These are the old-fangled and oxidized, the hoary and horrible musical instruments of history from the attics of all Europe and all eras.

The keeper of this musical menagerie is himself like an escapee from a Jules Verne novel. Monsieur Bissonnet appears harmless enough. He sports a quaint bowtie and often has a sleepy look in his eyes as he works obsessively long hours in his mad laboratory, his hair a hand-combed, unkempt Beethovian flurry of silvery locks. Bissonnet is a modern-day Nemo. His is an alternative technological reality, and he's one of few who still understand the workings of these ancient valves and keys and joints and miles of strings and pipes, keeping these musical failures breathing and making music. For this is neither a museum nor a cemetery: Like a snake charmer, Bissonnet can coax true music from all the instruments you see before you, playing a quick snatch of a tango on a bandoneon or a passage from Bach on a Pleyel piano.

And upstairs in his apartment he's rumored to keep his own private collection that is even more fantastic, more magical than that on display in his store below.

Bissonnet was born to a family of butchers—which seems about the most incongruous beginning imaginable for this musical *ingénieur*. Bissonnet *père* likely had great expectations for his son to follow in his footsteps with cleaver and apron. But the young Bissonnet lived in music: With a bit of head-scratching and some cacophonous first toots, he could play most any instrument he came across, the stranger, the better. Upon his father's passing, he took up running the neighborhood *boucherie*, but soon his growing collection of musical oddities began taking over the butcher blocks and countertops. For four years, he sold both briskets and banjos, and even today I can easily imagine hams and sausages hanging amid the violins and violcelloes in the shop front.

Yet it was a simple, lowly guitar that caught my eye. I spotted it from afar through the front window, hanging by its neck from the rafters all the way in the back of the shop.

Monsieur Bissonnet happily takes the guitar down for me to try out: He wants his instruments to be used, not to grow moss. I pick out a quick Djangoesque run on the old strings, and Bissonnet smiles to hear the guitar come alive. To my eye, it looks like a copy of the Selmer-Maccaferri steel-string jazz guitars as made by the luthier Bernabe Busato here in Paris, likely in the late 1930s or 1940s during the glory days of jazz. The spruce soundboard is worn smooth by a strumming arm, the fretboard pitted by the passage of many fingers; the guitar has that beautiful patina of having been well played. And it sounds like it desperately wants to make music again.

"*C'est un guitare Busato?*" I ask.

"Maybe, maybe not," Bissonnet says enigmatically. "The history of these guitars is cloudy, always difficult to know."

In these surroundings, this is exactly what I expect—and maybe even hope— he would say.

Django began playing his revolutionary jazz on a revolutionary new jazz guitar during the summer of 1935. The quest for volume was the Holy Grail of guitar construction in the day: Guitarists such as Django sought instruments to slice through the sound and fury of a jazz band. Designed by Italian luthier Mario Maccaferri, the novel Henri Selmer & Compagnie modèle Jazz guitar was France's answer. It boasted the steel strings of a mandolin, which were louder, brighter, and clearer sounding than the traditional gut strings of the *flamenco*'s guitar. And the Selmer was built around a unique patented resonating sound box hidden within the outer body. This novelty boosted volume while retaining the essential purity of tone.

In the early years, Django experimented with a variety of other guitars. Following the lead of Poulette Castro, he played one of luthier Julián Gómez Rámirez' steel-string guitars. Photographs also show Django playing other instruments that look like Martin Coletti guitars and a large-bodied steel-string made by Arthur Carbonell, a luthier from Valencia who opened an *atelier* in Marseille in 1922. But once Django started playing a Selmer-Maccaferri, he swore by it the rest of his life.

Mario Maccaferri was born May 20, 1900, in the town of Cento on the flat Emilia-Romagna plain near Bologna. Apprenticed at age eleven to famed luthier and guitarist Luigi Mozzani, Maccaferri learned to craft violins, mandolins, guitars, and other stringed instruments. These included Mozzani's own prize creation, the lyre-guitar, combining a standard guitar with an extended bass-bout soundboard and several non-fretted bass strings, increasing the guitar's sound range with the sympathetic drone strings of a harp. In 1923, Maccaferri struck out on his own and started his own lutherie in Cento. But it was not solely to building guitars that Maccaferri devoted himself: He was also studying as a classical guitarist.

In 1916, Maccaferri enrolled at the Accademia di Musica in Siena, where he graduated with honors. He embarked on a concert tour in 1923, earning plaudits from critics throughout Europe, and in 1926, he was appointed the Sienese school's first guitar instructor. At the time, Maccaferri and Andrès Segovia were lauded as the two luminaries of classical guitar.

Maccaferri closed his Cento lutherie and moved to Paris in 1927 and then on to London in 1928, where he set up a lutherie in the back of a furniture shop. Here, he crafted a prototype of a novel gut-string guitar. He brought his creation to Ben Davis, who along with his brother, Lew, managed the largest musical instrument shop in Britain, the London branch of Henri Selmer at 12 Moor Street, W1. Impressed by the guitar, Davis introduced Maccaferri to Selmer, who immediately charged ahead to begin production of a range of guitars initially destined just for the English market.

In spring 1931, Maccaferri established an *atelier* in a small wing of the immense Selmer factory in Mantes-la-Ville, just to the north of Paris. Within this factory, Selmer also made its famous clarinets and saxophones as well as other woodwinds and horns. Maccaferri designed and fabricated all of the lutherie tooling, set up an assembly line, and instructed a team of carpenters in guitar construction. Metal-working machines in the main factory stamped out special brass tailpieces and Maccaferri's novel covered tuners to the luthier's design.

In that quest for the Holy Grail of volume, 1930s guitar makers experimented with inventions and innovations ranging from the bold to the bizarre. Believing bigger was better, American luthiers Gibson, Stromberg, Epiphone, and artisan-luthier John D'Angelico vied to craft ever-larger carved archtop guitars. The race was won by Elmer Stromberg's monstrous Master 400. Boasting a lower bout that spread a full nineteen inches wide, it was a guitar so immense many players couldn't reach comfortably around its body. Meanwhile, Austro-Hungarian immigré John Dopyera was venturing off in his own idiosyncratic direction. In 1927 in California, he unveiled what was the most radical, complex, and by far, expensive solution in the search for acoustic amplification. Dopyera's National Tricone guitar was a metal-bodied guitar mounted with three stamped-aluminum resonating cones serving as crude speakers amplifying the strings. Due to its volume less than its tone, the National Tricone became the instrument of choice for Argentine expatriate jazzman Oscar Alemán as well as other Parisian jazz guitarists; it boasted the punch to be heard through a horn section on stage. Other boffin inventors were just beginning to experiment with electrically amplified guitars, marrying the expertise of a Dr. Frankenstein with the obsession of a Dr. Pretorius. Enlisting everything and anything from gramophone needles to crude radio transmitters to charged magnets, they captured and then amplified string vibrations. In 1933, amplification-visionary Lloyd Loar was ousted from the staid Gibson firm, where he had built some of the finest acoustic instruments ever. Now, Loar launched his own Vivi-Tone Company, offering the first commercially produced electrically amplified guitar. But the technology was still exotic and acceptance was therefore slow: Vivi-Tone was bankrupt just months after it was founded. It's these types of guitars that find their way to André Bissonnet's Instruments Musicaux Anciens.

Maccaferri's solution to the quest for volume, meanwhile, was old-fashioned yet ingenious. Taking a cue from the mandolin construction he knew so well, his guitar featured a soundboard arched at the bridge with the tailpiece attached to the backside tail of the guitar. The soundboard was also glued to the sides under pressure, aiding his interior sound box in amplifying volume. This volume was especially pronounced in the treble registers, giving the guitar a tone that carved through the powerful voices of accordions and horns like a knife through foie gras. The trebly tone made it ideal for recording sessions of the day: The treble stood out from the rest of a jazz band's sonority yet was also sweetened and smoothed by the recording process, sounding clear and warm by the time it was reproduced through a phonograph's speaker. In addition, the guitar's body featured a cutaway on the upper bout's treble side, allowing Django facile access to the upper frets. A short fretboard extension ran out over the sound hole, offering him a full two-octave range on the high E string alone. Simply put, he now had a wider palette of notes available under his fingers than any guitarist before.

The first Selmer guitars were made in France in 1932 and shipped back to the London branch, where they were eagerly promoted by Chappie D'Amato, Jack Hylton's guitarist. By mid 1935, the French guitars were finally available in France, and Django played his first riffs on a Selmer. He began using a Selmer-Maccaferri gut-string guitar, but soon Maccaferri launched his louder steel-string version that proved perfect for jazz. With their large sound hole, the better for projecting sound, these instruments became known among musicians as *grande bouche* guitars—large mouths. Or better yet, loudmouths.

Later in 1936 or 1937, Django began playing a revised Selmer with a small sound hole and a longer neck with fourteen frets to the body, offering him an even greater array of notes. With their elegant oval sound hole, these naturally became known as *petite bouche* guitars. And it was around this time that Django and Henri Selmer joined together in a promotional arrangement, likely a gentlemen's handshake agreement whereby Selmer provided Django all the guitars he required in exchange for his endorsement. Django reportedly visited the Selmer shop and tried out each and every guitar as soon as they arrived, picking and choosing the best-sounding ones for himself. The Quintette members were also given Selmers, although legend has it that their guitars were only on loan.

In the coming years, Maccaferri's Selmer guitar would have a fundamental influence on Django's music and his growing success. When Django traveled to New York City in 1946 at the behest of Duke Ellington, he left his Selmer behind; he believed American luthiers would fight among themselves to be the first to get him to play their guitars. There was no welcoming committee, however, and Django was forced instead to buy his own Gibson archtop, which he both loved and hated. When Charles Delaunay arrived in New York a short time later carrying Django's guitar, Django swooned over his Selmer while cursing the American guitars: *"Mon frère,"* he told Delaunay, "all the Americans will wish they could play on this guitar! At least it's got tone, you can hear the chords like you can on the piano. Don't talk to me any more about their *casseroles*—their tinpot guitars! Listen to this, it speaks like a cathedral!" Artist endorsements have rarely been so vehement and heartfelt.

After Django began using a Selmer in 1935, it was rare to see a French jazz guitarist—Gypsy or *gadjo*—play anything but a Selmer, both for the guitar's jazz qualities and in emulation of Django and his Quintette. And in an ironic twist, Mario Maccaferri's Selmer guitars featured a signature ornament— antiquated yet stylish accents to the bridge glued to the soundboard. These filigrees served no true sonic purpose, but they looked just right. They became known as *"moustaches,"* giving the guitars a slang nickname of *les guitares à moustache*. In hindsight, these adornments now seem an essential component on a guitar made famous by the man with the famous moustache.

I'm walking now through Galérie Véro-Dodat around the corner from the Louvre, on my way to Instruments de Musique à Cordes R. F. Charle. I've skipped the Louvre on this visit to Paris, but it'd be a sin to miss Rosyne and François Charle's *atelier*. This is without doubt the most beautiful guitar store in Paris— which of course makes it the most beautiful guitar store in the world.

Galerie Véro-Dodat itself is in part to thank. This enclosed *passage* running between rue Croix des Petits Champs and rue Jean-Jacques Rousseau dates from 1823, and is one of the only Parisian *galeries* surviving in original period condition. A floor of black-and-white checkerboard tiles leads up to dark-wood storefronts, fluorescent in their ornate designs and opulent trappings. The *galérie* is named for its two original investors, the unlikely duo of the *charcutier* Véro and financier Dodat. This simple tunnel through a block of buildings serves as a tunnel back in time: all of the shops here are devoted to ancient and arcane crafts, from hand-bookbinders and *imprimeries* to artisan *couturières* and leatherworkers—and even a famous night-owl restaurant that locks diners into the passage after dark.

At number 17 stands the Charles's shop. Labeling this a "guitar store" is akin to calling Paris just a "city." I enter the store and my head starts spinning, looking around at the guitars, violins, banjos, harp guitars, and more hanging above like stars in the sky. Rosyne has a repair room in the back, ripe with a fug of exotic animal glues of secret formulae for keeping these old instruments together; she's renowned throughout the capital, and even Europe, for her work. François, on the other hand, is the guitar and music fanatic. While his main love is American blues and old-time music, he's also known around the globe as the foremost expert on Selmer-Maccaferri guitars. In fact, he wrote the book on the subject.

We exchange a friendly *salut*, comparing notes on a Gypsy jazz gig we attended together the night before, and then he quickly moves on to the business at hand: introducing me to some new finds. The *petite bouche* Selmer once owned by Henri Crolla. A battered yet still regal Busato. A ridiculously rare Favino-Chauvet archtop, perhaps one of the first built. An elderly Di Mauro with a glorious patina of use after years being played in *bals musette* and jazz *boîtes*.

Like the C. F. Martin Dreadnought in the United States, Mario Maccaferri's Selmer jazz guitar soon became a style, if not a template, followed by other luthiers. And François's shop is the ideal place to see, hear, and strum out this history—it's hanging here on the walls and from the rafters, ready to be played.

Most of the other luthiers following Maccaferri's lead were also Italian emigrants to Paris. And most of them set up shop in Montreuil or Ménilmontant, the first of Paris they saw as they arrived from Italy.

Perhaps the earliest to build guitars in the Selmer-Maccaferri image was Bernabe "Pablo" Busato. While Busato guitars are some of the best in build and sound quality—sometimes surpassing even Selmers—they are also the rarest and their history the most mysterious. Little is known of Busato the man. His nickname of "Pablo" hints at a Spanish connection: Perhaps he lived in Spain and studied lutherie there from one of the flamenco masters. Or maybe he spent time in Argentina, the destination of many Italian immigrants. Busato likely came to Paris in the 1920s or 1930s; we know from *les tickets*—the labels luthiers glue inside their guitars with their signatures—that he set up a lutherie at 40 rue d'Orgemont in the 20th Arrondissement, a street too that no longer exists. He began building instruments faithful to the Selmer in style and quality, but from images of musette bands playing his instruments, he may have even preceded and influenced Maccaferri in building steel-string guitars with cutaway bodies. In later years, he offered innovations such as a small oval sound hole giving a more directed sound and a neck that joined the body at the fourteenth fret; legend has it that Busato might have inspired Selmer to update its own guitars. Busato continued crafting guitars as well as selling proprietary accordions and other orchestral string instruments until his death in 1952.

I have a special fascination for Busato guitars, no doubt inspired by their mystery and rarity, as well as their sound. Even after Django began using a Selmer, he also at times played jazz guitars built by Busato and others; a well-used Busato once owned by Django was given to Gypsy jazz historian Alain Antonietto by Django's other sister, Carmen Ziegler. Ninine Garcia of La Chope des Puces probably made the Busato most famous. He's been followed by other acolytes, including Romane, Potzi of the avant-garde swing ensemble Paris Combo, Neil Andersson of the Seattle band Pearl Django, and others. I own an ancient, well-traveled Busato that still has bronze frets and its original *ticket* hidden deep within the guitar's body on the neck heel, Busato's favored site. Who knows where this guitar's been or the music it's played, but it's been around the block a few times: Its fretboard is scarred and the soundboard scratched by many a pick's passage—it's not for nothing that Gypsy jazzmen affectionately called their instruments *une gratte*, literally "a scratch," as scratching the strings was their slang for playing. This Busato is so light that I hardly know I'm holding it. Yet it's voice is so deep and sonorous, it's as though the guitar is haunted.

Following Busato came Sicilian émigré Antoine Di Mauro. Settling in Paris in 1932, he opened his *atelier* in the impasse Rançon before moving to 47 rue de la Réunion, both in the 20th Arrondissement. Alongside Selmer copies, Di Mauro launched his own creation, christened the Chorus Special model, featuring an American archtop's F-holes—known as *ouies* in French—on a Selmer-style body. Yet most of all, Di Mauro was famed for working an alchemy. His guitars were inexpensive instruments built on a budget, and yet their sound was often lush and opulent, a rich tone admired by players then and now.

Antoine's brother, Joseph, also established his own lutherie, although it was likely in the same workshop and building much the same style of guitar. Joseph also added his own signature model: a jazz guitar with a heart-shaped sound hole that also had great soul to its sound. Baro Ferret played such a guitar built by Joseph Di Mauro, as shown in a famous photograph of him alongside accordionist Jo Privat in the late 1940s or 1950s.

Following Antoine's death, his son—also named Joseph, to make things further confused—kept the family's workshop alive until 1993. Joseph *fils* often came to hear musette and Gypsy jazz by one of the Di Mauro faithful, guitarist Jean Dubanton, who played in duet with accordionist Jean-Claude Laudat at the old Chez Elle restaurant near Les Halles. I met him here in 1999. He was always happy to share *un verre* and reminisce about the guitars his family built for some five decades.

There were other luthiers as well. Jacques Castelluccia and his son Jean-Baptiste. Pierre Anastasio. Spaniard David Enesa. Frenchmen Claude and Louis Patenotte and the Gérôme clan, both based in France's guitar-making capital of Mirecourt. Siro Burgassi, Olivieri, Jacobacci, Couesnon, and more obscure and small-scale artisan-makers. Today, there are numerous revivalist luthiers around the globe, including France's Alain Mazaud, Jean-Noël Lebreton, and Philippe Moneret; the United Kingdom's John Le Voi, Doug Kyle, David Hodson, and R. J. Aylward; Dell'Arte in the United States and Canada's Michael Dunn and Shelley D. Park; Leo Eimers and Thijs van der Harst's Moustache Guitars in the Netherlands; Germany's Stefan Hahl, Japan's Saga, and more. The best known of all may be Maurice Dupont in Cognac. Dupont crafts guitars faithful to the Selmer style, yet with modern features that update the style for the future.

Of all the makers of *les guitares à moustache*, none is so beloved among the Romani as Favino. Selmer and even Busato guitars are worth too much on the collector market, so Gypsies horse-trade them to the rich *gadjé* for cash. Favinos, they keep. And just as with the music, they pass them down through the generations.

I'm on the other side of Paris in the Faubourg Saint-Antoine and the old *atelier* of Luc Degeorges. Luc is the Paris outlet for Favino guitars and the base these days of Jean-Pierre Favino, son of founding father Jacques Favino. J-P comes to the capital from his workshop in Castelbiague in the Pyrénées once a month, and today's my lucky day to sit down with him and talk guitars. I'm trying out one of his new guitars, and as I pick out a melody, J-P tells of his family's history.

Like the luthiers before him, Jacques Favino was an Italian immigrant to France. He was born in July 1920 in Trecate in the northern Piedmonte. When Jacques was three in 1923, his parents brought him to Paris as they sought work. He grew up and became a carpenter and cabinetmaker—anything combining wood and handwork. But then World War II interrupted his career: Jacques was rounded up in 1943 and conscripted into Nazi Germany's slave labor force for the next two and a half years. Liberated by the Allies, he returned to Paris. Thanks to his father-in-law, Gino Papiri, he was hired on at Busato's *atelier*, fashioning banjo necks by hand. In 1946, he began working after hours, learning to make violins at Jean Chauvet's lutherie. In the early 1950s, Favino built his first guitars, following the style of American archtops with large bodies and f-holes. These early guitars bore the *ticket* "Chauvet-Favino."

In 1949, Favino met Matelo Ferret. Legend states it was Matelo who suggested that Favino build Selmer-style guitars, as he could not find playable examples of the old *grande bouche* Selmer-Maccaferris he loved. Favino began crafting his own Gypsy guitars, but with a larger, laminated-mahogany body and a deeper, more resonant signature sound. As J-P tells me, "My father always refused to copy Selmer totally. He wanted to build a guitar with a personal tone, a personal sound. Uniquely a 'Favino' guitar."

These guitars not only sounded great but were sturdy as well, something that can't always be said of Selmers. Favino made only fifteen to twenty guitars a week—a minuscule production run. Yet they were made to be played, night after night, year after year. And now, as they've proven, generation after generation. Most every Gypsy jazzman came calling at Favino's *atelier* at 9 rue de Clignancourt in Paris's seedy Barbès neighborhood, just a short walk from the Pigalle *boîtes*. Matelo owned several, Sarane Ferret a couple more. Due to Jacques's warm welcome, *atelier* Favino became a hangout for musicians, and the workshop's "wall of fame" included signed photos of many Favino "users." Even today, musicians such as Francis-Alfred Moerman and Boulou Ferré share with me fond memories of afternoons spent chatting and jamming there.

Along the way, Favino was hired by the Paul Beuscher musical empire in Paris to finish a run of Selmer guitars using a mélange of bodies, necks, and other parts found at Selmer's factory. And he was also enlisted by Joseph Reinhardt to craft three classical guitars for playing in the *cabarets russe*.

J-P joined his father as an apprentice in 1973, and when Jacques retired in 1979, J-P took over running the shop. Today, J-P still builds Favino guitars in his Pyrénées workshop. The J-P Favino guitar I am playing is an impossibly beautiful creation made from laminated redwood, the body's color so deep and lustrous you can stare into it like a crystal ball. And the sound it makes isn't bad either. With more hard playing, the guitar's voice will further open up, and I can foresee this guitar too being prized and passed down through the generations of a family.

And then there is the seemingly simple matter of the pick itself. Among Romani guitarists, the devotion to a good plectrum is near mystical. It's almost as if a pick contains music within, a mystery of mysteries beyond all knowing. One does not simply have a pocketful of store-bought, multicolored Model Number 351 picks to pick among; the perfect plectrum is handmade, time-tested, and gig-proven. I remember Dorado Schmitt misplacing his pick in between sets at New York City's Birdland club in 2004 and becoming nearly hysterical until he recovered it. To put it succinctly, there are picks and there are *picks*.

In formal French, the pick is known as *un plectre*, but no Romani guitarist I've ever met calls them that. In musicians' slang, it's *un médiator*, presumably as the pick offers a mediation between the soft soul of the fingers and the steel will of the guitar strings. *Flamencos*, who picked their cat-gut strings with their grown-out fingernails, used to varnish those nails for strength and longevity; today, the modern wonders of super-glue usually replace the vicissitudes of varnish. The pick is the fingernail made omnipresent, omniscient, and omnipotent.

Starting with Poulette Castro, the Romani of Paris adopted plectrums to play their new steel-string guitars. Picks added the volume they needed to be heard over an accordion, or later, a jazz band. To paraphrase guitarist Mark Knopfler, a pick is the world's smallest and simplest amplifier.

As a young waif learning banjo, Django was inventive in finding items to use as a picks. His family talks of him taking up anything that might strike the strings—the tip of a teaspoon, one of his mother's sewing thimbles, a two-*sous* coin, or a bit of whalebone that once served as a shirt-collar stiffener for a starched bourgeois all found new use in his hands. Later on, he graduated to a true *médiator* made most likely by himself from imported tortoiseshell.

Tortoiseshell is essential to a perfect pick just as wood is to a guitar body. Nothing else will do. Bone; ivory; coconut shell; brass and copper; Bakelite, celluloid, and other wonder phenolic and polycarbonate plastics; various exotic woods and precious stones; titanium and other Space Age unobtanium—they've all been tried. Even cowhorns have been experimented with, and the French being oh-so-French, proclaim that certain breeds from certain regions are the only cowhorns to use—in the Clignancourt *puces* a guitarist swore to me that the horn of the Normand cow was so superior it wasn't even worth considering the Salers, Limousin, Bazadais, or even the vaunted Blond d'Aquitaine. Yet none of them have that music within like tortoiseshell.

The shell of turtles was a curiosity brought back to France by sailors and merchants from the far side of the world. Thus, it was uncommon and expensive for a young Gypsy boy to get his hands on—and yet essential. Once procured, a chunk of hawksbill sea-turtle shell was shaped by sawing and then sanding. Some guitarists flattened their shell pieces by pounding them; others built up the edges to make them easier to grip by heating them on the wood-fired cast-iron stoves in their *roulottes* and molding them to suit their own fingers.

Guitarist Francis-Alfred Moerman still uses a pick made by Baro Ferret, which he says is the same size and fashion as the picks preferred by Django and the other Gypsy guitarists of the day. Francis's pick is minuscule, almost microscopic. It's about the size of a fingernail, perhaps a nod to the history of the plectrum as a replacement for the *flamenco*'s fingernails—or maybe due to the scarcity of tortoiseshell itself. It's also shaped roughly like a fingernail, but with a rounded "point" for picking. This point is not truly pointed, either. Rather, it's beveled on both sides, thus retaining its thickness. For me, playing with one of these tiny picks is like trying to hold onto air—and as soon I start playing, the pick itself takes to the air.

Nowadays, most Romani use monstrous picks both large in size and thick in width. Sometimes, the picks are just chunks of unshaped tortoiseshell, left natural and crude to aid in gripping the infamously flying objects. One portion is shaped for plucking the strings, sometimes with a second, duller edge for rhythm playing, adding force to the strummed chord as well as making vibrato easier to play. The thickness of course adds to the volume, making these picks the Marshall stacks of these simplest of amplifiers. But the Romani also solemnly swear they enhance the tone—that secret and sacred music within a special pick.

Today, of course, importation of tortoiseshell is outlawed most everywhere around the globe. Yet still many Romani play with plectrums made from the shells of turtles, some handed down through generations, others illicit. But times are changing too, and more and more young Gypsy guitarists have adopted American-style picks, the famous D'Andrea Model Number 351 shape made of celluloid or other plastics. It's another case of American pop culture infiltrating the darkest corners of the globe. Among the Gypsies, this is in large part due to the influence of American jazz guitarists who followed Django's era and in turn influenced the Romani players—guitarists like Jim Hall, Jimmy Raney, and perhaps most surprisingly, George Benson, whose melodic jazz lines are beloved by many Manouche. Patrick Saussois is one who swears by thin 351 picks. Yet instead of playing with the pointed tip, many turn the pick around to use the round "corners," mimicking with their modern picks the traditional style of the old Romani tortoiseshell plectrums.

In my hands I hold a small oblong metal bar measuring thirteen centimeters in length by three wide and one deep. It has a simple jack input at one end and a cryptic, unmarked potentiometer knob on top. Across the bar's face is the single script word "Stimer." It's one of the secrets to Django's electric bebop sound, a Stimer S.T.48 electro-magnetic pickup dating from the early 1950s. To Gypsy jazzmen, this chromed-metal bar is worth its weight in gold.

When and where Django went electric is a question of great mystery and much debate. The best guess has him plugging in shortly after the Liberation of Paris, in late 1945 or 1946. Django's former sideman, Corsican guitarist Marcel Bianchi, is lauded as France's first guitarist to play electric. He escaped the Nazis by playing jazz in Switzerland during the war, where he discovered the Swiss Bâle pickups that were years ahead of anything even conceived of in France.

Returning to Paris with the peace, he soon turned on the other jazz guitarists to the possibilities of electricity. Nin-Nin was a quick convert, and Django followed. American jazz guitarist Charlie Byrd told me of seeing them both with pickups screwed onto their battered Selmers jamming in a Pigalle *boîte* just after the Liberation—1945 or 1946; he couldn't remember the date for certain. During a Swiss tour in mid 1946, newspaper reports confirm Django was playing electric. And by the time he toured the United States with Duke Ellington in late 1946, he had adapted to and adopted the electric sound as his own.

In those early years, Django likely experimented with different boffin-made contraptions to electrify his sound. There are reports of him placing a standard microphone next to his guitar to create an electrified tone during a 1946 Belgian recording session. He may have returned from America with one of the Dearmond pickups he used with Duke. And photos from the late 1940s picture him with an array of bizarre-looking pickups of unidentified sources bolted onto his Selmer. But sometime around 1948, all that changed.

French radio engineer Yves Guen and his brother Jean unveiled their first guitar pickups in 1946, baptized in *Jazz Hot* magazine advertisements as the Stimer P46 and R46. The Guens set up a company at 39 rue d'Alençon in the Parisian suburb of Courbevoie to produce their electrical gadgetry. Yves had been experimenting with telephone receivers to aid his guitar-playing friends in amplifying their instruments. Now, with these first electro-magnetic pickups, a guitarist could simply bolt it into the acoustic sound hole, plug into an amp, and suddenly be set free with the twist of a knob.

The 46 Series Stimers may have been just prototypes. The fledgling science of electro-magnetic pickups progressed at a rapid pace from the crude pickups of just years before, and the 46 Series was followed by the real deal—the S.T.48 pickup and six-watt Stimer M.6 amplifier. To promote their product, *les frères* Guen naturally turned to Django, and he wholeheartedly endorsed the Stimer setup. In a 1952 photo session for Stimer ads shot by Hervé Derien, Django was pictured in his Samois cottage, his beloved fishing poles on the wall behind him, beaming with joy as he played his new electrified Selmer.

The Guens followed with the S.51 pickup and more powerful amps, including the ten-watt M.10 and twelve-watt M.12. By today's standards, these power output figures are quaint at best, but in their day they could raise the roof. Django proved this playing at Club Saint-Germain, his Stimer equipment turned all the way up—surely it would have been at "11" if the volume knobs had had numerals—the sound overdriven and reverberating off the *cave*'s stone walls. After years pounding out *la pompe* with a muscular right wrist, he must have rejoiced at the glorious ease of this sudden volume.

Other French boffins-turned-producers were also offering their own pickups and amps by this time. Alongside Stimer, there was RV, the Swiss Bâle, and more. But somehow the Stimer had the magic. It was a woefully simple setup: just a hand-wound, resin-immersed single-coil pickup wired through a sole volume potentiometer in the S.T.48. And yet it had a soul of a sort. How a certain basic electrical arrangement could create *the sound* while others could not has befuddled and tortured and inspired inventors and guitarists for ages. The sound of the Stimer became Django's signature—warm and rich: at times shocking; at others, sublime. Django's electric guitar now too spoke with a human voice.

I'm standing in front of what could and should be a shrine. Instead, it's a cold, almost scientific, museum display: a locked glass case, humidity and temperature controlled, and notated by the invariable small, impersonal card of identification. The case stands within La Cité de la Musique, the amazing symphony of concert halls, recording studios, interactive museum, and architectural attraction in the Parisian neighborhood of La Villette, once home instead to the city's slaughterhouses. Inside this case stands one of Django's Selmer guitars. While Paris has an estimated one hundred streets named for mathematicians; plaques in homage to artists, writers, scientists, even clowns; and statues and boulevards honoring every general that ever clipped on epaulettes and every politician that ever got a vote, there's nothing in the city to commemorate Django. No memorial plaque, no token tablet, not even a narrow, forgotten side street in a non-chic *quartier*. There's only his guitar in a museum.

Still, Romani and Gypsy jazz fans come from all over the world to see this guitar. It's the only public, surviving relic of Django. Shrine or not, seemingly unbeknownst to the powers that be, it's become a site of pilgrimage.

This Selmer guitar was one of the rare Modèle Django Reinhardt Series made by the lutherie. Built in 1940 and bearing serial number 503, it was one of Django's last guitars: From the telltale pick scratches and use patterns on the body, it can be identified in those photos taken of Django in Samois in 1952 for the Stimer ads. After Django's death, pictures of Django's widow, Naguine, and young son Babik feature the guitar, Babik tentatively strumming the instrument. In 1964, Naguine donated the guitar to the Musée du Conservatoire de Paris, and it was subsequently placed in this glass case in the Musée de la Musique de Paris.

Looking closely at Django's Selmer on display, I see something of the personality of the man imprinted into the guitar. Django was infamous for truly *using* his guitars. As a youth, his mother collected together the means to buy or trade for his *banjo-guitare* and he never had enough money for a case; just as a *charcutier* wrapped a ham in butcher's paper, Django carried his instrument wrapped in newspaper. Stéphane Grappelli remembered him arriving to play tea dances at the elegant Hôtel Claridge in 1934 still with his guitar protected by the daily papers. Even after he became a star, Django's guitar was not pampered. In 1946 after the Liberation, journalist Sam Adams chastised Django in public in the pages of *Melody Maker* concerning the state of his guitar with pure British sanctimoniousness. Adams described the abuse in detail: The guitar was dirty and disheveled, its pretty varnish long gone, a makeshift pile of matchbox covers under the bridge to keep the strings from buzzing on the frets. Django simply shrugged his shoulders and told Adams, "*C'est la guerre.*"

It seems Django's guitar was always doing battle. All those fiery nights of playing hot jazz are apparent here. The soundboard is polished smooth like an effigy's shined nose, the frets worn down like a cathedral's steps by penitents on their knees.

Regarding Django's Selmer on display, though, a fleeting yet unsettling thought lingers in my mind. I stand still, transfixed by the guitar. Then it becomes clear: I have an overall impression of sadness. This guitar deserves to be played, not retired.

And yet who would dare even to try to pick out a simple melody on it? Certainly not I.

EIGHT

Crossroads

On the Road to Les Saintes-Maries-de-la-Mer

'M EN ROUTE TO THE ROMANI RELIGIOUS PILGRIMAGE at Les Saintes-Maries-de-la-Mer, and it's an all-out, wide-open, no-holds-barred road race.

Gypsies often have little concern for the *gadjé*'s laws, and speed limits appear to fall into this category of disregard with a vengeance. In fact, through the windshield of my *petite* Peugeot, I can discern only one Romani rule of the road: It's illegal to be behind anyone else.

And so, we have the Grand Prix to the Gypsy Pilgrimage. In my rearview mirror, I stare into the gunfighter eyes of a hawk-faced, sixty-something Romani grand matron with thick black braids, a glorious rainbow-colored headscarf, and the seemingly essential golden hoop earrings. And she's driving like a demon. Agog with impatience, she's riding my bumper, darting sideways into the left-hand lane, seeking a hole in the steady oncoming traffic to shoot past slowpoke me. Her knucklebones blaze white-hot on the steering wheel, making like Juan Manuel Fangio in his Ferrari. In the distance is a stream of other Gypsy vehicles, all vying to pass *her*.

Road racing is fine by me—except for one thing. While I'm in my Peugeot, they're all driving monstrous mobile homes or tall, teetering vans pulling long camping trailers.

The Gypsy matron who has me in her sights at last finds a stretch of free two-laned blacktop and guns her mobile home past. She's followed by a herd of Romani campers, drafting each other, dueling for the lead. I'm left far behind—and wondering what all the hurry is about.

I finally roll into Les Saintes-Maries-de-la-Mer at high noon, and realize what fueled the Romani's rush. This low-rent beach town is home to just 2,500 people. But now, during the annual religious pilgrimage of May 24–25, some ten thousand Gypsies overrun the town. An estimated two thousand Romani caravans flood the town's official and unofficial camping grounds, roadside shoulders, beachside esplanades, and parking lots. They joyously ignore the signs warning *Voyageurs Interdit*. They're halted in any street, passageway, or path wide enough to wedge, jam, or cram in a camper. Pet monkeys climb over caravan rooftops, portable clothes-washing machines empty onto the sidewalks, and kilometers of extension cords are laid out like tripwires. Romani are everywhere. There are weddings, baptisms in the sea, drinking parties on the beach. The women's skirts are aswirl in every color imaginable; some women wear fur coats in the May sun, balancing on Everests of high heels; young girls saunter about in polka-dotted and ruffled flamenco gowns; boys dress like their idea of New York city gangstas; men with gold hedgehog charms around their necks carry guitars and bourbon bottles. And music fills the air: From the sand dunes to the chapel and through the pedestrian walkways that make up the *ville*, the world is suddenly full of melody. There are scrums of Gypsies clapping their hands to the opulent sound of flamenco guitars as women spin and strut. Balkan Tziganes *orkestars* of clarinets, brass, fiddles, and cymbaloms reel out their dark tunes. No one's passing the hat here for the crowd's coins; they're just passing those bottles to anyone who's thirsty. The jazzmen don't have time to drink; they circle around each other, pounding out *la pompe* with a fast, guttural, one-two punch, the Romani faithful cheering them on.

The wild times have just begun.

This town at the end of the road was long a crossroads of Gypsy music. When the Romani arrive here on their annual religious pilgrimage, they also bring with them their flamenco guitars from Spain, violins, clarinets, and cymbaloms from the Balkans, accordions and jazz guitars from Paris. Django came to Les Saintes-Maries-de-la-Mer at various times throughout his life, and the varieties of Gypsy music he heard here must have inspired his own playing. And so I am following his footsteps now, seeking the source of these religious and musical influences.

Les Saintes-Maries-de-la-Mer glows before me in the Mediterranean sunlight like a gilded kingdom. The town grasps tight at its tenuous plot of earth, a long finger of land reaching out into the sea, remote and distant from the rest of France. A grand dike—La Digue-de-la-Mer—saves the village from floundering into the sea. The *ville* itself is like a nautilus seashell, wound tight around itself in a protective coil. It's a resort town, but while the rich are sunbathing at

St. Tropez and Cannes and Nice along the Côte d'Azur, the rest of us are coming to places like Les Saintes-Maries-de-la-Mer. It's cheap and it's easy. Even today, it looks just like Van Gogh's paintings of the *ville* come to life—the seaside, fishing boats, *cabanes*, even the Gypsy caravans he immortalized.

Tall above the town towers its church, Notre-Dame-de-la-Mer. This is not your typical picturesque French country church of postcard or travel poster fame. Instead, Notre-Dame-de-la-Mer is a fortification. For centuries, it served as the town's *donjon*, or keep, to protect it from seafaring invaders. Les Saintes-Maries-de-la-Mer used to be encircled by battlements, with the church at its heart. Even today, if it were not for the bell tower, one could be excused for mistaking the church for a castle. The town was long a beachhead and gateway into La Camargue and Provence, making the fortifications necessary to protect the people from pirates and plunderers. Notre-Dame-de-la-Mer is daunting. The church is small, measuring just fifty meters in length, but its Romanesque and Norman architecture is grave and austere. There are no side chapels, scant riches in artwork; the church is humble in its beauty, harsh in its grace. A freshwater well in the apse allowed townspeople to survive under siege. And the golden stone walls soar straight skyward with little ornamentation beyond narrow window slits and rooftop crenellations suitable for firing down arrows or pouring boiling oil on invaders.

Les Saintes-Maries-de-la-Mer is the capital of La Camargue, the wild west of France and one of the country's last best places. La Camargue is a vast delta formed by the muddy mouth of the Rhône River as it empties into the Mediterranean Sea. This is the least known, least painted, least eulogized corner of France. It's a vast region, 346,000 acres that is as much water as land: salt pans, wetlands, and the long, crooked tendrils of the big river, all bordered by waterlogged scrubland and sand dunes. Roaming the town, I smell the perfume of the sea colliding midair with the scent of the marshes. Within this realm of blue waters, dusty green grasses, and the vast white of the salt lagoons, infinite flocks of flamingos brighten the wide open world with their startling pink plumage.

This may not be an American idyll of a frontier, but La Camargue is a refuge to a wondrous breed of wild white horses, le Camarguais. Stocky yet lissome, short-legged yet tough, these horses fend for themselves in this inhospitable world. I watch in awe as they feast on evil thistle plants with their velvety muzzles, chewing with evident pleasure as if the thorns were foie gras. Le Camarguais were beloved of Napoleon, who in 1812 rode his own wild white horse to Russia—and back again.

Long before the little emperor conscripted these little horses, though, they were already the pride of the cowboys of the Camargue, *les gardiens*. Originating sometime in the 1600s, these cowboys developed traditions and work gear akin to those of Spanish *vaqueros* and American cowboys, but with a Gallic flare and details tuned to their own range. They wear high-topped, deep-heeled leather riding boots; leather pants doubling as chaps; black or brown wool-felt, flat-brimmed *chapeaux*; checkered shirts; and their own style of bolo ties. In effect, the *gardiens* look like a cross between Don Quixote and Gene Autry, but wholly of the Camargue. Most still speak Provençau with its sun-baked, earthy tones, a regional dialect of Occitan that would make members of l'Académie Française pick the grit out of their craws. Atop their Camarguais horses, these *gardiens* wield tridents like Neptune. They herd the region's own breed of sulking black bulls, *les taureaux*. These long-horned cattle still run semiwild, identified by the brands of their *manadier*, or rancher. *Les taureaux* are raised for meat—providing the rich, dark beef for La Camargue's signature meat stew, the delectable *daube de taureau*—as well as for the bullfights that are the adored sport of the Midi.

La Camargue is also famous—or infamous—for its wind. The mistral blows raw and relentless from winter through spring. It drives down from the Gulf of Lyon, cooled in the Pyrénées and over the Massif Central, then funneled through the Rhône valley where it picks up velocity until it scours La Camargue and Provence. The people of the Camargue originally crafted their homes—known as *cabanes*—to ward off the wind. These houses are low to the ground, white-washed against the heat, roofed with wood thatch. And they're built backing into the mistral; their north faces have no windows to let in the cold, just a rounded-off, aerodyne backside to cut the wind. Like the black vultures in the sky over the salt marshes, the mistral is a carrion wind, carving the rocks of Provence with its bite, chilling you to the bone with its talons of cold.

Walking the streets of Les Saintes-Maries-de-la-Mer, I picture Django here as a child. His mother, Négros, likely led him into the church crypt to pay homage to the Romani's patron saint, known in Romanès as Sarah-la-Kâli. I see him as a young man, hiking from Paris to the Midi with his wife, Naguine, faithfully in tow, sleeping in haystacks along the way, she telling fortunes to the townsfolk for spare change, he playing his guitar at seaside campfires. I think of him during World War II, trapped in Nazi-occupied Paris, struggling to compose an organ mass to be played for his people during their pilgrimage. And I image him returning after the war with one of his many automobiles—a grand Citroën or an outrageous Buick, the bigger the better as befitting his ego—pulling his modern metal *campine* trailer, now the king of the Gypsies.

At some early point, for Django the pilgrimage must have turned from religious to spiritual—a musical pilgrimage. The celebrations here always blended religion with music. As Romani trekked from throughout Europe to bow before their Sainte Sarah, they brought all of their musical traditions with them.

The roots of the pilgrimage date back some twenty centuries. Among the first followers of Jesus were a number of women, including Mary Jacob and Mary Salome. These two Marys were sisters or cousins of Jesus' mother. Mary Jacob was the mother of the disciple James the Lesser, for which she is known in French as Marie Jacobé, Jacobus being Latin for "James." Mary Salome was the mother of James the Greater and John the Evangelist. According to the Gospel of Mark, following the crucifixion, these two Marys accompanied Mary Magdalene with spices to anoint Jesus' body when the stone was rolled away from the entrance to Jesus' tomb. Finding it empty, they became the first to spread the message of the resurrection.

The Romans now rushed to quell the Christians of Palestine. Mary Salome's son James was executed by order of Herod Agrippa. The other apostles fled. Roman soldiers seized the two Marys and, as legend has it, put them on a ship with neither sail nor oar, casting them adrift in the Mediterranean. On this ship along with Mary Jacob, Mary Salome, and Mary Magdalene, were Martha, Lazarus, Maximus, and others. Their voyage is not chronicled in the Bible, but their story became popular from the *Legenda Aurea*, the fanciful collection of hagiographies compiled around 1260 by Jacobus de Voragine that was a medieval best-seller: Guided by Providence, the Marys' ship miraculously found its way safely to the shores of Provence. Here, they met up with other scattered followers of Christ, and began preaching the word of Jesus. While Mary Magdalene traveled north into France, Mary Jacob and Mary Salome found asylum in a cave dug into the shore where they landed.

In the centuries after the two Marys' deaths, they were beatified. A sanctum was built here on a wooded island and known as Sainte-Marie-de-Ratis, or St. Mary of the Little Isle. In 1080, the sanctuary was given by the Archbishop of Arles to the monks of the nearby Montmajour abbey, who began erecting a church on the site in the twelfth century. Sainte-Marie-de-Ratis was renamed Notre-Dame-de-la-Mer—Our Lady of the Sea—and the town that grew up around the church was christened Les Saintes-Maries-de-la-Mer in 1837. Pilgrims coming to pray before the Saintes Maries were first chronicled in 1388, a detour on the sacred path devotees from throughout Europe walked en route to Santiago de Compostela in Spain.

Perhaps in keeping with their lot, the Gypsies come here to pay homage not to the Saintes Maries, but to the two saints' servant. Or *their* savior, depending on which legend you follow.

How Sarah fit into the lives of the two Saintes Maries is as clouded as the Romani's own history. Sarah is not mentioned in the Gospels, but according to orthodox legend, she was a black Egyptian servant of the two saints, accompanying them on their voyage after they were expelled from Palestine. One story states the Romans barred Sarah from the ship despite her pleas; Mary Salome then threw her cloak to Sarah, who used it as a raft to reach the boat.

Gypsy mythology tells a different tale, however. The Romani hold that Sara was a Provençal Gitane of noble blood, a queen of her tribe. She had a vision of the coming of the saints' ship and saved them when their boat capsized in a wild storm off the Camargue coast. Another story continues that Sarah was then converted to Christianity and spread the word among members of her own tribe. Sarah's own selfless and saintly role was first detailed by chronicler Vincent Philippon in his 1521 *La Legende des Saintes-Maries*. Still, to the Catholic Church, Sarah is a bastard saint; she remains unrecognized and unbeatified. To the Gypsies, the story is clear: Sarah is their patron.

Within Notre-Dame-de-la-Mer, effigies of the Saintes Maries in their boat stand in consecrated honor in their own portal. Jars of aromatic herbs, symbolizing the planned anointment, are placed in their boat by the non-Gypsy pilgrims. In 1448, King René of France was granted via a Papal Bull right to excavate under the church where legend placed the Sainte-Marie-de-Ratis sanctuary. Two bodies were discovered here, their heads resting on a stone pillow. Reliquaries bearing these remains are kept in a unique Chapelle Haute— an elevated chapel—high above the altar just beneath the church's bell tower. Meanwhile, Sainte Sarah's effigy is relegated to the crypt below Notre-Dame-de-la-Mer where the Saintes Maries once lived. Veneration of Sainte Sarah by the Romani was first recorded in the mid 1800s; Provençal folklorist and Nobel Prize winner Frédéric Mistral describes the Gypsies participating in the 1855 pilgrimage.

Like countless Romani since, Django too likely passed by the Saintes Maries in their boat to descend into the crypt on the wide stone stairs directly under the altar. Visitors must bow their heads here, not purely out of veneration but simply because the ceiling is so low. This ceiling, as well as the walls of the grotto, are blackened by the soot of generations of devotees' candles. During the Gypsy pilgrimage, hundreds, if not thousands, of candles fill every candelabrum in the crypt, pinpoints of light illuminating the dark. The heat is startling and hellacious. The candles also suck oxygen from the air, leaving pilgrims struggling to breath in deep, thirsty gasps. In the far southeastern corner stands the wooden statue of Sarah. She's known in Romanès as Sarah-la-Kâli—"Black Sarah"—and her effigy is stained a dark hue. Instead of alms or ex-voto medallions, the Romani cloak her in handmade robes, and by the pilgrimage's end, she is blanketed thick with ornate gowns. Sainte Sarah is a goddess of fate, as one Romani states, and touching her brings good luck and fortune. Her carved face is worn smooth by pilgrims caressing her cheeks, leaving her with a visage humble and truly saintly, as if she cares little for the Vatican's official decree, strong in her own faith.

On the afternoon of May 25, I am standing in place Jouse d'Arbaud facing the west portal of Notre-Dame-de-la-Mer. Inside the church, Romani are dressed in their best, packed shoulder to shoulder, standing room only. I poke my head in the tiny north doorway, but the crowd is so dense that I feel it only right to give up my two footprints' space to the faithful. The church service has been going on for some five hours, all of it loudly broadcast out of doors on tinny, metallic speakers mounted on the roof. The Gypsy priests—they're trading off now, like a tag team—preach in a sing-song way, their words emphasized not by *hallelujahs* as in an American Pentecostal church, but by ecstatic outbursts of flamenco guitar as though the guitarist is speaking in glossolalia.

Romani were initially Hindu, coming out of India a thousand years ago. But through their centuries of traveling, they assimilated Catholicism into their lives, sometimes blending it with their Hindu beliefs, sometimes supplanting them. In 1952, the Romani's faith found a home in their own church. *Gadjo* cleric Clément Le Cossec of Brittany was called upon by several Gypsies to come pray for them, inspiring him to start a church for the Romani. He founded *La Mission évangélique tzigane de France*, an evangelical Christian church to be run by and devoted to Gypsies. By the mid 1960s, La Mission won over many of Django's musical "followers," guitarists such as Piton Reinhardt and Laro Sollero, violinist Louis "Vivian" Villerstein, and Django's widow, Naguine. In the succeeding decades, the church spread from France throughout Europe to India and the United States. La Mission's goal was to convert Romani to Christianity, but not convert them from being Romani.

Now, as I stand in the square awaiting the pilgrims, through the church speakers comes Django's most famous melody, "Nuages." A single acoustic guitar picks out the theme. And then, to my surprise, the Gypsy congregation joins in, singing religious lyrics to the tune. Django's music has found a home in the service of the Romani church and been transformed into devout music in the truest sense.

Django's influence over La Mission's music was manifest from the beginning. La Mission's first musical director was violinist Pierre "Gagar" Hoffman, part of the Gypsy Hoffman clan. Django jammed with the Hoffmans night after night in 1944 in Thonon-les-Bains during Django's thwarted efforts to escape the Nazis by crossing into Switzerland. Gagar Hoffman was often joined by Romani priest Charles "Tarzan" Welty, who sang to his flock while strumming his Selmer modèle Jazz guitar. And the most popular of La Mission's minstrels was resistance hero, guitarist, and priest Armand Stenegry, who recorded several EPs of Gypsy hymns in the mid 1960s under the *nom de musique* of Archange. Listening to these records today, I am struck by Archange's backing band: Behind the lyrics offered up to God echo the violin of Villerstein and Sollero's joyous electric guitar lines, all in the best tradition of Django.

As the hymnal version of "Nuages" ends, a troupe of *gardiens* rides solemnly into the square on their Camarguais horses. They turn their steeds about face and stand in a place of honor looking toward the church, awaiting the opening of the doors.

And still the service goes on. A new preacher's voice is booming out from those speakers, at times talking in French, at others in Romanès, and still again in a language I don't recognize—likely a Catalan-Romanès argot in honor of the Midi Gitanos. Outside, the *place* and streets leading to the sea are jammed with people—mostly fellow Romani, but also some *gadjé* tourists like myself. People are on the church rooftop, clambering over the town's monuments and fountains, hanging from trees, waiting three or four deep on the streets. Seagulls soar above, iridescent like white angels on the sea winds. The bored little horses scratch at the cobbles, probably dreaming of those succulent thistles.

When finally the church doors open, both the pilgrims indoors and those waiting outdoors seem relieved to see each other, like long-lost siblings. Fronted by two *gardiens*, the preachers—both the *gadjé* parish priests and the Romani Mission priests—lead the procession. Acolytes carry portable speakers and microphones so the service never has to end. Romani pilgrims follow in all their finery: black fedoras so perfectly dapper they take your breath away, women with necklaces of silver coins, children dressed in stiff suits and seemingly stunned to lethargy by the epic service. They carry banners and flags and crosses draped in flowers, walking at a stately pace through the streets, singing hymns, verse after verse, never at a loss for song. As with many Gypsy events, organization is not a prized attribute: at times, the procession is backed up by traffic and grinds to a halt; at others, there's such a huge gap in the parade that I wonder if it's actually over.

After another lengthy wait that appears to bother none of the Romani, the effigy of Sainte Sarah comes up out of the crypt and through the portal. She rides on a plank atop the shoulders of Gypsy pilgrims, her numerous cloaks still tied at her neck. More *gardiens* leave their post to protect her path. The spectators and the procession become one now, snaking through the streets down to the sea, spreading out in the wide intersections and then jamming in close together in the narrow *rues*. I'm walking alongside *un gardien* on horseback, breathing in the rooty scent of the sweet little Camarguais—yet also keeping my feet clear of its hooves in the crowd.

Preceding the procession at the beach, there's more revelry than devotion. Packs of Romani surround guitarists, everyone dancing on the sand, bottles making the rounds until they are empty and cast aside. I fear there's about to be a collision between true believers and drunken musicians. But when the *gardiens* turn down to the sea, the party simply parts before them, suddenly taking on a devout mien.

The horses step into the sea without hesitation, used to their range blending water and earth. Pilgrims carrying the banners and Sainte Sarah follow, walking forward into the waves until they're at chest height. The water roils against them, threatening to teeter the believers into the drink. The whole of the horizon is filled with Romani—Gypsies in the water, on the beach, on the esplanade, on stone breakwaters. Banners wave above, along with numerous guitars, held upside-down overhead like icons themselves. And yet everyone is silent as their Sainte Sarah is washed in the saltwater of the sea. There's only the breath of the Camargue wind and the sound of the Mediterranean waves.

This purification ceremony highlights the likely ancestry between the Romani's Sarah-la-Kâli and the Indian goddess Kâli. In Hindu cosmology, this black goddess was a consort of the white god Shiva. Kâli was early on viewed with fear as a figure both malevolent and terrible in her powers, a goddess who could slay dragons as well as deal instant death to mere humans. In more recent centuries, she is prayed to as a mother figure of supreme benevolence, a goddess of creation. Both the goddess Kâli and Sainte Sarah-la-Kâli are noted for their black skin; both wear crowns and both are linked to water. In India each December, effigies of Kâli are carried down to the Ganges River to be immersed and cleansed in a ceremony eerily similar to the pilgrimage at Les Saintes-Maries-de-la-Mer on the other side of the world. In the stories of the many Hindu *vedas*, Kâli could transform herself into numerous emanations of her personalities and powers. It should thus come as little surprise that over the centuries and the many miles of the Romani's travel, she may also have become Sainte Sarah.

The ceremony complete for another year and Sainte Sarah safe again in her grotto, the Romani are now ready to return to their accompanying celebrations. The men tune guitars while the women impatiently cajole them to start the music. In the center *place*, in front of the *mairie*, and in the campsites, I now hear the strum of guitars, *palmas*, dancing feet, and that sad, strange flamenco singing.

Throughout Les Saintes-Maries-de-la-Mer, Gypsy caravans are parked everywhere in crazed disorder. It's an itinerant city—a rolling labyrinth and amusement park and souk and traveling junkyard all in one. License plates attest to the babel: France, Belgium, the Netherlands, Switzerland, Germany, England, Spain, Italy, and beyond. The caravans here are of all types: a few leftover ancient wooden *roulottes* intermixed with dilapidated Citroën *camionettes* stuffed with mattresses and quilts alongside the latest and greatest *campines* glowing like glorious oriental palaces. Most of the *roulottes* have forsaken their old spoked wooden wheels for the luxury of rubber tires and were long ago converted to allow an automobile to provide the horsepower. But it's the modern-day campers that astonish. The old *roulottes* were just boxes on wheels, measuring roughly seven feet wide by fourteen feet long and six feet high; here, a whole family would live. In comparison, the new *campines* are extravagance on wheels. They bear regal names—the Palasport Palace Five Star, Fendt Diamant, Tabbert Baronesse 710, Bürstner Ducato. And they're adorned with bump-out bay windows, satellite dishes, air conditioning, and huge awnings stretched over plastic outdoor dining tables and chairs. These are not mere mobile homes. They're mobile mansions.

Surrounding the caravans is all the detritus of the traveling life. Barking, sleeping, howling, growling dogs are tied out front. Those pet monkeys scurry across rooftops above. Playpens contain fantastically happy children. Youngsters zip through the maze on gas-powered miniature motorcycles and electric cars. Banks of up to six truck batteries are wired in line powering clothes-washing machines; other women wash the old-fashioned way, with elbow grease and washboards in plastic tubs. Clotheslines stretch everywhere, ready to garrote the unwary while extension cords underfoot are certain to ensnare you. And there's trash everywhere: ripening in the town's garbage pails, dumped along the beach, littering the once-picturesque pedestrian streets. And yet the caravans and campsites themselves are spotless.

Place des Gitans, the town's market square, is overflowing with a Romani market offering plastic housewares, cheap clothes, and brilliant-colored trinkets. Gypsies are making baskets, caning chairs, selling wares. Everywhere I walk, Romani women appear out of nowhere to pin a religious medallion on my shirtfront. As I realize all too quickly, if I accept, they then demand twenty euros or more for the medal. If I refuse and struggle to unpin it, their imprecations come quick and loud. I learn my lesson, and keep one eye always on the lookout.

In the heart of the markeplace, one Gypsy is caught red-handed stealing a pair of blue jeans from another Gypsy vendor. They're both on the ground in an instant, grappling in the dust. The thief's female accomplice runs away with the jeans while the vendor's wife screams above the market hubbub. Others jump into the fray, and the battle moves down the alleys: fists fly, hitting with sick, dull thuds; raw blood, shockingly red in the sun, splatters from a broken nose;

someone is pushed tumbling into the table of another stall, the wares catapulted into the sky like a juggler's spectacle. Now another Romani is down, rolling in the sand and being kicked with stomach-churning viciousness by three others in work boots. I run with the other shoppers to get out of the path of the mêlée. More Romani jump into the fight, swinging fists indiscriminately, kicking at anything, lashing out with insults. Finally, they drag away their beaten-up cousins—shirts in tatters, blood streaming down faces and chests, others' blood on their fists. They curse with bitter Romanès oaths. And they promise vengeance.

Another fight breaks out in the church *place*. But this one's not over a pair of stolen jeans; it's a lover's vendetta. A Gypsy flicks open his knife and tries to slice the woman who spurned him. There are more screams, running feet through the cobbled alleys, and the assailant's gone, his deed undone.

Manouche and Gitans love their knives, perhaps as much as their guitars. In the center of the market stands a knife vendor, the focal point for the Gypsy men. Let the women try on golden stiletto-heeled shoes or the polka-dotted flamenco gowns that fit like sheaths; the men crowd around these display cases erected on folding tables to *ooh* and *aah* over the blades glinting in the sun. The Romani vendor knows his audience. There's nothing here so prosaic as a Swiss Army jackknife: instead, there are superb artisanal Laguioles and Camarguaises, dastardly Corsican *vendettas*, Italian switchblade *automatiques*. There are lovely wood-handled Opinels in intricate styles for hunting, fileting fish, and truffling, these last fitted with a miniscule brush on the handle's heel to clean off the black gold. Many Midi Romani are master viticulturalists, hired to tend vines from Les Beaumes de Venise to Châteauneuf-du-Pape; for this work, they admire the numerous *greffoirs* on show—blunt-tipped, razor-edged folding knives for grafting plants. Other gaze with longing at the *serpettes*, all-round vineyard utility knives with blades shaped like crescent moons. And there are knives with handles engraved just for the Gypsies with images of *roulottes*, guitars, and of course, hedgehogs. In fact, one much-admired knife is even carved with the sobriquet *Niglo Special*. Sales are brisk, money changing hands for shining, sharpened steel.

I missed the knifeman's attack in the church *place*—with no regret—but I'm there by chance when he strikes again. It's just after dusk. A band called Gypsyland has set up amplifiers to play their rock'n'roll-tinged flamenco when shrieks from the milling audience cut through the music. In a moment, there's pure panic. The crowd stampedes from the eye of the fight, running hysterically—anywhere as long as it's *away*. Women scream, faces under the street lamps contorted in absolute terror. Men are soaked instantly in primal sweat. Children grasp parents, bawling with horror. In between the shadows, the knifeman too flees—but not before carving open the arm of his love. I had been watching the music from the back of the crowd. Now, as the *place* empties, I see the knifed woman's clan gather about her. They wrap her arm in a hastily torn-off shirt, then whisk her away in a black Mercedes.

It's no wonder that *gendarmes* and *Sécurité* agents and *Douanes* custom officials and narcotics enforcement and special police agents of myriad sorts are evident throughout the pilgrimage. They wear flak jackets, jump boots, pistols, night clubs, berets. Black, unmarked Peugeots move at a crawl through the campsites, the agents inside grim faced, their patrol ominous. And with all this activity, it's no coincidence that the Romani have a wealth of nicknames for the Law—*flics*, *Schmitts*, *bourres*, and more. But here they just greet them with ironic hoots of unimpressed snickers, *"Ooh la la!"*

And still more Romani caravans pour into town.

Through it all sifts the strains of music, the Romani's eternal soundtrack to life. Within moments after the last knife attack, the music is back. The sounds of fleeing feet are replaced by *palmas*, screaming by singing, and the world is right again. After a day of preaching, the church loudspeakers are finally, thankfully, mercifully, blissfully silent. In their stead, boomboxes the size of small refrigerators and as powerful as Porsches blast out rhumbas; men—always just the men—huddle on folding chairs between caravans strumming guitars with furious intensity.

The music has been going all day, but with the darkness, the music too transforms itself, taking on new life. The town also changes with twilight. Through the day, I walked the full streets, the beachfront, past the *corrida*, and through the Romani camps, and the energy was overwhelming. Now, it's almost frightening.

In the center of town on the walkways, flamenco players strum out their licentious sounds, everyone taking their turns dancing, young and old, women and men, stomping their heels and twisting their hands in accent. They're playing just for themselves; no one asks for a handout. Romani clap along with the intense, high-velocity *palmas* that mark the rhythm, the muted *sorda* accents, and the *contratiempo* that syncopates all—there's a whole liturgy of just clapping styles here! When the few *gadjé* like myself attempt to join in, we're quickly and resolutely humbled. Then a singer leans back his head and the sound is inconsolable, otherworldly. A Hungarian *orkestar* starts up. They're all dressed in black and armed with two clarinets, a guitar, bass, cymbalom, and some of the most battered brass horns imaginable. The band is named Urs Karpatha, and their music is straight from the Carpathian Mountains; they sound like a John Philip Sousa march played by Dracula. Each song starts out at a dirgelike pace before erupting into a devil-may-care jam. They speed up the melody, playing *accelerando*, faster and faster, until their arms are ready to fall off. Then an accordionist pulls open his bellows in a bar, and soon more people are dancing. A swing band jumps in, including some of the members of one of the flamenco scrums, unreeling a musette waltz at finger-twisting tempo. And all of this is concentrated within just four or five streets of each other. By midnight, the moon and stars are shining in the indigo Mediterranean sky above Les Saintes-Maries-de-la-Mer. The knife fights are forgotten, the bottles still have some juice in them. And the music goes on.

The cross-pollination of musics at Les Saintes-Maries-de-la-Mer continues today. I take a needed break to catch my breath from the craziness and drive up the road to the Greco-Roman-medieval city of Arles on the border between La Camargue and Provence. I make my way through the grand place de la Republique; past the outdoor cafés beneath the plane trees in place du Forum, the inspiration and model for Van Gogh's starlit *Café du Soir*; and skirt Les Arènes—one of the largest and best-preserved Roman coliseums in the world. I make straight for a small, dark bar on rue de la Cavalerie along the northern ramparts of the *ville*. Bar de la Salsa is one of those places your mother—as well as any well-traveled friends, the local Tourist Information Bureau, and all the world's guidebooks—warn you about. One could be melodramatic and say it's akin to the eighth entryway to Hades, but then again, it's just a simple Gypsy dive. Inside are four tables and accompanying chairs, a well-used bar—no *zinc* here, only plywood—three barstools, a handful of liquor bottles, a home coffeemaker, a couple of worn and torn bullfight posters, and an ancient pinball machine, Super Golf, the flipper buttons worn smooth with the supplication of play. Only two lights shine from the ceiling and try as the feeble bulbs might, they'll never penetrate the gloom of the corners. Pinned to the wall behind the bar is a handful of snapshots of grinning children gripping ukuleles. Those kids know what to do with those ukes; these are the Reyes children, for this is the bar of the Gipsy Kings.

Bar de la Salsa is nicknamed Chez Nenes after its owner, Nenes Reyes, one of the many brothers and cousins who make up the band and its fraternity within the Reyes–Baliardo clan. And sure enough, the bar's sole attempt at true interior decoration is a framed golden certificate for sales of the Gipsy Kings' *Best of* album alongside a well-traveled poster from their 2001 tour of Japan.

The story of the Gipsy Kings is a Romani rags-to-riches, Horatio Alger tale. Like many Gypsy legends, it begins in the distant past, long before the main protagonists were even born. Prior to the Gipsy Kings, the Reyes and Baliardo families fled from Spain's Catalonia and Generalissimo Franco's Gypsy-hating fascists to settle in Arles. José Reyes sang flamenco like few others before or after. He sang for Picasso and inspired him to paint. He sang for Chaplin and made him laugh. He sang for Salvador Dalì and made his moustache twitch. He sang for Bardot and made her dance. At his side was guitarist Ricardo Baliardo. Born in a *roulotte* in Séte in 1921, Baliardo played the guitar with such rich emotion he was soon christened Manitas de Plata—the Man with the Silver Hands. (Flamenco is nothing if not dramatic.) They performed for the pilgrims at Les Saintes-Maries-de-la-Mer and for Gypsy weddings in their native Arles' La Roquette district in the south of the city. Here, a *gadjo* neighbor named Lucien Clergue heard them and was pulled into the world of their music. In the 1950s, Clergue's mother ran a grocery in La Roquette, and he grew up alongside the Reyes and Baliardo clans. Clergue became their friend and soon, a sort of manager, shepherding José and Manitas de Plata to record a first LP. Then came more albums, tours, and as their fame grew, concerts at Paris's Olympia, London's Royal Albert Hall, New York's Carnegie Hall, the White House, television shows, and to top it all, a gala on December 17, 1965, at the United Nations celebrating the International Declaration of the Rights of Man. They were the first Romani recognized at the UN.

But that's only the prelude to the story. A new generation of Reyes and Baliardo cousins were starting to play, first on those tiny ukuleles, then on true guitars. José's four sons—Canut, Nicolas, Pablo, and Patchai Reyes—were joined by three Baliardo boys—Diego, Paco, and Tonino. Here in Arles—a city crazed for bullfights and flamenco—they all played Spanish guitar. But like Django before them, they also heard other, new musics, and blended them into the old. Busking on the streets of Arles as well as playing Romani gatherings, they melded the cool Gypsy jazz of northern France with the Mediterranean heat of flamenco and Latin rhythms, driving the music with more bounce and even more emotion. Clergue remembered how the crossroads of Romani music inspired the fledgling band: "In Stes-Maries they would meet cousins from Paris, uncles from Catalonia, Django Reinhardt's brother, Gypsies from Hungary with their performing monkeys and those wonderful Gypsies from Lyon who could play the waltz like nobody else!" They called their music rhumba gitana, and at first it was just one of the Romani secrets of Provence. Soon they were in a *gadjo* recording studio cutting their 1988 album *The Gipsy Kings*. Included was a tune called "Bamboleo" sung in a Gitan dialect blending Catalan, French, and Romanès. The song was an international hit of such magnitude that most anyone anywhere around the globe could sing the refrain or hum the melody, their bodies too starting to shimmy to the beat.

They're jamming on "Bamboleo" now at Bar de la Salsa. It's the middle of the night, and Nenes and his fellow Romani are still happy with the religious spirit of the pilgrimage—and fired as well by liquid spirits. In fact, with a *corrida* and

France's victory in the World Cup semifinal both that evening, spirits couldn't get much higher. Forget gold records, world tours, international superstardom; Bar de la Salsa is the true realm of the Gipsy Kings. The guitarist is drunkenly strumming a four-stringed six-string guitar at a ferocious pace, yet even with this gap-toothed instrument, he still makes it sing. Two Romani—Gigi and Marco—are teaching me a dice game that makes no sense to this *gadjo* no matter how many times they explain the rules. Maybe I haven't had enough *pastis* to comprehend it all. The only thing I do understand is that I'm successful in continually losing whether I roll snake eyes or double sixes. Meanwhile, bartender Frederica can't pour the bourbon fast enough to keep up with the guitarist's rhythm. As the town shuts down for the night, those still standing here at Bar de la Salsa are singing the refrain of "Bamboleo" off-key and off-kilter. They play as if it's a joke—or yet another classic Gypsy scam—on the *gadjé* world that this Romani song from a down-and-dirty neighborhood in Arles became such a hit.

From this distance of some eight decades, it's difficult to ascertain what music Django was hearing in Les Saintes-Maries-de-la-Mer. There were likely flamenco guitarists, traditional Tziganes bands, and perhaps Parisian Romani stars such as Gusti Malha, Poulette Castro, and Django's own seven uncles. From this pilgrimage-turned-schoolroom, Django may have learned songs for his repertoire and details of technique, some of which he retained, others which he revised to fit his own playing. His method of holding his hand clear of the guitar's body, rather than resting it on the bridge or soundboard and thus damping the voice, is akin to a *flamenco*'s hand posture. He chose to use a pick rather than pluck with varnished fingernails *à la* flamenco. A plectrum was essential to playing one of the novel steel-string guitars on which Django strummed out his jazz, which was in turn essential to be heard over the roar of the horns. And the quick whips of the wrist used in accenting *la pompe* served to mimic the *flamenco*'s stylish *rasqueado*—the rapid unfurling of the fingers that creates the accented beats. Years later during a recording session for the English label His Master's Voice in 1937, Django was forced on the spot to cut an instant solo piece to be titled "Improvisation." It's little wonder he stepped from jazz back into the mysticism of some of the first music he ever heard or played—the flamenco sounds of the Midi that he likely crossed paths with during his childhood travels to Les Saintes-Maries-de-la-Mer.

While the pilgrimage serves as a crossroads for Romani music, it also showcases the differences between flamenco, Balkan Tziganes music, and Gypsy jazz.

You can hear them all here on the streets on a gorgeous night in May. Still, however one defines Gypsy music—whether it be styles of performance, specific scales or arpeggios, or other more esoteric values—I discern two universals in the Romani music at Les Saintes-Maries-de-la-Mer: emotion and virtuosity. Ever since Django recorded his jazz, fans and critics and musicologists have searched for the grains that make his music "Gypsy." And it's here that that essence glows like the embers within a campfire: Certainly Django's jazz recordings are virtuosic, and they are above all alive with emotion.

Django sought to pay homage to Les Saintes-Maries-de-la-Mer in his later years. As early as 1936, he talked of wishing to compose a religious work for his fellow Romani to be performed during the pilgrimage. In 1944, during some of the worst days of the Nazi Occupation, he turned from jazz to begin work on a Gypsy mass. The pilgrimage continued as normal in 1941 and 1942, but was suppressed by the French Vichy government in 1943 and 1944. This may have played a part in Django's determination to focus on his projected *Messe des Saintes-Maries-de-la-Mer*. He sought to replace the *gadjé*'s music at the Romani mass, and at the same time illustrate the history and faith behind the pilgrimage. As Django described his inspiration to a newspaper reporter in 1943, "My people are savagely independent, private, and proud of our traditions, so we need a mass of our own, written in our language by one of our own. I hope that my mass will be adopted by my people throughout the world and that it will be consecrated at our annual gathering at Saintes-Maries-de-la-Mer."

Django had a fresh new clarinet player at the time in his Nouveau Quintette, a young man named Gérard Lévêque. Not only was Lévêque handy with a reed instrument, but he also had a fine ear, a reasonable understanding of music, and all the patience of the saints. Django enlisted him as his personal music transcriber. As Lévêque remembered, Django would lie down in his hotel room bed with his guitar across his chest, smoking cigarettes forever through the night, and compose out loud, playing or whistling the harmonies and melodies for the organ while Lévêque struggled to notate the score. In composing a mass, Django was limited by his musical illiteracy, as he explained to the newsman: "It's true that I cannot distinguish an F from a C on a page of music. However, we Gypsies, we have an instinct for harmonies, which we compose as improvisations on our instruments. To put together my mass, it's essential to have a good musician who is able to pluck my notes out of the air and transcribe them onto paper. In my Quintette, I have Gérard Lévêque who can do this task." Composing for organ must also have taxed Django, as there's no record or anecdote of him ever playing piano, let alone organ. Still, the composition took shape. Yet despite long nights picking out the theme on his guitar for Lévêque and studying the structure of masses, Django grew discouraged. After almost eighteen months of work, he abandoned the project—at least for the time being. But even years later, he hoped to revive his most ambitious work.

After Django's death, Nin-Nin too talked of wanting to complete the mass. If he ever worked further on it is not known; no traces of any of Joseph's possible composition survive, except perhaps in his guitar counterpoint to a spoken "Prière à Sara"—"Prayer to Sara"—recited by *chanteur* Jacques Vérières and released decades later on an obscure 45rpm to be sold to the Romani faithful.

With only eight bars of the mass completed, Django was requested to record it at the Parisian church Saint-Louis-d'Antin. A radio van arrived on the appointed day, but no one else. Léo Chauliac, the pianist in Django's big band who was to play the organ, had also gone missing. Django was in bed with a compress on his head to ward off the effects of too wild a night—and he intended to stay there. Not pleased with the mass, he told Lévêque, who had come to find him, "*Je m'en fous!*—I don't give a damn!"

A second recording session was arranged later in 1944 on the grand pipe organ in the chapel of L'Institution Nationale des Jeunes Aveugles, a Parisian school for the blind. Django was dragged out of his beloved bed and brought along to this session. Chauliac also deigned to show up, and finally the recording was made, although not released at the time and evenutally misplaced.

Listening today to that long-lost 1944 recording of Django's *Messe des Saintes-Maries-de-la-Mer*, I am struck by how different this work sounds from any of his other compositions. But then, as a religious mass played on organ, that's little surprise. The surviving recording is 7:33 minutes long; Chauliac had been asked to develop some of the themes Django only began to outline. The mass fragment is full of drama, swelling from soft contemplation to thunderous crescendos before descending again into a simple, prayerlike mood. Yet as with the rest of Django's compositions, the emotion is pure and profound.

That Django was never able to finish his most ambitious work to have it played for his people in Notre-Dame-de-la-Mer is of course unfortunate. And yet on the other hand, the humble little fortified church has no organ. Django's jazz instead become part of the music to illustrate the pilgrimage. It's alive here in those hymns written to "Nuages" and several of his other melodies, or simply in the Gypsy jazz they're still jamming on around the caravan campfires. To his fellow Romani, Django's music has truly become sacred.

After a week of music, devotion, weddings, baptisms, scams, robberies, fistfights, knife fights, arrests, drinking, dancing, and yet more music, the Romani pilgrimage is over. Piloted by weary-eyed Gypsies, the caravans are now leaving Les Saintes-Maries-de-la-Mer, heading to the four points of the compass at a slow, dirgelike pace compared to their race to arrive. And they're leaving the town reeling in their wake, trash-strewn and ragged—as well as mercifully quiet and calm. Seagulls descend to pick the abandoned campsites clean. Sainte Sarah is back in her crypt, cleansed and clothed in her new robes. And the guitars and accordions, violins and cymbaloms are packed away in the *roulottes* and *campines*.

Until next year.

NINE

Dynasty
Les Frères *Ferret and Their Musical Clan*

I DON'T NEED THE WISDOM OR WILES of a Romani fortune-teller to read something of the life of Jean-Jacques "Boulou" Ferré in his hands. His fingers alone tell a tale. They are short in length and wide in girth—not necessarily auspicious fingers. And yet, amazingly, each digit on his left hand is wider at the tip than at the base. I can't imagine these fingers moving with grace over the narrow neck of a Selmer guitar, nor even fretting a certain string with precision. Still, the physical appearance of Boulou's fingers belies the magic of which they are capable. These broad fingertips are all calluses, and they are unlike any I have ever seen. The calluses are blunt and thick, as leathery and hard as a drumhead. They are a testament to the life of a Romani musician, inspired to play guitar since he was just seven years old.

Yet it's not just Boulou's fingers that play his music; it's also those of his younger brother, Élié "Élios" Ferré. These two siblings form a fine duet. In physical appearance and character, they are as different as any two brothers could be. Boulou is short and round; Élios tall and slender, *trés* Parisian in his elegant dress and manners. Boulou seems to think and talk in abstractions of music, ethereal improvisations that he struggles to put into words; Élios is warm, effusive, and down to earth, yet as capable of startling musical journeys as his brother. Listening to them accompany each other in a near-forgotten Russian cabaret neighboring the Gare Saint-Lazare that's seen its golden years come and long since depart, the two brothers are almost like Siamese twins. They trade solos and accompaniments, somehow intuiting exactly where the other is going, almost as if each knows what the other will play before he even plays it. Or perhaps they're more akin to some fierce emanation of an Indian god of music—one body with four arms and twenty fingers playing two guitars.

Maybe I should not be surprised by their musical accord: They were both taught guitar by the same teacher, their father, Jean "Matelo" Ferret. And they are part of an incredible family musical dynasty.

With the discovery of Matelo Ferret, my search takes a turn. It's all part of the lineage of Django's Gypsy jazz. But when I first hear the guitars of the Ferret family, I'm awakened to music as original, as compelling, as that of Django.

There were three original Ferret brothers—Pierre "Baro," Étienne "Sarane," and Jean "Matelo." And they all played with Django, first as bandmates and later as his accompanists, before striking out on their own. Through the years during and after Django's death, they created musette, swing, bebop, and traditional Tziganes music that astounds. Their music is at some times dissonant; at others, harmonious. But throughout, it bears an intense sense of modernity and adventure.

During a number of meetings over several years, Boulou and Élios tell me the story of their family's musical dynasty. Like a Romani campfire tale, the history begins and ends, is picked up and dropped as a new anecdote is remembered, the thread continuing on at a meeting a year or so later. Of all possible times and places, it's in the midst of a winter blizzard in Saint Paul, Minnesota, that they share with me the first installments in their family saga. I'm sure they had no idea what they were getting themselves into when they arrived as part of a short tour of the United States in 1998: A blizzard struck just after they landed, shutting down the city, and leaving only brave souls to venture forth. Still, the Ferré brothers don't come to Minnesota every day, and their show at a local jazz club filled every chair in the room. They were meanwhile struggling to get their rented amplifiers to function, explaining their problems in French to the American bar manager. I was able to help, and they invited me for a drink later on. That first conversation continued at other rendezvous in bars, bistros, and cafés, from La Mouffe to Saint-Germain-des-Prés, just around the corner from a club Matelo played long ago. Their stories of a legacy of French Romani musicians included musical ancestors known to them only by legend; their famous uncles Baro and Sarane Ferret; other musical uncles such as Charles-Allain "Challain" and Jean "Memette" Ferret; cousins like Maurice "Gros Chien" and Eddie "Bamboula" Ferret. And on to future generations.

"My grandfather was a horse-trader," Élios begins, laughing out loud at this bit of stereotypical Romani lore.

Horse-trading was a common métier of Gypsies throughout Europe. Horses were of great importance to the Romani as they pulled their caravans and were perhaps the most valuable items a family possessed. The French Romani had a saying that defined the horse's value: *Un Tzigane sans cheval n'est pas un Tzigane*— A Gypsy without a horse is not a Gypsy. Horses were also a commodity that could be traded with local *gadjé* to make money or simply as a last resort when times were tight. The Gypsy horse-traders were known among the French townsfolk as *maquignons*—literally, horse fakers, from the verb *maquiller*, meaning "to make up a face" or "to fake a picture;" thus, the Gypsy horse-traders were said "to make up" or "fake" horses for sale. And indeed, sometimes their work seemed near magical. Farmers examined horses for the Romani's timeless trademark tricks— shoe polish hiding grizzled gray hair, a diet of water to fill out ribcage staves, lameness miraculously cured for a spell with a turpentine anesthetic, tired old nags brought back to life with a spike of ginger stuffed up under their tails or by a surreptitious poke from the prickles of a hedgehog pelt. It was all an ages-old exchange between the Gypsies and townspeople of Europe. And the tradition continues today, the horse-trader's job replaced by Romani who buy, refurbish, and then resell used cars.

"My grandfather was a horse-trader," Élios tells me again, "but *everyone* else in our family was a musician."

In recounting their family's history of music, Boulou and Élios do not begin with the first time their father met Django, as most Romani might. Rather, their story leads back to an even older generation of ancestral musicians. Considering the dynasty's history and the music it has created, this seems only right.

The Ferret clan is Gitan. Their roots reach to Spanish Catalonia, and before that, Odessa in Russia. And before that, no one remembers. At some point in the late 1800s, the family quit Spain and ventured east and north, perhaps seeking work, perhaps chased away by the Catalans—that story is lost; no one can recall it now. The Ferrets arrived one day in the northern French city of Rouen, and here they settled down, eventually staying for several generations. At some point too, they moved out of the caravan that had carried them, left behind now for the comforts of an apartment. They were becoming modern Gypsies, abandoning their lives as *voyageurs* to become *sédentaires*, a distinction Romani often make among themselves.

In Rouen, their grandfather, Hippolyte "Gusti" Ferret—the spellings of the family names are transliterations as none of this history has been written down before—began his horse-trading. But if he himself was not a musician, he still of course loved music, as Élios reassures me. Gusti's wife, Douderou, was a great fan of light opera, and together they raised two daughters, Nina and Nine, both fine singers. And then there were the family uncles—Baro, Pebbo, and Fillou Ferret—all well traveled and well versed in many forms of Romani music, from flamenco to the Tziganes melodies of Russia and the Balkans. In Rouen, these uncles were stars of the weekend night, banjoists who played their music alongside the accordionists in the *bals musette*. This musical tradition was soon to pass on to Gusti and Douderou's three sons.

Upon his birth in 1908, they christened their firstborn Jean-Joseph Ferret. But as with Django, it was not this legal Christian name, foisted on the Gypsies by French law, that spoke with any eloquence of his character. His true name, his Romani nickname, was Baro, attesting to his important family status as eldest son. "Baro" meant "Big One," or even "King," in Romanès. He was given his nickname in honor of his musical uncle, now known as Baro *l'ancien*.

Next came Étienne, in 1912. His nickname of "Sarane" paid homage as well to an ancestor, also a renowned musician.

Youngest of the three was Pierre, born on December 1, 1918. But Pierre did not retain his Christian name for long. Using the privilege granted to the eldest Romani sibling, Baro decided he did not like his own given name, and so appropriated his youngest brother's name. Baro then re-christened him with his cast-off name of Jean. As the Ferret brothers' long-time accompanist, Francis-Alfred Moerman, explains this confusion, "Gypsies change their names like they change their shirts." Still, this youngest Ferret brother would be best known by his Gypsy nickname of "Matelo," in honor of his godfather who was a sailor—*un matelot*—in the French navy.

Under the tutelage of their uncles, the three Ferret brothers all learned instruments at a young age. Following his brothers, Matelo first learned violin, then banjo, tutored by his uncle Fillou. Goaded into abandoning the banjo by his guitar-playing uncle Pebbo, who detested the percussive and noisy banjo, Matelo learned guitar as well as banduria. The three brothers busked for spare change on the street corners of Rouen, playing in the dance halls at their uncles' sides during the nights. Matelo made his debut as a professional musician in the Rouen *bal* Salle Barette in 1930. Like Django, he was also twelve years old.

In 1931, Baro and Sarane left for Paris to find better-paying jobs as musicians in the capital. Matelo was devastated, left behind without his cherished elder brothers. In secret, he now made his own plans. Just thirteen, he ran away from home to join his brothers in Montmartre.

And, perhaps ironically, it was Matelo who first discovered Django. The three Ferret brothers were encamped in a cheap hotel at 83 rue Damrémont on the northwestern, "back" side of la Butte de Montmartre, that part of the *quartier* tourists never visit. Matelo was climbing the hotel stairway one day when he heard a bewitching guitar melody. He followed the trail of the music like a child after a Pied Piper. It led down a hallway, to a closed door. Here, he stooped to listen through the keyhole, eavesdropping like a spy. And then the door opened on him, and he fell at the feet of Naguine Reinhardt. Matelo stammered his apologies, but rather than chastise the young waif, Naguine invited him in. She introduced Django, who was smoking one of his eternal cigarettes and picking his guitar while sprawled across the bed—one of his favored spots for composing new melodies. Matelo explained that he and his brothers were living in the hotel as well, and they were also guitarists. Yet hearing Django's fretwork, Matelo now vowed with all the solemn vigor of youth to throw his own guitar away. Django waved that threat aside and invited him instead to retrieve his instrument. The two began playing together, Django teaching him the tune "Sugar." It was the first jazz song Matelo learned.

It was also the beginning of a beautiful friendship.

At the start, the spotlight shone on Baro, not Django. The first musette or jazz recording from Paris to showcase the virtuosity of a Romani guitarman began with a stellar solo introduction played by Baro.

I wanted to uncover more of Baro's intriguing music and began the nearly impossible task of tracing the history of this mysterious musician. At times, I nearly gave up. In the end, however, the difficulty of the journey only made finding answers all the more rewarding.

Tracking the history of Baro Ferret is like venturing down a dark alley at midnight. His story is shadowy, remembered even by his family only in bits and pieces. Facts and dates are rarities—tough to come by, tougher to verify. Even anecdotes are sketchy, often uncorroborated by others. When I query, there's no agreement on the seemingly simply question of if he ever married or if he had children. No one remembers visiting him at home, or oddly, even exactly where he lived. Baro kept his life largely a secret. And for good reason, as I discover.

From photographs, he was a handsome man—dangerously handsome. I'm looking at a series of images taken over the years, from the 1930s through the 1950s. Hair slicked straight back from his brow in the dapper style of the day, he had the striking profile of a matinee idol. His eyes are dark, unreadable and unknowable. His smile in some pictures looks friendly and sincere. In others, it bears an ironic twist to it at the corners of his mouth, honed like a knife blade. Many who knew him firsthand describe him as a mystery; when asked to explain, they are often unable to even elaborate on their impressions. Baro was noted and notorious. Boulou and Élios speak of him with grave respect. Others, while praising his guitar playing, curse the man.

Upon their arrival in Paris, Baro and his brothers quickly found work at the sides of the accordionists presiding over the city's *bals*. Italian Zingaro accordionist Vétese Guérino, always appreciative of the guitar accompaniment of fellow Gypsies, hired Baro and Sarane in 1931 or 1932 to take over the sideman role left vacant by Django. Together, they played stints in the Cannes and Paris branches of La Boîte à Matelots. They dressed in sailor suits and strummed out their rhythms on a stage fashioned from a sailboat as befitting the nightclub's theme of a sailors' dive—but one reserved only for the slumming rich. The Ferrets traded off guitar duties alongside Guérino, sharing the role with Gusti Malha, Nin-Nin, *gadjo* guitarist Lucien "Lulu" Gallopain, and Django, who was two years junior to Baro.

Guérino led his group into a studio on March 19, 1933. The band recorded at least four sides released on the Odéon label as Guérino et son Orchestre Musette de la Boîte à Matelots. Backing Guérino's accordion were Baro, Django, and Gallopain on guitars, violinist Pierre Pagliano, and bassist "Tarteboulle." The recordings featured several guitar solos that were later attributed to Django by overzealous fans eager to discover lost recordings. But as Baro was the steady soloist for the band and Django was just joining them for the session, it's almost certain that it was Baro's guitar front and center.

I'm stunned by this guitarwork. It explodes off the recording of Guérino's tour de force *valse* "Brise napolitaine"—"Neapolitan Breeze"—in a daredevil blaze of flamenco-tinged arpeggios culminating in a climbing run of diminished triad fragments. I've never heard anything like it on musette or even jazz recordings up to that time from either side of the Atlantic. Even as a youth, Baro picked the strings with an aggressive confidence that his later accompanist, Francis-Alfred Moerman, would still remark on decades later, shaking his head in astonishment: "He played *so* hard. I've never seen anyone play the guitar so hard. He attacked it—which he had learned to do so he could be heard when playing in the *bals musette* behind the *accordéonistes*." This first recorded example of Baro's fretwork captures on acetate a young guitarist with a mature and sure style. It also painted in my mind an image of an intense and powerful man.

After Matelo met Django in the Montmartre hotel, Baro and Django became best of friends. It may even have been Baro who introduced Django to Poulette Castro, as Baro's nephew René Mailhes tells the family legend; Baro's father was an acquaintance of the Castro brothers, and Baro too learned technique from Poulette and often accompanied him. Another version of the story states that Poulette pointed out Django's guitar playing—with his picking hand held loose and free above the soundboard—as the modern style for Baro to emulate. Either way, as two of the most gifted young guitarists on the Paris scene, it was perhaps only a matter of time before these two best friends also became each other's greatest rival.

Yet by the time of the "Brise napolitaine" session, Django had devoted himself to jazz. Baro meanwhile was instead finding steady—and likely, better-paying—gigs as a musette accompanist. As Django's accordionist mentor,

Maurice Alexander, had warned him long ago, jazz was a new and unproven scene; musette was a sure thing. But Django was soon discovered by the fledgling Hot Club and his jazz svengalis, Pierre Nourry and Charles Delaunay. Baro lacked such patronage. And perhaps his character would never have stood for it anyway.

Baro did, however, agree to play rhythm in Django's Quintette du Hot Club de France, although being relegated to a sideman's role must have galled him at times. The Quintette was often a game of musical chairs disguised as a jazz band. In the beginning, no one took its prospects seriously. It was a side project, a loose, after-hours jam session they did for fun, and all of the members played in other, established ensembles to pay their keep. When a Quintette gig or recording session was scheduled, they were often already booked elsewhere, and so Django or Stéphane had to grab whichever friends they could find to fill those musical chairs. If Roger Chaput or Nin-Nin was playing elsewhere that night, Gusti or Baro was enticed to sit in. Baro became a regular Quintette member sometime in 1935; he first appeared at a Quintette recording session in July 1935, taking over Chaput's chair. Eventually playing in dozens of Hot Club concerts and on numerous recorded sides, he would continue on and off with Django's Nouveau Quintette and big-band group, Django's Music, up until 1940. And Baro's addition to the Quintette changed the ensemble's sound. With his guitar, the band boasted a hard-driving, more propulsive rhythm, especially when Baro was teamed with Corsican guitarist Marcel Bianchi, as on the famous four recording sessions for the British HMV label in April 1937. Baro's sharp-edged, almost violent rhythm playing set a style, bringing a personification of the man to the music.

Yet despite the numerous concerts and sides he played and recorded with the Quintette, Baro never seemed truly comfortable as a jazzman. Instead, he would remain true to musette, the music he first learned at the side of his elder uncles and began playing as a youth in the Rouen *bals*. Over the years, Baro proved himself the most stylish, even sensitive of all musette guitarists. And he was also without doubt the most innovative, as he would soon show.

The timeless beauty of Baro's musette was best captured by a quick recording session in Paris on March 2, 1939. This session was a bit of an oddity, as solo banjo and guitar recordings of musette were rarely made; Gusti cut a handful of sides, Chaput recorded a couple as well. Beyond these, few exist. And yet these four sides by Baro released on the Columbia label were masterpieces of *valse manouche*.

Listed as Le Trio Ferret, the session featured Baro as leader accompanied by bassist Maurice Speilleux and the guitars of Matelo and cousin Challain. The trio waxed four waltzes. Gusti's "La valse des niglos" was a gloriously beautiful melody and an archetype of the *valse manouche* with its minor-key tonality and roller-coaster runs. No recording of the song by Gusti has been found, and this version by Baro helped save the song from being lost. The quaintly sentimental "Ti-Pi-Tin" was on its face an odd selection. An American Tin Pan Alley tune by Mexican songsmith María Mendez Grever with Raymond Leveen, it was a number-one hit for Horace Heidt and His Musical Knights in the United States. The jingle also became a Parisian dance hall favorite, recorded by accordion stars such as Jean Vaissade, and now recreated with a Romani flourish by Baro. "Gin Gin" was a musette waltz credited to Django; it would later be known as "Chez Jacquet." And finally, "La minch valse" was retitled here as "Ma Théo," a wordplay on the name of the waltz's original composer, legendary Gitan guitarist Mattéo Garcia. According to legend, Garcia's son bequeathed the melody to Baro, requesting he add to it, and Baro likely created the final C section, among possible other additions.

The recordings of Le Trio Ferret proved Baro had paid his dues in the dance halls; no other guitarist ever played a musette waltz with such command. Matelo and Challain's manner of accompaniment was enchanting in its ambience, creating a timeless mood with a sound like a choir of angelic zithers. Since most musette *orchestres* did not include a bassist, the banjoist or guitarist was responsible for the bass lines and for providing harmonizing movement to the song. Thus, Matelo and Challain rarely sat on one chord voicing for more than one measure; instead, they played vagabond chord inversions that were constantly on the move, creating walking bass lines, descending or ascending beneath the melody. And their rhythm counterpoints often ended a phrase with an accented flourish straight from a Romani campfire jam session. These counter-harmonies and filigrees accented the melodies, seamlessly tying these *valses* together into small jewels of song. And above all, Baro's lead playing was pure confidence and mastery: His delicate lines of damascene arpeggios mirrored the playing of an accordion, whereas his strong vibrato called forth ages of Gypsy violinists.

Yet, even when they were recorded in 1939, Le Trio Ferret's *valses* were timepieces. Baro was on to something new.

Sometime in early 1938, Baro first heard the playing of a young Belgian accordionist relatively new to the Parisian scene. Gus Viseur amused himself by toying with the sacred musette songs of the elder generation: Sometimes, he swung the notes of the melody; other times he simply improvised over the timeworn theme, playing his own novel lines and wide-ranging harmonies. Viseur's audacity caught Baro's attention, and when Viseur launched his own band, Baro was at his side.

Joseph Gustave "Tatave" Viseur was born on May 15, 1915, in Lassines in Belgium's Walloon region. His father was a bargeman who plied the rivers and canals of Flanders and France, the family making its home on the water, traveling like Gypsies where the work and the waves took them. One day in 1920, Viseur *père* docked his barge for good on the River Seine near Paris's picturesque Pont de Puteaux in the shadow of the Bois de Bologne and Porte Maillot.

Just as guitar playing ran in the blood of the Ferrets, accordions were the heart of the Viseurs. Under his father's tutelage, eight-year-old Gus took up the squeezebox and learned the rudiments of music. After the family settled on the quays of Paris, Viseur *père* enrolled his son in lessons given by a music professor in the village-cum-suburb of Suresnes. By 1929 when he was fourteen, Viseur was playing in his father's amateur band, Jojo-Jass. After his father's death, young Viseur made a living roaming the café *terrasses* of Puteaux, Montreuil, Ivry, and Ménilmontant armed with his accordion.

The tall accordionist with the schoolboy face soon established himself. Star accordionist and bandleader Médard Ferrero hired Viseur to play second accordion in his ensemble Les Clochards—The Bums—throughout the early 1930s. Viseur also accompanied accordionist Louis Ferrari in the Pigalle *bals*.

While he was playing musette, Viseur's ear had been captured by the new jazz. In 1933, he met another accordionist, René "Charley" Bazin, who was crazy for this "Jazz-hot." Together, the duo tried their hands at improvising, a skill frowned upon by musette accordionists but one that rewarded Viseur when he met Django and Nin-Nin in 1934 and they jammed together. Soon, Bazin and Viseur were sharing a cheap room in Paris, one sleeping on the bed, the other on the couch.

This newfound love affair with jazz inspired Viseur to break loose from Ferrero's Clochards and front his own band when he was just twenty years old in 1935. Alongside the favored musette waltzes, Viseur's ensemble played javas, foxtrots, even a handful of four-four-time swing numbers. Viseur first recorded with his own ensemble that same year, waxing a cover of "Dinah" and three other tunes released on the all-but-forgotten Pagode label.

Viseur's swinging style of playing and his modern repertoire were not all that made him stand out. Viseur's accordion was also special. Like many of the musette musicians, he played an accordion made with three reeds per note. But unlike others, Viseur did not use the classic "wet" or *vibration* musette tuning with one reed tuned precisely to the note and supplemented by the other two reeds tuned slightly above and below it. This gave old-time players like Émile Vacher the trademark plaintive, quavering sound with a torch-singer's throaty tremolo surrounding every note. To Viseur's ear, that classic musette sound was passé. He loved to play dashing lines of single-note improvisations or organlike chord punctuations, either in chord-melody solos or as accents at the ends of lines; when he played in musette tuning, his style was overwhelmed by tremolo. Viseur had the reeds in his Fratelli Crosio accordion filed down and retuned "dry," without the augmented reeds. Now, when his fingers danced over the buttons, his sound was forceful and striking and modern. In a word, Viseur's playing sounded jazzy.

Baro likely was the one to introduce Viseur to Charles Delaunay, in 1938. Delaunay was then well on his way to becoming beatified as one of the popes of jazz, as French fans would later characterize—and criticize—him. To get ahead in the Parisian jazz world, Delaunay was the man to know. And yet Baro probably realized that promoting an accordionist to the jazzman would be a hard sell. To jazz fans, accordions symbolized all that was old and stale in French music: Musette was purely a snake-charm to the working class. As Delaunay swore aloud even years later in his 1985 memoir, *Delaunay's Dilemma*, "There was nothing more execrable to me than an accordion."

Viseur ventured to the Hot Club offices to play a surprise audition for Delaunay in the summer of 1938. And surprisingly, the man who detested accordions was awed by Viseur's sound. As Delaunay gushed in *Jazz Hot*, "I have no hesitation in saying that we have in Viseur a musical phenomenon on the order of Django Reinhardt." He also applauded Baro as a "revelation . . . whose guitar solos are so reminiscent of Django Reinhardt." By that time, there was no higher praise.

As before with Django, Delaunay wasted no time promoting his new find. In autumn 1938, he organized a concert highlighting the swinging musette of Viseur and Baro's new quintet. The band was a success and would go on to share the stage at numerous shows and festivals with Django's ensemble. On October 20, 1938, Delaunay recorded Viseur and Baro backed by Matelo and Challain playing a sweetly swinging version of Django's "Daphné" as well as Viseur's composition "Automne." In these early recordings, Baro proved that his solo guitarwork was an ideal foil for Viseur's accordion. Where Viseur played sweeping chords and dynamic scales that breathed with his bellows' enthusiasm, Baro's notes were quick and incisive, stabbing like a stiletto.

From 1938 through the early years of World War II, Viseur and Baro were prolific, waxing waltzes and swing numbers with one foot firmly in the old world of the *bals*, the other foot keeping time to the new world of swing. Their jazzy brand of musette was much more relaxed than the old musette—lighter and cooler, with a fun, jaunty air. At other sessions, Viseur was accompanied by Nin-Nin, Argentine virtuoso Oscar Alemán, or Romani guitarists Eugène Vées and Joseph Sollero. Upon his arrival in Paris and before he took up the button-box, the five-year-old Viseur had learned to play guitar from a newfound Gypsy friend. Now, like Guérino before him, Viseur always appreciated a good guitarist.

At the same time, Viseur and his accordion were called upon to back Edith Piaf, Jean Gabin, and other singers of traditional *chanson*. He added his touch to the landmark 1940 recording of *la môme* Piaf's "L'accordéoniste," marking him in the heart of all of France as being *the* accordionist.

Yet Baro and Viseur still had a grand statement to make. Delaunay organized another session for them on August 9, 1940, resulting in two epochal recordings. They cut Viseur's signature minor-key waltz "Flambée montalbanaise"— "Montauban Burning," a commentary on the devastation World War II inflicted on the southwestern French *ville*. The melody quickly became one of the most famous and timeless of accordion songs, Viseur unreeling cascades of arpeggios with rhapsodic elegance.

Viseur and Baro also recorded a waltz destined to become another famous Parisian tune. Called simply "Swing valse," the title itself served as a declaration of independence. Co-written by Baro and Viseur, the melody featured elements of classic musette but with a certain joyful swing to its audacious air. With Challain's driving rhythm, Viseur's playing is alive, his fingers dancing to the melody, while Baro's solo was dazzling. "Swing valse" was a symbol of change.

This happy melody now inspired a war. With the arrival of swing musette, a duel was waged on the dance hall floors between the old guard of musette and the new jazz-inspired musicians. To many, jazz was sacrilege, flashy and all too American, and an uneasy peace held only so long as the accordionists and guitarists did not swing their music. To others, it breathed life into the stilted strains of musette. The *bals* became battlegrounds. In dance halls from rue de Lappe to La Montagne Sainte-Geneviève and the down-and-dirty *dancings* in La Zone, the owners now posted warnings: *Interdit de danser le swing*. It was a sign of the times. As accordionist Georges "Jo" Privat recalled, "There were 'No Swing Dancing' signs in musette dance halls. Swing was a subject that provoked brawls. This risked aggravating *les mecs* who liked to hold their girls tight."

Symbolic of the era, a French liquor manufacturer launched at the dawn of the 1940s a new aperitif, aptly named "Swing" in tune with the times. To promote the drink, the company organized feuds pitting swing against musette in Parisian ballrooms. Defending the old musette colors were accordionists Privat, Émile Prud'homme, and Émile Carrara; on the swing front stood Viseur, Bazin, and another newcomer, Antonio "Tony" Muréna. Yet there was not really any competition to these contests. Privat remembered, "The musette and the swing *équipes* played in two sets. The public applauded, the sound-level machines judged." Swing always won during this golden age of swing. "This made *l'apéro* Swing sell well. They never created an aperitif called Musette. *C'est drôle.*"

And yet while these *bals musette* battles were being waged, Baro again was moving on. He seems to have rarely stood still in one place, always seeking something novel, something fresh. And then moving on again. From musette to jazz hot, swing to swing musette. And now he was hearing a different sound, a music that as yet had no name.

I heard rumors of these recordings by Baro from the mid 1940s and spent several years trying to track them down. Others before me had suffered the same ordeal. The recordings were lauded by old-time musicians—*"Formidable!" "Terrible!"*—and yet no one had a copy of them to share. These vaunted recordings of Baro's were the great mystery discs. Finally, French Gypsy jazz fan Didier Roussin uncovered one of Baro's 78s, found naturally in *les puces*. And amazingly, the disc was in pristine condition, as if destiny was playing a hand in the music's fate.

I'm listening now to a taped copy of this very record, a tape that has been passed down from Roussin to other aficionados, from Paris across the Atlantic on a Romani Trail of its own. The song is titled "Panique...!," which is far from the pastoral and romantic names bestowed on any previous *valse musette*. The music, too, is obviously related to the old musette but sounds like it's coming from another world.

The song begins typically enough with Jo Privat's accordion sketching out the theme. But even that theme sounds slightly askew, strange intervals within the seemingly simple melody lines. Then Baro's guitar enters. He strikes a series of jangling tremolo runs behind the melody, accosting me and sending a chill running down my spine. When they hit the B section, Privat's melody is torn apart into short bits of phrases, Baro's guitar playing scattered harmonic jabs that syncopate the rhythm almost as if he's taunting it and jeering at the whole concept of melody. Returning to the theme, Baro now plays the solo. He jumps between lines that echo old-time musette—or perhaps, mock it. He then unleashes a grandiose flamenco trill, followed by dark-toned and dissonant dashes of arpeggios, furious salvos of notes. This was not a waltz for waltzing to. Instead, it was like a panic-stricken flight down a darkened alleyway.

"Panique...!" is believed to have been composed by Baro during World War II, although it was not recorded until at least 1946. The mood Baro creates here captures the fear and uncertainty that was the everyday reality of life during the Occupation—and especially so if one was a Gypsy. The song's title fits the mood to perfection. There's a sense of foreboding, and even imminent doom, within Baro's music.

And yet I also hear something else. "Panique...!" was notated on the published sheet music as a "valse," but that doesn't begin to describe the music. Instead, I hear Baro deconstructing the stately old *valse musette*. In its place, he's recast the music into a jarring and unnerving new whole. Sure enough, on the label of the original Odéon 78 rpm record, "Panique...!" is listed as a "Valse Be-Bop." Baro's modern melodic sense along with his jarring chordal accents and counterpoint obbligatos behind the accordion's lines is all alive with the spirit of bebop. And amazingly, Baro was creating his *valse bebop* simultaneously with the bebop being fashioned by Dizzy Gillespie, Charlie Parker, Thelonious Monk, and others on the far side of the Atlantic.

The story of Baro's *valses bebop* remain more mystery than history. No one is sure exactly when they were recorded, much less composed. And no one is even certain how many *valses bebop* Baro crafted.

Baro's nephew René Mailhes recalls that Baro told him in later decades that he began composing and playing these waltzes during the World War II years, in the days after swing musette was born. The earliest recording of "Panique...!" bears no date, but was likely released in 1946, according to the Odéon label matrix number. It's possible that it was recorded earlier during the Occupation and not released until after the war; this same situation occurred with several sessions of Django's, as the release of swing records was frowned upon by the Nazi occupiers and acetate for the records themselves was near impossible to come by anyway.

Only four recordings of Baro's *valses bebop* from the 1940s survive—"Panique...!" backed by "La folle" (The Madwoman), which was co-written with Privat; and "Dinalie mineure" backed by "Turbulente Zoë." Yet others exist in sheet-music form, published by Éditions Léon Agel. Baro's *valse bebop* "Survol de nuit"—surviving only as sheet music, copywritten in 1951—may never have been recorded. Or perhaps it and others were indeed waxed, and copies of the old 78s still lurk out there, Baro's masterpieces waiting to be rediscovered in *les puces* somewhere.

Throughout the 1940s and into the 1960s, Baro again turned his attention elsewhere. The paucity of basic goods during World War II fed a blossoming black market in France, and Baro joined the underground entrepreneurs. As a Romani adept at skirting the *gadjé* system, he was ideally suited to this new métier. And he now focused the same fervor he brought to music on becoming a maestro of black marketeering.

By the war's end, Baro was a confirmed Gypsy gangster, as his old musician friends remember, their voices falling into a hushed, secretive tone. Part of the Pigalle aristocracy of gangsters, he operated a series of bars, each more louche and lowdown than the last: Baro-Bar in Pigalle, La Point d'Interrogation outside the city, Barreaux Vert, and most famously—or infamously—La Lanterne in the 17th Arrondissement near the Porte de Champerret. These bars were hangouts for the Romani underworld and fronts for Baro's own illicit activities that ran the gamut. Even after the black market of the war years, a gray market endured during peacetime within France's devastated economy for luxury goods—cigarettes, liquor, silk stockings, and more. Like many of his fellow Romani, including Django, Baro was a great fan of boxing, including the heroic exploits of Gypsy boxing star Johann Trollmann; Baro's bars served as headquarters for illicit betting on—and likely, fixing of—boxing matches. And he also procured women for the insatiable Parisian brothels, a specialty learned in his early days in the *bals musette*. A photograph taken at the opening of one of Baro's string of bars just after the Liberation pictures him hand in hand with a lovely demoiselle and seated alongside his old musician's cadre of Django, Sarane, Lousson Baumgartner, and Eugène Vées. Next to them sit a cabal of three Romani gangsters, their suits and hair slick, their faces hard.

Yet as the Romani saying went, neither the Devil nor gold remain in peace, and the gendarmes soon learned to keep an eye on Baro. His underworld rivals watched as well. Police raids only interrupted his ongoing business, but his musician friends say he spent too many years in prison from the 1940s through the early 1970s. One guitarist hired to provide musical ambiance at La Lanterne remembers overhearing Baro on the telephone warning whomever he was talking with that if things didn't go his way in a deal, he would "raise an army by daybreak." These days, Baro fingered his pistol more often than he played his guitar. Yet at times he still took the stage to play or jam with his old Romani cronies after the doors were locked for the night. A tape of one such after-hours jam session from the mid 1960s at La Lanterne survives, Baro still playing his old *valses bebop* with the same force and power as in his youth.

Baro set aside his guitar not only to start his second career as a gangster but also in daunted honor of—and indeed, frustration over—the music of his best friend and greatest rival, Django. Baro was never one to be second best. He continued to perform now and then, playing cabaret gigs in between running his own enterprises and serving time in jail. He backed trumpeter Rex Stewart on a series of September 1966 recordings for Delaunay's Disques Vogue. That same year, Delaunay also drew Baro back to re-record his then near-forgotten *valses bebop*. With a small band featuring the addition of vibes and organ, these were released in 1966 on an LP and an EP entitled *Swing valses d'hier et d'aujourd'hui*.

And in what may have been Baro's final session, he played alongside his brother Matelo on the 1971 session reviving the golden days of swing musette for Gus Viseur's *Swing Accordéon* LP. In later years, Baro confided to his nephew, René Mailhes, the reason he packed away his guitar and turned to other métiers: "Technically, Django did not scare me. It was his *mind*. He had ideas that I would never have, and that's what killed me."

And yet Baro's *valses bebop* remain tours de force. This series of ten near-forgotten waltzes are some of the most idiosyncratic, adventuresome, and stunning jazz masterpieces ever, bar none—including the best of Django.

Baro Ferret died in 1976, alone and uncelebrated. Fame may be fleeting, but even infamy doesn't last forever. No jazz or guitar magazines noted Baro's passing. Only a French accordionist's newsletter ran an obituary, which, considering his devotion to musette, was fitting.

I've been listening to Boulou and Élios reminiscing about their uncle Baro, and when we come to the end of the story, they're both quiet. It's obvious they hold great admiration for the man and his music, admiration they can't describe in words but which they've put into song. On their debut album, *Pour Django*, in 1979 they recorded a faithful rendition of his *valse bebop* "La folle;" this was followed by "Panique...!" on 1980's *Gypsy Dreams*. And along with Django, they hold Baro up as one of their prime influences.

As they turn now to Sarane Ferret, their tone changes. They laugh over a memory shared with me, grin about another, and speak of Sarane as though they're talking of a favorite genial uncle.

Sarane differed so much from his elder brother, Baro, that it's difficult to believe they were even related. Except for the music, that is. Jovial and good-natured, Sarane was a jazzman through and through, devoted to the Gypsy jazz that Django created.

Following his own image of Django, Sarane at times grew a moustache—one of the few of the Ferret clan to sport one. He shaved and shaped his mustachio *à la* Django, and sometimes even fretted his guitar with just two fingers, striving to get *that* sound. I'm looking now at a photograph of Sarane playing a gig at Paris's Monseigneur cabaret in 1938 alongside accordionist and guitarist Charley Bazin, American violinist Charlie Ritz, and American singer Jimmy Johnson. Sarane has his moustache and plays with his two forefingers. His curly hair combed flat, I might easily mistake him for Django. And perhaps that's what Sarane wanted.

He also loved to dress the part. Quintette bassist Emmanuel Soudieux remembered running into Sarane one day on the rue Montmartre: Sarane was puffed like a peacock, wearing a violent violet shirt under a pink two-piece suit all topped by a glorious Stetson fedora as white as snow. He was done up like his own image of an American jazzman. Or again, of Django.

Sarane's boldness extended to his music. None of the other Gypsy guitarists on the Paris jazz scene dared take a solo in Django's presence; their respect—indeed, downright fear—for Django's intuitive musical sense was too strong. Yet Sarane was not held back. He believed he was the equal of Django, as Soudieux remembered. Sarane, however, had the temperament and ambition to be a bandleader, something many other good musicians lacked. During World War II and the Occupation's call for jazz, he launched his own jazz ensemble, the Swing Quintette de Paris.

Like his clothes and guitar playing, Sarane's Swing Quintette too was based on Django's famous band. And yet there was little similarity in sound. While their repertoire included many of Django's compositions, the band imbued them with a unique personality. Sarane first led his ensemble into a Paris studio in May and June 1941 for the Odéon label. In the first session, he was backed by his faithful brother Matelo, Django's drummer Pierre Fouad, and bassist Speilleux. Following Django's experimentation with clarinet duets, the Swing Quintette's sound was colored by clarinetists André Lluis and André "Sylvio" Siobud. The band cut four of Sarane's original compositions, including the crepuscular "Blue Guitare" and the lilting "Swing Star." In the second session, he was backed by violinist Robert Bermoser, creating traditional string jazz akin to Django and Stéphane's Quintette. This time, the band also recorded a more traditional set: Django's "Swing 39," the Russian Gypsy classic "Deux guitares," the New Orleans standard "Tiger Rag," and Sarane's own "Cocktail Swing."

I hear in Sarane's fretwork a more deliberate, perhaps cautious guitarist. Certainly, his arrangements were more formal, and I've never heard him improvise with the freewheeling and rollicking abandon of Django. Sarane was certainly not the daring improviser nor guitar virtuoso Django was, yet his songs have something else. Listening to them now, they're imbued with a remote, even mysterious atmosphere, a clue perhaps to another aspect of Sarane's nature. I hear melodies floating on entrancing airs of minor-key wistfulness. Even the upbeat swing numbers such as his masterpiece, "Cocktail Swing," are infused with a rich jazz sensibility counterpointed by an eerie mood of minor-major-key Gypsy melancholy. It's as if Sarane realized that even behind the mask of the good times of a hot night in Pigalle, there remained a deeper sadness to the soul that could never be sated. Even by music.

Just as Django found a worthy foil in Grappelli, Sarane soon met a young violinist named Georges Effrosse. Equally at home playing classical music or jazz, Effrosse held a chair in the Paris Opéra *orchestre*. His talents were recognized by musicians throughout the city, and in 1943, bandleader Jacques Hélian hired him to perform with his group. Yet for Effrosse, even a symphonic orchestra did not tap the depths of his violin playing. Alongside Sarane, his violin evoked the jazz of Stéphane as well as echoes of Hungarian Tziganes music. Sarane and Effrosse recorded their first session together sometime in 1941 or 1942. They were backed by Baro, a second guitarist known only as "Raton," and either Matelo or Jean "Nénène" Maille playing rhythm with bassist Speilleux. The group recorded four sides: Sarane's "Royal Blue" and "Surprise-Party" as well as Django's "Daphné" and "Hungaria." In October 1942, Sarane and Effrosse cut four more compositions by Sarane—"Lucky," "Folies-Bergère," "Studio 28," and "Sex-Appeal." These Swing Quintette sides with Effrosse were the pinnacles of Sarane's career. With his fine touch on the violin, Effrosse could move within even a phrase from elation to sorrow, matching perfectly the moods of Sarane's guitar. Together, they created poetic Gypsy jazz speaking with a supreme delicacy and style.

Yet Effrosse's tenure with Sarane's Swing Quintette was short-lived. The Nazi occupiers applauded Django and the other Gypsies' swing, allowing them safe passage through Paris. But Effrosse was Jewish, and even though his violin played jazz during these golden years of swing, he was a marked man. To escape the Nazis' wrath, Effrosse tried to hide his identity. But to no avail. In 1944, he was just one of numerous French Jews herded up by the Germans. Interned at the Drancy camp outside Paris, he was soon packed into a railroad boxcar with dozens of others and shipped off to the Dora–Mittelbau extermination camp, where he perished.

Sarane continued to record at times and play in Montmartre and Montparnasse *boîtes* through the 1950s and 1960s, but he never again reached the peaks he touched in his duets with Effrosse. And while Sarane's brothers explored new musical directions, Sarane remained faithful to jazz in Django's mode. Still, his band became a sort of vagabond *conservatoire* for the upcoming generation of Gypsy jazzmen: Among his accompanists over the years were Jacques "Montagne" Mala, Paul Pata, Laro Sollero, René Mailhes, and Francis-Alfred Moerman. Sarane married Gusti Malha's daughter, Poupée, and lived on the northwestern side of Montmartre, a well-known regular in the *quartier*.

Upon Sarane's death in 1970, his clan organized a grand tribute concert at Paris's Olympia hall. The homage entitled "La Nuit des Gitans" featured performances by Matelo; Challain Ferret with Valia Belinsky; Maurice Ferret with

Joseph Pouville; René Mailhes; Stéphane Grappelli; Jacques "Montagne" Mala with guitarist Chatou Garcia; Babik Reinhardt; and Baro.

Turning now to Matelo Ferret, both Boulou and Élios struggle to sum up his life and music. This is not surprising: He was their father, after all. And in his musical journeys, Matelo ranged farther than either Baro or Sarane. Searching for words, Boulou finally describes, at least in part, what his father meant to him as a musician and teacher: "Without Matelo Ferret, neither Élios nor myself would have played guitar. One speaks often today of a 'master class' of guitar school; we lived that every day. He made us work our fingers all day long, practicing scales and our technique. He always said, '*Il y a des doigts sans âmes, et des âmes sans doigts*—There are musicians with fingers but without souls, and musicians with souls but without fingers.' And he would tell us, 'As a musician you must live through your ears. Work every day on your guitar: a day without playing will be a day that you no longer live.' Without Matelo, we would not have had this passion."

Matelo lived for music. He began playing violin, then banjo and banduria when he was just a child, and by the time he was thirteen, he ran away from his parents' home in Rouen to join his elder brothers and devote himself to performing in Paris. For the next five decades of his life, he probably had a guitar in his hand every day. His longtime and devoted accompanist, Francis-Alfred Moerman, tells me an anecdote of Matelo that sums him up well: "Matelo carried the melodies and harmonies to literally thousands of songs in his head. And yet he could barely remember his own address and would get lost in the street just a block away from his own apartment."

In the photographs Boulou and Élios share with me from their family album, Matelo appears to be smiling. Always. And perhaps that's in part because he has that guitar in his hands. A smallish man, he wears a large smile that brightens his whole being. And it's a happiness that comes through in his music, whether he's playing a jazz tune, a *valse musette*, or even a dark Balkan melody like the ominous "Sombre dimanche." He's happy simply to be making music.

There's also a photograph of Matelo at about age twelve, sitting with Baro on a curb along a cobbled street. Matelo holds a banduria, intent on playing a melody. He looks so young—an elfin figure, half cherub, half Cupid with his famous harp. At this age, Matelo was already a professional musician. Family legend has it that upon his arrival in Paris in 1931, he was immediately snapped up by accordionist Guérino as an accompanist and was also soon replacing Gusti at the side of Vacher on stage at L'Abbaye de Thèléme in Pigalle. Other family stories state that Matelo first joined the Romanian Gypsy Ionel Bageac's *orchestre* at the Casanova, one of Paris's hot new *cabarets russe*, or Russian cabarets. Matelo was likely performing in each of these bands at once. He traded off gigs from afternoon to evening, swapping suits and instruments to match the music and the nightclubs' themes—a sailor's suit and banjo to perform with Guérino at La Boîte à Matelots, a cossack's smock and guitar or balalaïka to play classic Russian and Romani music to accompany the vodka and caviar at the *cabarets russe*. Matelo played them all through the years.

The music of the *cabarets russe*—alongside musette and the jazz of Django— remained one of Matelo's most surprising and yet enduring influences. Ever since the Russian revolution, Paris had been flooded with fleeing White Russians— deposed princes and princesses, the newly landless gentry, and those whose political beliefs didn't run the same color as the Red revolutionaries. The city where Marx first drafted his revolutionary communist writings and where Lenin had plotted now became the refuge of some 60,000 Russians. It wasn't long before a *boîte du nuit* of their own was launched: In 1922, Le Château Caucasien opened—in Pigalle, of course—with two orchestras and three floors of enter- tainment, including the Russian Tziganes choir of Dimitri Poliakoff led by Nastia Poliakova's ethereal voice as well as Romanian Gypsy Nitza Codolban playing his cymbalom with Nico Bouika's *orchestre*. Other *cabarets russe* followed, each featuring its own band, usually composed of Gypsies—either those who recently fled Russia and Eastern Europe, or those already settled in France; as long as they could play, it didn't matter their origin. The Romani musical dynasties of the Codolban clan, the Sokolovs, Poliakoffs, and Dimitrievitches all descended on the capital and starred in the *cabarets russe*. And waiting on the wealthy were the formerly famous of Russia: The tsar's own chef served borscht and caviar at L'Ermitage Muscovite where the maître d'hôtel was a one-time admiral in the tsar's fleet, the bandleader the son of a Russian general, and the barmen and *garçons* all miscellaneous deposed dukes and domainless counts.

Matelo—as well as Baro, Sarane, and Django—played in various Russian Tziganes *orchestres*, especially at the grandiose Casanova and Shéhérazade caba- rets. From its premiere in 1927, Le Shéhérazade was host to the kings of Spain, Sweden, Norway, Denmark, and Romania as well as the king of playboys, England's Prince of Wales. The interior was a sheik's palace of arched grottos and flowing fabric draped from the ceilings like a harem tent all lit by the mysterious crystalline light of Arabian lamps. Sumptuous in decor, luxurious in service, and stunning in entertainment, Le Shéhérazade was the cabaret of kings and the king of cabarets. And during World War II, Le Shéhérazade was requisitioned by the Nazi High Command as its own after-hours headquarters.

While Django only played the *cabarets russe* sporadically in his early years, Matelo became enamored with the music. At thirteen, he was performing in Bageac's *orchestre* and was soon also backing Nitza Codolban and Tzigane violinists Yoska Nemeth and Tata Mirando. Matelo became one of the favored accompanists of Gypsy Jean Goulesco, formerly the tsar's violinist, now in Paris to present his romantic music. A virtuoso of violin trickery, Goulesco could perform bedeviling melodies and bow-slides that evoked the call of cuckoos and nightingales, musical conjuring that had even charmed the tsar's *éminence grise*, Rasputin. Matelo would play in the *cabarets russe* into the 1980s, long after the nightclubs' finest hours had come and gone. And in the process, he forged his own unique style of Tziganes music played on guitar.

At the same time in the 1930s, Matelo was pounding out the beat in the *bals* alongside accordionists from Vacher and Guérino to the younger generation of Viseur, Privat, and Muréna. And as well as playing jazz behind accordionist Louis Richardet, violinist Michel Warlop, and hornmen André Ekyan and Alix Combelle, he was serving time accompanying Django on gigs, recording sessions, and tours.

Inspired by Django's music, Matelo formed his own jazz ensemble to answer the World War II demand for jazz. Matelo had just celebrated his twenty-fifth birthday when he led his Sixtette into the Paris Pathé studio on December 15, 1943, and he played with a verve and *joi de vivre* telling of his age. The Sixtette boasted a thoroughly modern lineup in the style of Benny Goodman's small groups, including clarinetist Siobud, Camille Martin on vibes, drummer Saki Bambos, bassist Marcel Fabre, and rhythm guitarist René Duchossoir.

Matelo's first jazz sides were marked by tight arrangements and vivacious interplay among the musicians. His modern band lineup breathed new life into Django's "Swing Guitares" and "Swing 42" as well as Matelo's own composition "Le Rapide," a Gypsy train song. "Le Rapide" was innovative, even startling, a fast-forward from swing toward bebop. The song was highlighted by Matelo's audacious solo, jumping through vibrant arpeggios to syncopated chord-melody lines. Even early on in these first solo recordings, Matelo displayed his love for adventurous improvisations and off-kilter beats. If Django's jazz signaled a revolution in music akin to the Impressionists in painting, Matelo's music was now pure Cubism.

In the coming years, Matelo played constantly but recorded only sporadically. He cut four EPs of electric Gypsy jazz guitar—1951's *Diner en musique*, 1955's *Musique pour deux*, 1960's *Jean "Matelot" Ferret et sa guitare*, and 1965's *Marta*. And he recorded for Charles Delaunay's Vogue label in 1959, recreating "Les Inédits" of Django—four *valses musette* that might otherwise have been lost to time.

Matelo's live gigs in Paris's *boîtes du nuit* may have been where he truly shone, however, and those are indeed irrevocably lost. Fortunately, there is a period report chronicling one of Matelo's shows that is colorful and lively in its description—making me yearn all the more to have been there. The article was written by Herb Caen, later a famed and beloved columnist for the San Francisco *Chronicle* newspaper. When he wrote about this show in 1945, though, Caen was a jazz-obsessed U.S. Army Air Corps first lieutenant. On leave in Paris, he and a buddy went in search of Django at La Roulotte in Pigalle. Instead they found Matelo—who proved an even more thrilling discovery to Caen as he was an unknown. Caen sent a dispatch about his eye-opening find to *Down Beat*:

When you stroll into Django Reinhardt's jernt in Montmartre these nights, Gino, the Italian-American maitre d'hotel is likely to spread his hands in a Henry Armetta gesture and apologize: "Ah no, my frand, Django is not here tonight. You know how it is with these geniuses—they aren't dependable. But don't go. Tonight you can hear Django's cousin. Believe me, he is good, too."

So you step to the bar and order a brandy and water and get some watered brandy and settle back on a stool. On the tiny bandstand facing the bar sit two characters holding beat-up guitars they must have won in a crackerjack box. Behind them, leaning on a bass fiddle, stands a long, tall joker wearing thick glasses and an expression to match.

One of these gitbox gees is wearing a tuxedo that must have been Simonized—how else could it shine like that? The other, in a sad sack suit and dirty fingernails, turns out to be Django's cousin—Jean Ferret by name, and very fitting, too.

Just so they don't stomp off with somethin like *Estrellita*, we—Collie Small of the Satevepost and I—shout: "Howzabout *Honeysuckle?*" It was strictly a Djackpot of a request. The Ferret's face lights up—even the blackheads seemed to glow—and he kicks the floor four times.

From then on, the evening was in the groove and on the move.

Having heard most of the guitarists from Eddie Lang to the guy who used to play those sensational stink-finger breaks in the old Jan Garberchestra, I wish to stagger to my feet and say right out *fortissimo e sostenuto* that this Ferret is a guitarist of the first water. Now if somebody will just explain to me why "of the first water" means superlative—but leave us not digress.

Ferret plays a la Django as far as style is concerned, but for my francs the kid has a few tricks of his own that The Old Master has yet to conceive. His technique is flawless and his staying powers are incredible. Twenty consecutive choruses of any standard tune are strictly par for this guy's course, and he was breaking par all night.

There isn't a position on the frets that M. Ferret fails to negotiate. His long fingers race back and forth from the box to the keys in one, long black blur—and even with his dirty fingernails, he plays as clean as Goodman on the clarinet. His ideas are as innocent of cliches as a newborn baby whose first word is "Antediluvian."

After four hours of solid giving, the Ferret finally gave up and went home to bathe his bleeding fingertips, while Gino explained to us that the kid—he's 25—has a bad heart and really should take it easier than Muggsy Spanier in a jam session with Henry Busse.

"But the kid, he's going to be great," Gino said, a little unnecessarily, considering that the customers were still lying flat on their faces under the tables and frothing slightly at the mouth. "And the good thing is, he practices day and night and doesn't drink or play around with women. His whole life is wrapped up in that guitar."

. . . As you might imagine, Django's spot is the gathering place for every guitarist in Paris. In fact, on the night we dropped in, there were more stringpluckers in the house than you'll find at an Andre Segovia concert. They all took a whack at sitting in and giving out—but after M. Jean Ferret's performance, there was just nothing left to say on six strings.

Little did Caen know, but Matelo had only begun to speak with his guitar.

Through the 1950s and 1960s, Matelo was often at the side of accordionist Jo Privat, Baro's former partner on his *valses bebop*. They performed most nights in Paris, often at Privat's kingdom, the Balajo dance hall on rue de Lappe, as well as touring France and Europe. And together, they would record a masterpiece—two batches of old-fashioned musette, swing, and Gypsy jazz that would become known as the *Manouche Partie* sessions.

Of all the Parisian accordionists, it was Privat who best bridged the worlds of musette and swing. Perhaps it was his childhood on the streets of Paris that would destine him to become the most beloved of French accordionists, reigning for five decades at the cathedral of musette, Balajo. Whereas most of the other musette accordionists hailed from Italy, Privat was pure Paris, and Parisians embraced him. He had a sensitivity with musette and a touch for swing that won him accolades from dancers as well as respect from the likes of the Ferrets. Like Django or Piaf in their respective *métiers*, Privat would become synonymous with the charm of Parisian accordion.

Privat loved to boast in later years that he was *"élevé au sirop de la rue"*— "drank in the life of the streets with his mother's milk," as he pronounced in his colorful Parisian argot. He was a child of working class Paris, the 20th Arron-dissemont comprising Belleville and Ménilmontant, branding him a true "Mémilmouche," in *chansonnier* Charles Trenet's slang. Privat was born on April 15, 1919, his mother an Italian from Piedmonte and his father an Auvergnat mason—a storybook ancestry for a *bal* accordionist.

And yet it was Privat's aunt Yvonne who was the greatest influence in his childhood, at least in *his* memory. *Tante* Yvonne ran *une maison close*—a bordello—on the rue des Ecouffes near the Bastille. With her hard-won wages, she bought the young Privat his first diatonic accordion as a Christmas gift. "*J'en tombe amoureux*," Privat wrote in 1997 in his autobiographical preface to a collection of his music—"I fell head over heels in love." He played his first concert *chez* Yvonne's bordello, and as he recollected, "I was a great success among the strippers at Yvonne's whorehouse, especially with Rosita *le Glouton*—The Glutton. . . . In brief, it was *la planque* [a cushy job]." One day, Yvonne introduced Privat to her "*pôte intime*"—her intimate buddy—Émile Vacher, who regularly came to visit the charming Monique *la Ventouse*—The Sucker. While Vacher went about his business, Privat played "*une fleur*." As he left, Vacher hired Privat as his partner, and the young Georges began his life as "*un laborieux du dépliant*"—a laborer of the bellows. At Vacher's side, Privat played "almost every *bals musette* in Paris."

Along the way, he met Viseur and was inspired to swing his accordion. He also fell in with Baro and Matelo, and along with the *sirop de la rue*, he now drank in a new sound of Gypsy esprit, that famed sense of *rabouine*. As Privat summed up the 1930s Paris music scene, "Everyone was inspired by Django Reinhardt. . . . When Django played it was like being fed champagne intravenously."

At the same time, two associates with the unlikely names of Jo France and Jo Lallemand collaborated to open what would become "*le Temple du musette*," in Privat's words. They took over the former Bal Vernet at 9 rue de Lappe and hired famed artist and decorator Henri Mahé, who had designed the Bal au Moulin-Rouge, to create a wonderworld. Working his magic, Mahé designed a dizzying skyline with art deco flourishes; the ballroom was a city within a city. The dance hall was christened Balajo, in honor of the two Jo's who owned it. When the *bal* opened its doors to the dancers in 1936, a nervous eighteen-year-old Privat was waiting on the bandstand as the house accordionist. It was the start of a great love affair between Privat and the dancers at the ballroom. Privat would headline at Balajo for the next five decades.

On November 3, 1960, Privat and Matelo assembled a band of Romani jazzmen and *bal* regulars to cut the first of the *Manouche Partie* sessions. By this time, the music was viewed with derision as being stale and old. But their nostalgic revival of the *musette* milieu was such a hit that Privat and Matelo regrouped on December 16, 1966, to add four more tracks to fill out an LP. The band on the first session included Jacques "Montagne" Mala, Gypsy drummer Baptiste "Mac Kak" Reilhes, and clarinetist Jean Tordo. The ensemble was completed by a Hungarian Romani violinist whose name has been lost. Together, they resurrected classics from Django, Privat's old repertoire, Gusti's "La valse des niglos," and the Russian Gypsy classic "Les deux guitares." Yet it was in "Les yeux noirs" that Matelo created his most stellar work ever.

This Romani anthem has been played so many times in so many ways over the years it's difficult to imagine someone finding a new interpretation. In the beginning it was a waltz. Likely first sung in a Russian-Romanès argot, the lyrics described a Gypsy woman of otherworldly beauty and the supernatural dark eyes of the song's title:

> *Ochi chornye*
> *Ochi strastnye*
> *Ochi zhguchie*
> *I prekrasnye*
> *Kak liubliu ia vas*
> *Kak boius'ia vas*
> *Znat'uvidela vas*
> *Ia vne dbryi chas*

> Dark eyes
> Dangerous eyes
> Eyes aflame
> Beauty is their name
> How I love you, dear
> How I fear you, dear
> Since you came my way
> That unlucky day

Django may have been one of the first to translate the song into a jazz-inspired four-four-time signature, recording the song three times, twice in 1940 (once as part of Pierre Allier's *orchestre*) and again live in 1947. He then revamped it with a bebop sensibility—and intensity—in his "Impromptu."

I'm listening now to Matelo and Privat's version from the *Manouche Partie* sessions, recast as a four-four-time musette melody. They play it with the jaunty air of a foxtrot; perhaps it had been on their songlists back in the days of the *bals*. That unknown Hungarian Gypsy violinist leads off the song with a glorious tone of pure darkness before Privat's accordion takes over, adding a dance hall gaiety. The enigmatic Romani bowman is then back, improvising jazz that struts and swings as few others—even Grappelli—ever did. How sad no one remembers who he was! Privat recalled years later, "As to the violinist, I believe Matelo has taken this secret to his grave; no one remembers his name. . . . He was Hungarian, a guy who played in a Gypsy *boîte du nuit*; it was Matelo who brought him along. . . . His name, I never even knew." Just one more mystery to add to the mythology.

Now, as the violinist ends his solo, Matelo takes up the theme. And yet at the same time, he doesn't. He jumps into the tune, hitting only eccentric intervals *in between* the melodic line. Instead of playing the tonic and prime notes of the A minor chord upon which the melody is based, he hits the minor third, minor seventh, ninth, and thirteenth with proud, flaunting, defiant whole notes. He strikes the intervals of this riff like a church bell sounding a new hour, a new time for music. From there, his fingers dance up the fretboard into stylish licks blending age-old Tziganes tones with *modernistique* jazz sensibilities. He moves within a phrase from flowing lyricism to angular sounds, from the ancient pastoral world of the Romani to the stone streets of Pigalle. Replaying that opening phrase of idiosyncratic intervals, Matelo transfers them to yet another plane of startling intervals of the harmonic chord. Then, he launches into a series of octave riffs at a velocity far past anything of which Django, or Wes Montgomery after him, could have dreamed. Matelo's octaves move like dancers in a hora, spinning ever faster. It transforms now into a dizzying display of virtuosity—triplet runs that would tie most any other guitarists' fingers into a knot. At the same time, he's shifting the ictus of the beat within those triplets, throwing the rhythm off center with an edgy bebop syncopation. He ends the solo by tossing off a bent blue note and a casual jazz outro, as if saying, "*Ça? Ça, c'était rien*—That? That was nothing." In the process of just two quick choruses, Matelo tears apart a century of Romani musical history, then recreates it for a new future. If he had recorded nothing else in his lifetime, this one simple solo would remain a masterpiece.

Matelo didn't stop there. He was performing most nights now in the dwindling number of Parisian *cabarets russe*. And he often now had one or more of his three sons at his side—Michel "Sarane," Boulou, and Élios Ferré.

In 1978, Matelo returned with Charles Delaunay to the Vogue studio to craft what would become yet another masterwork, a two-album LP set entitled *Tziganskaia*. The collection was a menagerie of ancient Tziganes melodies, jazz tunes, near-forgotten *valses musette*, and original compositions, all played with a Gypsy finesse. Backed by Boulou and Michel Villach on cymbalom, Matelo recast Django's musette waltz "Gagoug" into a rubato reverie and played Sidney Bechet's "Petite fleur" with floral delicacy. He resurrected "Sombre dimanche"—Sad Sunday—a dirgelike song he used to perform with Tziganes violinist Georges Boulanger. The tune was infamous, so unredeemably dreary that it reportedly drove people to suicide in Hungary and was thus forbidden to be played in Budapest. And in Matelo's own "Pouro Rom," he crafts a haunting melody akin to an epic history of the Romani diaspora. In sum, the album was Matelo's autobiography, writ in music.

Above all, Matelo was a performer, often playing two or even three gigs daily in the nightclubs of Paris. I'm walking with Boulou and Élios through the streets of Saint-Germain-des-Prés on a cool March evening. Many of those old nightclubs are just now turning on their neon lights, the waiters setting out on ice the enticing oysters and other bizarre briny shellfish in front of the grand brasseries. With us are Gypsy jazz guitarists Scot Wise and Francis-Alfred Moerman, who was long one of Matelo's accompanists. Francis is acting as tour guide, pointing out the sites of the ghosts of bygone cabarets they once played together, telling us of other never-ending nights when the music went on until the sun rose.

"I moved to Paris from Belgium in 1955 as a student," Francis tells us as we walk up from Odéon toward the Luxembourg. "I met Sarane first, in 1959. He was playing at La Montagne Pelée near place de la Contrascarpe, and I liked his music. I was playing with a Guadeloupean guitarist named Roland Balthazar, and he said he'd introduce me to Sarane. I wasn't a very good guitarist then, but Sarane handed me his Selmer and told me to play a tune with his accompanist, Laro Sollero. I played a blues improvisation, but it wasn't much. A week later, Sarane called me up and asked if I wanted to be his accompanist through the summer for a gig in Corsica. And that was the beginning."

Through the years, Francis often backed Sarane and Matelo—and even Baro at rare moments. He also hung out with everyone from their cousin Maurice Ferret to Jacques Montagne and guitarist Paul Pata, who told Francis he was Baro's illegitimate son. Francis and Laro Sollero became great *amis*, although Laro later joined the Romani evangelical church and devoted his guitar, upon which he once played ebullient bebop lines, now solely to religious hymns. And there were others, obscure, little-recorded Gypsy guitarists who were all virtuosi— Jean "Cérani" Mailhes, Jacquet Mailles, a phenomenal violinist nicknamed Tête Cheval, South American guitarist Jorge Lagos, who once performed alongside Oscar Alemán and stayed on in Paris to play his own jazz. Francis evokes them all for us.

From talk of great guitarists, he now begins to remember legendary *guitars*. Like others may recall a favored childhood puppy or beloved grandparent, Francis is now sentimental, even misty-eyed, when speaking of certain instruments. He tells of a particular Selmer guitar owned by Sarane. The guitar was imbued with a tone that was beyond magical: warm and woody, rich and deep, it had a true voice. This oval-hole Selmer was fabled among the Gypsies—until, like a golden instrument in a fairy tale, it simply disappeared one day. Francis talks of Matelo's love for Selmers—but only the *grande bouche* models; he despised the "pinched" sound of the *petite bouche* guitars. When old *grande bouche* models became impossible to find, he spurred luthier Jacques Favino to build his Gypsy guitars. And Francis remembers his own first Favino, custom made for him by Jacques in 1961, with a special sound that he still strives to recreate; he accidentally backed over the guitar in his car while packing to leave for yet another tour with the Ferret brothers.

Continuing our impromptu tour, Francis now recalls for us the rowdy, cramped jazz clubs of the *quartier* in the 1960s, the new era of movie stars, playboys, and jet-setting royalty that came to hear the Gypsies play their guitars. He tells of one night in Saint-Germain-des-Prés when he and Sarane were performing just across the street from the club where Matelo was playing—a Spanish cabaret called Don Camillo. He now points out the site of the bars as Matelo's sons listen to his stories. "During his breaks, Matelo used to run down the street with his guitar and come sit in with Sarane and me, and we'd all jam together until he had to go back and play again. Then, when it was our break, Sarane and I'd take our guitars down to Don Camillo and jam with him. That was the first time I met Matelo. Throughout the night, he'd never set his guitar down."

Matelo did finally set aside his guitar. In 1989, after a lifetime playing his music across Paris, he passed away following a short, quick bout with cancer.

Boulou and Élios talk now of another uncle—the honorary "fourth brother"— Challain. Like the other brothers, Challain too was born in Rouen, in 1914. His father, Fillou Ferret, taught him guitar, and Challain accompanied his own sister Marie Ferret, a fine *chanteuse* in the vein of the other Ferret sisters. Challain's brother, Ange, became a legendary horse-trader, celebrated among his fellow Romani. Challain, however, took his guitar and left home for Paris sometime in the 1930s to join his cousins.

As with Matelo, Challain played the whole scene. He backed accordionist André Verchuren in the *bals*, accompanied violinist Yoska Nemeth in the *cabarets russe*, and played jazz with Django. Challain was left-handed and owned what was perhaps the sole left-handed Selmer.

Over his long career, Challain sadly recorded but a few times. In the 1960s, he joined with pianist Valia Belinsky to cut two albums, *Folklore Tzigane* and *Guitare mélodie Tzigane*. On both, Challain's guitarwork was delicate and inspired. In the same spirit and style, he and Belinsky also backed Russian *chanteuse* Ludmila Lopato on the *Dve Guitary* EP and LP. Challain may not have been a composer or improviser in the spirit of Matelo, but he too played the traditional Tziganes music with rare grace.

Challain later married a woman from Toulouse and moved to the Midi where he continued to perform. His son, Paul "Challain" Ferret, learned at his side, and together they launched the ensemble Django's Jazz, performing a set at the Samois-sur-Seine tribute to Django in 1991. Challain died in 1996.

Boulou and Élios pause now. Our conversations about their family's history has covered thousands of miles from Russia to Spain to Paris, several generations of ancestors, and more than one thousand and one nights of song. Now, I point to those incredible fingers of Boulou's and ask him about his own music.

Echoing the trio of the original Ferret brothers, Matelo and his Jewish wife, Jacqueline, had three sons—three guitarist brothers of a new generation: Michel, born in 1948 and nicknamed "Sarane" after his uncle; Boulou, born in 1951; and Élios, in 1956. This new generation would also modernize the spelling of their family name in keeping with French orthography as "Ferré."

Being the eldest, Michel was the first to take up the guitar. Boulou followed, at age seven. He describes how he began playing when he was first able to hold a guitar and reach those frets. Élios at first cared little for music and didn't start until he was older. Matelo instructed them, teaching in the call-and-response fashion common among the Romani. Matelo would play a chord or a snippet of a melody, and Sarane, Boulou, and Élios were instructed not to follow their father's fingers on the guitar but to listen to the music, then recreate it themselves. This method was slow and difficult and perhaps inefficient, but it tutored their ears to hear the pitches and detect the shades of color in the nuances of tones. And besides, there was little other choice. Matelo may have played guitar his whole life, yet he could not read music to teach it to his sons in any other way.

Like their father and uncles, the brothers were inspired by Django's music: "Django was a guru for all of us," Boulou tells me now, the first time the brothers speak of Django's influence. "A master...we listened to him all the time—it's part of our history, our world, our culture, our lifestyle." And Élios adds, speaking first in French, then switching to English to emphasize his point: "Django Reinhardt is the greatest guitarist in the world. I like all of the famous American and English guitarists, but my hero is Django, all of my life."

Yet along with Django's music, Matelo also opened his sons' ears to everything from Bach to Charlie Parker. The brothers listened to Bird and Dizzy Gillespie's records, transcribed their solos, and added a bebop sensibility to the music of their father. "Our father told us he was going to teach us the history of jazz—not only of swing," Boulou says emphatically.

Boulou gave his first concert at age eight. That same year, he also appeared on his first record, backing French *chanteur* Jean Ferrat. The A&R man from the singer's label was so impressed by Boulou that he signed him to a four-year contract. In 1963, Boulou enrolled in the Conservatoire National de Paris and began many years of classical training. He was twelve when he released his first record as a leader, *Bluesette*, and fourteen when his second LP, *Jazz/Left Bank*, made its debut.

Élios soon shared his brother's passions. Yet he first became enamored with flamenco. He entered the Conservatoire, receiving classical training as well as studying with flamenco master Francisco Gil. Élios performed his first concert when he was thirteen. Then, in 1969, he first heard Jimi Hendrix's *Are You Experienced?* and was carried off by the possibilities of electric guitar.

At the same time, the brothers were accompanying their father in the surviving *cabarets russe*. Boulou backed Matelo on his 1978 *Tziganskaia* masterpiece and also played with veteran Russian cabaret Gypsy singer Valia Dimitrievitch on the 1978 LP *Rêve à la Russe*. But even melding all of these disparate influences, it was still through Django that the Ferré brothers viewed music.

Boulou and Élios joined forces as a guitar duo in 1978, trading solos and rhythm lines like Siamese twins. (Sarane Ferré was an excellent player, too, but chose not to become a professional musician.) While playing in Copenhagen in 1979, the brothers met Nils Winther, producer for the Danish jazz label Steeplechase. At Winther's invitation, they recorded their first album together, *Pour Django*, taking Django's music to extremes of melody, harmony, and emotion. The brothers' version of Django's "Douce ambiance" here is a bewitching revision of the original; their "Rythme Futur" goes beyond what even Django might have imagined of jazz's future. They cover Wayne Marsh's "Marshmellow" and recreate the Beatles' "Here, There and Everywhere" as Gypsy jazz. The album's coda is Boulou's composition "Michto Pelo," a medley of Tziganes music following the caravans from Greece through the Balkans to Russia. The brothers play as if they are jamming around a Romani campfire lost in time, their ageless riffs charged with bravado and pyrotechnics. All in all, *Pour Django* remains one of the most adventurous Gypsy jazz records ever.

Still, Boulou and Élios are cautious about simply mimicking the classic music of the Quintette du Hot Club de France, as many Gypsy jazz bands are doing today. Élios warns, "Django's music is great—but it is also *dangerous*. Jazz is a living music, and one cannot simply copy and recreate it. You must step beyond it and make it new. To play jazz, you must be playing your *own* music, your *own* feelings. So you must start with the history and develop it, like a torch handed on from Django to you." And he sees no reason simply to recreate Django's music—nor the music of his father and uncles: "It's better to listen to the originals," he says. And he adds, half in jest, "It doesn't mean anything to copy or imitate: You could be arrested for stealing!"

Throughout the 1980s and 1990s, the brothers continued to release records, experimenting with different band arrangements—from their duo to trios and a quartet—and added drums, piano, horns, and electric guitars at times. Then, for several years in the late 1990s, Boulou and Élios did not return to the studio, instead playing festivals, Parisian jazz clubs, and *cabarets russe*. Boulou also found a new love, playing organ for a Parisian church: he tries to describe for me the sensuous joy he finds in listening to the deep sound of the pipes reverberating off the ancient stone walls, but words fail him and he evokes the feeling simply in a whirl of his hands.

At the dawn of the new century, the duo returned to the studio with a vengeance, releasing almost an album a year. They play originals, such as Boulou's *valse bebop* "La bande des trois" dedicated to Baro, Sarane, and Matelo on their 2002 CD *Intersection*. In the style of their ancestors, they put the music of Bach to jazz, a common feature of the Ferret brothers, as well as Django's repertoire, as evidenced by songbooks by Baro and Sarane published in the 1950s. Boulou and Élios also cover tunes by everyone from Romani violinist Georges Boulanger to American jazzmen Lee Konitz and Lennie Tristano; they range widely from Simon and Garfunkel's "Scarborough Fair" and Ennio Morricone's "Ballad of Sacco and Vanzetti" to Eddie Durham's "Topsy"—a tune played by Django— taking it now from swing into bebop. And Boulou plays Ray Noble's standard "Cherokee," moving through the theme into Charlie Parker's famed recasting of the tune as "Ko-Ko." And then Boulou recreates the melody again, as his own.

There's but a last few *cabarets russe* surviving in Paris today. Most of the grand old nightclubs have long ago turned off the flames below the samovars, shut off the spotlights on the stages, and locked their doors for good. La Casanova, Le Shéhérazade, Le Château Caucasien, L'Ermitage Muscovite—they're all history.

I'm at one of the last, lost in the backstreets near the Gare Saint-Lazare. It's hard to call this a true cabaret in the spirit of the 1930s; it's more of a Russian bistro with music, yet a bit wilted and sad—the drooping red-velvet curtains threadbare, dust even coating the showy lightbulbs, casting a shadow of what once were the most famed cabarets in the city. The *cabarets russe* were always for remembering—and forgetting. Remembering the good times, the old music, and the glory that once was life for the privileged in Imperial Russia. And forgetting the present in never-ending toasts of iced vodka, overflowing spoonfuls of caviar,

The boy with the banjo: Jean "Django" Reinhardt, age thirteen or fourteen in 1923–1924, holds his diminutive *banjo-guitare* with pride. During this era, he was performing nightly in the underworld *bals musette* of Paris alongside Gypsy accordionist Vétese Guérino. (Alain Antonietto Collection)

French Romany on the move in their wooden *roulottes*, circa 1910s. Django's family lived in a similar caravan, but cut away the rear to make a tiny traveling stage on which to play their music. (Author Collection)

Django and other Gypsy jazzmen grew up in caravans parked in *La Zone*, the lurid no-man's land that surrounded Paris. This circa 1960 photo of *La Zone* shows a Gypsy encampment made up of old wooden *verdines*, modern *campines*, converted buses, and the Romanies' modern horse—the automobile. (Author Collection)

Gitan maestro Jean "Poulette" Castro stares into the eyes of *chanteuse* Rosita Barrios in this publicity photo of Le Quatuor à Plectre, circa 1925–1930. Poulette was one of Django and Baro Ferret's teachers and a great influence on the first generation of Gypsy jazzmen. The Plectrum Quartet included Poulette's brother Laro Castro as well as Coco and Serrani Garcia, forefathers of the Garcia musical dynasty. (Alain Antonietto Collection)

Auguste "Gusti" Malha was a banjo wizard and an inspiration to the young Django. As one accordionist remembered, Gusti played as though he had six fingers on each hand. (Francis-Alfred Moerman Collection)

Romany pilgrims and their *roulottes* overrun the Camargue town of Les Saintes-Maries-de-la-Mer every year during the week surrounding May 24–25. In Django's day as today, the festival is part religious gathering, part musical celebration, and part party. (Author Collection)

Vintage medallion honoring the Romanies' Sainte Sarah.

Django played many a night at La Java, one of the roughest of the tough *bals musette*. Here, a Parisian *mec* is patted down for weapons before entering—a wise precaution, but one that didn't curtail the many fights. The doorway to La Java looks almost identical today. (Author Collection)

A vintage *jeton de bal* from La Java—*bon pour une danse.*

In 1927 when he was seventeen, Django eloped with a Romany girl, Florine "Bella" Mayer. Here, he stands like a young prince with his new moustache; Bella is to the right with her hand jauntily on her hip, surrounded by her family. Within a short time, Bella was pregnant; their son would be named Henri "Lousson." (Mayer-Renaud Family Collection)

Returning from playing La Java on October 26, 1928, Django or Bella accidentally set their caravan outside La Porte de Clignancourt ablaze and Django was nearly burnt alive. Convalescing over eighteen months, he taught himself to play again, using only his two working fingers to fret. By 1935, when this souvenir postcard was for sale, Django was a rising jazz star, inspiring the world with the possibilities of the guitar. (Author Collection)

The Quintette du Hot Club de France poses for a 1936 publicity photograph. Often tardy for gigs—and sometimes forgetting his guitar or not even bothering to show up himself—Django here had forgotten his tux and arrived wearing an everyday striped suit. He exchanged coats with bassist Roger Grasset, but still wore his now-mismatched striped pants. It was only the beginning for his petulant antics. From left, Stéphane Grappelli, Joseph Reinhardt, Grasset, Django, and Roger Chaput. (Irvin Blumenfeld Photograph; Bibliothèque Nationale de France, Département de l'Audiovisuel, Fonds Charles Delaunay)

The well-dressed Gypsy jazzman: Sarane Ferret, circa 1940. (François Charle Collection)

Poster announcing Gus Viseur's swing musette, circa 1940. (Author Collection)

During the World War II years, Django reached a peak of stardom. His song "Nuages" was a hit, whistled along to by the Occupied French and German soldiers alike. This mammoth poster—measuring four by five feet—was pasted up through-out Paris announcing Django's concerts and recordings. (Author Collection)

During World War II, jazz was golden. It was also outlawed by the Nazis, yet ironically still officially allowed. German soldiers loved swing while the occupied French heard resistance in the freedom of jazz improvisations. At Django's club, La Roulotte on rue Pigalle in 1943–1944, Sarane Ferret plays to an audience of German officers and French *collabos*. (Author Collection)

Violinist Léo Slab swings with teenaged guitarist prodigy Jacques "Montagne" Mailhes, center, during World War II. The war turned Montagne into *un petit animal sauvage*, as Slab said. Montagne died of consumption at age fifteen, and was buried with his guitar nestled alongside him in his coffin like a teddy bear. (Léo Slab Collection)

Gypsy jazzmen and gangsters: Baro Ferret (left front) invites his friends to celebrate the opening of one of his underworld clubs, circa 1945. Baro's cabal of Gypsy associates included from left, Eugène Vées (top left in profile), Baro, Lousson Baumgartner, Django, Sarane Ferret, and three Romany hoods. (Roger-Viollet Photograph)

Baro Ferret jams with accordionist Jo Privat, circa 1949. Baro and Django were best of friends—and greatest of rivals. Baro's *valses bebop* won Django's admiration, yet Baro was forever daunted by Django's playing. In later years, Baro set aside his guitar and became a Gypsy gangster. As he confided to his nephew, René Mailhes: "Technically, Django did not scare me. It was his mind. He had ideas that I would never have, and that's what killed me." (Francis-Alfred Moerman Collection)

In the postwar years, Django turned to bebop, then cool modern jazz. But even with his fame, he preferred to retreat from Paris to live in his *caravane* in the muddy slums of Le Bourget. Here, he picks a melody for his beloved son, Babik. (Author Collection)

Django and Joseph Reinhardt (left) play a melody around a cookstove in a Romany encampment, circa 1950. (Author Collection)

Following Django's death in 1953, several of his former bandmembers were assembled to pay tribute in director Paul Paviot's 1957 documentary on his life. From left, Stéphane Grappelli, Henri Crolla, bassist Emmanuel Soudieux, Joseph Reinhardt, Eugène Vées, Gérard Lévêque, André Ekyan, and Hubert Rostaing honor their bandleader. (Author Collection)

Babik Reinhardt strums his father's old Selmer, serial number 503, in the family's caravan following Django's early passing. (Alain Antonietto Collection)

Django's 1940 Selmer Modèle Django Reinhardt, serial number 503, one display in Paris' Cité de la Musique. The guitar was donated by Naguine in later years. (Jean Marc Angles Photograph; courtesy Cité de la Musique)

Violinist Schnuckenack Reinhardt leads his jazz ensemble, three hard-pounding guitars strong. Hans'Che Weiss—soon to leave to start his own group—is at left. (Author Collection)

Matelo Ferret picks his Jacques Favino guitar amidst a Gypsy encampment, circa 1960s. Whether he was playing musette, jazz, or Tziganes melodies, Matelo's music was always adventurous and daring. (Ted Gottsegen Collection)

Baro was lured back to the studio in 1966 by Charles Delaunay to re-record his lost *valses bebop*. With a band including guitarists Matelo Ferret and Jacques "Montagne" Mala and organ player Jean-Claude Pelletier, various versions of the *valses* were released on an LP and EP both entitled *Swing valses d'hier et d'aujourd'hui*. Baro died in 1976, alone and uncele-brated. (Ted Gottsegen Collection)

Manouche Partie, circa 1966. Accordionist Jo Privat brought his band including Matelo Ferret (standing with back to camera) and Jacques "Montagne" Mala (above Matelo) to deliver a copy of their new LP to Django's widow, Naguine (center, beside Matelo). (Author Collection)

Francis-Alfred Moerman learned Gypsy jazz as an accompanist for Sarane and Matelo Ferret. In later years, he led his own ensembles, creating near-magical music with a sensitivity and poetry few others could match. (Author Collection)

The Piottos, circa 1950s: cellist Latcheben Grünholz, violinist Henri "Piotto" Limberger, and guitarist Eddie "Bamboula" Ferret. (Private Collection)

The homemade, photocopied cover for Bamboula Ferret's underground masterpiece, *Oe djoevia*. The homemade CD and sold only at gigs and religious gatherings—typical of some of the best Gypsy jazz. (Author Collection)

Django's sons jam: Babik Reinhardt, left, comps for Lousson Baumgartner, circa 1965. (Francis-Alfred Moerman Collection)

French stars Sylvie Vartan and Johnny Hallyday (with autograph) bravely descend into Marseille's shady Au Son des Guitares to hear Patotte Bousquet (left) plays his fierce music. Bousquet's faithful accompanist Gérard Cardi comps. (Author Collection)

Child prodigy Boulou Ferré hits a soulful note, circa 1960. (Alain Antonietto Collection)

Paul "Tchan Tchou" Vidal swings at an outdoor café in Mougins on the French Riviera, 1985. (Luc Moïseef Photograph)

Setting up to play a gig in 1989 in Béziers on the French Riviera, Swiss guitarist Fere Scheidegger of the Hot Strings band was surprised to see the famous Jacques "Montagne" Mala appear out of the night. After taking over Baro Ferret's underworld enterprises, Montagne disappeared with the *gendarmes* on his heels. Fere and Montagne (left) jammed for several shows, then Montagne was gone once again. (Fere Scheidegger Collection)

Biréli Lagrène was a child Gypsy jazz prodigy before experimenting with everything from rock to fusion. He made a triumphant return to his roots with his phenomenal Gipsy Project ensemble in 2001. (Author Collection)

Stochelo Rosenberg (left) plays his Selmer guitar— serial number 504, just one number away from one of Django's Selmers. John Larsen, leader of the Hot Club de Norvège, accompanies. (Jon Larsen Collection)

Jimmy Rosenberg (left) was just nine when he was discovered by the *gadjo* world playing hot jazz on a guitar several sizes too large in a Dutch Gypsy camp in 1989. A younger cousin comps for him. (Jon Larsen Collection)

Dallas Baumgartner surrounded by his Madame Rose (left) and Romany friends on the Montmagny hills overlooking Paris, 2007. (Author Photograph)

John "Peeky" Adomono, American Gypsy guitarist extraordinaire, circa 1959. (Kevin Adams Collection)

Tchocolo Winterstein (left) and Dallas Baumgartner unreel their electrified swing in a rare gig, playing in the cellar of Paris' Eglise de la Madeleine, 2007. (Author Photograph)

Danny Fender (center) and his Band of Gypsies in full swing, eight guitars strong in San Francisco on Valentines Day, 2006. (Author Photograph)

Django's former *chanteuse*, Beryl Davis, is back on stage in her eighties, performing with guitarist John Jorgenson's ensemble in 2005. (Author Photograph)

Where Gypsy jazz meets rap: Christian "Syntax" Windrestein's 2004 masterpiece, *Gens du voyage*. (Author Collection)

Johnny Guitar (seated) trades licks on "Hava Nagila" with Danny Fender for an adoring Romany audience. (Author Photograph)

Django's grandson, David Reinhardt, stands with his mother Nadine before their *caravane* parked on the edge of Paris, 2005. (Author Photograph)

Every weekend afternoon, come rain or shine, war or peace, Ninine Garcia (left) and his father, Mondine, can be found playing their enchanting Gypsy jazz at La Chope des Puces in the Clignancourt flea market— just paces away from where Django's caravan burned in 1928. (Author Photograph)

Ninine Garcia, left, and Christian "Syntax" Windrestein jam on a Gypsy jazz rap for an enthusiastic audience. Photo courtesy Laurent Soullier.

Yesterday as today as tomorrow: a guitar leans against a *roulotte* doorway at Les Saintes-Maries-de-la-Mer, 2007. (Author Photograph)

and the reborn music through the nights. On stage here tonight are Boulou and Élios, still playing the music of their father and uncles, and their ancestors before that going back several generations or more. They haven't forgotten. They play Tziganes melodies handed down to them through their family's dynasty, Romani songs like "Les yeux noirs," "Les deux guitares," "Djelem, Djelem," and their own Gypsy campfire medley "Michto Pelo"—songs that begin with a slow, sorrowful preamble before building up speed, catching fire, and turning into ferocious fifteen-minute-long jam sessions with the inevitable toasts and shouts of "Opà." Even the scattered few diners here are clapping along. With the vodka liquid ice on my tongue, I'm feeling the mood just fine as well, even though I have no Russia to remember or forget.

Midnight has long since come and gone when the brothers launch into a jazz tune—Stan Getz's "Parker 51." The transition seems a natural one to Boulou and Élios. And they play with such virtuosity the jazz now takes on a Tziganes flavor. Boulou improvises with a grand sense of droll humor, quoting from American blues, the Beatles, even Aaron Copland. The brothers trade improvisations and accompaniments with guitarwork that is nearly clairvoyant. And yet still they have their own voices. Boulou is at times far out there, lost in his music, playing with an otherworldly fury as if he's left us behind. He hums his improvisations as he plays them, scatting along with his solos. He's transcended all. Élios leaves ground too, but his improvisations stay more rooted in the firmament of the melody, exploring its nuances, traveling through its twists and turns.

In their own way, Boulou and Élios have remained faithful to their family's musical traditions by constantly stepping outside those traditions. They continue to play Tziganes music, *valses musette*, and Django, Matelo, and their uncles' jazz. But under their fingers, they've taken those traditions beyond the music of their ancestors, blending them with bebop, modal and free jazz, even classical music and rock'n'roll to create their own sounds. Their father and uncles would have demanded no less.

TEN

La Dernière Valse des Niglos
Saints and Sinners of the Malha Clan

A S I TRAVEL AMONG THE ROMANI OF FRANCE, I begin to notice a peculiar symbol. At first, I stumble upon it only at rare moments. It's here and there: a minuscule emblem on the tail end of a caravan traveling down the road, furtive graffiti on a cement wall encircling a hidden encampment, a charm on a gold chain around someone's neck as he passes by. But soon my eyes are attuned to it, and this enigmatic symbol becomes obvious and commonplace—hidden, unspoken, yet flaunted out in the open. To most *gadjé* who deign to notice, it's nothing but the image of a hedgehog. To the Gypsies, however, it's a totem of cultural identity.

I soon learn that in Romanès, the hedgehog is known with great affection as a *niglo*. In French, however, this bizarre yet undeniably cute little animal is spoken of with fierce Gallic wrath as *un hérisson*—followed often by an emphatic and learned discourse on the swiftest poisons or surest traps to keep your garden safe from its passage. The *niglo* is a mammal—but not akin to a rat, as the French may warn you. The hedgehog makes its home neither in the open grasslands nor the safety of the forest, but hidden away safely in burrows beneath shrubs or the borderlands of hedgerows—nether regions no other animals desire as homes. And it's nocturnal, trespassing on France's native soil only under cover of darkness. On its back, a hedgehog wears a protective coat of keratin "prickles," a deterrent to attacks from the far greater and far larger world. With all this rolling around in my head, it becomes clear to me why the Romani feel a special kinship with the *niglo*.

And soon I see *niglos* everywhere. "Niglo" is a common Romanès name among French Gypsies, yesterday and today. At Les Saintes-Maries-de-le-Mer, Romani men wear with pride that golden hedgehog charm on a chain amid the symbols of the cross and other religious icons. A *niglo* ornament is also the preferred adornment to a ring holding the key to the Romani's modern horse. Stickers depicting hedgehogs meanwhile often appear next to license plates on their cars, much as the national oval sticker with an "F" for France does on the *gadjé*'s automobiles. And within the paintings and other artwork by some French Gypsy artists I now notice hedgehogs hidden away in corners like in-jokes, playing miniature guitars around campfires, dancing beneath the full moon. The *niglo* floats around these Romani images like folkloric putti.

Perhaps ironically, the hedgehog is also the delicacy of French Gypsy cuisine. It's one of the rare animals the people of France turn up their collective noses at the thought of eating. Yet, as French photographer Juliette Lasserre remembered, Django caught *niglos* in *La Zone* outside Paris in the 1930s for his mother Négros to cook around their caravan fire. Lasserre was present at one such feast, and the *niglo* was sublime.

Hunting a *niglo* is a far more complicated affair than stealing chickens or tickling trout. This hunting venture requires wiles and, in particular, a good nose. Gypsies train dogs to track *niglos* much as pigs are used to root out truffles. Once a dog corners a *niglo*, the hedgehog is chased into a cloth sack and clubbed on the head to still it. A good hedgehog-hunting dog is invaluable and treated like royalty, living a life of canine luxury. Once in a great while, a legendary *niglo* dog comes along and is spoken of ever after, remembered with reverence.

Hedgehogs boast a dark, rich meat. One Gypsy jazzman describes it for me as gamy yet succulent and delicate—"But if it's cooked poorly, it can be *détestable!*" he alerts me with a visible shudder. Old-time hunters advise that *niglos* are best when caught in autumn after the animals have put on fat for the winter's hibernation. To enhance the flavor, a special process is involved, as the poet Serge remembers: "Before cooking the *niglo*, place it for one night on the roof of *une verdine*, so that it bathes in the moonglow, which makes it taste better!"

The dilemma for hedgehog cuisine is getting rid of the inedible prickles. Several tricks have been crafted. Some Romani poke a hole in the hedgehog's hide, then blow into the carcass, inflating it until the skin is taut so the prickles may be easily shaved away with the honed blade of the hunter's knife. Serge describes another solution: "One scalds the *niglo* to easily pluck out the prickles, guts it, and then there's nothing more to do but fry it." As well as being fried, *niglos* are cooked on a spit over open flames, stewed in a ragoût with onions and tomatoes, or made into a lasagne, as another Romani guitarist tells me, practically licking his lips at the thought.

The classic recipe, however, requires Gypsy enterprise in using ingredients found along the road. In this fashion, the *niglo* is roasted in a clay sarcophagus—*en civet*, as the Romani say. With its prickles still in place, the hedgehog is sliced open across the belly and gutted, saving the liver as the supreme delicacy. After stuffing the *niglo* with fresh rosemary, thyme, and wild garlic, the incision is stitched shut. The hedgehog, prickles and all, is rolled in wet river clay, creating a soccer ball-sized lump that is roasted in the reddest coals of a campfire for an hour or so. When the clay rings to the rap of a knuckle, the shell is broken open, the hardened clay prying away the prickles. With a prayer of *Latcho rhaben*—Romanès for *bon appétit*—the hedgehog is feasted on. As Serge exclaimed, "To dine on a *niglo*, ah, what splendor!" And as still another Gypsy tells me in a near whisper as if letting me in on an arcane secret, "*C'est formidable!*"

Legendary Gitan banjo virtuoso Auguste "Gusti" Malha first sang an ode to the hedgehog. With his epochal composition "La valse des niglos"—The Waltz of the Hedgehogs—Gusti not only crafted a masterpiece of *valse manouche*. He also paid homage to a way of Romani life.

Gusti came from one of the great Romani musical clans, and here again my own travels take yet another wandering turn. Like the Reinhardt and Ferret families, Gusti's was a long-lived lineage with a legacy intertwined with musette and Gypsy jazz from the beginnings to today. The family's roots were in Catalonia, but family members traveled widely, as depicted in the rainbow of orthographies of their names. In Spanish, they are known as Malha, Malla, or Mala; in Portuguese, Mailhes; and in French, Maille. And the clan included no less than a musette pioneer (Gusti himself), a beatified saint (Ceferino Jiménez "El Pelé" Malla), an astonishing child prodigy (Jacques "Montagne" Mailhes), two more "mountains" of Gypsy jazz (Jacques "Montagne" Mala and Jean "Montagne" Maille), two Gypsy beboppers (René "Néné" Mailhes and Christian Escoudé). And more. It's a family saga of saints and sinners, alternately proud and sad, its history succinctly summed up in the melody of "La valse des niglos," Gusti's simple remembrance of things past.

To learn more about Gusti's legacy—as well as the Romani's intriguing hedgehog totem—I've searched out recordings of "La valse des niglos." These prove to be surprisingly rare items. Today, the song's a recognized classic, and most every current Gypsy jazz band has their own version. But the song appears not to have been recorded with any frequency in the 1930s; perhaps at the time it was more of a Romani campfire favorite than a dance hall hit. And sadly, there are no known recordings of Gusti performing his own melody—at least one has not yet been found among the piles of dusty 78s in *les puces* or in a Romani record collection secreted away in a caravan.

Gusti secured a copyright on the song in 1939 via Léon Agel Musique, although it's likely he composed and was playing it in the dance halls years before. Sheet-music publication usually coincided with a recording of the song. On the sheet music, Gusti is listed as co-composer with Jean Davon, an obscure accordionist. Davon likely simply knew how to read music and was able to transcribe Gusti's song into notation, a common occurrence with Romani musicians including Django. Eventually, I track down the earliest known surviving version of the melody—Baro Ferret and Le Trio Ferret's recording from March 2, 1939, alive with a charm all its own. Through the oracle of Baro's guitarwork, I can imagine Gusti alongside accordionists Davon or Émile Vacher on a wild night in a *bal musette* unreeling the waltz on his banjo with all the flourish and virtuosity that inspired Django.

According to legend, Gusti learned this flair from that man of the shadows, Mattéo Garcia. This Garcia may have been Gusti's teacher or just his *copain*, but together their influence on the music is primal. Vacher and the other accordionists composed numerous—as well as numerous *forgettable*—musette waltzes that were cheerful dance ditties riding on major-key harmonies. Yet Gusti and Mattéo added something more, that inscrutable Romani sensibility the *bal* musicians labeled *rabouine*. Along with Poulette Castro, these Gypsy banjomen introduced minor-key melodies, adding deeper flavor to their compositions. At the time, minor-key melodies were rarities. In early music, the Catholic church proscribed their use. Even by the 1920s, the minor *notes bleu* were heard as atonal to most ears; simply put, they were *wrong* notes. At best, a minor-key melody was reserved for novelty tunes, such as faux oriental music-hall songs. But to Gusti and the other Romani musette musicians, these notes added that essential emotion.

The Gypsy banjomen further spiced their minor-key melodies with passing seventh and even diminished chords that added tension to the harmony. And within the melody lines, Gusti and the others often struck sixth, ninth, even thirteenth notes. If the minor keys sounded wrong, these notes must have stopped dancers mid-step. Mattéo's "La minch valse," Poulette's "Valse Poulette," and Gusti's "La valse des niglos" were all avant-garde in their day. It was as if Stravinsky had invaded the dance halls.

I learn to play "La valse des niglos" thanks to Francis-Alfred Moerman. Francis had picked out the melody and accompaniment to the waltz in *bals* and bars alongside the Ferret brothers more times than he could ever count. Now, with the required extreme patience, he teaches me.

We begin with the harmony chords. Francis explains that in the old days of the *bals*, the accompanist duty of the Gypsy banjomen was a complex role. Behind a musette accordionist, the single banjo player was often the whole rhythm section. Francis shows me a typical chord progression he played with Sarane and Matelo for "La valse des niglos," as adapted from Baro Ferret and Gus Viseur's December 29, 1939, recording of the song. Rather than sitting on a tonic E minor barre chord and plonking out the three-four-time, Francis's hands are constantly on the go. For each measure, he reaches for a new fingering of the E minor chord, starting at the fifth string of the seventh fret, moving to the sixth string, then up to the fifth fret, descending the fretboard to end with a re-sounding open chord that punctuates the climax of the melodic phrase. And here Francis adds a flourish with a picked melodic counterpoint before jumping back to the next line at the seventh fret. As most *bal* bands lacked a drummer or bassist, the Romani banjoist provided the harmony, rhythm, and walking bass line all at once. And as Francis proves to me, their job in the dance halls was not an easy one.

When my fingers can finally grasp these complex harmonic lines, Francis moves on to the melody. He picks out the theme with an assurance built up from a lifetime performing these songs. And yet he doesn't play it fast. He has no need to show off, as too many modern-day Gypsy jazzmen do when playing these songs at peak velocity for pure bravado effect. Instead, he plays "La valse des niglos" as it was meant to be played—a waltz to which to dance.

As Francis teaches me the theme, Gusti's melody line falls easily beneath my fingers. Whereas some accordion waltzes are a trial to transcribe to guitar, "La valse des niglos" shows the hand of a banjo player as composer rather than an accordionist. The notes are right there within easy reach in the typical "box" pattern of a guitar scale, just as they were long ago on Gusti's *banjo-guitare*.

Francis now teaches me the third, or C section, of the waltz. Legend states that it was the Romani banjomen such as Gusti who amended the early *valses musette* by adding these bridges. Following the thematic A section, the accordionists played a B section typically made up of a dashing melody line of torrid triplets before reaching a crescendo and returning to the theme. Francis explains that *bal* dancers spun to this B section in a twirling dance step nicknamed *la toupie*, named for a child's spinning top. Gusti added his C section, a lyrical counterpoint to the frenzy of the B theme, providing a relaxed melody line giving dizzy dancers a chance to catch their breath before launching back into the A theme. And as Gusti's and the other Gypsies' waltzes were composed in minor keys, they moved to a major key for the C section, further enhancing the mood of their masterpiece *valses manouche*.

Francis and I trade off the solo and rhythm roles—me struggling through Francis's prescribed chord progressions, my fingers then getting all twisted up in the melody like the launch string raveled around that spinning top. Soon, though, despite my rickety, precarious fretwork, I have it down.

And then, as Francis and I play Gusti's ancient *valse*, the song comes to life anew for me. The ambience this simple tune creates is like a spell. Gusti's melody paints aural images that dance before me: I hear a *cirque tsiganes* drama, as if the tune is the buildup for a feat of circus-ring derring-do. I hear the rolling, wandering melody line of ascending and descending arpeggios and chromatic runs, like the wayward journeys of a *roulotte*. I hear the nuances of sublime arabesques and ornamentation, akin to the hand-carved wooden scrollwork that once adorned those old-time Gypsy caravans. And through it all, perhaps masked behind those minor-key arpeggios and the dark seventh-chord harmonies, I hear a certain bittersweet air and world-weary pathos perhaps only describable with music.

Through the years, Gusti certainly became *le professeur* to generations of succeeding Gypsy jazzmen. "La valse des niglos" and his other numerous waltzes set a benchmark for musette that inspired the coming generation of Romani ban-jomen, including Django and the Ferret brothers. With Gusti showing the way, Django soon took the lead. And by the mid 1930s when Django's jazz was first sounding, Gusti sometimes played rhythm behind him in the Quintette du Hot Club de France. The student had followed the teacher—and become the new master.

Gusti's influence continued on, however. In 1940, a nephew of Gusti's appeared one day like an apparition out of *La Zone* to astound the Paris jazz scene. He was a fourteen-year-old prodigy named Jacques Mailhes, and he had learned his way around the fretboard thanks to his uncle Gusti. Now, due to his skill with his guitar, his fellow Romani nicknamed him "Montagne." The moniker meant "mountain;" as a *nom de jazz*, it proclaimed him as simply the pinnacle.

In the few surviving photographs of Montagne, he looks ridiculously young. Montagne's bandmate, violinist Léo Slab, now in his eighties and just recently retired in the south of France, shares with me three carefully kept mementoes of the group. Two of the photographs show the band in poses, publicity shots that once would have appeared in cabaret lightboxes by the entrance doors advertising the night's spectacle. In one image, the musicians stand in a row; in another, in their stage formation. Montagne is dramatically shorter than the rest, still not fully grown. He wears a quaint diminutive bow tie and a satin-lapelled black tuxedo obviously several sizes too large for him as the front overlaps in extra folds, which he tries to hide behind his guitar. His fingers gripping his *grande bouche* Selmer guitar are impossibly delicate, almost fragile looking. And yet while he looks barely fourteen, Montagne certainly does not appear in the least bit self-conscious; on his face is a look of musical knowledge far beyond his years.

In a final photograph from Slab's scrapbook, the band is captured in full flight on a concert stage, Slab arcing his bow above his fiddle, Montagne strumming away with poise and command. And yet still he looks like a schoolboy playing hooky to jam on hot jazz.

Gusti's young protégé first arrived on the Paris scene at a 1940 amateur jazz contest arranged by Charles Delaunay at the grand Salle Gaveau. Remembering the debut of Django, Delaunay kept an eye on this young upstart. Montagne was flanked by two Gypsy cousins—Gusti's son Noye Malha and Djouan Sollero, the son of Gitan guitarist Joseph Sollero. To round out the ensemble's sound, Delaunay steered them to another newcomer, twenty-year-old violinist Léo Slabiak.

Born in Poland in 1920, Slabiak's Jewish parents brought him to Paris when he was young, entering him in the Conservatoire with heady dreams of their child becoming a classical violinist. In a twist of the times, Slabiak's Conservatoire friends taunted him that his music was old-fashioned; they were all enamored with jazz and urged him to listen to Django and Stéphane. One day, Slabiak was at a cinema where the Quintette played during the *entr'acte*, and he became an instant convert. In another ironic twist, with the dawn of World War II and the German Occupation of Paris, Slabiak was banned from studying at the Conservatoire due to his religion. The only music he could now play was jazz—and the German soldiers came to cheer him on at nightclubs.

After Delaunay's introduction and a quick rehearsal backstage at the Salle Gaveau, Montagne and Slab—his *nom de jazz*—took the stage together and stole the show. Together, they formed their own Swing Quintette de Paris and began playing the Parisian cabarets, winning more fans among the German soldiers. Django too heard tell of Montagne, and came to one of the band's rehearsals. Yet when Montagne saw him, he was too frightened to play and set his guitar down. Django had to feign that he was leaving, then hid in the shadows to listen to the young Gitan's impressive fretwork.

When a German officer invited Montagne and Slab on a tour of Germany, Slab diplomatically turned him down. Their band would have posed a triple threat to Nazidom: It was impossible to imagine a jazz band made up of three Gypsies and two Jews (Slab's brother, Charlie, played bass) finding safe passage through Germany. But they found plenty of work in France, playing Paris nightspots and then setting out on an arranged tour of Vichy.

Léo Slab describes for me how he hid his Jewish background behind a false identity. Still, while playing with Montagne in Nice, he was collared by gendarmes and conscripted on the spot into military service for Vichy. Sent to a camp in the Jura Alps, he spent endless days chopping wood. He appealed to the military board, stating he was a classical violinist and woodcutting endangered his hands. Miraculously, he was freed. Slab made his way back to Paris but found the situation too dangerous for a Jew. He went into hiding, setting aside his violin and taking up a machine gun to fight with the *maquis* in the east of France near Vezoul for two years until the war's end.

Montagne and Slab's Swing Quintette sadly lasted but a short time and never recorded. But the music they made is still spoken of as legend among the old-time Romani of Paris.

Throughout it all, Montagne was growing up too fast. He not only played music far beyond his age but also smoked cigarettes, drank, and chased women like an adult, living the musician's life of late nights and little sleep. Slab remembered that the war and Montagne's life as a musician turned him into *un petit animal sauvage*. In 1942, just two years after his debut, Montagne died of consumption. He was just fifteen. Montagne was buried with his guitar nestled alongside him in his coffin like a favorite stuffed animal.

The most famous of all the Malha clan is a man who never played jazz, yet his story is an essential part of the family's identity. I'm back in Les Saintes-Maries-de-la-Mer in the church plaza when a Romani woman dressed in a rainbow of flowing skirts and headscarves stuffs a piece of paper into my hand. I've learned to move like lightning in these incidents; if you don't, the seeming gift of a talisman against the evil eye or a token of sparkling jewelry pinned to your lapel becomes a loud, insistent demand for a return present of money. But when I say *non* to the proffered paper, this woman happily waves to me and walks on. It's then that I examine the piece of paper, which turns out to be a saint's *carte de prière*—a prayer card. On the front is a drawing of a short, stout man, who bears more than a passing resemblance to Gusti. On the flip side is the story of El Pelé, Ceferino Giménez Malla.

While Sainte Sarah may be a saint only in the eyes of the Gypsies, El Pelé is the first beatified martyr of the Romani to be recognized by the Vatican. On a day-to-day basis, the Gypsies may care little about the Vatican's benediction for one of their own, but this status has earned El Pelé a special place in Romani hearts. El Pelé is little known to the rest of the Catholic church, but then again this should come as no surprise: His story is the Romani's story.

Much of El Pelé's past is lost to history, beginning with his birth. Some say he was born in the Catalonian town of Benavente de Segria on the northeastern Spanish border with France; others claim it was in the village of Alcolea de Cinca in Aragon. Even the year of El Pelé's birth is unclear: It was sometime between 1861 and 1865. The confusion is likely due to his being born on the road in a caravan, as his family were Kale, the Spanish Romani, also known as Gitanos.

His father was Juan Jiménez, known among his fellow Gypsies as Tichs. His mother was Josefa Malla.

El Pelé grew up on the road, traveling Catalonia, selling in town markets the baskets his family made or doing farm work in the winter months. As with other Kale children of the time, he rarely stayed in one place long enough to attend school and never learned to read or write. When times were especially hard and there was no food, his family sent him out on the streets to beg.

When he was of age—likely in his middle teens—his father chose and bargained for a wife, a Romani girl named Teresa Jiménez Castro. According to legend, his bride turned her back on El Pelé because she thought he was ugly. Yet a deal had been made between the families, and the two were wed. El Pelé would soon prove his beauty.

He now became a horse and donkey trader, that traditional *métier* of the Romani throughout Europe. Yet as the Catholic Church goes to great pains to point out, El Pelé was always honest in his trading—as proven by the numerous testimonials collected by the church. In the Vatican-approved hagiography, author Father Ángel Fandosa writes, "In the markets where he traded in animals, El Pelé honed the skills of his profession, dexterously using every permitted method of gaining customers: a good joke, some made-up story, colourful comparisons, innocent tricks. But never swindles or lies." Even the title of this hagiography—*Un Gitano con madera de Santo*, A Gypsy with the material, or soul, of a saint—makes it clear the Church believes El Pelé was special, as if few other Gypsies are made of such material.

Not only were El Pelé's saintly horse-trading ethics an example to his fellow Romani, but he also won the respect of the Spanish, serving as an ambassador of goodwill between Gypsies and *gadjé*. And to cap it all, he regularly taught prayers and Holy Scripture to Gypsy and non-Gypsy children alike.

But times were bad in Spain, indiscriminate of background. Fascist Generalissimo Franco had sparked a coup, erupting into civil war by 1936. Both the Church and the Romani were on the losing side. Many Gypsies were fleeing to France, although El Pelé stayed on, even though the church bells in his new home of Barbastro had been silenced by the government. On July 19, 1936, El Pelé was walking through town when he saw soldiers arresting a priest. Pleading for the priest's life, El Pelé too was beaten. When the soldiers found an outlawed rosary in his pocket, he was hauled off to prison. After weeks in jail, the Guardia loaded El Pelé and nineteen other prisoners into a truck early in the morning of August 9, 1939, and drove them to the cemetery. Lined up against the cemetery wall, they were all executed.

El Pelé was canonized as a saint on May 4, 1997, by Pope John Paul II. In his homily, the Pope stated: "The beatified Ceferino Jiménez Malla sowed understanding and solidarity among the Roma. In conflicts, he was a mediator who strengthened relations between Roma and non-Roma." The Pope then reminded Roma who attended the ceremony in large numbers from all over Europe that "it is necessary to overcome old prejudices causing your suffering which is brought about by various forms of discrimination and undesirable marginalisation." No doubt he was preaching to the converted.

In the postwar years, another member of the clan began playing jazz on the Paris scene. No saint, his sins would set him on the run.

Jacques Mala was among the most famous of the Lost Generation of Gypsy jazzmen. These guitarists played their music during the late 1950s, 1960s, and 1970s when there was little opportunity to record in the shadow of rock'n'roll's ascendancy. But that may have suited this Mala just fine.

Jacques Mala took the *nom de jazz* "Jacques Montagne" in honor of his cousin Jacques "Montagne" Mailhes. And he wasn't the last to adopt the nickname: he was followed by another cousin, Jean "Montagne" Maille. In all there were three Montagnes, and counting.

This second Montagne was the quintessential rhythm man, pounding out *la pompe* alongside Nin-Nin, Baro, Matelo, and others of his elders. His rhythm work was renowned for his soft and subtle touch. Jamming with the last of Django's generation, Montagne served as a link between the old and new.

In his own playing, however, Montagne spoke with the voice of a new era of Gypsy jazz. He preferred a *petite bouche* Selmer, or in later years, a large-bodied Favino, fitted with one of the *frères* Guen's Stimer microphonic S.51 pickups. Beloved by Django in his bebop years, the Stimer gave Montagne that same muscular sound, the bane of many modern jazz guitarists. While other Romani beboppers such as René Mailhes, Laro Sollero, and Django's own Lousson and Babik were turning to American Gibson electric guitars—ES-175s and ES-335s with their warm, woody tone—Montagne remained true to Django's legacy as well as faithful to the power possible from a loudly amplified Selmer. He even fretted his guitar with just two fingers in an attempt to channel Django's sound. And fired by Django's bebop, he fashioned a hard-edged jazz.

In retrospect, this seems only fitting. Montagne himself led a hard life. Details of that life are difficult to come by, even among the Romani who knew him well. When I ask about Montagne, no one seems to know much. His birthdate and birthplace appear unknown, details of his jazz career—and "other" careers—are sketchy. He would surface to play a gig, then disappear again, his long silences leaving fans to give him up for lost. No one's even certain if he's alive or dead today.

In the 1960s and 1970s, Montagne stepped out from the back of the bandstand to spark his own ensemble. With his cousins Jean "Cérani" Maille and Jacquet Mailles as well as Chatenout Garcia backing him, Montagne unreeled his bebop. He supplanted Duke Ellington's stately old "Caravan" in his repertoire with Dizzy Gillespie's new "Night in Tunisia," and on private recordings of him playing at Baro's La Lanterne and other dives, he'd jam on the song for upwards of seven minutes. Montagne recorded just once as a bandleader, on a 1970s four-song EP released on the all-but-forgotten Context International label. His bebop here on his original compositions such as "Canone" and "X Man" was wild and unruly, teetering on the brink of being out of control. When he soloed, his sound was shocking, abrupt. It was Montagne's own style, his soul given voice, unique and eccentric and uncommercial, as if he didn't care if the rest of the world wanted to plug their ears from its assault. And through the nights, he played this bebop in some of the shadiest bars Paris had to offer—La Véranda in *les puces* at Saint-Ouen and especially La Lanterne.

Montagne and Baro formed a certain friendship at La Lanterne. And according to legend, after Baro's "retirement," it was Montagne who took over running his underworld enterprises. Yet one day the heat got too close, and Montagne went on the run. He simply disappeared for his own good into the shadows of the Gypsy world. He lived on the road, hidden from the gendarmes—and from the jazz world as well.

I'm talking now with Swiss guitarist Fere Scheidegger, leader of the venerable Hot Strings band. Fere is a guitarist who combines the dazzle of Django with the beauty of B. B. King, playing those perfect notes highlighting his virtuosity. At his guitar shop in Berne, Fere is reminiscing about one of his band's tours that took them across the south of France in 1989. After a day in the Riviera sun, they came to the town of Béziers. Setting up to play one evening, out of the night appeared Jacques Montagne. Fere gladly—if quizzically—shook his hand. Montagne looked tan and fit and relaxed, and he still wore his grand Djangoesque moustache. Fere invited the "retired" Montagne to play, and he joined in with the band, his licks as fluid as ever. He obviously was not out of practice. At the end of the *soirée*, Montagne said his *au revoirs* and disappeared once again, back into the shadows.

The Malha clan still can be heard playing their Gypsy jazz several nights each week in Paris. René Mailhes has cut several albums of stylish modern bebop and performs in concerts in the capital. But it's to hear another guitarist of the clan that has pushed me tonight to climb Paris's own "mountain," La Butte de Montmartre.

What La Butte lacks in altitude, it makes up for in steepness. I'm hiking from the ancient convent at place des Abbesses, zigzagging my way up the narrow streets running like a labyrinth of switchbacks. I take one of the many shortcut stairways, teetering and leaning and impossibly steep. I come out by the old Moulin de la Galette, once the site of Montmartre's most famous *bal* as painted by Renoir, the windmill arms now still and eerily skeletal against the night sky. I swing around past Le Lapin Agile, the bohemian café where in 1910 artists tied a brush to a donkey's tail, dipped it in paint, backed him up to a canvas, and created modern art. As I continue to climb, through the darkness ahead of me now looms Sacré-Cœur, glowing like a white ghost in the moonlight.

Walking the cobblestones, I suddenly enter the carnival of place du Tertre. Here, Paris is at its Disneyfied worst. The old *place* is simply too beautiful—the perfect picture of France in the minds of millions of tourists. And the tourists come in hordes, including myself. Beneath the gnarled trees in the gorgeous *place* are the essential painters with their easels, strolling musicians playing *valses* on their essential accordions, and bistros with *terrasses* full of diners and the essential hustling waiters serving *steaks-frites*. Still, one would have to have a hard heart not to thrill to it all.

At one of these tourist oases, Romani musicians have played Gypsy jazz for generations now. Au Clarion des Chasseurs lacks atmosphere, good food, or even decent wine, but the music makes it all worthwhile. In an out-of-the-way corner of the dining room, a small dais serves as the musicians' stage. A clothesline runs overhead: for decades now the audience has pinned to it banknotes with song requests penned on them; the guitarists reel the bills in and do their duty.

From the 1970s through the early 1990s, this stage was home to Maurice Ferret and Joseph Pouville. Joseph was known by the nickname "Babagne," French argot for "prisoner," given to him because of his love of striped shirts. Maurice was called "Gros Chien"—Big Dog—simply because he was a big man. When Maurice held his *grande bouche* Favino fitted with a Stimer, he almost dwarfed the large guitar. And of course, Maurice was yet another cousin to the Ferret brothers. The duo recorded two classic LPs—the straightforward *Hommage à Django* from 1970 and the stylish *Le Train Gitan* in 1975, both released in limited runs on the label Les Tréteaux by the restaurant itself and still for sale at the counter for years after. Yet the studio sound of the albums failed to capture the good times that ran here late into the nights, filled by Gros Chien's trademark sound of a Stimer pickup run through an American Fender Twin amp. Maurice Ferret's guitar tone sums up a whole era of Gypsy jazz.

After his longtime *pôte* and accompanist died in the mid 1990s, Gros Chien could not bear to perform any more on the stage they shared for thirty-seven years. Maurice moved down into Paris and played with other Romani and *gadjé* from a new generation at new restaurants. But it wasn't the same. He too passed away in 1999.

Their place at Au Clarion des Chasseurs was taken by Jeannot "Titote" Malla, a Gypsy jazzman of the Gibson Generation who learned to play from his elder uncle, Gusti, as well as Baro. Playing with him was Tchouta Adel, the long-haired son of old-time guitarist and violinist Spatzo Adel, part of the Adel clan into which Joseph Reinhardt married. Tchouta left after a couple years, and his chair was filled by none other than Ninine Garcia, venturing out of La Chope des Puces.

I settle onto a stool and sip a welcome glass of Normandy *cidre*, listening to Jeannot and Ninine. When they play in *les puces*, their repertoire is jazz *à la* Django. But here the tourists request *chanson* and pop tunes—*soupe*, as the Gypsy jazzmen call it. Yet like the Romani musicians who traveled from town to town in bygone days playing whatever songs were called for, Jeannot and Ninine oblige. And perhaps this is only fitting, as here things have come full circle: Just as a Malha and a Garcia—Gusti and Mattéo—played together in the *bals musette* a century ago, now here are Jeannot Malla and Ninine Garcia playing through the Paris night.

Much has changed in the world around the Romani since the days when Gusti played "La valse des niglos" in the old-time *bals*. La Zone in all its horrors—and glories—is now long gone. In its place is the asphalt of La Périph, itself a sort of wall around Paris. Beyond the ring road rests a new zone known in sociological analyses as *La Ceinture Rouge*—the Red Belt—a noose of poor villages-cum-suburbs girdling Paris. As the city center has become gentrified, these *banlieues* are where the poor, the immigrants, the working class, and those who merely can't afford the extreme rents of Paris have been pushed. These were the suburbs—places such as Clichy-sous-Bois and Neuilly-sur-Marne—that erupted in riots during fall 2005. Over the years, many of the Romani moved from *roulottes* in La Zone into grim concrete apartments in outer suburbs. Or they simply parked their *campines* further out of the city. In far too many ways, *La Zone* lives on.

On September 19, 1979, the European Union approved the Convention of Berne, which, in Annexes II and III, outlines regulations and fines outlawing the "detention, transportation, and keeping" of *Erinaceus europaeus*, the hedgehog. This seemingly put an end to a long cultural tradition of *niglo* hunting and cuisine.

Yet in a Gypsy encampment outside Paris to the north, old ways live on. I'm walking among the *caravanes* with a Romani jazzman. Behind us, skirting the encampment, is La Butte-Pinçon, a vast, dark forest of trees and dense under-brush. Here, French royalty once had a favored hunting lodge. And here today, this Gypsy tells me, waving his hand at La Butte, the woods are still home to hedgehogs. And with a sly wink, he invites me back in the autumn when the *niglos* are ready. There will be music, he says, and a grand feast.

ELEVEN

Au Son des Guitares
On the Trail of Patotte Bousquet

T HE NOTORIOUS MARSEILLE NIGHTCLUB Au Son des Guitares does
not open its door until midnight. When it closes, I have yet to discover.
In a city famous for infamous bars, *boîtes du nuit*, *boui-bouis*, sailors' dives,
bordels, and worse, Au Son des Guitares defies most descriptions. It's a Corsican
bar renowned for its Gypsy music—two traits that would never win it inclusion
in any travel guidebook. Its location hidden away on a shady backstreet just off
Le Vieux Port is not on the tourist itinerary. And the bouncer who greets you in
the early hours of the morning when you ring the doorbell is not likely to win a
congeniality contest. Suffice it to say that this is not a bar to which you go to try
the happy hour hors d'oeuvres, or even to cry in a lonely beer. You venture here
to plot a robbery. Or a revolution.

Au Son des Guitares translates literally as "At the Sound of the Guitars," but
the meaning runs much deeper to *Corsicos*. There was a movie from 1936 that
explained it well. Entitled *Au Son des Guitares*, it starred classic heartthrob Tino
Rossi, that Corsican idol beloved of all women and envied by all men. Rossi plays
Bicchi, a poor Corsican fisherman who happens to be graced with golden vocal
cords and is ready to strum his guitar and burst into joyous song with his fellow
Corsican fishermen at any moment. Bicchi is taken under the wing of a va-
cationing Parisian siren, who carries him back to the Big City like a quaint
holiday souvenir. Of course the siren soon forgets her curio when she's home
amidst the glamor of Paris, and the usual catastrophes await poor Bicchi—far
from his beloved Corsica, he wanders Paris, a stranger in a strange land without a
bed to sleep in, food for his empty stomach, or a *sou* in his pocket. Even his faith in

himself falters, until he has a brief moment of heady success as a cabaret singer in a nightclub. Yet the songs he sings—his native Corsican *chansons*—remind him of home and family and goodness and truth, and so he makes a joyous return to his native Ajaccio—to the sound of the guitars.

In Marseille, Au Son des Guitares was a home away from home, a reminder of Corsica for the price of a glass of *gratte-gorge*—literally, throat-scraping rough wine. Just as Paris served as a stepping stone to prosperity for Auvergnat immigrants and the *bals musette* as their nighttime Eldorados, Marseille was a foothold on a new life for Corsicans. It was also a land of exile for a dangerous few. And so founder and owner Jean Casanova created Au Son des Guitares as a nocturnal haven for his expatriate compatriots, a reminder of *l'Isula Rossa* far from home on this new, unfriendly beachhead.

The club soon became a port of call for Corsican musicians. Guitarist Paolo Quilici played his glorious Corsican waltzes from this stage. Singer-guitarist Antoine Bonelli recorded two albums of Corsican *chanson* here in the 1950s, fittingly paying homage to the bar in their titles *Un Soir au Son des Guitares*. *Chanteurs* Jean Casi, Michel Deïdda, Lorenzo, and the star duo Régina and Bruno Bacara intermixed Corsican popular songs and polyphonic a capella. The music at Au Son des Guitares also attracted Gypsy musicians from across the Midi—flamencos and Gypsy jazzmen alike. In 1959, a Gitan guitarist named Étienne "Patotte" Bousquet first performed at the bar. His guitarwork was such a hit with the *Corsicos* that he was hired to play every night thereafter.

Bousquet played his Gypsy jazz inspired by Django as well as an acquired Corsican repertoire. While he jammed with many others—including Joseph Reinhardt during one of his visits to the bar—his sole accompanist was also a *Corsico*, guitarman Gérard Cardi. Corsicans and Romani often jammed together, sharing the bar's small stage and eventually influencing each other's music. As befitting the bar's ambience, Au Son des Guitares became the source of the Corsican connection in Gypsy jazz. And like the pilgrimage festival just down the coast at Les Saintes-Maries-de-la-Mer, Au Son des Guitares became another crossroads of Romani music.

And so I took my wife to Au Son des Guitares for a romantic evening.

My wife's up for such adventures. Her name's Sigrid, an old world Scandinavian name and part of her family heritage. But in her travels as an archaeologist through Italy and South America, she's largely given up on the name: No one speaking a Latin language seemed able to pronounce it. When a Tuscan friend misspoke her name as "Tigra," she accepted the new name. It's fitting, anyway. Raised on a ranch in Montana, she learned to ride horse at age five and saddled up for her first cattle drive in the mountains when she was seven. So when I explain about Au Son des Guitares and its Gypsy jazz history, she is ready and willing.

We arrive in Marseille via Le Panier, the old Provençau district to the west of the port. Coming over the hilltop, the whole of the city opens out before us, burnished in gold, alluring in the afternoon Mediterranean sun, even now in November. The city is crowned by Notre-Dame-de-la-Garde on the signal hill overlooking the sea. The neo-Byzantine basilica on the limestone outcropping is visible from most anywhere in the city and long served as the sailors' church, bedecked with ex-voto offerings from seamen who returned safely from their journeys.

If Notre-Dame-de-la-Garde guards over the city's soul, Le Vieux Port is at its heart. In the glory days, the sailors and fishermen set sail from the Old Port, which then as now is lined with quays fronted by small sailors' bars, fish-sellers stalls, and boat-stock chandlers. The port is a long rectangular basin cut into the city. It was once the outlet of the River Lacydon, since covered over. Today, Le Vieux Port is largely a yacht marina, yet one filled still by a fleet of morning fishing boats and even wooden three-mast sailing ships. The port's guarded at the entrance by the opposing Forts Saint-Jean and Saint-Nicholas, grim bastions tempered by their ramparts of ocher stone. At the harbor entrance stands the lighthouse, Phare de Sainte Marie, guiding boats home—or serving as a symbol of a far-off and unreachable home to the inmates sentenced to the prison fortress on the island of the Chateau d'If.

The River Lacydon's place in the city has been taken by La Canebière, the city's main street, once made up of markets where one could buy all the wonders of the world, licit and illicit. The route early on connected the port to the fields where hemp was grown to be used in the ships' rigging ropes; *les chènevières*—the hemp fields—gave their name to the street. The *marseillais* were so proud of their main street that Dumas wrote in *Le Comte de Monte-Cristo*, "If Paris had La Canebière, Paris would be a second Marseille." Gone today are the seedy and salacious gangster bars and shell games that earned it the nickname of "Can o' Beer" thanks to the American GIs and sailors. Now, La Canebière gloats in the dull respectability of banks and business.

Much of the rest of Marseille still lives up to reputation, however. As Flaubert wrote, Marseille is "a babel of all nations"—from the native Nams tribe to the founding Greeks and Phoenicians; the late-arriving Romans, Ségo-bridgians, and Vikings; and more-recent immigrants from Italy, Spain, North Africa, and Corsica. Each has brought its native vices to this wide-open port city. As oh-so-British traveler Basil Woon warned the world in his proper 1929 handbook to the respectable highlife, *From Deauville to Monte Carlo: A Guide to the Gay World of France*:

> If you are interested in how the other side of the world lives, a trip through old Marseilles—by daylight—cannot fail to thrill, but it is not wise to venture into this district at night unless dressed like a stevedore and well armed. Thieves, cutthroats, and other undesirables throng the narrow alleys, and sisters of scarlet sit in the doorways of their places of business, catching you by the sleeve as you pass by. The dregs of the world are here, unsifted. It is Port Said, Shanghai, Barcelona, and Sidney combined. Now that San Francisco has reformed, Marseilles is the world's wickedest port.

It may have relinquished that crown of thorns, but Marseille still remains the French connection to the world's evil corners. This is a city that has long been dedicated to serious crime—although with its growing affluence today, the dark dealings may now not be in drugs and white slavery but in real estate and redevelopment.

As such, Marseille still is passed over in modern guidebooks as a city that's best skirted around in favor of the quaint graces of Provence. But that's just missing the good stuff.

I climb with my wife up Le Panier, the streets like stony scales over the carapace of some ancient reptile. They lead us upward past the aptly named marketplace at place des Pistoles to the place des Moulins where windmills once powered grain mills. Above our heads, clotheslines are strung from building to building, hung with laundry like multicolored prayer flags—never underestimate the picturesqueness of laundry. As we try to find our way through the maze, black cats appear out of the growing darkness, never crossing our path, but skulking along the side of the road ahead, then disappearing into the shadows— only to reappear again down the road.

Suddenly, Tigra and I find ourselves at the edge of Le Vieux Port. The sky has turned into a rainbow from the blood-red horizon to orange and gold azure to violet and dark blues, reflected in the sea, cut now by the old ferry crisscrossing the port. We make our way along the quays past ships' chandleries ripe with their tar smells from the miles of rope, bolts of sailcloth, monstrous anchors, and ancient brass diving helmets. Hidden away among them is Le Bar de la Marine, one of France's great unsung landmarks. This bar was first celebrated in Marcel Pagnol's theatrical and subsequent film *trilogie marseillaise*—*Marius* (1931), *Fanny* (1932), and *César* (1936). Together, this trilogy was a salty drama of everyday Marseillais life, played out around games of *belote* and glasses of cloudy *pastis*.

Settling into a table at the back of the reborn bar, we feel like we've taken a wrong turn back in time. The ferry still docks out front and *pastis* remains the favored drink. While Paris is tragically hip, Marseille is unapologetically itself—sun-bronzed, well-fed, and in no hurry whatsoever. I get the distinct impression the *marseillais* wouldn't trade places with the *parisien* for anything.

Just as much as bouillabaisse, *pastis* symbolizes Marseille. Gold like the Mediterranean sun and Provençal hills, it's an age-old nostrum tasting of the land's native herbs—aniseed, vervain, cassis, poppy, coriander, birch, savory, cumin, and whatever else a distiller chooses to infuse into the pastiche. And of course the local slang is legion: *une pastaga, une fly*, or simply, *une jaune*. We order *une mauresque*—Ricard mixed with a dash of the almond liquor of the Moors. Pouring in the requisite splash of water, the golden elixir turns as cloudy as truth.

With a long time to wait before Au Son des Guitares opens its door, Tigra and I settle into a quayside restaurant for dinner. After bouillabaisse, Marseille is also renowned for its *bourride*, a fish stew dabbed with *rouille*—that saffron-and-pepper sauce so richly, so gloriously, so impossibly red. We sit out along Le Vieux Port, braving the cruel, early seasonal gusts of the mistral and watch the little ferry come and go across the bay. At last the stars shine, and it's time for music.

Down a backstreet off Le Vieux Port, Au Son des Guitares awaits. Turning off rue Paradis, we come to a warren of dark side streets weighed down by time and grime and home to obscure bistros, *boucheries*, and hotel rooms to rent by the night, hour, or maybe even minute. These streets boast all the charm of *coupe-gorges*—cut-throat alleyways—but we're not waiting around to discover if they live up to their advertised ambience. Oddly, at the center of this neighborhood is the old Opéra de Marseille. The city is justly proud of its grand theater building and long ago adopted opera as one of its beloved musics. Just around the corner to the shadowy side of the Opéra is Au Son des Guitares. While the Opéra gives the bar the cold shoulder, Au Son des Guitares seems to be biding its time, as if it's waiting to stab the Opéra in the back.

The streets of this neighborhood are named for famed French playwrights, perhaps a joust at respectability. Au Son des Guitares is at 18 rue Corneille. Yet the bar is just a locked door in a dark street. In photos of the past, the entrance was surmounted by a neon sign, the bar's name spelled out in a stylish 1950s cursive surrounded by musical notes and a guitar. But that's long gone. These days, there's only a doorbell.

Tigra and I check our watches and see that midnight has come and gone. Still, there's no sign of life here and certainly nothing to make you think you're welcome at Au Son des Guitares.

And so I ring the bell. After a lengthy wait, the door at last opens, and a maître d' steps out onto the threshold. This is not your usual, welcoming host of the gracious grin and warm handshake. Instead, he's a shaved-head African dressed in a zoot suit, his wide frame and massive shoulders filling and blocking the doorway. He's obviously less of a host, more of a heavy. With a bouncer's eye watching out for trouble before it begins, he looks me up and down. He appears a bit startled to find two Americans at his door. Finally—and reluctantly—he steps out off the threshold and simply says, "*Entrée.*"

We cross over the threshold and into a pitch-black hallway. It's not that it's just dark here, it's that there's a deep, total, absolute absence of light. The bouncer shuts the door behind us, staying outdoors to examine the night. Inside, there's nothing for my eyes even to adjust to. Straight on, I run into a wall, and am forced to walk with my hands outstretched to feel my way. To the left is another wall, but to the right the darkness opens out. With Tigra's hand on my shoulder, I'm the blind leading the blind—somewhere.

I take a couple more steps forward, and seeing a glow of blue light, follow it. The wall ends, and then to our left the bar opens out. The room's bathed in the blue, shining in beams down from the ceiling while a fog of cigarette smoke drifts upward. The main room is small with an oppressively low ceiling, all made smaller by the smoke. A bar runs across the far wall. The interior is U-shaped, with another, smaller room of *couchettes* around the corner. In this low and tight room, I have a momentary feeling of being trapped.

Facing the bar, a wall is populated with photographs of the *boîte* from the 1950s: Bousquet and Cardi jamming for that blonde Barbie, Sylvie Vartan, and other notables, including France's answer to Elvis, Johnny Hallyday; Bousquet standing in front of the old club with painted name above the doorway; Bouquest and Cardi accompanying Joseph Reinhardt. At the end of the room is a small plinth that serves as a stage. Here is where Bousquet and Cardi set up to play most nights, and it's here where Nin-Nin and other passing Gypsy musicians joined them to jam. Tonight, the music plays on: A Corsican band, equipped with an electric piano and electric guitars, again plays Corsican *chansons*, a remembrance of the island just across the Mediterranean waters.

Still, Au Son des Guitares is far removed from Hemingway's clean, well-lighted place. There are no frills, no frippery here. The sole attempt at atmosphere comes from the blue lighting, the only decoration seems to be the cigarette smoke.

The French are particular in their slang descriptions defining different types of dives. We Americans have just that one term, but French argot is ripe with categorization to a near-scientific degree. A dive of a café or a grubby little restaurant is derided under the genus *boui-boui*. A crummy dance hall is *un guinche*, taken from the slang term for dancing, *guincher*. *Bals musette* were known affectionately in slang as *un baloche*, an Auvergnat term; or *un bastringue*, pure *langue verte*—the "green language" of the gutters. Nightclubs were originally denounced as *une boîte de nuit*—a box of the night—a derisive term that's become common usage, although *une boîte* is also used unkindly to describe any bare-bones bar or café. *Un bobinard* is a lowdown bar, but one usually enlivened by music of some sort. A sailor's bar is *un bar à matelots*, the description itself serving as ample warning. *Un tripot* is a bar with illicit gambling or betting while *un tapis franc* is a thieves' den. *Un assommoir* is a gin mill, or more literally, a place to bludgeon yourself into unconsciousness.

Au Son des Guitares defies any of these categorical descriptions. Instead, it falls under the general term, *un bouge*—a dive of a bar haunted by riffraff, gangsters, B-girls, prostitutes, and more. *Un bouge* is a clip joint where the wayward traveler shouldn't be surprised to find a full underworld résumé of drug dealing, immigrant smuggling, gun running, plot hatching, and revolution making. And so we settle in for a night on the town.

Ironically, the man who made Marseille's Corsican paradise famous was a Gypsy from Spain. Patotte Bousquet spent his life roaming the Midi coast, playing his guitar in bars like Au Son des Guitares and at the Romani pilgrimage to Les Saintes-Maries-de-la-Mer. Why would the *Corsicos* hire a Romani *musico* to remind them of their home island? Why not? Like Gypsy musicians before and after him, Bousquet had the ability to learn most any musical style, assimilate it, and play it back again better than ever.

In the few surviving photographs, there appear to be two sides to Bousquet. Examining that wall of pictures at Au Son des Guitares from the 1950s and 1960s, Bousquet wears a warm smile that doesn't look to be merely a showman's stage grin. Playing music, he looks kindly. He exudes a paternal image, approachable, down to earth. Above the collar of his simple yet distinguished suit coat, his face is deeply tanned from the year-round Mediterranean sun. In some photos, the shadow of a thin, Djangoesque moustache runs across his upper lip. He was not a tall man, yet he was graced with long, spidery fingers, the better to grasp the neck of a guitar.

And then there was seemingly another side to Bousquet that appears in other photographs, such as the images glowering from the picture-sleeve covers of his 1960s EPs. Older now, he looks tired, disillusioned—even though the 45's cover proclaims him *L'extraordinaire guitariste gitan*. The smile's gone now. His cheekbones are chiseled, his skin leathery. Bousquet's rough intensity shows through in the furrow of his brow above dark, dark eyes and the iron grip he has on his electric guitar, as if he's strangling its neck. In truth, his intensity could at times be frightening: Bousquet was legendary for strumming his guitar with such force that he at times broke all six strings in one swipe of his pick.

Bousquet was of a new generation of Romani musicians who followed after Django. Performing for nightclub audiences from Paris to the Riviera, Django's melodies were a well-known repertoire of crowd pleasers sure to win them applause and tips. Yet Django's fame did not mean instant success for other Gypsy jazz musicians in the 1950s. Instead, they played on much as Django's father had half a century earlier, wandering Europe seeking work, strumming out dance tunes in *bals*, busking on café *terrasses*, or creating the background musical ambience in cabarets. For the most part, Bousquet and the other Romani musicians remained a caste of entertainers, often playing for pitiful pay.

Still, Bousquet had Django as inspiration. Django, with his Gypsy jazz, was a vision of a sense of cultural value: Django had become a Romani king with a guitar for his sceptre. Yet even among his fellow Gypsies, Django's music was fast becoming only an oral tradition—and verging on becoming just a memory. Now, the music Bousquet made over the coming decades of the 1960s and 1970s served to keep Django's legacy vital—at least among fellow Romani—when it was on the verge of dying out and being forgotten. If Gypsy jazz began with Django, Bousquet was an essential link that kept it alive.

Like Poulette Castro, Gusti Malha, and Django himself, Bousquet began as a banjoman. He was born in 1925 in the Spanish Catalonian city of Figueras, birthplace as well of Salvador Dalì. Here, Bousquet learned first banjo and then guitar from his father, starting to play when he was about age six. At fifteen, he and accordionist Émile Decotty set off to play in North Africa during the World War II years. After the war but while he was still in his twenties, Bousquet joined the band of accordionist Fredo Gardoni, whom Django too once accompanied. At other times through the years, he plonked out the rhythm lines for an accordion band in a Marseille *bal*. These days, no one seems to remember whose band it was or even where the dance hall stood—perhaps a sidestreet in Le Panier, in the shadow of Notre-Dame-de-la-Garde, or maybe one of the alleyways neighboring Le Vieux Port. In January 1943, much of Le Panier was razed by the occupying Nazis and Vichy's Police Nationale led by another man named Bousquet, the fascist René Bousquet, to ferret out Jews and destroy the *résistance*'s base of operations in the backstreet warrens. With this destruction went much of the city's old *quartier* as well as its history.

In 1959, Patotte Bousquet met *Corsico* guitarist Gérard Cardi, and they formed a duet that performed for the next sixteen years at Au Son des Guitares. These days, Cardi proudly tells me they played *every* night. But even given time off for good behavior on Christmas and their visits to Les Saintes-Maries-de-la-Mer, that's still some five thousand shows—far better than Scheherezade's thousand-and-one-night run. Their repertoire for all those nights included Django's Gypsy jazz, swing *valses*, Corsican waltzes, and other Corsican popular tunes. In Cardi, Bousquet was lucky enough to find one of the perfect accompanists, akin only to Joseph Reinhardt, capable of playing a rock-steady rhythm with flair and flourish. And Bousquet knew he was lucky. Cardi was one of several fine Corsican guitarists along with Paolo Quilici, Gérard Poletti, Jean-Michel Panunzio, and Jean-François Oricelli who traveled back and forth between the island and France—and usually France meant just Marseille.

The Gypsy and Corsican musicians played many of the same nightclubs along the Riviera, often joining forces in bands. Bousquet's cousin, Paul "Tchan Tchou" Vidal played and recorded for years with Corsican guitarman François Codaccioni behind him. Django's sideman Marcel Bianchi was a *Corsico* born in Marseille in 1911 who first led his own ensemble at age seventeen in the sailors' dives off Le Vieux Port before coming to Paris in search of jazz. Sarane and Matelo Ferret often performed in cabarets in Corsica as well as Corsican restaurants in Paris; they undoubtedly had a repertoire of Corsican *chanson* they could pick out on their guitars when the island moonlight was shining right. This Corsican connection was essential to Gypsy jazz as the Romani and the *Corsicos* reciprocally influenced each other's musics.

Quilici was the most renowned and stylish of the *Corsico* guitarists. A small, broad man who picked on a grand Favino Enrico Macias jazz guitar, Quilici was prolific in the recording studio, releasing countless EPs and LPs from the 1960s through the 1980s, all flavored by the sun and *joie de vivre* of the island. He and the other Corsican guitarmen played in a style much like the Romani with a strong picking hand and fleet fretting fingers, infused by an admiration for virtuosity. They too played many *valses*, but unlike the dark-timbred *valses manouche* composed in minor keys, the Corsican waltzes such as Quilici's trademark "Les guitares à Paolo" were often gay and lively with a happy-go-lucky Italian air to them. Quilici's repertoire at his base in Ajaccio's cabaret Le Pavillon Bleu also included boléros, tangos, paso dobles, mazurkas, and of course, Corsican *chanson*. But no jazz. American music must have remained foreign to the remote island. Above all, Quilici and the other Corsicans played good-time music without the deep melancholy of the Romani; rarely in the eternal sunshine of *l'Isula Rossa* did guitarists appear inspired to use minor keys.

Bousquet and Cardi epitomize this Romani–Corsican connection. In photographs of them performing at Au Son des Guitares and on the covers of their various EPs, the two musicians share the same two guitars—flamboyant red archtop electrics befitting nightclub stars, with grandiose pickguards ideal for reflecting the spotlight to catch the audience's eyes, pearloid inlays dandying up the necks and showing off their fast fingerwork, and plenty of impressive buttons and switches to push and twirl, guitars like a jet pilot's cockpit. In one image, Bousquet grasps one guitar, Cardi the other. In the next image, they've traded instruments.

If Bousquet had been based elsewhere than Marseille, his music might never have been recorded, never have survived to influence future generations of Gypsy jazzmen.

In Paris, record labels in the 1960s and 1970s turned their backs on Romani music. Fiery Gypsy violin music was once a hot-selling genre, the likes of Yoska Nemeth evoking an exotic night of Caspian caviar and icy vodka in a Russian cabaret in Paris. But now, the labels were onto something new, something infinitely hotter—the proto-rock'n'roll sounds of *yéyé* as played by early swingers like Johnny Hallyday, Claude François, Françoise Hardy, Sylvie Vartan, and the like. "Le Twist" was *le tube*—the hit—and labels, including one-time jazz stalwarts like Disques Vogue, tuned in. Among the Romani, few of the old-school guitarists were offered opportunities to record beyond rare one-night stands such as Nin-Nin's few LPs of the mid 1960s, Baro Ferret's *Swing valses d'hier et d'aujourd'hui* of 1966, and Matelo Ferret's *Tziganskaïa* of 1978. Sessions such as Jo Privat's 1960s *bal musette* revival *Manouche Partie* and Gus Viseur's *Swing Accordéon* of 1971 were anomalies. Even to true jazz fans, Django's music was now stale, outdated. Django was history, a pioneer like Louis Armstrong; aficionados were hip to hard bop and cool, "modern" jazz. Only up-and-coming Gypsy guitarist Paul Pata was able to record an oeuvre during the bad old 1960s, but that's because he played *soupe*—literally "soup," the Romani musicians' derisive slang for popular tunes that were tasty but not filling.

Marseille, however, boasted the hinterlands' label Président, which was sadly out of the spotlight of Paris chic but still attuned to music that sold to its audience in the Midi. Président, as well as the Corsican label Consul, recorded the sound of the southern Gypsies and *Corsico* guitarists that otherwise would likely have left a silent legacy.

In 1959 or 1960, Président released a 25-cm LP entitled *Au Son des Guitares* capturing the ambience of a night in the cabaret. Bousquet's rollicking instrumentals with Cardi are interspersed by Corsican songs by singers Jean Casi, Michel Deïdda, Lorenzo, and the duo Régina et Bruno Bacara. While the *chansons* fall into the categories of either homesick or lovelorn, and thus tender and touching, Bousquet's guitar is downright snarling and mean. This was that other side of his personality that showed up in certain photographs of the man.

Bousquet blazes through the Dixieland classic "Tiger Rag," Gus Viseur's "Flambée montalbanaise," and Guérino's "Brise napolitaine." These latter two were once accordion *valses*, but Bousquet here recasts them as guitar showpieces in the style of the Corsican waltzes, displaying his prowess on the fretboard, his fingers dancing in time.

He then cut two EPs for Président in the mid 1960s showcasing an array from his repertoire. Included were traditional Tziganes tunes like "Les deux guitares" and a growling, guttural "Les yeux noirs." These accompanied a range of songs such as the homesick Catalán anthem "L'Émigrant" and Duke Ellington's "Caravan," imbued with a new sense of Gypsy style. They must have been bravura showpieces to make even the gangsters and B-girls at Au Son des Guitares take notice and offer him a well-earned toast.

As stylish as these EPs were, it was Bousquet's one and only LP that became his most influential recording for the future of Gypsy jazz. Sometime in the late 1960s—the album is undated—Bousquet recorded and released *Hommage à Django*. Many of the twelve songs here were covers of compositions by Django or taken from the old Quintette du Hot Club de France's classic repertoire. Yet Bousquet played with his signature intensity, almost if he was picking out a *yéyé* romp. His slashing version of Django's "Minor Swing" was just over two minutes long, but it was alive with a carnival ride of chromatic runs, chordal octaves, and a dapper brutality. Bousquet's lusty emotion proved inspirational to later generations of Gypsies who took from his LP this version of Django's song almost note for note.

Hommage à Django also included a song listed only as "Valse à Django," a glorious minor-key *valse manouche* that was a tour de force of virtuoso guitar. The melody had actually been composed by Django but never recorded by him. It was through Bousquet's recording (and a near-simultaneous version by Matelo Ferret) that the song—later known as "Montagne Sainte-Geneviève"—survived being forgotten.

The release of *Hommage à Django* was a minor sensation in France at the time. Bousquet and Cardi were suddenly stars. They were brought to Paris to play on several television shows, including Jack Dieval's "Fenêtre sur le Jazz" and a documentary on guitar history hosted by Robert Vidal. They also jammed live on TV with the teenaged Gypsy phenom of the day, Boulou Ferré. Watching clips of these television shows—such as one of Bousquet playing a pop medley of Django's compositions with slick bandleader Claude Bolling—Bousquet looks uncomfortable in the Parisian spotlight. It's as if he were just biding his time until he could hurry back to the dark cavern of Au Son des Guitares.

Bousquet may not have been a composer or a particularly adept jazz improviser. But he had something else—ferocity. Bousquet's playing was from another era. There was no hint of bebop here, nothing of modern jazz. Instead, he played Django's wartime swing sung modern and electric. Modal jazzman Christian Escoudé remembered jamming one night with Bousquet at Au Son des

Guitares: "Now there was *un guitariste* who never had technical problems with his instrument or amplifier: he just plugged in and played! No adjusting the tone, no adjusting the volume; he just played—and he played like a machine gun, *tchu, tchu, tchu!*" The intensity of Bousquet's music, the quicksilver runs, and the Catalan brio with which he dashed off his solos all inspired future generations of Gypsies and *gadjé* alike, convincing them that here was great music. Bousquet held the key, and aspiring players learned his solos note for note and lick for lick along with Django's originals. In the 1960s and into the 1970s, Bousquet's *Hommage à Django* was the most current Gypsy jazz one could find.

And if he played like a fire-and-brimstone preacher proselytizing jazz to his flock, in retrospect that seems only right.

While Bousquet was instrumental in keeping Django's legacy alive, his own fortunes faltered. During his lifetime, his fame was never widespread, his success only meager. It was all emblematic of the life and fortunes of Gypsy jazzmen of the time. He was hailed at Au Son des Guitares and well known among his fellow Romani along the Midi. But he never won the recognition of Django, nor a fraction of his riches.

In 1975, Bousquet gave up on the hardscrabble life of a Romani musician. Bitter and disillusioned, he set aside his flashy red archtop guitar for a better-paying career: He became a *ferrailleur*, scrounging and selling scrap iron like many another Gypsy before and after him. In his later years, he retired from scrap dealing to set up a stand selling shoes and used clothing in Marseille's La Plaine *marché aux puces*. Out on the edge of the city, the flea market is a flash of noise reverberating with color: rag sellers with fashions new and ages old, African gods and trinkets, rap clothing ripoffs, Gypsy fortune-tellers on the prowl, knives of all wicked types, North Africans and Corsicans and Italians on the make—all the remnants of the city's glories spread out for anyone to buy. I ask at a stall selling dusty used records for the music of Patotte Bousquet. The wizened old dealer scrunches his face and says, *"Eh?"* It's obvious he's never heard the name.

Bousquet passed away in Marseille in 1998. Bousquet's son, Antoine—known variously as Tony Manou or simply Tèt—doesn't play. But he did inherit his father's shoes-and-used-clothing stall. He lives in *une campine* and still works the Midi's traveling *puces* today.

Gérard Cardi is still playing his guitar around Marseille. He accompanies a choral ensemble but more often simply jams with friends in the cool of the Mediterranean evenings. Cardi doesn't perform at Au Son des Guitares any more, but he brings alive for me the many nights he and Bousquet played there, remembering them as the best years of his life.

TWELVE

The Unsung Master of
the Gypsy Waltz

Tracing the Legacy of Tchan Tchou

IT'S JUST ANOTHER SATURDAY NIGHT in Paris. Autumn leaves litter the sidewalks of the quays along the Seine like leftover confetti, the remains of the glorious summer. I'm walking up from the river and into the neighborhood of Beaubourg-Les Halles. With the coming of dusk, the individual points of light across the city take on more brilliance and join together, becoming a jeweled carcanet along the skyline. La Tour Eiffel stands tall above all, as skeletal as a French fashion model. Paris is a city of cities— each *quartier* a world with a life of its own. Beaubourg too is its own universe. I pass the hidden Stravinsky fountain with its funky automat water sculptures; square des Innocents, once the cemetery of prehistoric Paris; the grand Belle Époque carousel with its painted wooden horses. I navigate the ravines of teetering buildings and the much-missed food markets of Les Halles, the so-called belly of Paris, and pass the eerie gothic cathedral dedicated to Saint Eustache. I come at last to rue Berger, the ancient street of the shepherds. In the last light of day, the old Italian men are racking up their *boules*, forgetting their feudalistic rivalries for the moment and heading off arm in arm for *un verre*. Neon lights of pink and red and green are being turned on at the neighborhood's famous restaurants that once served their trademark *soupe à l'oignon* to Les Halles *porteurs*—Au Chien qui Fume, Au Pied de Cochon, Le Poule au Pot. Down the street at the bistro Chez Elle, guitarist Jean-Yves Dubanton and accordionist Jean-Claude Laudet are tuning up to play their swing musette. Just across the river in the *Quartier Latin*, Rodolphe Raffalli picks his guitar in a below-ground *cave* while Steeve Laffont and his trio Sré Kidjalés are warming up at La Taverne de Cluny. And this evening there's also music by Serge Krief, Pierre "Kamlo" Barré, Ritary Gaguenetti and Macho Winterstein, the venerable Raphaël Faÿs, newcomer Rocky "Falone" Gresset, Frédéric Belinsky (grandson of Challain Ferret's pianist, Valia Belinsky), and even, east of the city along the River Marne, Patrick Saussois and his Alma Sinti ensemble stirring up a dancing crowd at a favored *guinguette*, a quayside open-air dance hall along the water. Just another Saturday night in Paris.

Tonight, I'm longing to hear classic Gypsy waltzes and so have come in search of a modern maestro of the *valse manouche*, Moréno Winterstein. And through the augury of Moréno's guitar, the near-forgotten waltzes live on from one of the all-time masters, Moréno's teacher and mentor, Paul "Tchan Tchou" Vidal.

Moréno's Parisian headquarters is Le Bistro d'Eustache in Les Halles, a dark little café from another era. It's also one of the best cafés for Gypsy jazz. The bistro is old-time Paris come to life. Tables and chairs are set up on the *terrasse* before the black-painted wooden *façade* of the café. Inside, the floor is well-worn mosaic. Basic wooden banquettes line the walls leading up to a curvaceous wood-topped bar—there's not even *un zinc* here. The bar is topped with taps for the favored beer of the house, an Alsatian *bière blanche*, which oddly enough is a perfect accompaniment for my palate to the chef's *sud-ouest cassoulet*, served in steaming earthenware crocks. The walls are plastered with faded posters announcing the annual tribute festival to Django at Samois-sur-Seine, the list of performers reading like a who's-who of Gypsy jazz, too many of them deceased now just years later—Challain himself, Nin-Nin, Matelo, Lousson, Eugène Vées, Jean-Pierre Sasson. The music of the present, however, is booked at the bistro every weekend night, which here starts as early as Thursday.

Standing in front of the bistro under the street lamps at twilight, I meet up with François Charle. Earlier in the day at his lutherie shop near the Louvre, we had made our plans for the evening.

As we wait outside the café, Moréno comes strolling down rue Berger carrying his own guitar case. Tall, dark, and handsome, he's dressed to kill. He wears a sleek jet-black double-breasted suit buttoned to the top, a silky black shirt, and a black tie highlighted with white polka dots. On his feet—and he doesn't care who stares—are the quintessential Gypsy guitarist's footwear: hot *noir et blancs*, two-tone spectator wingtips. This is Parisian haute couture Romani style, the runway a littered street in Les Halles. Moréno's hair too is black, but with streaks of glowing silver. On his upper lip, he sports the dash of a silver moustache.

Moréno greets us with cool aplomb and a handshake. He knows François well from horse-trading guitars and me from one such dealing for a majestic old cedar-topped Favino. We examine the night, then turn inside the bistro.

Moréno and his sideman—cousin and fellow guitarist Tchocolo Winterstein—find two barstools at one side of the café. There's no sound check, none of the interminable fooling around during band setup: Moréno simply unpacks his *petite bouche* Favino, Tchocolo tunes up his own Favino, the string bassist stretches his shoulders in his suit coat a couple times, and the music begins.

Moréno launches into "La gitane," the blazing waltz composed by Tchan Tchou. Accented by the clockwork strike of the bass, the rhythm guitar is rock steady, pounding out *la pompe* with percussive purity. Moréno's melodic arabesques soar above. The waltz is Romani rodomontade put into song, starting with a finger-contorting cascade of triplets. And this is just the way Moréno prefers it. His fretting fingers dance on the strings, his pick hand moving impossibly fast. Moréno gazes with studied nonchalance about the bistro, not deigning to watch his fingers as he reels off the waltz's signature melody. He is a keeper of traditions, a line back to Tchan Tchou—and to Django himself. There are many Gypsy jazz guitarists who are true virtuosi, many who play with flash and fire, but few who can play with such vaunted technical perfection and smooth, sure velocity as Moréno. As the Romani themselves swear, Moréno has a right hand like God Himself.

This Saturday night is young—and looks promising.

Moréno was born in 1963 in Alsace. He grew up speaking Romanès, traveling with his family via *caravane* through France, and learning to play the guitar music of his father. As Moréno tells his own story, "My father died when I was very young, but as far as I can remember he always had a guitar with him. My older brothers taught me all they knew. All I had to do was open my ears, watch and try to copy the finger positions. Sometimes they were tough on me and they would slap my hands when I made a mistake, but they quickly saw that I was talented.

"All I ever thought about was playing the guitar. At night, when there were guitar parties, I pretended to be asleep in our *campine*, yet I watched carefully through the window. When I saw a chord I didn't know I quickly reproduced the finger positions on my left forearm. Then I took my guitar that I always hid next to my bed and silently pressed the chords while lying in my bed. Nobody knew."

Like other Manouche youngsters, Moréno studied the recordings of Django, playing them over and over until he knew the songs as well as the master. Armed with his guitar and his fleet fingers, Moréno set off for the south of France to play.

"I busked in the cafés around Toulon," Moréno says. "One day I was playing at a café *terrasse* when a short, well-dressed man, wearing a hat and a moustache, came up to me. He said, 'You're from Alsace. I can tell by the way you play.'"

This was Tchan Tchou, already a legend among the Romani even far from his base in the Midi.

"I had heard a lot about Tchan Tchou and had listened to his records," Moréno continues. "I often dreamed of meeting him. I could talk for hours about him. The same night we met, we played together and immediately hit it off. I was nervous and very impressed by him. He played two notes for ten of my own. I quickly understood that I was nothing next to him. I was like a young puppy jumping around like crazy while he took his time to carefully place his phrases."

Even today, years after his passing, Tchan Tchou's memory burns eternal during the Romani pilgrimage to Les Saintes-Maries-de-la-Mer. Throughout the crazed days of religious and oh-so-secular festivities, a Gypsy gentleman with a glorious gray curlicued mustachio sits in state in front of his *campine* along the beachfront selling bootlegged and pirated CDs. The banner draped across his caravan "boutique" advertises "Musique Voyageurs," which seemingly includes everyone from Django to Frank Sinatra to French popster Claude François. He wipes homemade CDRs on his shirtfront, then pops them into his boombox, spinning the discs like a New York nightclub DJ, playing the music proudly at top, rip-roaring, speaker-splitting volume, the trebly sound blending with the waves on the shore and seagulls overhead. After playing a quick sample of a Tziganes band and then a rap duo to show the unmarked CDs actually contain some music, he drops in a disc of Tchan Tchou and gives the volume knob another furious twist. Compared to the rap, the simple guitar sounds quaintly old fashioned, Stone Age versus Stoned Age. But our DJ never notices. He's lost in the music. His eyes are shut now as he listens, appreciating the guitarwork as if savoring a fine Bourdeaux. "Ah, Tchan Tchou," he proclaims to all who will listen—and yet mostly just for himself. "The master!"

Among the Romani of the Midi, Tchan Tchou is a fabled guitarist. His fame here may even eclipse that of Django, and certainly the other Midi Gypsy jazzmen such as Tchan Tchou's own cousin, Patotte Bousquet. And yet Paul Vidal remains another one of the enigmas of Gypsy jazz. His EPs and LPs are all long out of print and nearly impossible to track down today. Thus, Tchan-Tchou's contributions to the music have often been overlooked simply by being difficult to find.

One reason for this mystery is that Tchan Tchou chose not to move to Paris to seek his fortune with his guitar. Like Bousquet who ruled Marseille, Tchan Tchou stayed primarily in the south of France, far away from the limelight and the big recording companies in the capital. He was instead a hero of the Midi's sun-soaked café *terrasses*, the pilgrimage for Sainte-Sarah, and the many all-night campfire jam sessions.

Born in a caravan near Aix-en-Provence on November 22, 1923, he was given the name Paul Vidal. According to legend, as a babe he looked like he was Chinese to his Romani family: his features wizened and wise, his eyes slanted, his visage even then inscrutable—all the standard stereotypes. And so, an elderly aunt bestowed on him the oriental-sounding moniker of Tchan Tchou.

Vidal's family traveled across southern France, his father performing the ages-old Romani craft of caning chairs. But at night, Vidal *père* unpacked his guitar from the family *roulotte* to play with other Gypsies in the encampment. Django was a family acquaintance and when he visited the Midi during the lucrative summer months and met up with his old friends, Vidal *père* backed Django in his makeshift bands.

Tchan Tchou did not learn to play guitar until he was twelve years old—inconceivably late among his fellow Romani. In the now-usual fashion, he studied by watching his father and even Django himself.

Like Django, Tchan Tchou apprenticed as a rhythm man in accordion bands in dance halls. Traveling north to the city of Lyon in the mid 1940s, the twenty-three-year-old Vidal was playing with two other guitarists as the Hot Club de Jazz de Lyon. The trio mimicked both the name and musical style of Django's Quintette du Hot Club de France. While Tchan Tchou sometimes ventured to Paris, his visits were rare. Instead, he moved from Lyon to Monte Carlo and across the Riviera for the next seven decades, performing in cafés and dance halls and on radio and television broadcasts, including Radio Monte Carlo concerts.

Over the years, Tchan Tchou's style of playing developed to bear his own signature. He improvised over classic American jazz tunes with carefully chosen phrases, aiming for eloquence instead of flash. Yet it was in his *valses manouche* that his playing glowed, a result of his early years in the dance hall bands. And it was as a master of the Gypsy waltzes that he would be idolized by his fellow Romani at Les Saintes-Maries-de-la-Mer.

Tchan Tchou recorded only sporadically. This was the result of keeping to the Midi where there were few record labels and due to the times as the French proto-rock'n'roll known as *yéyé* was the fad, not Gypsy jazz. Tchan Tchou's first opportunity to record didn't come until he was in his forties. And it arrived in

Lyon, his long-time base of operations. Here, he cut an EP released in 1964 for the tiny *lyonnais* label JBP, namesake of local producer Jean-Baptiste Piazzano. Tchan Tchou was accompanied by guitarist Robert Palayan and an unknown drummer. His music was inspired as much by Django as by an idyll of swank nightclub soirées in far-off America with Sinatra and Dean Martin. The disc included Django's World War II anthem "Nuages" as well as the timely American pop hits "Strangers in the Night" and "Tout le monde, un jour," his version of "Everybody Loves Somebody" translated into Gypsy jazz. On the record sleeve, the small-statured Tchan Tchou grips his giant Favino guitar, a tiny Django moustache on his lip and a fierce look on his face belying the grace he displays in his music.

Sometime in the mid 1960s, Tchan Tchou brought his guitar to back another one of his many musical cousins—this time, accordionist Tony "Tieno" Fallone. Born in 1924 and pumping an accordion by the time he was six, Fallone was early on enlisted in his family's traveling band. La Troupe Fallone was a miniature musical ensemble of child prodigies—and curiosities. They became a famous sight in France playing flea markets and *fêtes foraines*, and postcards of the children were sold like freak-show souvenirs. Now, years later, Fallone and Tchan Tchou recorded a collection of musette classics, released solely on the newfangled medium of tape cassette. Time-frayed postcards of La Troupe Fallone still surface today in *les puces*, whereas this cassette of Fallone and Tchan Tchou's sonorous *valses musette* is a prized rarity.

Still, Tchan Tchou's music somehow caught the ear of a mainstream commercial label, and in 1964 he was invited to record his first full solo album. Released on the tiny Bel Air label and titled *Guitare Party*, the LP was a showcase of Tchan Tchou's nightclub repertoire. He performs a variety of jazz standards such as "Premier rendez-vous," "Bésame mucho," and "La complainte de Mackie" ("Mack the Knife") intermixed with Romani classics like "Les deux guitares" and "Les yeux noirs." But it was in his own compositions such as the fiery waltzes "La gitane" and "Dolorès" that his style blossoms. His playing shifts in a blink of the eye between simple, restrained melodies into bursts of gorgeous and impossibly long arpeggios. Tchan Tchou's style aimed at the essence of a song, resulting in weightless and luminous improvisations.

Yet it was a full decade before he was back in a recording studio—and then he cut *two* further albums. In 1980, he released the LPs *Swinging Guitars* and *Nomades...*, both recorded for Charles Delaunay's Disques Vogue. He was backed by his long-time accomplice, *Corsico* guitarist François Codaccioni, as well as Django's former sidemen bassist Alf Masselier and Roger Paraboschi on drums. Again, amid the jazz standards and pop *soupe*, it was Tchan Tchou's originals that shone. In his composition "Tant pis ou tant mieux," his ferocious flourishes and rapid runs adorn the elaborate simplicity of his melody.

Throughout these years, Tchan Tchou continued to wander with his guitar. He made Toulon his fiefdom, but he also performed in cabarets across the Midi, from Nuits Tziganes in Mougins to backing Tieno Fallone in Dijon to playing at Au Son des Guitares in Ajaccio, Corsica. And each year on May 24, he returned to Les Saintes-Maries-de-la-Mer.

Tchan Tchou died in 1999, but his legacy lives on in his signature song, "La gitane." The song has since become a Gypsy jazz standard, part of most every band's repertoire. Each time I listen to Tchan Tchou's recording of the waltz, I am amazed yet again by the finesse he brings to six strings. Tchan Tchou recorded his masterpiece of *valse manouche* twice, on his debut LP *Guitare Party* and again on his final album *Nomades . . .* , half a lifetime apart. On both versions, his guitar conjures forth a musical specter of a Romani woman of stunning beauty; she comes alive in the waltz's dazzling opening triplet, which resounds in my mind like the seductive *floreo* flip of *la Gitane*'s wrist in a midnight flamenco dance. Tchan Tchou doesn't rush the *valse*'s tempo as too many modern guitarists do to show off their prowess. He knows no hurry. Rather, he relishes the smoothness and lucidity of soul—that elusive *duende*, or spirit, at the heart of the music. Akin to the mystical flamenco dancer he evokes, Tchan Tchou spices the lyricism of the melodic movement with gyres of arpeggios like quick *zapateado* dance steps resonating with supreme emotion. And through his fine touch and virtuosity, his image of *la Gitane* is at once tender and loving, fierce and frightening.

No one plays "La gitane" today with more power than Tchan Tchou's chief accompanist from his later years, Moréno. And he performs the waltz with this passion in tribute to his mentor.

"The first time I heard Tchan Tchou, *j'ai flashé sur lui*—I was dazzled by him!" Moréno remembers again their first meeting in Toulon in the late 1980s. "I found his playing more cheerful than Django's; I heard less sadness. . . . He knew how to sum up the entirety of existence in just two notes. Me, I was playing a chorus of Django at three hundred notes an hour—yet I could not obtain the same emotion. For Tchan Tchou, one note sufficed. He was the maestro. . . . Tchan Tchou played with a deep sensitivity and perfect technique, especially to his right hand—his was an extraordinary right hand, that could play triplets and runs of the first order."

The young Alsatian guitarist became the old Midi master's accompanist. He also learned everything he could glean.

"I decided to stay in Toulon," Moréno says. "I found myself a *campine* and accompanied him for four years. He taught me the basics, in particular the art of the waltz, the notion of measure, and the musicality of a phrase. It is when you are separated from someone like that that you realize how much you learned from them. Today, I still think of how he played and he remains a reference. I was extremely lucky to have met someone like Tchan Tchou."

In the beginning at least, Moréno too stayed in the south of France, away from the spotlight of Paris. After releasing a self-produced cassette of music for sale at gigs, he was invited to record commercially in 1994 by the Nanterre-based label Al Sur, which chronicled the disparate musics of the Midi, from traditional Gypsy music and flamenco to North African immigrants' rai. Moréno's first mainstream album, *Yochka*, included nine original tunes interspersed between standards, such as a stylish Romani rendition of "Somewhere over the Rainbow." *Yochka* served notice that a gifted new Manouche guitarist had arrived.

In 1996, Moréno returned with *Moréno Boléro*, an homage to Tchan Tchou. There are covers of the almost-obligatory Gypsy jazz standards such as "Les yeux noirs" and "Nuages," songs by which Gypsy guitarists are too often measured. These are surrounded by three songs penned by Tchan-Tchou: "Tant pis ou tant mieux," "Les yeux de Dolorès," and "La gitane."

Moréno continues to record Gypsy jazz, including 1997's *Electric!* where he shifted effortlessly among an undercurrent of Manouche sound blended into arrangements more typical of an American-style jazz combo; 1998's stellar *Romano Baschepen*, Moréno jamming with fellow Gypsy guitarist Angelo Debarre; and 2007's *Django Club*, featuring the addition of a clarinet recreating Django's wartime swing sound.

At the same time, Moréno also cut albums of traditional Tziganes music with other musicians. In 1997, he backed the astonishing Romanian Gypsy accordionist Robert de Brasov on *Prima Jubire*. De Brasov long played for Romani circuses traveling Europe, and his songs here are spinning, swirling Gypsy jams. And Moréno lent his guitar to a 1999 album, *Latcho Dives*, chronicling the flamenco style of Midi Romani.

Yet despite his prolific run of commercial recordings, Moréno continues the underground Gypsy jazz tradition of cutting self-produced CDs for sale only at gigs. Recorded *chez lui* or in a rented studio, these CDRs with color-photocopied songlists best show Moréno's wide musical journeys. He mixes Gypsy jazz with classic Balkan Tziganes music, flamenco with American jazz standards—as well as melodies by Tchan Tchou. At times, Moréno's wife, Marina, adds her soulful vocals and a classic Gypsy street-singer's tambourine. These albums eschew the *gadjé*'s commercial labels and mainstream distribution, and remain pure Gypsy horse-trading at its best.

Back at Paris's Le Bistro d'Eustache on that fine autumn evening, Moréno and his trio count into another song. Now, with midnight come and gone, François Charle orders yet another coffee at the bar while I again sample the *bière blanche*. The tiny bistro is packed to capacity with late diners supping on *steak-frites*. Moréno is in his shirtsleeves now, his *noir et blancs* tapping in time to a beat that is steadily and inexorably accelerating as the night progresses into morning. He has his own legion of groupies as well. *Gadjé* guitarists swooning on Gypsy jazz stand just an arm's length from the band in the cramped bar, craning their necks and attentively studying his every note. Moréno bears the twinge of a smile on his lips as he plays ever faster. I too am among these fans, trying in vain to memorize how Moréno's fingers fly over the fretboard, and finally shaking my head in astonishment.

It's all in the best Gypsy jazz tradition, just as young Django watched his father and uncles play, or as a youthful Moréno learned from Tchan Tchou.

THIRTEEN

The Lost

*The Secret History of Lousson Baumgartner
and the "Other" Family*

I SPENT MORE THAN TWO YEARS searching for Dallas Baumgartner. I heard rumors from other Gypsy jazz aficionados that this grandson of Lousson Baumgartner-Reinhardt, and thus great-grandson of Django, was playing jazz. Where he was, however, no one seemed to know—maybe Paris, sometimes in Lille, the Midi, or Italy, often just out on the road. He was not necessarily hiding from anything or anyone. But that didn't make him any easier to find.

I stumbled across a copy of Dallas's self-recorded, self-produced, self-distributed CD *Dallas Trio* from 2005—his one and only recording so far—at François Charle's guitar shop near the Louvre, but even François knew nothing further about the musician's whereabouts. Listening to the album, I was stunned by the muscular energy: Dallas played rollicking Gypsy jazz *à les puces*. His music bore an old-fashioned sound, yet was alive with a modern electricity. I tracked down one of his accompanists, a *gadjo* named Manu Gravier, but he too didn't know where to find his own bandleader—last he heard, Dallas was maybe in Belgium, visiting the rest of his family and jamming there with his younger brothers Loumpie, Fillou, and Simba, all of whom also play a similar brand of wild, intense guitar.

So, after months of frustrated hunting, I telephoned from across the Atlantic to Manouche guitarist Tchocolo Winterstein, who's up on all doings within the Gypsy jazz world in Paris. Tchocolo surprised me. He said that he and Dallas were playing together in Paris the next week, their only planned gig for the next six months. Tchocolo passed along Dallas's mobile phone number, and with this secret code in hand, I finally—and with anticlimactic ease—reached him. Yes, Dallas tells me, the show was indeed planned for next Wednesday. I told him I'd see him there, but he invites me to come visit him at his encampment as well. I got lucky, found a cheap plane ticket, and was on my way.

Dallas had said to meet him in the Parisian suburb of Pierrefitte-sur-Seine, and we'd continue on together from there to his *caravane*: "It's impossible to explain how to get here," he explains. It was not an apology.

I arrive in Pierrefitte after a convoluted trip via airplane, *métro*, train, bus, and a healthy hike. Across the town *place*, I recognize Dallas in an instant. He's Django incarnate: tall, slender stance; dark eyes; and that requisite moustache. And he also looks like Joseph, his wavy hair slicked back from his brow in a style dating to the halcyon days of the Quintette in the 1930s. Dallas wears pressed jeans, stylish pointed-toed loafers, and a black turtleneck sweater, a delicate cross on a chain around his collar. He gives me a warm welcome, even though our friendship had begun just days ago via cell phone. He is accompanying his grandmother, doing the daily shopping in town. A petite woman of perhaps seventy, Madame Rose is also known among her fellow Manouche as Kalí— "Black" in Romanès—for her dark complexion.

"*Djess,*" Dallas says, dropping into Romanès, the equivalent of the universal French phrase, *on y va*—let's go. Carrying the sacks of groceries, we walk out of town toward the nearby *ville* of Montmagny, always upward, ascending cobbled backstreets and clandestine pathways between gardens until we are high above Pierrefitte—and Paris. We come out on the hilltop called La Butte-Pinçon in a forest stretching away to the north. On the edge of the *ville* within these ex-quisite woodlands, there's nothing but trash, garbage, refuse, and more trash. This appears to be the town's ashtray. An unofficial landfill, all of the cast-offs are here—a rusted-out and stripped hulk of a car dumped in a ditch amid a sad rainbow of sodden multicolored rags, faded plastic bottles, and used toilet paper. We step with caution through the mess, up a dirt road, around a hedgerow cor-ner, and into a small Romani encampment. Here, all is spotless. The ground is laid with clean gravel, the modern *caravanes* are glistening white in the autumn sunshine, and the Gypsy women always seem to have a broom, mop, washrag, or dust cloth in hand.

Dallas has it good. In a city of million-euro rooms with a view, penthouses looking out on the Seine, and grand hotels of Sun King opulence reigning over Les Grands Boulevards, Dallas may just have the best view of all. From his *caravane* perched high on the heights of Montmagny, just ten kilometers north as the crow flies from Le Sacré-Cœur, he gazes out across all Paris. His doorstep's at roughly the same height as the top of La Tour Eiffel, and the view from his kitchen window takes in the whole city, Belleville to Notre-Dame-de-Paris to La Tour Montparnasse. Here, there is no traffic, no car horns, dump trucks, *gendarmerie* sirens. It's the countryside, more remote than the posh Jardin du Luxembourg, more tranquil than the gentrified Bois de Vincennes. And there are still *niglos* to be hunted—legally or otherwise—in the woods surrounding him.

"*C'est haut, c'est tranquille, c'est beau, eh?*" Dallas says, calm and relaxed, looking out from the doorway of his *caravane*. Paris in the distance is gilded by the afternoon sun on this spring day, yet this is where he'd rather be.

There are about a dozen trailers here in this fenced-in enclave, the *campines* of his clan. Madame Rose has a long, beautiful *caravane* topped by a satellite dish, a welcome mat by the doorsteps, and out front, a picnic table with buckets arranged to catch rainwater for washing up. Electrical, water, sewage, and even telephone lines run into the encampment. Other trailers belong to family members and cousins, all relatives in some fashion of Django's. Dallas's own *caravane* is a small, one-person trailer. Inside, between his kitchenette, bathroom, and bed, are his portable amplifier, a tidy CD collection of Django's music, and a portable TV for watching vintage black-and-white films, Fred Astaire's movies being his favorites. Dallas's well-traveled no-name Gypsy guitar with its Stimer pickup affixed with blue masking tape rests silent in the corner.

I catch my breath after the labyrinthine, uphill journey. As Dallas jokes with me, "*C'est pas facile de trouver Monsieur Baumgartner.*"

He doesn't know how true his words are.

Finding his grandfather, Lousson Baumgartner, was next to impossible as well. In fact, since he never recorded commercially, rarely played on the Paris jazz scene, and was even seldom photographed, Lousson has been almost forgotten by Gypsy jazz fans. This son of Django was and is a cipher.

I first learned some of Lousson's early story due to another improbable meeting. Orchestrated from the United States, I had found the family of Django's first wife in Paris several years earlier. Beyond her Romani name of Bella, no *gadjé* knew anything of her life; even in his 1968 biography, *Django, mon frère*, Charles Delaunay couldn't shed light on her story. Over dinner one night, I mentioned my interest in Django to French friends Valérie and Pierre-François who were living in Minneapolis: I was trying to track down hospital records through the Archives de l'Assistance Publique–Hôpitaux de Paris and had become lost in the unfathomable bureaucratic maze there. They laughed and said, *Bien sûr!* They then said they had a French doctor acquaintance, Jean-Christophe, who was adept at ferreting out historic documents from official archives as his hobby was researching French corsair pirates; they'd tell him of my plight next time they talked. Via e-mail, Jean-Christophe wrote back with news surprising us all: He and his father before him happened to have been the family physicians of Django's first wife's family over several generations. And thus, I bought my first spur-of-the-moment ticket to Paris.

Several weeks later, I am on another series of *métro* trains and buses through the never-ending *banlieues* of Paris to the southern suburb of Vitry-sur-Seine. Meeting up with Jean-Christophe at his clinic, we set out into the surrounding canyons of low-income apartment blocks. These were the same suburbs that would erupt in riots a year later, in autumn 2005. But for now things are calm, if uneasy. African and other immigrant youths huddle about, soothed by hazes of marijuana smoke. All around them, these inhospitable apartment buildings they call home stretch up and away into the mists of a rainy evening. The apartment blocks are known as *les cities*, and indeed each one is a city in the sky. Coming at last to the apartment building of Madame Marie-Thérèse "Minou" Garcia, we ring the bell.

Thanks to Jean-Christophe's introduction, there is little hesitation in accepting an unknown *gadjo*, let alone an American, into their home. Madame Minou welcomes us. The apartment is small but again, scrubbed to a stunning state of cleanliness. Several others wait inside, quiet in their nervous state— Madame Minou's sister, Augustine "Poupée" Renaud, and cousins José "Jeannot" Garcia and Michel Heil. As soon as a copious roast-chicken dinner is served, all reticence is gone. Talk turns to Django, legends and tall tales repeated. Jeannot begins playing tapes of Django on a boombox, and stoked by hot jazz, the evening grows ever warmer. Madame Minou retrieves the family's paperback copy of Delaunay's memoir of Django, carefully safeguarded against time in a plastic bag. Besides her Bible, it's the only book she owns.

Then, I present them with a gift that I brought from the United States: a recording of Lousson, made at a Paris gig during the 1960s. Jeannot immediately halts Django mid-song, drops in the CDR, and then turns up the volume. The quality of the recording is far from perfect, but no one minds. The family listens in reverence. It's the first music they'd ever heard by their own ancestors.

Heated by the spirit, Madame Minou now produces the family photo album. The book is thin, only a meager handful of studio portraits of the family's lineage, supplemented by numerous modern-day Polaroids and snapshots— summer campsites, pilgrimages, weddings, baptism parties. I feel like a peeping tom eagerly looking into the family's past, a voyeur into their history. Madame Minou turns another brittle page, and there is a photograph staring back at me with startling intensity: Django, with a moustache just starting to darken his upper lip, standing proud like a young, eighteen-year-old pasha in a professional photographer's studio surrounded by his first wife's family. And there, at Django's side, stands the fabled Bella herself.

She has lustrous black hair curling around her face. Rich olive skin. Smiling eyes above a smile on her lips that would stop the breath of any man, The name Bella—Italian for "beautiful"—was certainly just.

Her full name, her descendants now tell me, was Florine Mayer. After their "runaway" marriage, as it was known and recognized by their fellow Manouche, Django and Bella were received by her mother, Josephine Renaud, and father, Henri "Pan" Mayer. In another image from the family album, Pan appears out of the past. He looks like a fine example of a *petit bourgeois*—a stocky yet fierce man beneath a perfect bowler hat and bearing a glorious handlebar mustachio. Yet he was a bourgeois only of *les puces*.

(Dallas too has a photograph of Pan, likely taken in the late 1920s and perhaps the sole surviving copy. Pan and his wife stand at their stall in *les puces* at the Porte de Clignancourt. The family's children are arrayed around them holding the guitars, banjos, and violins Pan was famous for repairing and reselling. Perhaps this was where Django too found one of his first instruments?)

Django and Bella made a new home for themselves near the *caravanes* of their families just outside the Porte de Clignancourt in the *marché*. Soon, Bella was pregnant.

Then came the fire. On that October 1928 night, they were both admitted to Hôpital Lariboisière with serious burns. With Jean-Christophe's assistance, I traced hospital records, detailing Django and Bella's injuries and Bella's eventual discharge on November 16 after three weeks of doctor's care.

While Django was still confined to a hospital bed, Bella gave birth to a son. He was named Henri in honor of her father. This *petit* Henri they called *l'Ourson*, or "bear cub." In time, the nickname transformed into Lousson.

Yet following the fire, a rift grew between Django and Bella. Despite their newborn son and the goodwill of Pan who paid for much of their hospitalization, Django and Bella went their separate ways. She soon remarried—another Gypsy named "Niglo" Baumgartner—and Lousson was given his stepfather's family name, becoming known officially as Henri Baumgartner.

Here's where Dallas picks up the story again. We're having lunch now in the *campine* of his grandmother, Madame Rose. Those groceries we carried up the hill are being put to good use. Madame Rose cooks veal cutlets while Dallas prepares his specialty—*une salade* of crab meat, tuna fish, Gruyère, and shallots, all coated in a fine vinaigrette. We eat in the dining nook of the *campine*, and over glasses of red wine, Dallas and Madame Rose trade off telling of their family.

Dallas was born on March 13, 1981, and so he was just eleven when Lousson died in 1992. But his memory—and admiration—for his grandfather is strong, supported by some impossibly rare studio recordings made by Lousson that survive only *chez famille*.

"Lousson learned to play guitar from Django," Dallas explains. Or at least, that's the family legend. While Django started a new family with Naguine and had a second son, Babik, he seems to have remained in contact with Lousson throughout. A photograph from the World War II years shows Lousson strumming a Selmer guitar at Django's side during the grand opening of one of Baro Ferret's bars in Pigalle. And when Django led his Nouveau Quintette on a tour to Bruxelles in 1948, Lousson was on rhythm guitar. After that, Lousson's historical path is next seen in a photo from Django's funeral, standing beside Joseph Reinhardt.

Through the 1950s and 1960s, Lousson sometimes played in Paris *boîtes*, but more often was on the road. "Lousson, he played with great heart—like Django," Dallas says. And the few surviving recordings—private club bootlegs and tapes from a July 4, 1966, gig at Paris's Caveau des Deux Ports—bear this out. He appears for a brief stint in Sten Bramsen's 1978 Danish television documentary *Django*, playing his father's melodies all alone in a nighttime café. Lousson may not have been a virtuoso or played at impressive tempo, but Dallas is right: he certainly played with heart. "At times, Lousson used a Selmer with a Stimer; at other times, an electric Gibson," Dallas says. "He was half in the old style, half modern—*un mélange*."

Dallas also retains an old recording the world doesn't know exists: a mid-1960s Paris studio session with Lousson and violinist Louis "Vivian" Villerstein. Although planned as an LP, the tracks have never been released—and are unlikely to be any time soon due to family wranglings. Listening to these tapes now in Dallas's *caravane*, I hear Lousson's stylish phrasing—calm and targeted flurries of notes followed by singing single-note punctuations that resonate through the melody lines. Dallas is in heaven. "Such heart," he says again.

Before these recordings were completed, however, Lousson hooked up his own *caravane* and left for Italy. He would stay for the next twelve years. Dallas shows me a photo of Lousson in Italy, playing in a Brazilian samba band. Lousson and his bandmates are all disguised by ruffled blouses and sleek black slacks. Lousson strums his Selmer before a vast percussion section of more conga drums than I can count.

It was during Lousson's absence from Paris that Babik went to visit a lawyer. French law didn't recognize Django's elopement with Bella as a legal marriage, just Django and Naguine's formal marriage under French civil law on June 21, 1943. So, in 1982, Babik hired French attorney André Schmidt, and with Charles Delaunay as witness, he was named sole heir to Django. And all of

Django's royalties. Bela, Lousson, and their families were left out. It was a move that would reverberate through Gypsy jazz history.

Lousson did not return to France until the dawn of the 1990s when he was in ill health. He died in 1992 and was buried alongside his father in the cemetery of Samois-sur-Seine.

And yet in the years before he died, Lousson offered a prognostication about his young grandson. Dallas was just six or seven at the time and had not shown any interest in a guitar. Still, his grandfather sensed an innate musical nature. And though none of Lousson's own five sons—including Dallas's father, Paul "Navire" Baumgartner—played, Lousson foresaw that Dallas would one day become a guitarist. He predicted a future full of music.

Madame Rose listened. It was she who had watched over Dallas for much of his life. In fact, she gave him his name, which she borrowed from the glamor of the television series *Dallas* from the other side of the globe and another world away. And now it was she too who bought him his first guitar, presenting it to him on his eighth birthday. Soon, sure enough, he was jamming with his Romani elders, men of Lousson's generation.

Now, Dallas is telling me his own story: "One day, I approached *une caravane* and heard music pouring out. It came from the man who would become my teacher, Adolphe Romela. *L'ancien* knew how to play harp, violin, guitar, piano. I was fourteen or fifteen years old, and played day after day, learning from him the music—and the life of a musician."

A few days later and it's that Wednesday night gig for which I came all the way to Paris. Dallas is playing his jazz in a most unlikely place—a cellar *cave* below L'Eglise de la Madeleine in the heart of the city—unlikely because La Madeleine does not often sponsor jazz soirées. More unlikely still as this is one of the most chic of Paris's *quartiers*: Surrounding the church are bank headquarters and fashion designer ateliers—Kenzo, Ralph Lauren, and many more. With Red Ferraris and somber black Citroën limousines parked around the *place*, somehow the world of high finance and haute couture has here found a happy marriage.

Yet this is an evening when the Romani have invaded this chic universe. In the *cave* is an opening of a Gypsy art exhibit—paintings by Macha Volodina, Tchocolo's wife, and Sandra Jayat; sculptures by Gérard Gartner. Dallas and Tchocolo are to provide the *douce ambiance*. And soon, the Gypsies have a way of making this cold, inhospitable place their own. Bags of potato chips, bottles of Coca-Cola and red wine, happy children running free, two guitars, and this stony cellar is suddenly alive with warmth and *bonhomie*.

At one end of the *cave*, Dallas and Tchocolo are jamming, the sound of Dallas's Stimer ricocheting off the stone walls, Tchocolo's Favino resonating with bass notes. Dallas plays a couple of Lousson's compositions, several of his own such as "Mystérieux" and "Tout en douceur," and then of course some of his great-grandfather's tunes. And like Lousson, Dallas too plays a unique blend of past and present. He sings old tunes like the gorgeous "Mélodie" with gusto. And he picks out electric swing with ferocious, perhaps slightly tetched, vigor, his Stimer turned up loud like a clarion call. Christian Escoudé has stopped in to view the paintings and sculptures, but he now stares and listens in awe at the vibrancy—and sheer volume—of the new generation's Gypsy jazz.

Huddled outside the French city of Lille on the remains of a disinfected chemical factory site sits another Romani encampment. The glories of *Vieux* Lille are far off in the distance. Here, there's nothing picturesque beyond one surviving smokestack standing tall like a monument. *Caravanes* are parked on the ground cover of cement that was once the factory floor. Dallas has come here in his peripatetic wanderings to visit family. And of course he brings his guitar.

Lille has long been a magnet for Romani. Other ancestors of Django's settled here in years past, chief among them being Jacques "Piton" Reinhardt. A contemporary of Django's, Piton played fast and furious guitar. By legend, he was such a devotedly "uncivilized" Gypsy that he couldn't function within *gadjé* culture for even a moment and so rarely ventured forth from his own Romani world. It's thus little surprise that Piton never recorded commercially. Happily, however, a handful of private recordings remain from the mid 1960s, including a 1966–1967 jam session at La Chope des Puces in Clignancourt. Listening to these surviving tapes, I'm almost assaulted by the fierceness of Piton's picking. His style is robust, even rustic, sounding like bebop in the intensity with which he played Django's classic swing repertoire. Today, Piton's equally adept sons, Coco and Samson, still live in *caravanes* outside Lille, both playing and recording Gypsy jazz, albeit with a new smoothness of style.

For Dallas, Lille means family and music. He has three brothers who live in *une campine* here, and all of them play guitar. Dallas began tutoring his youngest brother, Simba, on six strings when Simba was only six years old. Simba's just nine now, but plays with verve. Loumpie is a fine accompanist while Fillou is also learning.

As evening comes down on the encampment, lights inside the *caravanes* glow and the Baumgartners' resounds with guitars. They sit on the built-in banquette below a large framed painting of Django hung on the wall like a saint's image.

All the brothers are playing at once. Dallas is trading off licks with Simba, beaming as his younger brother takes the lead. Simba's short fingers struggle to reach some of the notes on his gigantic archtop, missing a few but hitting most. Dallas is obvious in his pride, telling me, "Most young Manouches, they just want to watch television and play Nintendo. They don't want to play guitar—it's too much work." Simba is named for the feline hero of Disney's *The Lion King*, and already he makes his guitar roar with sound if not yet profundity.

And outside Paris, there's another one of Lousson's great-grandchildren who also plays Gypsy jazz—Lévis Adel. Lousson is Lévis's maternal great-grandfather whereas Joseph Reinhardt is his paternal grandfather. At ten years of age, Lévis first performed at the Django Reinhardt tribute festival at Samois-sure-Seine. Someday soon, he'll release his debut album.

There's little concern that this side of the family will remain silent looking into the future.

Back at the *caravane* of Dallas's grandmother, Madame Rose, we're sipping sugary sweet coffee while looking through a batch of photographs that I brought with me just for this occasion. Outside, Romani kids are playing *boules* in the street while the women are cleaning yet again. The autumn sun is gentle in its warmth, dappled in the surrounding forest, reflecting off the gleaming white *caravanes* of the encampment, a halo over the city in the distance. I share pictures collected by Delaunay from Django's family, images loaned to me by Romani, as well as photos borrowed from other Gypsy jazz historians—images of Django, Lousson, and Gypsy jazz history. There are photographs Gypsy jazz fans have all seen so many times they've almost become commonplace: the picture of Django at about six with an impish grin and wearing a fedora several sizes too large for him, standing alongside his mother, Négros and her father. There's the famous studio portraits of Django, age fourteen, with his *banjo-guitare*, the young hero of the *bals musette*.

And suddenly I have a startling and sad vision of how easy it is for this history to be lost among the people who themselves made the music.

Madame Rose is a gentle, smiling matron, immensely proud of her Dallas and ever so pleased to have an American *gadjo* come to hear his music. But now, looking at these photos, her hand is covering her mouth in shock. She holds the images close so her eyes can focus, then shakes her head in disbelief. "*Moi,* I've never seen photos of Django as a young man," she says.

And there's that photo of an eighteen-year-old Django in 1928, newlywed to Bella, both young and remote and beautiful. It's the picture I first saw on the other side of Paris, a copy graciously made for me from Poupée's family album.

Now there are tears in Madame Rose's eyes. "And I've never seen a photograph of my mother as a young girl."

And so of course I leave her with my copy, to be framed and hung in pride of place in her *caravane* overlooking Paris.

FOURTEEN

Minstrel

Bamboula Ferret and the Travels of a Romani Troubadour

MINSTREL, TROUBADOUR, *MUSICO*. EDDIE "Bamboula" Ferret is one of the last of an era. He sports a grand fedora, its wide brim cocked just right over his dark eyes. A red scarf is often tied around his neck, an echo of *bal musette* style. His tanned skin is highlighted by the most stunning white whiskers imaginable—old-time sideburns that blend into a glorious full mustachio that suddenly makes Django's trim accent mark appear so very avant-garde.

Bamboula is a compatriot and peer of Django. He's also a man who spent his life making music. Like Django's parents and so many other itinerant Romani musicians, Bamboula lived on the road playing where there were paying crowds at small-town market days, country *fêtes*, and big-city *puces*. With his guitar, violin, and voice, he accompanied the feats of circus acrobats, the drama of theater plays, and the on-screen magic of the first silent motion pictures. He was, and is, a human jukebox with a repertoire like a soundtrack to the Twentieth Century.

So I naturally sought out Bamboula, eager to hear some of his tales. I hoped to learn of the life of Romani minstrels, whether it was the Parisian Gypsy jazzmen of Django's ilk or the wandering troubadours playing Tziganes music. He recalls it all as a hard life and a good life. Fame never found him, just as it never discovered most Gypsy musicians, no matter how good. Bamboula's story is certainly his own. And yet it is also the story of a time now past.

These days, Bamboula has been slowed by the years as well as arthritis in his vital hands. It's only rarely that he plays any more, usually in the Porte de

Clignancourt *puces* on *jours de fête* when his fellow Romani ask him—no, *demand* it of him. He first put away his guitar after some six decades of playing when his fingers could no longer dash over the hurdles of the frets. After his guitar, he sadly set aside his beloved violin. Now and then today, he still sings, his voice roughened by the years and too many cigarettes, yet at the same moment strangely soothing and lyrical. His songs are sung in French and Andalusian and Catalan and Romanès and other Gypsy dialects like a trail back through Romani history. His old repertoire is alive still with tunes from times past: Charles Trenet's sentimental "Que reste-t'il, de nos amours." "Oe Djoevia." The glorious *chanson* "Mélodie." "Alpha Négro (Orfeu Négro)." "I Leida." Songs romantic and nostalgic, sad and beautiful, timeless and yet near-forgotten.

I spoke with Bamboula several times over the years at his home in the dreary Parisian suburb of Drancy. As with his music these days, Bamboula is reticent about telling his story. Yet once he is entreated and finally begins, the tale comes out like a ménage of *chanson*, Romani campfire melodies, flamenco fandangos, and Tziganes violin glissandi all in one epic song.

"*Alors*, my father had died, and my mother remarried one of her cousins. He already had some children as well and so, for us, this did not work out; we were not the preferred ones. I had two other cousins—Henri 'Piotto' Limberger [born July 26, 1914] and his brother, Alfred 'Latcheben' Grünholz [born in Antwerp, Belgium, in 1912]—that were in a similar situation to me. They would later become my brothers-in-law. But for now, we three had already decided to leave, to go and live without our parents. And so we formed a small musical group to go on the road. They were already good musicians. We saved some money from our playing and bought a small *caravane*, an old one with wheels made of wood, and a small horse. But our poor horse was too weak to pull the caravan, *et alors*, we'd have to climb down and push it for him.

"We traveled from country to country, living out in the wild, and we played all the time. We had just a cello and a violin and a guitar. Henri was our violinist and bandleader. He was known as Piotto, and so we called ourselves 'Les Piottos.' Piotto was already a virtuoso. *Moi*, I was younger, thirteen years old, and I learned and came along well. When I found a new chord on my guitar, they encouraged me, they kissed me! Ah, those were glorious days! We did not know much about music, not even the names of the chords. We called a chord 'flat' if we played it with a barre and a seventh note. We said 'D' for a 'Re' chord. And when we moved to a 'Mi' minor [A minor] chord, we simply called it the 'small Ré,' or the 'backed-up chord.' We knew no better!"

Photos of the ensemble give a glimpse back in time. Bamboula, Piotto, and Latcheben all have virile moustaches and long black, flowing manes combed straight back. In some pictures, they wear blouses with dramatic flowing sleeves highlighted by intricate embroidery set off by scarves, vests, and pantaloons. In another, they are dressed like gauchos with flat-brimmed cowboy hats and bow ties. In yet a third, they wear the smock of cossacks from nights playing in *cabarets russe*.

"*Alors*, when we arrived in a small city, we took out our instruments, tied our small horse behind the *caravane*, then the three of us made the rounds of the cafés and the parties began. When we played, the people never wanted us to stop; they told us, 'Remain here and play, and when you're hungry, go to the kitchen and eat. And afterwards we'll give you a little money.' We'd sometimes play for three days straight!

"We traveled, rolling along by ourselves—we were independent from *tout le monde*, no one held any reins over us. We'd stop for the night somewhere and start a small campfire. We were always dressed in Gypsy clothes, with white smocks with lace, tall black boots, vests, grand pantaloons—just like the Three Musketeers!

"And then one day, we passed by a coal merchant and my brother-in-law says, 'It's getting cold; I'll buy us some coal.' But we told him, 'You see, we cannot put 50 kilograms [125 pounds] of coal in our *caravane*—our small horse already cannot pull the load!' And so we purchased just 25 kilograms [60 pounds] of coal. But even in Flanders where it is all as flat as a plate, there were at times small hills that we had to climb. We'd say, '*Allez*, let's go push from behind!' We pushed the *caravane* up the hill, leaving us breathless. Then we discovered that Piotto had remained there in the caravan! We'd shout at him: '*Qu'est-ce que t'fais?* We exhaust ourselves pushing—and you remain inside!' He was sitting there holding the bag of coal across his shoulders and pushing on an inside wall. He tells us, 'I *was* pushing, here, and look at me, I'm also carrying the bag of coal.' *Alors*, he thought that indeed he was not only helping push but also making the load lighter for the little horse!

"One time after we played a show in a dance hall, a group of people from a theater came to see us. There was among them *une grande dame* in furs and *un monsieur* in a velvet smoking jacket, and they wanted to talk about hiring us. The man told us, 'I am the director of the Royal Opera of Ghent, and I would like you all to come play with us. We're producing *La Comtesse Mariza*, and there is a passage including Gypsy musicians. We need you for it.' We went along, and I had never seen anything like it! We toured in a big bus, like the English buses, with all the artists, maybe fifty people, traveling around the whole of Belgium.

There were thirty-six musicians in their orchestra—huge drums and tubas, cellos and double basses! Then there were the singers who sang without microphones but with such amazing force! There was a passage in the opera where they have a fight while singing, and one could hear all of the argument back and forth, the shouting and cries! Then all of a sudden, behind us on the stage, the choir enters—sixty people dressed in lacquered helmets topped with horse tails, and the stage floor shook underneath us all! When we finished the performance, I had tears in my eyes. I said to myself, '*Moi*, I'm ready to climb up to heaven; I don't need anything more!' My heart was pounding: I thought I was going to die of music!

"When I was young, we learned music from the movies. By that era, all the movies had soundtrack music. For me, the musical films thrilled me. I cajoled my mother into giving me a couple *sous*, and then I was ready to go off to the movies. When there was a truly beautiful song, I called my cousins: 'This is *un morceaux* that we must learn! We'll go back to the movie together, us three. You remember the first passage; me, the second one; and him, the third one—because one of us alone could not remember the whole melody.' We'd go, but sometimes it took us a long time to get the song down as we couldn't remember all of the music by heart. Then we'd have to go back and see the movie again, but we'd have to wait to get more money. *Alors*, then I thought of Piotto. He was like a walking recording machine! We could just send him to the movie and he'd remember the melody all by himself. So we got together and paid for Piotto to go to the movies. When he exited the theater, he was already whistling the whole song!

"Some people had small, portable phonographs in their *caravanes*, but it was rare that anyone had many records to play. And those early records broke as easily as a piece of cake! And then the needles wore out, so we sharpened them on a rock. Finally, the phonograph's spring would break. So we'd get a kid to stand there and turn it with his finger. He'd get lazy or bored, and we'd scream at him, 'Turn it smooth!'

"Then I had a manager, Nino. This man worked with the circus for years as a clown. He took care of me a little, organized for me to play music for the Cirque Médrano, traveling around the world!"

One day in 1965, Bamboula and his ensemble arrived to make their music in a *café* called De Klokkeput in the village of Sint Martens Latem near the Belgian city of Ghent. The proprietor here was Emiel De Cauter, and his restaurant drew a regular clientele of artists and musicians. This was fine by Emiel, as he too was a violin player as well as a painter. And it was fine by Emiel's son, Koen De Cauter, as he was fascinated by the music.

The band of Gypsies set up to play. Sitting in behind Bamboula and the older men was a thirteen-year-old Romani boy named Fapy Lafertin. Koen De Cauter's eyes were drawn to this boy of his own age. Fapy had been playing guitar ever since he was old enough to hold one. His first guitar was a full-sized resonator guitar, and a photo of Fapy at age five shows him struggling to reach around the big body—while on his face is a magnificent grin. Fapy was a nephew of Bamboula on both sides of the family: His mother, Kalie Ferret, was Bamboula's sister; his father, Tsavele Lafertin, was Bamboula's cousin. Fapy and Koen were born one day apart in 1950, and they shared this same passion for music. A long and intense friendship was born.

A short time later, Piotto Limberger returned to perform at Emiel's café, and soon, Fapy and Koen joined the band. They both began a schooling in old-time Romani music under Piotto's tutelage.

By 1975, Fapy and Koen decided they wanted to modernize their music: They wished to play Gypsy jazz in the style of Django. Enlisting another local Belgian youth, Michel Verstraeten, on bass and an American expatriate acquaintance, Jeff C. Wickle, on rhythm guitar, they formed their own band. Now the band needed a name.

Koen had a three-year-old son whom he called "Waso," a diminutive form of the Norwegian name "Was" that caught Koen's fancy. As Waso De Cauter remembers thirty years later: "I was walking around—probably minding my own business—when they were looking for a band name." Added to this was the link between the name 'Waso" and another Romani elder musician they admired, Jozef "Wasso" Grünholz, the son of Latcheben. And so the band's name was chosen.

The Waso Quartet began playing cafés in Belgium and the Netherlands, just as Bamboula and Piotto had done. Yet while their music was more modern than that of Les Piottos' old-fashioned melodies, it was still some four decades behind the times. Django's music was now old-fashioned as well. But in Waso's hands, all of the traditions and history of Gypsy jazz came together in harmony to revive the music for a new era and a new audience.

In 1975, the band recorded a first LP, *Live at Gringo's*, capturing one of their café shows. Fapy had studied Django well, and he now played the master's solos almost note for note off the old 78s, almost as if he were channeling Django's spirit. When Wickle left in 1976 to return to the United States, he was replaced on rhythm guitar by the son of Piotto, Vivi Limberger. And the band continued on in this classic Waso lineup to record four further albums.

While their Gypsy jazz was well done, the band's masterpiece may just be an obscure, hard-to-find LP from 1977 entitled *Rommages*. Paying tribute to their elders—Bamboula, Piotto, and Latcheben—the band backed *chanteur* Jacques Mercier in a set of songs recreating the Romani minstrel traditions. The singing was enchanting, the music charming.

When Fapy fell ill in 1985, Koen took over the solo guitar chair. Over the next two decades, the band and its music continued to evolve, with Koen's sons Waso on rhythm guitar, Dajo on bass, and Myrddin on clarinet and flamenco guitar; his daughters Vigdis on piano and Saïdjah performing flamenco dance; as well as Vivi's multi-instrumentalist son Tcha joining in. And Fapy too was back when they played a series of tribute concerts to Django in 2004, along with guest guitarist Patrick Saussois.

Throughout it all, Koen and Fapy have never simply copied Django's musical legacy. Fapy moved beyond Gypsy jazz, also playing Portuguese fado and Gitano flamenco. Koen's repertoire is also broad and varied, stretching far beyond the confines of traditional Gypsy jazz to include classical music and *musette*, Tziganes, flamenco, klezmer, New Orleans jazz, and the songs of Georges Brassens. And more. Far from the modern-day fast-paced pyrotechnicians, Koen often plays his music slow and deliberate. His sense of swing is sure, his sound lyrical. Above all, Koen De Cauter is intensely *musical*.

Waso's goal had been simply to make song, and yet the band's music would play a hand in inspiring a renaissance in Gypsy jazz. Waso influenced other young Romani and *gadjé* alike, convincing them that they too could play this music.

Among those influenced to play Gypsy jazz again were several other children and grandchildren of the original members of Les Piottos. Latcheben Grünholz's grandson was a skinny boy named Isaak Rosenberg, better known as Stochelo. Born in a Dutch Gypsy camp on February 19, 1968, Stochelo was the first son of guitarist Wilhemus "Mimer" Rosenberg and Joana "Metz" Grünholz. Stochelo was ten before he began playing guitar, tutored now by his father, grandfather, uncle Wasso Grünholz, and self-tutored by deciphering Django's solos off records.

In 1974, Dutch jazz fan Hans Meelen met the Rosenberg clan and they soon formed a band to accompany church services with Wasso, Sani Rosenberg, and violinist Storo Berger. By 1980, the band expanded to be called Manouche and include Stochelo, Sani's rhythm-guitarist son Nous'che, and Rino van Hooydonk. Awed by the young Stochelo's playing, Meelen organized a 1979 in-studio show at local radio station Omroep Brabant. He then took copies of those recordings to introduce the band to a 1980 Dutch television-show talent contest called *Stuif es in.* Twelve-year-old Stochelo, his cousin Nous'che, and bassist friend Rino performed and took home top prize.

Stochelo was immediately besieged with recording offers. Yet his parents hesitated. They wished to shield their son from the *gadjo* spotlight. In addition, being staunch members of the Romani Pentecostal church, they were unsure about his playing secular music, even that of Django. And so Stochelo—along with his cousins Nous'che Rosenberg on rhythm guitar and Nonnie Rosenberg on bass—honed their playing instead at religious pilgrimages and church services throughout the Netherlands, Belgium, and into France and Germany. Known as the Rosenberg Trio, the band became stars among the Romani. But they were unknown to the jazz world outside.

It couldn't last. On June 17, 1989, during the Django tribute festival at Samois-sur-Seine, Meelen fast-talked the band onto the stage between acts. Performing the music they had grown up on, the unknown Rosenberg Trio stunned the audience of jazz aficionados who believed they knew the pulse of the music. Here was Django's swing, alive again, recreated by three young Romani who had simply appeared out of the campsites.

Meelen then worked together with Jon Larsen, leader of both the Hot Club de Norvège band and the Hot Club Records label, to record the trio. The band's 1989 debut, *Seresta*, was Gypsy jazz as never before heard. The album featured Romani classics such as "Les yeux noirs," a transcendent cover of Django's "Troublant Boléro," a tribute to their elder in "Wasso's Waltz," and even a Latin piece in Dorado Schmitt's "Bossa Dorado." Here as well were Gypsy jazz versions of modern classics, including a roaring take on Sonny Rollins's "Pent-Up House" and a remake of "On Green Dolphin Street," previously the domain of Miles Davis and Bill Evans. Gypsy jazz was suddenly a vibrant music reflecting on its own past and looking forward into the crystal ball of a now-exciting future. The Rosenberg Trio's *Seresta* would be another primary inspiration for a new age of Gypsy jazz.

While Waso and the Rosenberg Trio were reviving Django's music for a new era, Bamboula remained steadfast in playing his music from an older time. In Paris, he was singing and playing violin with the band Bâchtre Sinto, led by guitarist Mano Dray-Weiss. Bamboula takes up his tale again: "Over the years, there were eight of us cousins and brothers that made our careers as musicians. I also had two brothers that sometimes joined us: One played accordion; the other, Ringo, played guitar. My father-in-law also played violin. After my marriage, he and I became great buddies together. Piotto's children [he married Bamboula's other sister, Miso Gabrielle Ferret] and nephews also made music their career—including Jan, Storro, Vivi, and Biske, and Jan's grandson, Martin. And Piotto also has a grandson that plays well—Tcha Limberger. He was blind at birth, but he's a true artist."

In 1980, Piotto passed on, followed in 1998 by Latcheben Grünholz. Koen De Cauter composed a eulogy to Latcheben—and in many ways, to this whole generation of Romani minstrels. In his melody "Adieu Lachpin," Koen sang through the sad voice of his soprano saxophone a plangent and achingly beautiful tribute to this elder generation.

Now, Bamboula was truly the last of his era.

And yet oddly enough, Bamboula's career and renown was just about to take off. In 1998, his nephew Fapy Lafertin arranged to record Bamboula playing his old repertoire as a way to keep the past alive, or at least to assure it wouldn't be forgotten. Bamboula played violin—he had already set aside his guitar—and sang in his deep, dark voice, at times raspy, at others glorious and smooth. Fapy added his trademark guitar, and the duo were backed by more cousins—rhythm guitarist Dadie Lafertin and bassist Wiwits Lafertin. The result was Bamboula's recording debut, after just some seven decades as a musician. The first self-released CD was entitled *Oe Djoevia*, followed soon after by *Me am kolle marsch*. Never released commercially, they were sold only privately at gigs and Romani religious pilgrimages.

Bamboula continues telling me the story: "Fapy and I, we recorded the old songs, *les vieux morceaux* that I have been carrying with me all these years. I had to teach them all to him, and that pleased him. I sang songs in Manouche. I played only old pieces, old *valses*, songs no one else remembered! But me, I knew them. We confined ourselves in the *caravane*, drank coffee, smoked cigarettes, and played all day long. Fapy had some cassettes and CDs made to sell at the pilgrimages and after concerts. This pleased me a lot, and those recordings, they have now been around the globe. They were just home recordings, not done perfectly—yet they were my first recordings, and I'm proud of them."

Among the songs on Bamboula's album is a simple yet gorgeous little waltz, entitled "La valse à Bamboula." While Bamboula swears he did not compose it, the song has become his trademark. And today, played by Gypsy jazz guitarists everywhere, it has found a place in the canon.

Bamboula remembers the story behind his namesake *valse*: "There was a waltz that I heard a very long time ago and remembered still after all these years because it pleased me so much. It's not me who composed it; it was just me who remembered it, for at least twenty years now. I was in a market on a fair day, walking around, looking at the stalls. There was a merchant with old records for sale, and he played this *petite valse* on his phonograph to entice buyers. That waltz, she remained in my head, and afterward I tried to play it. I did it to the best of my ability, but I don't know if it is perfectly authentic. After hearing me play it twenty years later, Fapy baptized the waltz—'C'est "La valse à Bamboula!"'"

As I listen now to Bamboula tell his story and then to his album *Oe Djoevia*, I am struck by the simple dignity of this man and his music. "La valse à Bamboula" and the other songs here evoke images of wandering minstrels within our lifetimes playing for pitiful pay in small-town markets or the joys of late-night jams by the flames of Romani campfires. I hear songs that are storytelling at its finest, a voyage back into a bygone way of life. Bamboula has every reason to be proud of his music. *Oe Djoevia* is unique, stunning. It's sentimental without being precious, nostalgic without being simply quaint. And throughout, Fapy's guitar is the perfect complement, enhancing his uncle's singing with virtuosity that never overpowers or outshines the man with the voice. With his album *Oe Djoevia*, Bamboula Ferret created one of the great masterpieces of Gypsy jazz, while his life's music was an inspiration for the future.

FIFTEEN

Resurrection

The New Elegance of Biréli Lagrène, Stochelo Rosenberg, Angelo Debarre, and Ninine Garcia

A T ONE TIME, Django's music was nearly dead.

In the decades following Django's own passing, many Romani had all but forgotten the jazz played by one of their own. The younger generations of Gypsies coming of age in the 1960s and 1970s grew up rarely if ever hearing it. Django's legacy was on the verge of fading away into silence.

The resurrection of Gypsy jazz came thanks to several surprising forces. Any one of these forces alone likely wouldn't have saved the music. But because of fate and chance, they converged to revive Gypsy jazz. And bring it back stronger than ever before.

In quest of the story behind this musical resurrection, I've come now to Strasbourg, the heart of Alsace-Lorraine. I'm walking the cobblestone streets of the city's Grande Île, skirting the red sandstone cathedral and medieval timber-framed buildings, over the many canal bridges, past the white swans under the willow trees, and out beyond the modern glacial chic of the European Parliament's headquarters. Here, on the far edges of town and in the surrounding countryside resides a vast population of Romani. The Rhineland, with Strasbourg at its center, has drawn Romani for as long as anyone can remember. Over the centuries, Alsace served as a natural passage between the impenetrable Black Forest and the heights of the Alps, Jura, and Vosges mountain ranges. *Strossburi,* as the city's known in the curious Alsatian dialect, means literally the town (*burg*) at the crossing of the roads (*strassen*). The region was thus an ideal Romani headquarters. And hideout. There were two governments from which to accept welfare, two countries in which to escape to evade police.

Today, Gypsy apartment complexes and caravan encampments surround Strasbourg and stretch out into the Rhineland. They're a constant reminder of the thorny issues concerning the Romani within the European Union congress. Most of the apartments and campsites are consecrated now by the French and German governments, an attempt to entice, if not actually force, the vagabonds to settle in one place by providing water, electricity, and sewage hookups for their *caravanes*. The apartments have the charm and character of the nearby Maginot Line—concrete bunkers with gun slits for windows, living rooms like artillery emplacements, latrine-style bathrooms. And the official encampments are really nothing more glamoros than mobile-home parks, with all *their* usual enchantment. They look and act like well-ordered villages—almost. Each has its own official postal address and of course bureaucratic and police surveillance. This is an essential element of the encampments *raison d'être*: control. Once upon a time, France and Germany outlawed being a Gypsy, deporting perpetrators to Africa or Louisiana, the slave galleys, or concentration camps. Today, the governments of these two countries want the people they once forced onto the road to settle down and stay put at the side of that same road.

Romani are willing to comply—for the time being, that is. These camping sites offer easy access to those government handouts. This is almost a code of honor among the Gypsies. As a Romani saying goes, *Rrom corel khajnja, gadjé corel farma*—The Romani steals a chicken, but the *gadjé* steals the farm. It's a saying, and a warning. These days, *gadjé* no longer fret that Gypsies will steal their children. Yet the Romani live in real fear that the governments' social services may indeed steal theirs.

And the apartments are fine *pied-à-terres*, the campsites handy way stations. But they too are both viewed by the Gypsies as only temporary addresses. Come summer, everything is packed up. Satellite dishes and portable clothes-washing machines and motorized children's tricycles are stowed, *campines* hooked onto a Mercedes, BMW, or grand Citroën, and the families are happily on the road again.

Arriving now at the heart of one Romani encampment, it's obvious that the modern world has not been kind to the Gypsies. I see kids with bored, deadpan expressions, gazing out through the chain-link fences encircling campsites. Men loiter with no intent. Instead of camping in the beauty of the Rhineland countryside, that countryside has been paved over and turned into a parking lot. There's no horse-trading, chair-caning, pot-mending, basket weaving, jewelry-crafting, lace-making, or other artisanship these days. Government aid has taken their place.

And yet, coming from somewhere within the labyrinth of caravans, I hear the sound of guitars, pounding out *la pompe* with a hard-driving, freewheeling sense of swing.

One of the forces behind the resurrection of Gypsy jazz was something as prosaic as changing technology. Living in peripatetic *caravanes*, many Romani never owned record players on which to listen to Django's recordings. The 1970s brought the invention of magnetic cassette tapes, which, while a marketing boom for the rest of the world, proved a minor miracle for Gypsies. Suddenly, these transient people had a portable source of recorded music. Labels such as Vogue and EMI-Pathé reissued Django's classic sides on the novel medium, and a new generation of Gypsies discovered the old melodies. The music had survived this long largely as an oral tradition, heard only by live audiences from the few elder Romani still playing—Joseph Reinhardt, the Ferret brothers, Bamboula, Bousquet, Tchan Tchou, and too few others. Now, it could be heard anywhere and everywhere.

To these young Romani, Django's music was a revelation. This revolution of rediscovery brought a renewed interest in playing Django's music among his own people. These Gypsies heard everything within Django's playing that enamored us *gadjé*—whether it was B. B. King or Tal Farlow or even myself. The dapper swing, incandescent improvisations, and deep emotion.

They also heard something more.

From those apartment blocks and encampments, a new, unforeseen spirit of Romani pride was emerging and radiating across Europe. This movement evolved into the establishment of the Romani World Congress, which held its first gathering near London in 1971. Gypsy representatives from twenty countries, including India, attended the meeting sponsored by the Indian Government and World Council of Churches. Among the goals of the congress were efforts to garner Nazi war-crime reparations and combat Romani social problems and education issues. A Romani flag was flown, featuring a red *chakra* wheel eternally rolling across a field of green beneath a blue sky. And a Romani anthem was adopted, the song "Djelem, djelem," with lyrics by balalaïka player Jarko Jovanovic set to an old Gypsy melody:

> *Djelem, djelem, lungone dromensa*
> *Maladilem bakhtale Romensa*
> *A Romale katar tumen aven*
> *E tsarensa bahktale dromensa?*
> *A Romale, A Chavale*

Vi man sas ek bari familiya
Murdadas la e kali legiya
Aven mansa sa lumniake Roma
Kai putaile e romane droma
Ake vriama, usti Rom akana
Men khutasa misto kai kerasa
A Romale, A Chavale

I travel, I travel down long roads
I met happy Romani
O Romani, from where do you come
With your tents down happy roads?
O Romani, O fellow Romani
I too once had a great family
But the Black Legions [Nazi SS] murdered them
Come with me Romani from all the world
For the Romani roads are open again
Now is the time, rise up now, Romani
We will rise high if we join together
O Romani, O fellow Romani

All of a sudden, Django's guitar spoke with a new eloquence to his own people. French writer Guillaume Apollinaire once stated that Gypsies have no history, only geography. Now suddenly, the Romani had a history—and a proud one at that.

This new generation of Manouche and Gitan guitarists proudly embraced Django's music and pronounced it *mare gilia*—Romanès for "our music." Never mind that many of the songs dated from another era or originated from across the ocean. Gypsy jazz was reborn.

Along with Gypsy camps in Paris as well as Belgium and the Netherlands, many of this new generation originated from Strasbourg and the Rhineland—another reason I've come here, in pursuit of this Alsatian branch of the music. The region is the birthplace of a who's-who of modern Gypsy jazzmen. Violin virtuoso Titi Winterstein and his guitarist cohort Lulu Reinhardt. Marcel Loeffler, the blind accordion master, inspired as much by Gus Viseur as by *neuvo tanguero* Astor Piazzolla. Guitar maestro Dorado Schmitt. His cousin Tchavolo Schmitt, who was born in Paris but spends much of his time in Alsace, where he also starred in Algerian Gypsy Tony Gatlif's 2002 film, *Swing*. Mandino Reinhardt. Titi Bamberger. Moréno Winterstein. Mito Loeffler. Macho Winterstein. And many more from Winterstein, Loeffler, Schmitt, Weiss, and of course, Reinhardt clans.

These Romani guitarists began by copying Django's song heads and solos off tapes, faithfully picking out his choruses in near-religious devotion to his musical canon. With Django leading the way, these new generations of Gypsy jazzmen now play with a style and finesse and technical proficiency as never before. Django's guitar articulated their being, becoming an emblem of Gypsy identity.

I can hear all of this—and more—in the simple jazz jump "Noto-Swing" by the Titi Winterstein's Quintett with guitarist Lulu Reinhardt. Leading off the band's stellar 1985 LP *Djinee tu kowa ziro*, the introductory chords come pounding off the acetate like a machine gun. Then the melody line is struck up, echoed in muscular duet by violin and guitar. As the band hits its first chorus, the rhythm goes into stoptime; only the solo guitar barks out, blasting off a torrent of notes so strong, so impressive, it leaves me gasping for breath. This may be just another swing song, but it's alive with a muscular assertion of cultural identity. This is no longer just Django's music. It is the sound of renewed Gypsy pride.

With tape recorders ready, Romani musicians now made cassettes of their own music and sold or traded them among themselves. There was no need for mainstream *gadjo* recording companies. The music of these homespun bands symbolized a lost generation to *gadjé* jazz fans as the recordings were rarely released commercially or distributed far afield. Yet with their homemade cassettes, these Gypsy musicians reached the sole market they cared about.

With the arrival of the compact disc in 1982, the recording and duplicating of a band's own album skyrocketed in quality and dived in expense. Gypsy jazzmen's self-produced albums were everywhere, sold at gigs, at religious pilgrimages, even in mainstream music stores like France's ubiquitous FNAC. Suddenly, there were no boundaries to where this new era of Gypsy jazz could travel.

Out of this new generation came four guitarists who set the tempo for the future, proving the most influential for fellow Gypsies and *gadjé* alike—Alsace's Biréli Lagrène, Dutch Gypsy Stochelo Rosenberg, Paris's Angelo Debarre, and an unlikely fourth, Ninine Garcia of the Porte de Clignancourt *puces*.

Modern Gypsy legend tells the tale this way:

Some twenty years after Django's untimely death in 1953, his brother Nin-Nin overheard a slight Romani youth playing Django's jazz on a Jacques Favino guitar several sizes too large for him. The boy's four small fretting fingers struggled to reach all those notes Django played with just his two, but his sense of swing was sure. Nin-Nin was so moved by the music that he burst into tears. He declared this prodigy must be the reincarnation of Django.

His name was Biréli Lagrène. Born near Soufflenheim, minutes north of Strasbourg, on September 4, 1966, he began forming chords on a guitar when he was just four. His father was Fiso Lagrène, a renowned guitarist among the Manouche of the region. Fiso now began to tutor his son.

"My people consider Django the King of the Gypsies," Biréli explains to me. "My father was a big fan of Django's, and I feel as if I grew up with the man. As a kid, I played Django's records unceasingly until I could recreate the songs note for note."

When he was just twelve, Biréli was booked for a tour of Germany, playing with his elder brother Gaiti as his rhythm man. In 1980, now all of thirteen, Biréli released his first album, *Routes to Django*, capturing him live with his brother at the Krokodil club in Kirchheim. Performing a repertoire that included several early originals, his guitarwork displayed a maturity far beyond his age. This teen who could barely reach around his guitar stunned the jazz world with riffs that swung with new eloquence. Even Django's own son Babik praised the skinny little newcomer, saying, "He's the true keeper of my father's flame."

Within the next few years, Biréli would release two more albums—*Swing 81* and *15*—and bring his brand of Gypsy jazz on tour throughout Europe and to the United States to play Carnegie Hall. He was indeed following in Django's footsteps.

And yet, as both a Romani and a musician, Biréli began to feel constrained on his chosen path. "My fellow Gypsies were telling me, 'No, the way to play the music is like *this!*'" he explains to me. At age fifteen, Biréli was stuck. There was no opportunity for him to grow within this music—Gypsy jazz as prescribed by his Romani elders ironically lacked freedom of expression.

It's a refrain heard time and again, the variations lying in the verses: A Gypsy guitar prodigy appears one day on the jazz scene, younger and fresher each time, playing with a grace or speed as never before—or both combined. This new arrival first learned to fret the guitar at age eight, seven, six—it's impossible to imagine them able to play any younger. And in these new generations is the future of Gypsy jazz. The list is long. Biréli himself. Boulou and Elios Ferré. Raphaël Faÿs, son of *bal musette* guitarman Louis Faÿs. Samson Schmitt, son of Dorado. Yorgui Loeffler, Ritary Gaguenetti, Wawau Adler, Dino Mehrstein, Joscho Stephan. Eddy Waeldo, who at just fourteen in 2005 released his first album of sophisticated bebop. A whole lineage of Reinhardt cousins, of course, including now Falko and Faifie. And then there's the Dutch Rosenberg clan—Noë, Jimmy, Watti, Kaatchie.

It's not exactly a new tradition. Django of course performed with his pianist father and dancing mother when he was just seven. Playing violin and later, *banjo-guitare*, he was part child prodigy, part child curiosity. In Django's day, teaching a child to play was the perfect way to add to a family's livelihood. Today, the various European governments prescribe school, although too many Romani youths only ever get a small dosage. And with nothing to stand in their way, children can spend hours learning their instrument.

A discordant number of Romani children become guitar prodigies by their teens. Yet too many rarely progress beyond that. They might record an album, play gigs, and go on a short tour. But soon they've reached a peak, and without benefit of further musical education or management direction, there's little more to which to aspire. Many simply get bored and set aside their guitars. Others take up crime or drugs instead.

The situation was similiar for Biréli. The music he grew up on and loved was now becoming a trap.

"I came to understand that it's better to respect the great guitarists than imitate them," he tells me. "I discovered that it was better to try to create something new than replay their music. *This* is the essence of jazz."

So fifteen-year-old Biréli plugged in an electric guitar, turned up the volume, and shocked his elders and the Gypsy jazz purists. "I really had to start my career all over," he remembers: "It was a big risk." Joining forces with former Weather Report bassist Jaco Pastorius, the duo went avant-garde with a run of jazz-rock fusion albums. They painted their masterpiece in 1988's *Stuttgart Aria*, jumping from reggae to funk to Charlie Parker, all spun through a hurricane of guitar.

After Pastorius's premature passing in 1987, Biréli moved on again. He traded off between solid-body and archtop electrics, fusion and traditional jazz— he even cut a tribute to Frank Sinatra, 1998's *Blue Eyes*, Biréli trying himself at the mic. He also toured and recorded with the likes of Larry Coryell and Al Di Meola, as well as the Jimi Hendrix of accordionists, Richard Galliano.

And yet Biréli was still searching for his own sound.

If this is Monday, this must be Moscow. It's actually midnight, so we're now on the brink of Tuesday. But it is indeed Moscow, yet another stop on a 2005 world tour supporting Biréli's new album. He has just landed at Domodedovo International Airport and is being whisked into the city proper via limousine; he's chatting with me on the other side of the Atlantic by way of his manager's cell phone. Despite the hour, Biréli sounds crisp and clear, speaking his impeccable English.

These days, Biréli has returned to his roots. With the recent renaissance of Django's music, Biréli was inspired in 2001 to form his Gipsy Project ensemble, based on the classic Quintette du Hot Club de France. But his return to Gypsy jazz did not come easy. "I hadn't played a note of this music in more than fifteen years, so I had to go back and listen to Django's records," Biréli admits. "It took me about three months to get my chops back." He need not have fretted: His chops were back in fine style on his band's 2001 eponymous debut and the 2002 follow-up, *Gipsy Project & Friends*. Biréli's swing was once again uninhibited and virtuosic, carefree yet sincere, and he found a ready audience at the booming Gypsy jazz festivals in Europe and the United States. Biréli's 2004 DVD, *Live: Jazz à Vienne*, captured the spirit at one of these festivals. He trades exhilarating licks with cameos by today's Gypsy jazz stars—Dorado and Tchavolo, Stochelo, Angelo Debarre, Django's grandson David Reinhardt, and more. The music was inspired.

Yet after these faithful homages, Biréli was again ready to experiment. His next CD, *Move*, took up where Django left off, transporting Gypsy jazz into the twenty-first century: "This album was an attempt to move forward, to try something new, without violins," Biréli says. "We play Django's more modern side, moving on to this kind of bebop sound."

After Django and violinist Stéphane Grappelli famously parted ways at the outbreak of World War II, Django also updated his sound. In his Nouveau Quintette, he replaced Grappelli's violin with horns—first, a clarinet in emulation of Benny Goodman; later, an alto sax inspired by Bird. Fifty years later, Biréli followed suit. He formed his own lead duet with conservatory-trained French saxman Franck Wolf. The soloists are backed by fellow Romani Hono Winterstein's rock-solid rhythm and bassist Diego Imbert. With this string-jazz base, Biréli's band still eschews drums. Yet Django remains the foundation here, Biréli building on this with his own contemporary compositions, inventive guitar solos, and dynamic interplay with Wolf.

"When I was a kid, I was surrounded by all of my Gypsy cousins who always wanted to hear Django's music played in the 'right way,'" Biréli explains. "Now, I try to play *around* Django, not play *like* him." Biréli's maturity and musical travels have helped him create something better than ever. "I feel much freer now," he confides. "Suddenly, I feel I can finally play like I want to."

Ironically, Biréli found new inspiration not just in Django's old records but in rediscovering the beauty of Grappelli's violin. "Grappelli had a big impact on my guitar playing," he explains: "It's the way he phrased—it's just lovely. I try to capture that in my solos."

This all comes through in Biréli's thoroughly modern "Nuages." "It's a song that's been played too many times and I didn't want to record it again," he says.

Talked into including the song by producer Francis Dreyfus, Biréli insisted on taking it in new directions. In the grand bebop spirit of reharmonizing classics, he revamped Django's chords with added ninths, elevenths, and thirteenths, at times crafting graceful chord-melody rhythm lines behind the chromatic theme intoned by the sax. "'Nuages' suddenly sounds very different," Biréli laughs.

He's not bound to old-fashioned Gypsy jazz rhythm on up-tempo songs either. Instead of sticking to the genre's signature sixth chords—beloved for their dark, even sinister mood—Biréli tosses in straight-ahead minor chords, an influence from his own electrified past and love of rock guitarists like Joe Satriani. The effect is like hard-edged Gypsy jazz power chords; as Biréli says, "Adding in a simple Gm chord can really flip things over."

He explains, "I put everything into my rhythm playing. I love to play different types of music and it's hard for me to remain faithful to just one style of music; I don't want to be tagged simply as someone who can 'play Django.' The most important thing to me now is to put my own ingredients into the music—my tone, my phrasing, my inspirations. I want to demystify the old style by mixing in the new, and I hope whatever I do gives ideas to the other Gypsies to dare to try something new, to explore the music."

For now, Biréli and his new Gipsy Project are back on the road. With concerts in Moscow and ongoing tours of Europe and the United States, Biréli has taken Gypsy jazz global. He's become an ideal ambassador for the music, his virtuosity and sense of swing inspiring Gypsies and *gadjé* to take up the guitar and study Gypsy jazz roots. "This music is far more popular than ever before," Biréli says to me. "It's hard for my Gypsy friends back home in France to believe that our music has traveled so far on so many different continents."

I'm on the outskirts of Paris in Montreuil-sous-Bois at the bistro La Grosse Mignonne on a warm and wondrous night in spring 2007. This is a rare evening, an opportunity to see two of the biggest names in modern Gypsy jazz playing not in a grand concert hall or on a festival stage, but here, in a small café. Romane and Stochelo Rosenberg have formed a sort of alliance, recording together and playing shows in duo. And tonight they prove theirs a fine collaboration.

Both musicians have been key influences in the growth of Gypsy jazz. Frenchman Patrick "Romane" Leguidecoq was one of the first modern players to spread the word far and wide in the United States and United Kingdom, as his records were easily available when most Romani guitarists' albums were unobtainable. While others may play faster and wilder, Romane's eked out his own style, which is not easy to do in the shadow of Django. Rather than recite the master again and again, Romane's proven himself an able composer. And his numerous method books elucidating the mysteries of the music have found homes in many acolytes' collections.

Stochelo's on another level, however, and it was to promote this shy Romani's music that Romane first began to produce Stochelo's recordings in 2000. Stochelo can play with both velocity and virtuosity, but it's the elegance of his improvisations that have inspired fans and other guitarists around the globe. His shyness comes through in his music: Rarely does he grandstand, opting instead for grace.

Tonight at La Grosse Mignonne, the interplay between the two proves it all. Romane is careful to be the one to count into each song; if he doesn't, Stochelo will—and at a tempo that's inhuman, the result of a lifetime jamming around campfires. But when they find their stride in tunes like Romane's sublime "Swing for Ninine" or Stochelo's "For Sephora," the result is wondrous.

Stochelo has become one of the great stylists of Gypsy jazz. After the Rosenberg Trio's landmark *Seresta* in 1989, the band cut several further albums before their 1994 CD *Caravan* was released worldwide. With this international attention, the Rosenberg Trio suddenly became the world's most famous Gypsy jazz band of the 1990s. And yet, because these young Romani men distrusted airplane travel, they played only a handful of shows beyond their base in the Netherlands. Still, alongside the recordings of Django, guitarists everywhere were now trying to play like Stochelo.

For his part, Stochelo remained true to his first hero. As he tells his fans, "Forget about Stochelo Rosenberg and all the others. If you want to learn and understand Gypsy jazz start with Django, the best guitar player that ever lived." With the band's stellar 2007 CD *Roots*, the Rosenberg Trio pays homage to Django and the Gypsy music they grew up on. And Stochelo himself now plays Selmer *petite bouche* jazz guitar serial number 504, the sibling of one of the last guitars Django played, serial number 503.

Back in Paris, I'm walking with American guitarist friends Brian and Kevin Barnes along the Canal Saint-Martin at twilight. The moon's reflected in the canal's calm waters, the October night sweet in its soft warmth. Yet we're passing by the evening's charms on our way to another dark, smoky dive of a bar.

This bar's in the Hôtel du Nord, a Parisian landmark misplaced within the backstreets of the 10th Arrondissement. The old hotel is nondescript and easy to miss: Back in the day, it was just another Parisian flophouse, a temporary home for bargemen working the canal. But the hotel soon became a movie star. Marcel Carné's classic 1938 film *Hôtel du Nord*, adapted from Eugène Dabit's 1929 novel, portrayed the lives and fortunes of two working-class Parisian couples living in the hotel. World-weary Pierre and Renée get a room, in which they plan to kill themselves and put an end to life's miseries. Meanwhile, pimp Edmond and prostitute Raymonde, played by *chanteuse* Arletty, are scratching to rise above the milieu of Paris's *bals musette*, seedy music halls, and dead-end bars. In the movie's most famous scene—and one of the most renowned in all of French cinema—Edmond and Raymonde feud on a footbridge across the Canal Saint-Martin nearby the Hôtel du Nord. Edmond tells her, "*J'ai besoin de changer d'atmosphère*—I need a change of scenery." To which she responds in her backstreet patois in a curse that resounds through the whole city of Paris, "*Atmosphère? Atmosphère! Est-ce que j'ai une gueule d'atmosphère?*—Scenery? Scenery! Am *I* nothing but scenery?"

It was precisely this *atmosphère* that draws us to the Hôtel du Nord tonight. The old hotel looks much the same as in the movie: In the last glow of dusk, its grand old façade shines in the canal streetlamps like a black and white film of *chiaroscuro* darkness and light. Entering the bar, we're greeted by a maître d'hôtel straight out of a Carné movie—part unctuous waiter, part oily gangster wearing a sleek suit with slicked-back hair above a face that makes me check for my wallet after he ushers us to a table. Red-velvet curtains smother the walls; deep banquettes surround booths, ideal for cutting occult deals; candles on the tabletops serve less to provide light than to cast deep shadows that better suit the clientele. *Douce ambiance* indeed.

On a small dais in a far corner is Angelo Debarre, accompanied by Corsican-Italian-French guitarist Rodolphe Raffalli. Angelo is dressed in a dark suit matching his dark eyes, his face showing no emotion as music flows from his fingers, filling the night with hot jazz—there's just a twitch of his pencil-line moustache after a musical phrase that seems particularly to please him. They play Django's melodies, *valses musette*, the odd French *chanson* and traditional Gypsy tune, as well as American jazz standards straight from the Quintette du Hot Club de France's songlist. It's the music Carné himself would likely have chosen for the scene.

Angelo was born August 19, 1962, in Saint-Denis. This birthplace tells much about his heritage: Now a gray suburb of Paris, Saint-Denis was once a gay village outside the capital's medieval fortifications. Even at the time of Angelo's birth, remnants of *La Zone* survived here, a caravanserai of campers, trailers, vans converted into homes-on-wheels, mile-scarred cars, and even rare relics of the ancient wooden *verdines* from Django's day, still pulled by the odd horse. Nowadays, the last, lost enclaves of Gypsy trailers hold out in forgotten corners of Saint-Denis and its surroundings, but most of the Manouches and Gitanes have moved into the French government's apartment towers—Gypsy encampments in the sky.

Still, even within these apartment skyscrapers, there was music. As Angelo says, "In any gathering of three to four hundred caravans, there's no shortage of music," and he himself began to learn guitar at age eight under the tutelage of his father and an uncle, Jim. Angelo also fell in with another Gypsy prodigy about his same age, Raphaël Faÿs, and learned the music from Faÿs' father, Louis. Faÿs *père* played guitar in dance hall bands and jazz groups in the generation following Django. By the time Angelo was thirteen, he was accompanying Raphaël at gigs, playing bars in Montmartre, jamming at La Chope des Puces. He set aside his guitar for a time to play drums. But in 1984 when he was twenty-two, Angelo was back on six strings to spark his own group, the Angelo Debarre Quartet.

During the 1980s, the hot club for Gypsy jazz was the Montmartre *boîte*, La Roue Fleurie. The cabaret became not only a rendezvous for Gypsies but also those entranced by Gypsy music. Owner Serge Camps knew his way around a fretboard, and hired Angelo to front a house band with guitarist Frank Anastasio (son of luthier Pierre Anastasio) and Camps's father, Pierre, on bass. Yet at La Roue Fleurie not only did Angelo fine-tune his jazz riffs, he was also schooled in all sorts of Gypsy music by Serge Camps.

The fruition of this collaboration came on the 1989 album *Gypsy Guitars*, recorded in Norway by Jon Larsen. Interspersed with the usual suspects—"Sheik of Araby," Django's "Blues en mineur," "Cherokee"—were Rumanian and Hungarian folk songs and Gypsy medleys as well as a stunning finale in Vittorio Monti's *Csardas*. It was a guitar *tour de force*. The album—Angelo's first—became a classic, essential listening for fans of Gypsy jazz.

Yet all good things seem to come to an untimely end, and so it was with La Roue Fleurie. *Montmartois* neighbors complained about the glorious noise, and the café was forced to lock its doors in 1990. Angelo then went on a tour of Paris's *cabarets russe*. Along the way, he met Yugoslavian Gypsy Petro Yvanovich, a balalaïka master whose musical style further inspired Angelo.

Over the next years, Angelo released a score of further albums, from his own *Caprice* to duets with fellow guitarists Moréno Winterstein on *Romano Baschepen*, Tchavolo Schmitt on *Mémoires*, and swing accordionist Ludovic Beier. He's also added his guitar to albums by Romane, Jimmy Rosenberg, Florin Niculescu, and Bratsch as well as several other traditional Tziganes groups.

The next time I see Angelo perform, we're both on the other side of the globe. He's the headliner for Djangofest, an annual three-day festival of Gypsy jazz on Whidbey Island in Washington state's Puget Sound. Angelo is one of the few Romani jazzmen who's not afraid to travel—or at least, to travel by airplane— and he thus plays concerts around the world as well as cafés around Paris. And so, combined with his pyrotechnical proficiency on the guitar, he's become one of the stars and greatest influences of the Gypsy jazz renaissance.

Angelo is especially inspiring tonight. He kicks off with a rousing "Swing Gitan," a traditional *puces* anthem. Even played here on the rim of the Pacific, Angelo's rendition summons forth images of Paris's *bals musette* and flea market bars. The evening is off to a fine start.

Trading licks with violinist Tim Kliphuis and bassman Simon Planting, Angelo's flurries of improvisation seem limitless, his smiles—usually a rarity—are countless. Behind the soloists, guitarmen Tchavolo Hassan and Chiquito Lambert keep up a rock-solid rhythm.

Angelo then shifts into "Mélodie au Crépuscule," the sensuous ballad devoted to the twilight, one of those rare songs that makes you shiver with its magic. The song was part of Django's repertoire and bore his name. Yet it's long been thought that Django's brother Nin-Nin was the true composer; the tune's dark tones and introspective melody certainly sound akin to Nin-Nin's other compositions. Either way, Angelo and band make you believe in every note.

Their versions of Django's bebop pieces "R-Vingt Six" and "Impromptu" showcase the band's technical mastery of the music. Angelo's fingers turn into a blur across the frets. Yet while the tempo is dazzling, the sense of musicality is never lost.

And then Angelo counts out "Honeysuckle Rose." He has a particularly deft touch with American jazz standards; his chordal intros and improvisations over the melody lines swing with a sure touch as if he was born and bred in New Orleans. This song's been played to death since Fats Waller composed it, yet in Angelo's hands, its simple beauty blossoms again. I wish the night would never end.

Wherever I am in the world, I find a certain comfort in knowing that on any weekend, from approximately two to six in the afternoon, Ninine Garcia is in his usual chair playing Gypsy jazz at La Chope des Puces, the ancient bistro in the heart of the Clignancourt *puces*. Through winter and summer, war and peace, Ninine is here at *"le p'tit café mythique,"* as guitarist and Gypsy jazz fan Thomas Dutronic so rightly labels it. La Chope is a nondescript hole in the wall on the ancient rue des Rosiers, hidden away amid antique sellers' stalls and the bric-à-brac of the ages. Like much in the old thieves market of Clignancourt, the bar has changed little over the decades. Ninine will be plugged into the usual amp, sitting alongside his father, Mondine, who's in his usual chair with his usual battered Jacques Favino Modèle Enrico Marcias guitar fitted with a Stimer pickup held in place by swaths of packing tape. Mondine will be wearing one of his plaid flannel work shirts buttoned all the way to the neck, a baseball-style cap on his head. And together they'll be playing the music they've played together for the past thirty-five years. Thirty-five years and counting. Perhaps the only thing that's changed over the last two decades since I've been going to La Chope is that Ninine has retired his grand old Busato guitar, the veteran of so many years of Gypsy jazz, the frets worn flat, the bridge held high by a fold of cardboard. Nowadays, with some extra money from the release of his first CD and more concerts around the capital, he's picking on a glorious blonde American archtop. And yet it too, after all the jazz that Ninine has played on it in just a few short years, is also becoming worn with character.

That Ninine would become one of the most influential of all Romani guitarists may seem unlikely. Others can certainly play faster, play more notes, compose more prolifically, record more albums, and play more places around the globe. Some like Biréli, Stochelo, and Angelo—as well as Boulou Ferré, Raphaël Faÿs, Jimmy Rosenberg, Dorado and Tchavolo Schmitt—are true virtuosi. Yet Ninine plays with a clarity and simplicity, a charm and soul that's the stuff of inspiration. He's a humble man with a smile that lights up his whole being; he sports the requisite moustache and short, bristly hair akin to a *niglo*'s prickles. And like Django's, his music is imbued with a deep joy.

Jacques "Ninine" Garcia is part of a clan of musicians stretching back to Coco, Serrani, and Mattéo Garcia, forerunners of Django. It's thus little surprise that Ninine speaks of his upbringing in near-mystical terms: "The world of Django Reinhardt, that's where I was born. I grew up in the world of swing. Thanks to my family, who were all guitarists, I in turn became a musician—as well as a spokesperson for a living tradition of music as created by Django. I am devoted to preserving the rich culture and heritage that Django left us."

Yet before I can greet Ninine upon entering La Chope, I must of course pay homage to his father. Mondine is the patriarch of the bar. Born in 1936, he has played jazz here since 1960, at first with his band Les Manouches including his rhythm guitarist cousin Niglo Adel and a variety of bassists and violinists, including Spatzo Adel. As Ninine explains, "When my father was ten years old, he played his first gig in a *bal musette*, and over the years he has known so many musicians and played in so many places that he could tell stories for hours and hours.

"He learned to play from his elder brother, who was an ace at the *valse musette*. He didn't hesitate to educate my father with slaps to teach him to play correctly. That was the style of music education of that era! Apparently, it was effective, for today my father is *Le Roi de la Valse*. My father is envied equally for his wonderful right rhythm hand as for how he plays his solos with a light touch that is a pleasure to the ear. The esthetic of his picking is an example for all of this musical style. It is part of this marvelous generation that carried the music of Django through to us. I regret that I didn't get enough of those slaps!"

Ninine himself was a latecomer to music. He tells his own story like the biblical tale of the prodigal son: "My father often said to my mother—and in front of me—'I have a son, and am thankful; that's more than one can ask for.' But I could tell he wished for more—a son that also played music like him.

"One day, my father returned home with this fine Busato guitar, the guitar that everyone has seen since and coveted at La Chope des Puces and on which a great number of great guitarists have played. Me, I call it *La Vieille Relique*—The Old Relic. If this guitar could speak, she'd have some stories to tell! People were not attracted by the guitar's appearance—all of her varnish is worn away and she is filthy. Yet she has a grand richness in her soul, a glorious tone. And her history. She has for me great sentimental value.

"*Alors*, my father gave this guitar to me on my tenth birthday, hoping I would follow in his footsteps and become his musical successor. He hid himself in order to watch me, to see my reaction to the guitar. Then, one morning, he heard a bizarre noise. He got up and found me in the process of beating on the Busato with a big spoon. He confiscated the guitar and told me he should have brought me a drum set instead.

"I was fourteen years old when I had my first epiphany. It came thanks to my cousin, who was the same age as me. I had come with my father to Saint-Ouen where half of my family lived. My cousin invited me to follow him to the room of his father, Niglo Adel, where two guitars were waiting, two beautiful Favinos. My cousin picked up one and began to strum some chords. *Ebloui!* I didn't know he played. And I remember his next words as if it was yesterday. He said me, 'Come on, you know how to play.' Filled with shame, I replied, '*Non*.' My Gypsy pride was devastated. Our fathers had played together for twenty-five years and continued even now to play—in their band, Les Manouches. I saw then a grand anomaly: his father played, he played; my father played, and me, Ninine, the son of Mondine, I did not play. What humiliation! My father was the band soloist and my cousin's father was the accompanist, just like me and my cousin should be. Yet I, Ninine, was nothing!

"For my first music lesson, my cousin was kind enough to show me my first chords. It was my first introduction to torture! He twisted and turned my fingers in all directions, and this started a fight between me and my cousin, our first fight. My fingers couldn't bear this torture. And yet I play today thanks to him. I owe him everything. My cousin left us at a very young age, and yet he will remain always in my heart as my first *professeur*."

Ninine was soon at Mondine's side in La Chope and on the rare, limited-edition records his father released. "I know about perseverence," Ninine says. "I was an accompanist for ten long years before I played my first solo chorus. This was thanks to my father, Mondine, who also played accompanist for years to get where he is today."

This afternoon in La Chope, Mondine is proving once again that he is one of the great accompanists of Gypsy jazz, playing behind his own son. One of the greats, and yet unsung. His style is old-fashioned—*out* of fashion. He plays *la pompe* with the classic *boom-chik, boom-chik* rhythm, few power barre chords to mar the light and dry percussive tone. Again, others may play it faster, louder, and with more pizzazz, but Mondine's got the style. If you need a lesson in how to play *la pompe*, it's right here.

I ask Ninine about his own playing, and he talks not of mysterious ancient Gypsy scales or *modernistique* jazz diminished arpeggios. He speaks instead about the essential beauties of rhythm playing as the path to soloing: "It's essential to study first to be a good accompanist before becoming a soloist. Too many people commit the same error: They want to run before they walk. All of Django fans are filled with wonder by his skill, by the colors in his improvisations—but don't forget that Django too paid his dues as a rhythm guitarist in the *bals musette*. Simply listen to how he accompanies Stéphane Grappelli: Sometimes he plays like a train behind him, other times like a bomb going off. This is thanks to his years of 'schooling' as an accompanist in the *bals*. And I'm certain that Django heard an orchestra playing in his soul.

"When Django takes a chorus—what wonder, what joy! It's just as good when he plays *la pompe*. How can you be a good soloist when you have a bad accompanist behind you? How can you find inspiration, support that will help you develop your ideas? If your accompanist slows down, then you must push back the tempo. If his two hands are not synchronized, then the beat gets off-kilter and makes you unstable as well. If his rhythm lacks punch, then there's no swing to emphasize your beautiful phrases. If you have accompanist playing 2.50-*franc* chords—that is, poor chords without a rich sound—it kills the inspiration. I'm persuaded that a good accompanist must have a lot of qualities and be perseverant.

"For me, there is immense pleasure in listening to a good accompanist. At times, he is everything to the music. At other times, his sole goal is to emphasize the soloist. Listen to Stochelo Rosenberg's accompanist, Nous'che; Dorado's accompanist, Hono Winterstein; or Biréli's, Gaiti Lagrène. They are a big part of the success of their soloist. The accompanist is the soloist companion, not a divider.

"In summary: Walk before you run."

Now, after thirty-five years in La Chope, Ninine is ready to run. In 2004, he released his first CD, *My Dream of Love*, a collection that takes him away from La

Chope to showcase his own compositions and improvisations. Most of the tunes on the album are originals, honed and fine-tuned with Mondine, but now played on his own. And he's backed here by his nephew of a new generation, Mundine Garcia. Ninine's solo style is fluid without striving to impress, lucid and melodic without reaching for virtuosity. As Ninine warns, "There are those that confuse Django and Jimi Hendrix..."

Ninine remains firmly in Django's camp: "Jean Cocteau compared Django to *un fauve*—a wild beast—that will surprise you at every instance with his music. He surprises you with the mysterious dissonance in his music and his majestic phrasing, all played with an inimitable tone. And his extraordinary improvisations will transport you to another world, the world of Django. He's also a painter, with a thousand colors in his palette, a rainbow of colors. When Django plays, I understand everything he says. Django's notes speak a magical language. When he plays 'Tears,' he's speaking in poetry, different from the intensity of 'Mystery Pacific' or 'Rythme Futur.' Django is the Baudelaire of swing."

Ninine may be ready to run, but he's in no hurry to go anywhere. He's playing weekend nights at Au Clarion des Chasseurs on Place du Tertre and other gigs around the capital, from bars to concert halls. Yet La Chope suits him best. He and Mondine have a special connection through their music—or perhaps it's just the three, going on four, decades of playing together that does it. On some choruses one of them may play an extra measure, and the other understands, adapts, and they come back to the top together in perfect time, right on that beat. Ninine is comfortable here, alongside his father, in his usual chair, with his usual cadre of friends, playing timeless *valses* and Gypsy jazz every weekend afternoon from two until six, come rain or shine, war or peace.

The Music Thieves

SIXTEEN

*Into America with Danny Fender, Johnny Guitar,
John Adomono, and Julio Bella*

I T'S AS IF THE BEATLES WERE BACK!

Or had never left.

When Danny Fender and his Band of Gypsies hit the stage at San Francisco's Palace of Fine Arts Theatre, it's chaos and delirium and pandemonium all in one. Even though the band's an hour late, the audience of three hundred American Romani (and one *gadjo*, myself) are on their feet in an instant, cheering at such volume it overpowers the music. This hysteria hits me unprepared. I traveled across the country to hear Danny Fender and his secretive brand of American "California Style" Gypsy guitar—"secret," as few *gadjé* anywhere have ever even heard *of* this music, never mind hearing recordings or the music itself live. I never suspected the music had such a following. Screams, shrieks, whistles, that throaty undulating-tongue Eastern European chant—this is Gypsy Beatlemania. I've never seen an audience anywhere go so crazy for a band the moment they step on stage. Danny's cool, though. He stabs his pink-paisley Fender Telecaster and tears into Rimsky-Korsakov's "The Flight of the Bumblebee" at full Romani virtuosic velocity. And the band is with him all the way, *nine guitars strong*. The rhythm-men are strumming with a ferocity that builds with each of Danny's choruses, digging deeper into a groove that's part Balkan Tziganes, part Gipsy Kings rhumba, and part good old, all-American surf music. Teenage Romani girls are dancing in the aisles and on their seats, impromptu flamenco-style shimmies to a rock'n'roll beat. Elderly gents in gangster suits and two-tone shoes from a forgotten era are waving fedoras in the air, their other hand across their belly in a trancelike Hungarian step. Grandmothers in high heels are dipping and diving, their shawls held above their heads like wings carrying them away. The screaming never stops, and I make a note to be ready to catch the crazed Gypsy girl next to me when she topples over in a faint. Then, a duet of female dancers jumps on stage and goes into a dervish spin. There's no hired security here; this is an all-Gypsy affair, and the Gypsies take care of their own. The on-stage dancers wind themselves into a frenzy, full skirts floating on the air, red and orange silken scarves flying behind like flames caressing Danny's electric guitar.

The Beatles played their last concert ever at San Francisco's Candlestick Park on February 29, 1966. But this audience of Romani never missed them. Tonight is Valentine's Day 2006, four decades later almost to the day and just across the city, and with Danny Fender at center stage, the music has only just begun.

Discovering Danny—let alone getting a chance to hear him play his guitar live—was a minor miracle. But once I heard him, I wanted to learn more. More about Django's influence on fellow Gypsies a world away from Paris, more about American Romani music itself. While Danny does not play only Gypsy jazz, his music is inspired by Django and is a fascinating aspect of Gypsy jazz history. And it's phenomenal music in its own right. So I began my search.

Little did I realize, it would take me seven years to find Danny Fender.

The first clue about his music was uncovered on the other side of the United States, in Charlotte, North Carolina, back in 1999. Fellow Gypsy jazz fan Scot Wise overhead a Romani teenager in a guitar store picking a bit of supercharged Gypsy song. Scot asked him what music he was playing, and the boy responded, "California Style." Nothing more. When Scot queried him further, the boy reluctantly said it was a tune by a guitarist named Danny Fender. This set off the quest.

I began questioning every American Romani I knew, but the best—actually, only—lead I got was that Danny was likely in Las Vegas or L.A. But "Danny Fender" is just his stage name, adopted from his favored guitar; I search the phone book, music stores, the Web, everywhere, and find no mention of him. It's almost as if he—and his people—do not exist.

Although their population is estimated at one million, Romani in America are a hidden people. Their culture too is insular, and intentionally so, to protect what's theirs. Yet in rented dance halls and event centers, for weddings and anniversaries and births and Super Bowl parties across the United States, American Romani are celebrating with their music. This is not an underground; it's all very mainstream—within Romani culture, that is.

Then, a year or so later, I heard tell of John Filcich, a fan of traditional Eastern European folk dance who ran a mail-order business in Los Angeles named Festival Records. Call John, an American Romani acquaintance told me; he carries recordings of Gypsy music for sale at dance festivals. I dialed up John, who indeed knew of Danny Fender, but was even less forthcoming and more protective of his information than most Romani. Yes, he had some of Danny's self-produced cassettes available. But when I asked how I could purchase them, his wary response was, "Why do you want them?"

Coaxing copies of Danny's cassettes from John, I was eager finally to listen to this elusive music. Much like the Gypsy jazz circulated among European Romani in the 1970s and 1980s, Danny's numerous recordings are released only on homemade cassettes and CDs bought, sold, and horse-traded among American Gypsies. Danny's "albums"were inexpensive machine-dupe cassettes with typewritten labels noting *Danny Fender and the Caravans*. No song lists, no personnel, no further clues. And so, I loaded one into my tape player.

The music I heard was startling, breathing with energy and emotion and electricity. Danny's California Style is an electrified and hot-rodded blend of Tziganes, flamenco, Gypsy rhumba, Gypsy jazz, and surf. The tracks were culled from Gypsy wedding shows, fading in just in time for the vocal refrains or the start of a good jam, then fading out again—or at times cutting off abruptly mid song. It wasn't a polished album from the production side, but it was music honed and tight, made for dancing. I wrote a short article on Danny's music for a guitar magazine.

And then, more silence. That was all I heard of Danny for the next several years—although I always kept an ear and eye open for more.

Then, one day in 2006, I ran across a Web site mentioning the Band of Gypsies concert in San Francisco. There was no contact information, just a date and time. The show was a week away, so I gambled on it. I bought a cross-country plane ticket, and now here I am, seeing Danny on stage in the midst of this whole unknown world of Beatlemania, Romani style. Few in the outside world even suspect the wonders of Danny's music, but here among his own, he's a star.

On his 2006 CD, *A Band of Gypsy's*—again homemade with photocopied cover and available only from Danny—there's ample proof that Danny Fender exists, and at full volume. The album won't make any *Billboard* charts, hit no Top 10 lists, win zero Casey Kasem raves; there'll be no accompanying music videos, no millions in T-shirt sales, no nationwide tour—at least none that us *gadjé* will ever know about. But if his fans' response at the San Francisco concert is any gauge, Danny's latest CD is solid gold.

And it's not just a coincidence that the album kicks off with Django.

When Django arrived in the United States in 1946 to tour as special guest soloist with Duke Ellington's Orchestra, he spread his jazz not only to the jazz faithful but also to a hidden audience. And those reverberations continue today.

"My grandpa met Django in New York in '46," Danny Fender tells me with pride. "They were in a nightclub and Django came up to my grandpa, who was with a bunch of cousins, all Gypsy boys. Now us Gypsies have a Gypsy thing: We can always spot another Gypsy. So Django asked my grandpa in our language, Romanès, if he was a Gypsy. My grandpa had blue eyes, which was a bit strange. My grandpa and his cousins didn't know Django from Adam, so they asked him in Romanès, 'Who are you?' Django told them, and they ended up drinking together with him through the night. My grandpa was not a musician, but he played a little guitar and he loved music, and the next day he went out looking for Django's music. When he listened to those records, he was just amazed!"

I hear that amazement still in Danny's music. On *A Band of Gypsy's*, he begins with Django's "Minor Swing," played with reverence. Yet he doesn't seek to duplicate or ape the 1930s Quintette sound as so many *gadjé* Gypsy jazz bands do. Instead, Danny recreates "Minor Swing" in a modern American Romani vernacular. He quotes Django's solo with effortless fluidity, then moves off to improvise under Django's inspiration. There's a little bit of Balkan Tziganes music here intermixed with a little of the Ventures. And there's a long legacy of American Gypsy guitarists echoed in Danny's playing—other unknowns, at least to the non-Romani. Gypsy heroes like John Adomono, Johnny Guitar, and more. As Danny says to me, "Django influenced *every* Gypsy guitarist."

I'm sitting back with Danny and some beers in his home in Los Angeles—East L.A., to be exact. After the San Francisco concert, I introduced myself and congratulated him on the show. Miraculously, Danny had stumbled upon my article on his early recordings—the only outside notice he had ever received—and we were quickly talking music. The next thing I knew, Danny invited me to visit next time I was in California for a real Gypsy jam session. Outside, in the East L.A. sky, helicopters hover overhead, the long fingers of their searchlights probing the darkness, the bass-heavy thump of their blades adding a war-zone *je ne sais quoi* to the twilight. Cop cars patrol the streets beneath the palm trees in the veil of summer heat; sirens in the distance are a constant, white noise. But inside Danny's house, it's another world, and far, far away.

Danny and his wife Janet's home deserves a prominent place in *House Beautiful* magazine. Out front sits his Lincoln Navigator. Within are white walls with white trim, white drapery and swags, white Louis XIV couches with golden frames, white pillars in the corners topped by white Romanesque busts, Midas-touched chandeliers, and above the white fireplace mantel, a massive gilt-framed, mirrored portrait of Elvis in gold-lamé suit. And the house is full of music: A built-in sound system is playing Danny's latest recordings. In the dining room is a grand glass display case with three of Danny's favorite guitars—a Gretsch Chet Atkins Model 6120 with "G" cow brand, steer head, cacti, and other western motifs running up the fretboard; a glitter-gold-trimmed Gretsch Black Falcon like a six-string Cadillac; and the Holy Grail of all American guitardom, a Gretsch White Falcon, its all-white body set off by gilded hardware in perfect harmony with the household décor.

Their home doubles as Janet's *ofisa*—her fortune-telling office. In the front lawn stands a grand sign offering palmistry, tarot readings, cures for curses, wards against the evil eye, and guarantees for health and wealth. The sign's in Spanish, the long list of soothsaying services surrounding a painting of Mexico's beloved La Virgin de Guadeloupe. Janet boasts the *wortacha*—a sort of relegated monopoly among fellow Gypsies—on psychic powers among her *kumpania*, or Romani community, for an agreed-upon area. And here, nestled in East L.A., the flourishing market for fortune-telling is with neighboring Latinos. Among them, her *nom de crystal ball* is Tina.

Tonight, Janet is looking into her oven to see if the lasagna's done. Served up accompanied by platters of garlic bread and copious salads, it's some of the best I've tasted this side of Italy. Proof of the lasagna's qualities are in the silence of the eaters, a dramatic reversal from the boisterous chatter that preceded the meal. Danny's invited over a cabal of his guitar-playing cousins this May evening to talk American Gypsy music with me. Along with Danny's grandmother, various children, nephews, and nieces, Danny's father is here, along with his uncle, Johnny Guitar; his cousin and bassist Lonnie Fender; and bandmate George Fat Joes. And they've all brought their guitars. It's a rarity to invite a *gadjo* into their home for dinner. Rarer still one who's interested in their music, and everyone's excited to tell stories and play. But for now, the lasagna's taken center stage.

Los Angeles with its suffocating surroundings of urban sprawl is home to perhaps the nation's largest Romani population. There are also substantial Gypsy centers in Las Vegas, Chicago, New York, and Miami. Most *gadjé* never would even guess there are Romani in their cities—as one fellow *gadjo* asked me, "Do you mean there still *are* Gypsies?" Yes, Victoria, there most certainly are. Some operate fortune-telling *ofisas*, run roof or driveway seal-coating businesses, or do seasonal agricultural work; others are college professors, lawyers, doctors, and professional musicians in wedding bands or symphonic orchestras. The American Romani are hidden in plain sight.

Romani began migrating to North America in the mid 1800s. Like the other immigrant groups making up the United States, the Romani here are of eclectic backgrounds, coming from all parts of Europe. The Romanichals, also known as Romichals or "English Travelers," first reached the United States in the 1840s. They were followed by the Vlax, escaping the Romanian principalities of Wallachia and Moldavia in the 1860s at the end of five centuries of slavery. The Vlax population was made up of eastern and western groups: the Kalderasha, originating from Russia; and the Machvaya, coming from Serbia. In the 1870s came the Bashalde, or "Hungarian-Slovakian" Roma. A new wave of Romani arrived from Hungary, Poland, Romania, and the Czech Republic after the fall of Communism in the 1990s, settling primarily in New York City and Chicago. Only a few Lowara and Manouche, and next to no Gitanos, ventured across the ocean. As Ian Hancock, the Hungarian-Romanichal professor of Romani studies at the University of Texas in Austin, states, "There is thus no homogeneous Romani population but a number of sharply disparate groups differing from each other in numbers, in degree of acculturation, and in aspects of their language and priorities."

Danny Fender is part of the Machvaya *veesta*, or clan, his family coming to the United States from near Belgrade. Here, on the other side of the ocean, Danny and members of his *kumpania* remain close-knit. A *kumpania* is made up of a certain number of *tsera*, literally "tents" or households, the families often distant relations, usually through the men. The *kumpania* looks out for its own. The Romani have their own code of law, a sense of moral and hygienic purity— *wuzho*—countered by pollution—*marime*—from the *gadjo* universe. They arrange their marriages among their own; there is no intermarrying with *gadjé*. And they keep as far away as possible from the outside world's police, policing themselves for the most part with a Gypsy court known as a *kris romani*. Danny's just as likely to speak in American slang as he is in *Romanès*. And like many Gypsies in the United States, his family has stayed on the move. His grandfather originally came to New York City, but his father led the family wandering west. Now, Danny's up against the Pacific, as far west as he can go.

Throughout their travels, Danny and his clan's love of music remained strong. "We brought our music with us from the Old Country," Danny tells me. "We bring it everywhere we travel." As with the French Manouche and Gitans, playing guitar was part of this American Gypsy boy's growing up, a rite of passage like playing rock'n'roll in a garage band in middle America. As Danny says, "Go into any American Gypsy house and you will find some great guitar players."

Danny was tutored by his uncle, whose own stage name of Johnny Guitar is fitting both for his history and his influence. "He's the man we all learned from," Danny says, gesturing across the dinner table to Johnny.

By "all," Danny means the whole Band of Gypsies ensemble, which is in truth made up of three combined groups—Danny's combo Gypsy Roma, featuring bassist Lonnie Fender, their guitarist cousin Ronny Fender, and vocalist Robert Adams; the Gypsy Nights quartet with guitarists Donny and Bobby Lovers, whose choice of stage names are as catchy as their rhumba guitar playing; and the Gypsy Boys featuring Paul and George Fat Joes, Frankie John Franks, and Nick Playboy—yes, more stage names; never hurts to have an alias, or three. And that's not counting the accordionist, bassist, keyboardist, and two drummers. When they get together with all nine of those Gypsy guitars going at full bore, it's enough to make Lynyrd Skynyrd blush with envy.

Johnny Guitar is nonchalant about his inspiration. He laughs loudly at Danny's statement—which is easy for him to do, because he knows it's true. Now in his seventies, Johnny is spry and full of stories, talking with a mischievous grin about the good old days. He tells me of Django's influence on him from listening to LPs, and how guitar became central to his life from an early age: "The way I got my first guitar is this: My mother's best friend killed her husband, did him with a knife. She was going to prison, and said the only thing she had to give my mother was her dead old husband's guitar. So she gave it to me; I was just four years old. And playing that guitar kept *me* out of prison!"

The dinner dishes are being cleared as Danny's grandmother brings out a large cake she's baked, which Danny introduces to me as "a true American Gypsy cake." Served up in huge pieces, it's a wonderful confection of custardy egg filling, pineapple, and cinnamon. And with the end of dinner, everyone's ready to talk music again.

Johnny tells of his band, the Fantastics. Made up of himself and his Gypsy cousins, they were based in San Francisco but performed up and down the California coast starting in the 1950s. "Movie stars would hire us to play Hollywood parties. They'd pay us $500 for a show, and with rent being just $125 a month back then, we were doing pretty well!"

In the mid 1960s, the Fantastics recorded a 45 of their most-requested number, "Hava Nagila." This song—believed to have originated with Hasidic Jews in Eastern Europe—was early on adopted by the Romani as one of their own and has since become a staple of Gypsy weddings and celebrations from Macedonia to America. Johnny played it all his life, for the numerous family functions, *veetsa* celebrations, and movie stars' shindigs.

"Truth is," Johnny confides to me now, leaning forward in a conspiratorial whisper, "us Fantastics weren't all that fantastic. We were cousins, and everywhere we played, people'd tell me I needed new accompanists. But I couldn't just kick them out of the band—they were *my cousins*. I had to wait until they died off."

The Beatles had it easy: they could simply disband and go their own ways. The Romani are bound together for life.

They're dancing now in the kitchen. And in the living room and dining room— anywhere there's space to dance. Danny Fender has his guitar out. George Fat Joes strums a complex accompaniment. Lonnie's pounding out a bass line. The sound of their music reigns, the trio jamming with élan on a Balkan Tziganes tune. Janet's spinning around the kitchen hand in hand with her sons as other nephews and nieces boogie about the dinner table. It's jubiliation akin to that San Francisco concert, replicated now in Danny's East L.A. home.

Danny's in his thirties, but plays with a masterful hand. Throughout the high-speed Balkan melodies, he never misses a note, never stumbles. And yet within the virtuosity there's still that emotion so central and essential to Romani music.

Danny lists for me his influences, many of whom are guitarists the world barely remembers these days: Buddy Merrill, the eternally baby-faced guitar-man of Lawrence Welk's band and an early multitrack boffin; Don Wilson, Bob Bogle, and Nokie Edwards, masterminds of the Ventures' guitar-powered, twang-toned surfer hymns; Les Paul, who studied Django's every lick back home in Wisconsin before taking on the world, inventing his own solid-body electric guitar and helping pioneer multitrack recording and similarly unorthodox electronic guitar effects; and the Beatles, of course. But most of all, there's Johnny Guitar and Johnny Adomono.

George Fat Joes is also a phenomenal player. He lets Danny, his elder, take the spotlight, but behind him, his rhumba rhythm lines are lithe and dynamic, snaking in and out of Danny's lead. George's father, Imao Stevens, was an accordionist legendary among his people. The accordion, like the violin, is an instru-ment sadly foresaken among young American Romani today in favor of the guitar, as even guitarists Danny and George bemoan: They lay the blame on rock'n'roll— and Django. The fabled Imao was known affectionately as Fat Joe Stevens, thus the stage names of his sons, George and Paul Fat Joes. Now, when George takes over the melody on a tune, his guitar resonates with his father's music.

Along with playing concerts for their fellow Romani, Danny's ensemble is also fully booked for weddings and parties among Southern California's insular Russian, Eastern European, Greek, Persian, and Jewish communities. Thus, they've built up wide-ranging repertoires catering to each. Danny's even taught himself bouzouki to play Greek music. And they perform for swank Hollywood parties, where their references have spread by word of mouth. "My group's sometimes known as the 'Band of the Stars' because we play for so many stars' parties," Danny explains. And sure enough, floor to ceiling on one living-room wall are framed snapshots picturing Danny and bandmates with James Coburn, Oscar De La Hoya, at Brad Pitt and Jennifer Aniston's wedding, and with many more suntanned, sunglassed producers, stars, and other movie-world luminaries.

Tonight, though, they're playing just for themselves. Seated around Danny's dinner table, the trio now pick out a Romanian hora, the Greek song "Never on Sunday," Danny's own composition "D'Artagnan," then "The Flight of the Bumblebee," just for laughs seeing how fast they can accelerate the melody and still keep the pace. And still Janet and the children are dancing. Danny plays an old Eastern European Jewish tune, a Chet Atkins piece that resounds with a perfect Nashville vibe, a Russian Gypsy melody, a Ventures ode to the ocean, and now the theme song from the 1950s Victor Mature film *Samson and Delilah*, a gorgeous, dark-toned melody the rest of us have sadly forgotten. But not Danny and George.

Stopping for just a moment to catch his breath between songs, Danny turns to me and jokes, "People say we Gypsies are robbers and thieves—and I agree. We steal everyone's music, and make it Gypsy music!"

And they launch into another song.

Following Danny's insistent advice, I'm listening now to one of the most incredibly strange LPs I have ever discovered. It also bears one of the longest album titles: *Donn Beach Presents "A Night at the Beachcomber" with Adomono (Guitarist Fantastique)—Actually Recorded at the International Market Place, Honolulu, Hawaii*. And on the cover, Romani guitarist John Adomono picks one of the funkiest guitars I've seen—a bizarre harp guitar with long, lyre-shaped wings like an ancient Greek kithara, an instrument from another time and place.

Danny speaks often of Adomono, but while he evokes him as an influence, he himself doesn't have any of Adomono's recordings any more. Nor, it seems, does anyone else. That's not because Adomono didn't release records—he did, and for mainstream labels such as Decca. Yet even among those of us who still own and exercise our turntables, Adomono's music is shunned as kitschy curiousity at best, baroque obscurity at worst. He was a Gypsy legend and mainstream lounge idol in his day. But now his music has been lost to all but old-record wax museums where they're placed in last-gasp desperation with theremin B-budget Martian-invader soundtracks, defeated armies' marching bands, and other unclassifiable and incurable exotica, the netherworlds where unwanted old music fades away in silence. After months of hunting out Adomono's recordings, I finally stumbled by pure serendipity across this LP in the back-of-the-store tiki music bin at Hymie's Vintage Record City, itself situated amid the stringed-lightbulbs of used-car dealerships and faded neon of sinister-looking Chinese restaurants on Minneapolis's motley East Lake Street. And this forty-plus-year-old copy of the record was still in its sealed plastic wrap, never opened, never played.

Setting down the needle on the virgin vinyl, I hear Adomono's electric guitar start out slow and quiet, then it builds in ardor and verve. Soon, I'm hooked. On this album and others I eventually uncover, Adomono plays Gershwin's "Rhapsody in Blue," a rollicking "Miserlou" that'd make Dick Dale park his Stratocaster, Adomono's own Balkan and flamenco Gypsy compositions, and that *Samson and Delilah* movie theme. It's all music echoed today by Danny Fender and his Band of Gypsies cohorts.

Only later was I by chance able to piece together something of Adomono's own story. Danny's vocalist, Robert Adams, is Adomono's grandson. On the Web, I unearthed another son of Adomono's, Kevin Adams, who is an Elvis impersonator and Vegas lounge star in his own right. Neither knew the other, but both shared tales with me.

Johnny Adomono was born in the 1930s—no one can remember exactly when—in New York City. He was known by his fellow Romani as Peeky. Learning guitar from his elders, he busked on Manhattan streets to help support his family. At twenty, he left home to wander the country with his guitar, eventually running up against the western ocean. He soon graduated to performing in hotel bars and casino lounges, making his home at Las Vegas's Thunderbird Hotel, where he became a fixture attraction in the 1960s. A black-and-white promotional from this era shows Adomono an intense-looking man—hair severely parted and combed down; perfectly trimmed pencil-line mustachio; dark, fathomless eyes. In his hands he holds a mammoth sunburst archtop as if it's a weapon.

Adomono may have grown weary of the guitar's basic sound around this time as he began experimenting with a novel, new sound effect, the Ecco-Fonic. Hidden within that pandora's box was a tape-delay system, functioning—with the arcane spin of numerous knobs and dials—as the world's first outboard reverb unit. Adomono adopted the Ecco-Fonic as part of his lounge act, becoming an early wizard of reverb-laced guitar. I hear it in Adomono's playing on his *Guitarist Fantastique* LP: The effect duplicated the age-old mystery and emotion of the spectral Romani violinists' tremolo, yet with a Space Age edge.

Adomono's guitar and Ecco-Fonic brought him stardom. He played with the Mills and Ames Brothers, Jimmy Durante, and on *The Ed Sullivan Show*; jammed with Duke Ellington; and performed once for JFK at the White House. When Texas-born tiki impresario Donn Beach launched a craze for faux Polynesian restaurants with his Don the Beachcomber chain, Adomono was there on stage.

While waiters served up alluring Pu Pu Platters and potent Mai Tais, Zombie cocktails, and Tahitian Rum Punch, Adomono played the luau soundtrack. His nightly song list was a mixed drink of pop ditties, movie themes, Hawaiian hula dances, undisguised Gypsy melodies, and his own "Beachcomber Blues." He shared the stage under the grass roof with the King of Tiki Swing, Martin Denny. Admono performed at the original restaurant on Los Angeles's McCadden Place and in the Honolulu hotspot at International Market Place. It was one of these nights captured by the live 1961 LP.

Adomono also released several other albums over the years. *¡Guitarra Estupendo!* on the Foremost label was a 1960s collection of Spanish-tinged melodies. *Gypsy*, from 1974 on the Magnemedia label, celebrated Adomono's heritage. And there may be other lost 45s or LPs out there, waiting to be rediscovered in the oblivion of a musty Salvation Army record bin.

For all his time in the spotlight, Adomono has been forgotten these days by the mainstream guitar world. But not by his fellow Romani. Robert and Kevin Adams still sing his praises, while Johnny Guitar and George Fat Joes hail his memory. For Danny Fender, Adomono was a conduit back to Gypsy music history, and Django in particular.

"I met Adomono just once, in the 1990s, before he died, at a Gypsy funeral," Danny's telling me. "Us Gypsies are not supposed to play music for several months after a fellow Gypsy's death, but I couldn't let this occasion pass me by. Adomono said, 'I've heard about you. Now let's hear you play.' He got out his big Gibson L5, and we jammed. He was just amazing."

Django's tour inspired more than just American Romani guitarists; his string jazz with Stéphane Grappelli was also an epiphany to Gypsy violinists in the New World. After playing the tour finale in Detroit on the night of December 7, 1946, Django and bandmates from Duke's orchestra were directed across town to Dearborn's Hungarian Village, a swank nightspot that was the height of Detroit fashion. While they dined, they were serenaded by Romani violinist Ziggy Bella. Ziggy was also known as Bela Ziggy and sometimes even by his real name of William Margitza. He was a local star who made the restaurant shine. But Ziggy also played for weddings and parties, recorded several LPs of classic Hungarian Gypsy music, and was a respected classical violinist in the Detroit Symphony Orchestra. Yet it was Ziggy's son, ten-year-old violinist Julius Margitza, who was most thrilled by the French Gypsy's visit. Julius was also playing that night at the Hungarian Village, and according to family legend, Django joined in. Hearing Django, Julius was moved to tune his violin to jazz. Eighteen years later in 1964, Julius—playing under the name Julio Bella—would release the first album of American Gypsy jazz, *The Hot Jazz Violin of Julio Bella and His Quartette.*

Julius was born in Pittsburgh on July 18, 1934. He was christened with his father's name, William Julius Margitza, as his father had great hopes for his young prodigy to follow in his footsteps as a classical violinist, according to family legend. Ziggy began teaching his son violin at the age of five, and Julius soon became a child attraction in the spotlight at the Hungarian Village. Yet after Django, Julius dreamed only of jazz.

Through the years, Julio played his swing in nightclubs from Detroit to Cleveland to Pittsburgh. He later moved on to jam at a Chicago cabaret, where he met up with John Bajo, a *gadjo* jazz fan and record collector. Bajo shared with him his carefully garnered stock bought from Paris of original Swing 78s of Django and Stéphane Grappelli. And while Django had first caught Julius' ear, being a violinist Julio was now more smitten by Stéphane's role. He studied Bajo's recordings to build his library of licks. Bajo remembered listening to Julio: "He was playing in some high-class restaurant and I used to drop in every so often as they had great roast duck and fabulous martinis. He was a fine fiddler, especially in person."

There are differing accounts in the Margitza family of the effects of young Julius's new music. Julio told Bajo that his father expected him to start a classical career, yet when he tuned his fiddle to jazz, it engendered a family feud, and Ziggy disowned Julio. Other family members, including Julio's brother, Bill Margitza, who played piano on the LP as Billy Marr, state that "disown" was too strong a word. Still, Ziggy's "disappointment" was deep.

The hot jazz Julio played was steeped in the poetic style of Stéphane, yet had a more raw, rougher accent, perhaps the influence of a Detroit upbringing. And there was more. When he cut the LP tracks, Julio was recently divorced from his wife and had lost custody of his son, Randy. His anger and depression came through in his jazz, as Julio's grand-nephew Ross Michael Margitza, also studying now as a jazz trumpeter, tells me.

Julio's ensemble was made up of his Romani cousins. Alongside his pianist brother, Bill, guitarist Marty Kallao, bassist Andy Hallup, and drummer Billy Kallao were all part of the musical clan. Together, they jumped through a repertoire of then-modern American jazz such as "Green Dolphin Street" and a wide-ranging swath of Quintette du Hot Club de France tunes informed by John Bajo's collection of Parisian Gypsy jazz. These included gems such as Django's proto-bebop tune "Porto Cabello," Stéphane's hymn to his daughter, "Eveline," and downright obscurities like Henri Crolla's 1955 melody "Alembert's." The LP was in mono with indifferent equalization and scratchy sound. It was released on Jack and Devora Brown's family-run Fortune label from Detroit, best known for its pre-Motown R&B.

By the time he was thirty, Julio quit the music scene; Bill Margitza tells me that Julio had a problem with "nerves." Bajo's remembrances are equally sketchy: "Julio left his job [at the high-class restaurant] and I didn't see him for a few years after that. One day he came visiting. He looked bad, seems he'd fallen on bad times. After that visit, I never saw or heard from him again." Julio died back in Dearborn on April 16, 1988. He was only fifty-four.

Jazz didn't die out in the Margitza clan, however. Bill Margitza continued to perform, and in the next generation, tenor and soprano saxophonist Rick Margitza has become respected on the international scene.

Like Julio, Rick began as a classical violinist before discovering jazz. "I grew up hearing my grandfather play a lot of Hungarian Gypsy violin music. My father is a classical violinist. He played in the Detroit Symphony for almost thirty years and then my mother's father was a jazz bassist, who also played some cello on some *Charlie Parker with Strings* albums. So I started playing the violin. I picked it up from my grandfather and I started studying classical piano as a result of my father's classical influence, and then I heard one Charlie Parker record. It happened to be the one that my grandfather played on, and then I heard the music and immediately I said that is what I wanted to do. So I went to school the next day and got a saxophone and started playing along with records." He went on to study music at Berklee College of Music in Boston and Chicago's Loyola University. Since then, Rick has toured with Maynard Ferguson, joined Miles Davis's group and recorded three albums with him, and collaborated with artists including Maria Schneider, Chick Corea, and McCoy Tyner. These days, he's based in Paris, playing with the Moutin Reunion Quartet.

On his 2000 album *Heart of Hearts*, his seventh as a leader, Rick's modern jazz melodies were spiced with improvisations from his Romani heritage. As he explains, "The story behind this record is one about my grandparents, great-grandparents, about all the different hearts that have influenced my life and my music. I grew up hearing all this sad Gypsy music from the older musicians in my family. On *Heart of Hearts* I tried to bring out that romantic tone." And here, his toneful sax lines seem to float on a timeless air, at once sorrowful and yet rejoicing.

It's a hot night in a cold city, and the Gypsy jazz is making it all the warmer. Eighteen-year-old American guitar prodigy Sam "Sammo" Miltich has come out of the northwoods of Minnesota to play Minneapolis's tony Dakota Jazz Club. Sam's not Romani, but that does not hold back his guitarwork. Arrayed alongside him on stage, his Clearwater Hot Club band is locked in on the rhythm—French expatriate violinist Raphael Fraisse, rhythm guitarman Mark Kreitzer, and Sammo's dad, Matthew Miltich, on string bass. In the unflinching eye of the spotlight, Sammo appears impossibly young, especially to be playing this venerable music with such eloquence. "All of Me," Django's "Swing 41," "Night and Day," "Somewhere over the Rainbow"—he plays it all, launching elegant improvisations that carry you far away from a Minnesota winter night back in time to the City of Lights in the 1930s. Then Raphael takes up his violin, and with an effortless swing to his stride, plays with a tone pure and radiant. The band is one of the most exciting and joyful of Gypsy jazz groups anywhere.

With the dawn of the new millennium, a worldwide Gypsy jazz renaissance has caught on at the tempo of one of Django's hot jazz jumps. The voice of Django's music continues to speak over the decades to new players, Gypsy and *gadjé*, from France to Germany to the Flanders countries and on to North America and Japan. In truth, the sound never faded away, but now it's found new listeners. And it's alive, swinging with a soul as great as great rock'n'roll.

Yet Django's influence on guitarists goes beyond simply his music. His life as a musical Gypsy living free outside the confines of the status quo remains an inspiration. Django was not only one of the premier inventors of guitar, but he may also have been the progenitor of the rock'n'roll lifestyle—decades before rock first rolled.

Perhaps nowhere has this revival been as quick and strong as in the United States. Back in the 1960s, disparate groups such as mandolinist David Grisman's idiosyncratic Dawg bluegrass ensembles took inspiration from Django and Stéphane; Grisman even enlisted Stéphane to revive his old music for a landmark tour across the United States. Dan Hicks and the various iterations of his Hot Licks and Acoustic Warriors bands also adopted aspects of the Quintette's hot jazz. And latin-tinged jazzman Charlie Byrd long flirted with the Hot Club sound in his quintet.

The Gypsy jazz renaissance took hold in the late 1990s with the Hot Club of San Francisco and Seattle area Pearl Django. Since then, Gypsy jazz bands have been counting off songs in hotspot cities such as Seattle, San Francisco, Austin, and Minneapolis-Saint Paul. Most every city can claim a band: Parisan-turned-Brooklynite Stéphane Wrembel, Nashville-based world-traveling John Jorgenson, Austin's Dave Biller, Chicago's Alfonso Ponticelli, Atlanta's Bonaventure Quartet, Madison's Harmonious Wail, New Orleans's Tony Green, Charlotte's Musette Guitars, the Seattle area's Hot Club Sandwich, and Minneapolis-Saint Paul's Parisota Hot Club and Café Accordion Orchestra. And there are many more, bands bearing their cities' names from the Twin Cities Hot Club to the

Hot Club of San Diego, as well as the Hot Club USA, western-swinging Hot Club of Cowtown, and Canadian luthier Michael Dunn's intergalactic Hot Club of Mars.

On the other side of Minneapolis-Saint Paul at the classic American supper club Matty B's, Romani pianist Bill Duna is leading his jazz ensemble. The paneled walls here are mahogany, the dance floor pure cherry, the jazz lush and swinging.

Bill has been a mainstay of the Twin Cities jazz scene for decades. He's also been a college professor teaching musicology and Romani and Holocaust history for twenty-plus years at the prestigious University of St. Thomas on Saint Paul's Summit Avenue. And he was the first Romani presidential appointee to the U.S. Holocaust Memorial Council. Bill's proud of his Gypsy roots.

His musician grandparents immigrated from Hungary to perform at the 1880 Chicago World's Fair. They stayed on in the United States, launching a musical legacy. Bill boasts a huge collection of recordings of Romani music, perhaps one of the country's, if not world's, largest. And he leads Basipen, the Society for the Preservation of Gypsy music. Basipen is Romanès for "to play," an apt name for the organization.

I ask Bill about other Romani musicians who have influenced American music, and he immediately begins listing names, many of which are familiar to me although some I never realized were Gypsies. This is an all-too common trait, Bill explains: "Many Romani do not let people know they are Romani. Anti-Gypsy feelings are still common."

First and foremost, Bill lists Marty Kallao, the Detroit-area guitarist who played on Julio Bella's pioneering LP of American Gypsy jazz. Kallao often remained anonymous, like many other American Gypsy musicians. He became a top-bill studio musician, playing on further Fortune-label tracks as well as Motown hits. Romani guitarist Albert Garber sometimes shared duties with Kallao but, as was typical of Motown backing personnel, neither received any fame beyond their paychecks. Still, there was little racial code in the Detroit R&B factories; as Bill says, "For Motown, it did not make a difference what color you were; they just hired the best musicians."

Marty Kallao's brother, Alex Kallao, began playing piano on Motown tracks but later became best known as a jazzman. Blind since birth, he found inspiration in other sightless pianists such as Art Tatum and George Shearing. His 1954 LP, *An Evening at the Embers*, remains an underground jazz classic, still in print half a century later.

Most famous of all was another Romani jazz pianist, Josef "Joe" Zawinul. A Manouche, he was born in Vienna in 1932. Part of the European jazz scene,

Zawinul immigrated to the United States in 1959, where he played alongside everyone from Miles Davis and Cannonball Adderley to Dinah Washington. A founding member of Weather Report, he composed the pop hit "Mercy, Mercy, Mercy" and fusion-jazz opus "Birdland" as well as the classical symphony *Stories of the Danube*.

Following Julio Bella's lead came several other violinists. Richard Margitza backed his saxophonist cousin Rick on some of Rick's Blue Note LPs. Louis Kallo—no doubt another Kallao cousin—played cello behind Romani guitarist-violinist Elek Bacsik on Bacsik's 1966 *Zigani Ballet*. And Bill Duna's own cousin, Gregory Ballogh, is a superb violinist, equally adept with Gypsy music and jazz.

And the list goes on.

While numerous Romani play jazz in the United States, few if any are playing solely Gypsy jazz in Django's idiom. Bill Duna's band, for instance, is titled the Latin Jazz Combo; like many Romani through time, he loves many styles of music and plays what pays. While Django may have provided a fine introduction to his music with his brief 1946 U.S. tour, America was a big place with numerous other musical influences feeding it, and American Romani musicians had much to choose from.

The extent of the role of Gypsies in American music is a larger, deeper question, and the answer's as complex and slippery as simply attempting to define what constitutes "Gypsy music." The answer is also as secretive and hidden beneath the melodies as the Romani themselves are hidden within American society. Numerous Balkan Gypsy immigrants turned their violins to classical music and like Ziggy Bella/William Margitza, performed in symphonic orchestras across the country. And again like Ziggy Bella, they often hid their identities. As Bill Duna tells me, "Throughout the United States, there are whole families of incredible Gypsy musicians. They are not famous, they don't play concerts, they don't release records. But they're well known within the Gypsy world. Marketing's the thing, but they're not into marketing. And many don't want to let others know they're Gypsies. It's a sad thing."

Meanwhile, everyone from Louis Armstrong to Dizzy Gillespie to Stan Kenton recorded their own takes of "Dark Eyes," recast into an American jazz idiom. Among the most stunning versions anywhere of the Russian Romani anthem was that of African-American violinist Eddie South. Born in Missouri, South went on to study classical violin before coming to jazz, venturing to Paris and then Budapest to learn Tziganes violin firsthand. He recorded with Django several times in 1937, and throughout the rest of his career utilized Gypsy melodies as a jumping off point for hot jazz improvisations. Bluesman Muddy Waters was inspired to sing about going to visit the Gypsy woman to have his fortune told. Then there was B. B. King. And Charlie Christian, Chet Atkins,

Barnie Kessel, Tal Farlow. And of course Jimi Hendrix, who was obviously inspired with the image and lifestyle in launching his Band of Gypsies. While Jimi did not play Gypsy jazz, he may in fact be Django's closest spiritual follower: He too was a vagabond musician who knew no boundaries and again opened the world's eyes anew to the limitless possibilities of the guitar.

Back at the San Francisco Palace of Fine Arts Theatre, Danny Fenders and his Band of Gypsies are two hours into their show yet showing no signs of slowing down. The dancers too haven't let up, spinning and shimmying through a flamenco jam, a Balkans Tizganes tune, a Russian melody. The concert is akin to a global tour of Romani music. And perhaps this is the miracle at the heart of Danny's guitar playing—the survival and wide-open fusion of so many styles of Gypsy music from so many parts of the world. Packed up into instrument cases and brought with Romani immigrants from across Europe to the United States, the old-world music has been blended with the new. And yet it still retains its identity. Danny and Ronny Fender set aside their electric guitars now and take up electrified bouzoukis to play a Greek dance, the tempo building in speed, chorus after chorus until the audience can hardly stand it and finally stop dancing, panting and clapping along, urging Danny to play faster still. Then Danny's niece comes out to sing and dance with a flamenco lilt. The next song is a rollicking Gypsy rhumba, straight from the Gipsy Kings' repertoire. Vocalist Johnny Ugly—yes, another stage name—is now at center stage, paying tribute to Romani crooner Singing Sam Stevens. And when the band dives headfirst into "Minor Swing," it's half Django, half Nokie Edwards. And the crowd loves it all.

Johnny Guitar himself is introduced in the second half of the show as a special guest. Dressed in a dapper tan suit topping a black shirt, his snow-white tie matches his stylish white bucks. He sits down in a chair on stage, and someone hands him his 1952 reissue Fender Telecaster, all tuned up, plugged in, and ready to go. The guitar's butterscotch body and black pickguard match Johnny's own attire. Holding the guitar at two o'clock, he launches into "Hava Nagila" at a rock'n'roll intensity. He smiles a Vegas smile and picks that electric guitar.

Then it's time to slow things down. Robert Adams takes the mic and sings one of the band's biggest crowd pleasers—as if the past songs haven't thrilled them enough. A soft blue spot shines down now on just Danny and Robert as they launch into a tune that for a moment I can't place. Their fans sure know it, though. At first they applaud wildly, then the mood too goes blue. Robert is singing in Italian, but the melody's so familiar. Then the next verse is in English, and the song becomes obvious: Nino Rota's "Speak Softly Love," the "Love Theme" from *The Godfather*. This song touches something special with the audience.

The Romani are swaying and singing along to the melody—there seems to be little they love more in music than a beautiful melody. It strikes me then that the audience takes their dress cues straight from *The Godfather*. The women, young and old, large and small, wear tight-fitting black or red dresses, dripping with jewelry hidden under shawls, and towering high heels—all dressed to kill. The men sport sharkskin suits and shined patent-leather oxfords or black-and-white spectators. Their dark clothes are set off by gold Rolexes, gold chains, gold bracelets, and gold rings. Handkerchiefs are starched and folded, peeking just so from breast pockets; red carnations flowering on lapels. This is a group where fedoras and red cravats have never gone out of style. I spot six-year-old boys dressed better than I could ever hope for. *The Godfather* has done more for men's fashion—and not just here, among the Romani—than all the decades of Paris and Milano *haute couture* combined.

I also realize it's not just fashion sense that *The Godfather* inspires. The movie reveals an insular world of a separate culture, albeit Sicilian. And the Romani understand and relate. It's not their world—but then again, it is.

Now, as Danny hits the final chord of "Speak Softly Love," Robert holds the mic high to catch his last high notes. And the crowd swoons. Then they start clapping in time, ever louder and faster, demanding that Danny play the song once again.

When the music comes to an end, Danny and his buddies like to talk fishing. We're at Danny's East L.A. home, and Danny and George Fat Joes have set aside their guitars for the night—only to have Danny's son and nephew pick them up and start playing. Danny, though, is now telling fish stories. On weekends, boats and family in tow, he and his bandmates like to head up to the California reservoirs to angle for bass. He wants to hear all about fishing in my home state of Minnesota—especially about muskies. I tell my own fish stories now, covering everything from sunfish to sturgeon, and another round of beer is served.

Soon, however, the talk returns to music. Danny's inviting me to his son's wedding this summer, which he promises will be the bash to top all bashes. Great food, great music, and lots of both. "Have you ever been to a Gypsy wedding?" Danny queries me, his eyes twinkling, which I've quickly come to recognize as the prelude to a jest. "It's basically one big family fight, interrupted by some wedding vows." Danny's hired a Russian Romani vocal group; his bandmates will play, and of course, he'll take the stage as well when father-of-the-groom duties aren't pressing. I have to be there, Danny says: The music will never stop.

SEVENTEEN

Gypsy Jazz Rap
Syntax and the Search for "Le Meilleur Chemin..."

I T'S AN ODD IMAGE: A Gypsy jazzman singing rap. And it's equally odd to imagine a rapper playing jazz. But tonight Christian Windrestein is on stage, playing under his *nom de rap* Syntax, proving these misconceptions all wrong.

It's another Parisian night at another tiny bar, this one tucked away in the backstreets of *le quartier* Sentier. I've searched out this bar on this night to hear Syntax rap his tour de force tune "Gens du voyage" accompanied by none other than Ninine Garcia on guitar. This is Gypsy jazz rap, and Syntax is the man who created the genre, the most modern and far-reaching expression of Django's music. At least, so far.

Syntax's "Gens du voyage" is built not over some big-bass dub or faux-music electro sample but on the ancient Tziganes melody "Les deux guitares," Ninine picking out the lines on his grand Epiphone archtop, for goodness sake. Then Syntax adds a stinging solo line—*a rap musician actually playing a guitar*—of Gypsy jazz riffs on his *petite bouche* Favino. He dresses in rap couture, but in his own fashion: He wears the inevitable two-sizes-too-big black hoodie, yet underneath is a black T-shirt with an image of the French Gypsy's iconic *niglo*. Syntax himself is a bear of a man with a shaven head like a French Devil's Island convict on the lam and the most intense eyes into which I've ever looked. Another swing riff on his guitar, and he launches into his rap with a torrent of words:

> *Ils nous accueillent rarement avec le sourire*
> *Nous appeler les voleurs de poules...*

They rarely welcome us with a smile
They call us the chicken thieves . . .

At the heart of Syntax's Gypsy jazz rap is a dream of proving other, more important misconceptions wrong as well. His *rap manouche* is highly political music, charged with changing France's—and the world's—stereotypes and prejudices toward his people, the Romani. This is far from heavy gangsta rap with its posturing and posing and fixation on 'hos, drugs, and Mercedes-Benzes. Syntax raps about basic issues of human rights. His list is long, starting with cultural identity, discrimination, unequal schooling, unfair taxes, and ending ultimately with equal rights for his people. Think of Django fused with Bob Marley.

For Django remains at the soul of Syntax's music. Syntax grew up in a *caravane* parked near Montreuil on the frayed fringes of Paris, and as a boy, he learned to play Gypsy jazz from his father. He can play mean swing and often sits in and jams with his straight-ahead Gypsy jazzmen friends, from his buddies Ninine and Tchavolo Schmitt to pop stars afflicted with *jazz manouche*, such as Thomas Dutronic and Stéphane Sansévérino. Hearing Syntax play jazz, there's no question he knows how to swing it right.

"From the age of fifteen years, I played swing, I played guitar, just like my father, *swing!*" Syntax tells me. "Then I heard rap, and I heard similar beats in swing and rap, the same rhythms, swing and rap—*bap, bap, bap, bap!* And so I brought them together."

Syntax may look like a desperate prison escapee, but when he laughs, those intense eyes truly sparkle. I quickly realize there's a sweet soul here behind a mask worn by many a Manouche in the foreign world of the *gadjé*. Syntax is a quiet and seemingly soft-spoken man—until you get him started, that is. Then he talks like he raps, in that flash flood of thoughts and words, punctuated by his own rhythmic flow that becomes a certain poetry all his own.

"My rap lyrics, they're translating the melodies of *jazz manouche* into words, explaining the melodies. The rest of the world is telling us, 'Gypsies are like this, Gypsies are like that.' But I'm explaining the way *we Gypsies feel.*"

Montreuil is the gristle and sinew of Paris, a rambling, hardscrabble village cum Parisian *banlieue* that was and is home to many an immigrant, whether they are Italian or African or Romani. This is the eastern corner of the capital where most immigrants first wash up. I'm walking across the city square on a warm spring day. But, looking around me, I may be mistaken about my whereabouts: This seems less likely to be France than Algeria, or Hungary, or Timbuktu—or maybe I took a wrong turn at the Stalingrad *métro* station and ended up in a Russian *diryévnya*. The *place* here is more akin to a souk. I'm just as likely to pass women in full birqas as French grand matrons among the food market stalls. Eastern European men in their athletic suits converse in Polish while Berber gentlemen in turbans and desert *djerbas* sip mint tea in the cafés.

Montreuil is composed of squat, low buildings—there's none of the money or elegance of Paris here to build the imposing six-story *grande maisons*. The buildings run away to the horizon, as far as I can see, so close-set, so lacking in order that it's almost claustrophobic, unnerving. There are the classic old shop fronts with gilt-painted signs now long tarnished—*Boucherie Chevaline, Accordéons, Plombier*. These are intermixed with latter-day neon and gaudy backlit signs for halal butchers, East Indian spice shops, hammans, Asian grocers, and a circus of billboards advertising all of the usual bling and blam of the modern world: cheap furniture, cheap cell phones, cheap creams to scourge cellulite. Montreuil, and other outer *villes* like it, is where the true workers of Paris live. Gentrification of the old city has pushed all of the working class out past Le Périph, and while Paris is now more chic than ever, it's also losing the famous grit that gave the city its near-forgotten accent, food, humor, character, even charm.

It's thus little surprise that the *marché aux puces* at Montreuil is unlike any other as well. Most big cities have their thieves' markets, but Montreuil may just rule them all. Rome has Porta Portese, Tokyo has Ueno, London has Petticoat Lane. People bemoan the demise of good thieves' markets, their decline in quality, their gentrification. Fear not in Montreuil. I see everything and anything here, from the ragpickers' *haute couture* delights to drug dealings, Victrolas to iPods, horses to cars. And it all looks hot to the touch.

But there's more in this *puces*: There's the whole fate of Imperialism on display, as well. France's former subjects are all here, hunkered down around scraps of cloth spread on the ground, selling the faded glories of France back to the French for mere *centimes*. Algerians and Vietnamese, Haitians and Senegalese barter the helmets, medals, and crutches of French soldiers; French matrons' lacework linens, needlepoint pictures, and never-finished knitting projects; the country's used pornography, its children's toys, its cast-off crèche scenes. This is not France the way the French want to imagine it.

Walking on further out of the city center, I come to Romani encampments notched in between commercial areas and residential neighborhoods, no one batting an eye. Other encampments huddle on scrublands along train tracks or are lost within industrial zones, nomadic parking-lots that have become established villages. The Gypsies have been here for generations—they're almost town fathers now. Coming to Paris from the east, this is where many first parked their *caravanes* centuries ago and where they stay today.

Syntax grew up in a *caravane* here, and now he is a fighter for the rights of his fellow *nomades*.

Once upon a time, France and the rest of Europe—if not the rest of the world—were eager to be rid of Romani. Today, most European countries want their Romani simply to stay put, to park their *caravanes* and halt their travels. In this way, it's easier to control essential services for Gypsies such as sewage, public health, and schooling. Easier, above all, to control *them*.

Times have changed, and the laws have changed as well. On July 5, 2000, the French Assemblée Nationale passed law code 2000–614 stating that any town of 5,000 or more inhabitants must provide a space for *"gens du voyage"* who live in *caravanes*—the law terms these spaces *les aires permanentes* or *les places désignées*. Electrical lines, sewage, and water are obligatory. Municipalities had two years to comply.

Yet even now, more than five years later, few towns follow the law. As of 2007, only an estimated 7,000 *caravanes* have been provided sites out of an estimated 30,000 needed. And so far, the French government is blind to the towns' infractions.

L'Assemblée Nationale sees clearly when it comes to the rights of landowners over Gypsies, however. The same law also went on—along with reinforcement by March 18, 2003, law code 2003–239—elaborating the rights of municipalities and private landowners to oust Romani parking in illicit areas or trespassing on their land. The detail here is exquisite. *Gens du voyage* parking without permission on public or private land will be liable to six months' imprisonment and a fine of 3,750 euros. In addition, vehicles—except those that are dwellings—can be impounded; meaning if you were parking illicitly, you'd now be without your tow car to move you. And *voyageurs* are also in danger of forfeiting driver's licenses for up to three years, which will further inspire you to stay put in the first place. And in a final article, the law reminds *gens du voyage* concerning the authority of the LSI—*Le Sécurité*, a sort of French FBI and paramilitary police all in one—to assist local *gendarmeries* in dealing with the Romani. As the law code's title states, and as is repeated ad infinitum within the subarticles, this is essential for the good of France's *"sécurité intérieure."*

In 2006, *voyageurs* were hit with a new law from a new quarter. The French Assemblée Nationale crafted a special tax just for *gens du voyage*—the legal bureaucratic euphemism for Gypsies, without actually creating "race"-targeting laws. Romani were now affixed with property tax on their *caravanes*. At first glance, this *taxe d'habitation* was similar to the property tax most French pay, whether they live in apartments or homes, rented or owned—all suitably complex and convoluted in calculation. This new tax charges *voyageurs* 25 euros per square meter of a *caravane* used as a primary dwelling. This was further supplemented in 2006 by another special *taxe-vignette* of 75 euros on any caravane used as a dwelling or larger than four square meters. The expected 50-million euros in proceeds from the *taxe-vignette* will be used, in part, to finance building *les aires permanentes* decreed back in 2000. The combined result is that Gypsies now pay more to live in their *caravanes* than most French pay to live under a true roof.

The message is clear to Syntax: Leave behind the now-traditional life of *un voyageur* and become a modern Gypsy, *un sédentaire*, with a grim apartment in one of the grim public-housing blocks in one of Paris's grim outer suburbs. And there's that ancient Romani saying, *Un Tzigane sans cheval n'est pas un Tzigane*— A Gypsy without a horse is not a Gypsy. Twisting that saying around, it's exactly what the powers that be so desire. If history is written by the victors, laws are written by the powerful.

And so Syntax wrote a song.

He raps with the fluency and velocity of scat. In full swing, Syntax hits a rhythm with a driving sing-song tone, tough yet from the heart, at times full of humor but still with a message. And indeed, his version of rap is akin to 1940s Harlem scatting. Yet instead of a bebopper's lexicon of jazz onomatopoeia, Syntax has much to say.

I'm watching Syntax and Ninine Garcia perform their funky-cool Gypsy jazz rap amalgam at Le Port d'Amsterdam. This is one of those bars found most anywhere around the globe that confuses matte black paint with ambience. But this bar's located in the heart of the Sentier, Paris's fashion *quartier* where the new black is usually just more of the old black. Thus, the interior decorator deserves not antipathy but condolences. And anyway, with hot music and *une jaune* in hand, the place comes alight. Ninine has his shoulders hunched up, playing with focus, sweating to strum out *la pompe* at high velocity as Syntax unreels his rap.

The song "Gens du voyage" is Syntax's masterpiece. And what a masterpiece it is. The song blends influences and bends traditions like no other rap that I know. He began with that loop of the Tziganes melody "Les deux guitares." Syntax added castanet-like percussion, albeit played with two empty beer bottles—this isn't the elder generation's flamenco after all. Then, Syntax's blazing Gypsy jazz riffs punctuate his rapping. The song's refrain is sung *à la* flamenco in a Catalan-Gitano argot by two Gitan *copaines*, Comino and Juan from the duet Casta Cali. Snatches of Hungarian Tziganes violin intermix with turntable scratches, the old and new coexisting side by side in Syntax's world.

While the music is funky and startling and mind-opening, it's his poetry that matters most:

Ils nous accueillent rarement avec le sourire

Nous appeler les voleurs de poules

Leur colle toujours le fou rire

On leur demande pourtant pas grand chose

Juste d'être tranquille

Mais dès que dans un coin on se pose

Ils veulent qu'on décolle, persuadés que tous les Gitans volent

Ils refusent nos enfants dans leurs écoles

Les laissant ne savoir ni lire, ni écrire

Demain, ils s'étonneront de les voir capables du pire

On subit leur haine, dès le plus jeune âge

Nos origines attisent, méfiance et rage

Les préjugés sont pas prêts de mourir

Sur nous, les rumeurs continuent de courir

Ils te diront, y'a pas de gentils Gitans

Ils nous détestent et on finit par en faire autant

Et on finit par en faire autant

On est juste différent

Parce que chez nous, c'est partout différent

Parce que nos maisons ont des roues

Différent

Parce qu'on est pas de chez vous

Différent

Parce que plus que tout, notre façon de vivre

Se passe de votre accord, on choisit nous-même

Nos routes et nos décors

On n'est pas corrompus par votre système

On balancerait pas le voisin pour avoir son BMW

On s'entraide, on cache nos peines derrière des grimaces

Dieu comme témoin, le paradis nous promet une place

En attendant, à chaque jour son lot de brimades

Jugés brigands, alors que juste nomades

Manouches, Tziganes, Roms, Sintis,

Le meilleur chemin est celui qu'on choisit

Manouches, Tziganes, Roms, Sintis,

Le meilleur chemin est celui qu'on choisit

They rarely welcome us with a smile
They call us the chicken thieves
And this always gives them the giggles
We ask for just one small thing
Simply to be left alone
But as soon as we arrive
They want us gone, persuaded that all Gypsies do nothing
    but steal
They refuse our children in their schools
And our children are left not knowing how to read or to write
Tomorrow, they will be astonished to see our children capable
    of the worst
We live with their hatred, from early on
Our origins inspire mistrust and rage
And these prejudices are not yet ready to die out
Rumors about us continue to spread
They will tell you that there are not any good Gypsies
They detest us and as a result we start to hate them back
And as a result we start to hate them back

We are simply different
Because with us, everywhere is different
Because our houses are on wheels
Different
Because we do not stay in any one place
Different
Because more than anything else, our style of living
Is different from yours
We choose our own roads and our own views
We are not corrupted by your system
We won't finger our neighbor to the police to get his BMW
We help each other, hiding our sorrows behind a smile
With God as witness, we are promised a place in paradise
But right now on Earth, every day brings pain
Judged bandits, we're nothing more than nomadic
Manouches, Gypsies, Roms, Sintis
The best path is the one you choose for yourself
Manouches, Gypsies, Roms, Sintis
The best path is the one you choose for yourself

And in the refrain—as near as Syntax himself can translate for me; he doesn't speak this Catalan-Gitano flamenco dialect either—the song is ultimately a celebration of a way of life despite the reins the rest of the world tries to put on the Romani:

Vive l'amour!
Vive la fête!
Vive l'amour!
Vive la fête!

The day after the concert, I meet up with Syntax and his producer, Laurent Soullier, in a café at the Porte de Bagnolet on the edge of old Ménilmontant. Beers and *pastis* are served, and Laurent previews for me their new work-in-progress. Syntax is typically sanguine in explaining his roots and inspirations: "When I grew up, we had just five records in our *caravane*: one by [French pop *chanteur*] Michel Legrand, one by Baden Powell, and three by Django."

Like many a Manouche youth, he learned guitar young: in Syntax's case, at age eight. He played the music with his family, cousins, friends. It was all a Romani rite of passage. As Syntax tells me, "Most every Manouche learns to play. The first song they learn is 'Minor Swing'—it's now traditional."

But it's one thing to play Django's music as a cultural folk tradition, and quite another for it to be an evolving and vibrant music. And that's where the likes of Syntax step in.

He's by no means the sole Romani musician taking Gypsy jazz in novel directions. A new generation of guitarists are experimenting with Gypsy jazz in tonal styles (sixteen-year-old Wawau Adler), free jazz (Boulou Ferré), bebop (Yorgui Loeffler, Samson Schmitt, Eddy Waeldo), and even religious music (Ensemble Enge). Then there are those looking back as Matelo Ferret did to Tziganes music and reviving it for a new era—musicians from Moréno Winterstein and his *chanteuse* wife, Marina, to the bands Bratsch, Les Yeux Noirs, Ams Ketenes, and Les Ogres de Barback. And there are those looking forward, electrifying the Balkan Tziganes music, Gypsy jazz, and flamenco, and imbuing them with a rock'n'roll edge, such as Danny Fender.

In addition, non-Gypsy groups are forging new directions with the old music. Following the jazz vein, guitarist Jean-Philippe Watremez explores extremes of tones and intervals. From his early trio Cordacor to his own, ever-changing ensembles, he's released a variety of string jazz albums, the best being 1998's *Mosaïque* and especially his self-produced *Watremez Trio*.

Dominique Cravic's loose-knit ensemble, Les Primitifs du Futur, is among the most adventurous, a surrealist-Dadaist-futuristic take on the old musics.

Including musicians from the late Gypsy jazz historian Didier Roussin to cartoonist R. Crumb, the band celebrates the roots of musette and jazz. They've blended in American blues, tango, Cuban son, and other Latin musics along with scat singing and instrumentation from bowed saws to slide guitar to eerie, groovy theremin. Cravic conducts these newborn primitives like a mad scientist, his crazed mane of hair astray as he bobs his head in time to his guitar.

From Austin, Texas, French expatriate guitarist Olivier Giraud launched his group 8½ Souvenirs, similarly blending Gypsy jazz with rockabilly as well as influences from film noir to Fellini soundtracks and the pop music of Serge Gainsbourg and Paolo Conte. In sum, 8½ Souvenirs' music was a confection both sweet and stylish. Today, the group's dissolved, but their music still has a cult following.

Thierry Robin's Gitans group created a fusion of North African, Spanish, Moorish, Jewish, flamenco, and French Romani music. Throughout, Robin was strongly influenced by Matelo and Francis-Alfred Moerman. But he also moved beyond. Robin's stage shows often include a vast percussion section, a range of near-forgotten wind instruments, and Indian dancers.

Two other groups have propelled Gypsy jazz into the mainstream, at least in Europe. Paris Combo began as a sort of French swing revival band infused with Piaf's *chanson* and Django's Gypsy jazz legacy, propelled by Manosque guitarist Potzi. But following their 1997 eponymous debut album, Paris Combo quickly became so big they're now shelved in pop music. The band is led by mastermind composer and *chanteuse* Belle du Berry, whose songs are at various times moody and clever, funny and infectious.

For his part, Stéphane Sansévérino switches between a Selmer-style Gypsy guitar and a Gretsch Model 6120, the rockabilly's choice. His music too bounces between musette and Gypsy jazz, rock and pop. Singing with cleverness and humor at high speed, he's become a new French star in a style of retro music known as *nouveau guinche*. Similar experiments continue with various far-sighted bands crafting gloriously apocryphal hot jazz, from Chicago-based violinist Andrew Bird to France's Samarabalouf, Opa Tsupa, and Les Szgaboonistes.

And yet no one has taken the music as far—or charged it with such a mission—as Syntax.

Syntax discovered rap in the 1980s—late, by American standards, but then he was living by his own Romani rules. "My generation of Manouche all listens to rap. On the radio, on television, it's everywhere." Run-D.M.C. and Dynasty were his favorites, what's now labeled Old Skool, rap with politics instead of just posture. "I don't like hard rap," Syntax pronounces. "But rap can be a full music, a rich music when mixed with other musics, whether it's *jazz manouche* or

Mexican, and this I love. The difference for me between hard rap and *rap manouche* is not about talking tough, about cool clothes, it's about our lives, respecting us as a people."

He put out a first rap single, "Chtar Academy," in 2003, and was immediately hailed by French rap magazine *Groove* writer Karim Madani: "Syntax has literally invented *rap manouche*."

But Syntax didn't just go on to a life in pursuit of bling. He worked with the too many Romani youths in French jails, leading hands-on seminars on writing and producing rap. In 2004, he was back with his fellow Romani rapper DJ Godzy, also known as Hugo Mércier, launching their debut album, *Gens du voyage*. Along with the title track and other politically charged raps, the CD included the song "Django," a true jazz tune, Syntax and Ninine paying homage where homage was due. *Rolling Stone* writer Jean-Eric Perrin heard all the currents within Syntax's music and praised the fusion: "*Gens du voyage* is a debut album with all the prickles of a hedgehog that depicts with witty eloquence over a nervous, mixed beat of Gypsy jazz, the universe of young Gypsies today, caught between the weight of traditions, a forceful rejection of the inherited racism directed toward 'chicken thieves,' and modernity (rap). Idiosyncratic but universal, the music is full of joy and emotion. This completely independent disc gives French rap new color."

In producing an accompanying video, Syntax and producer Laurent ran up against the same French discrimination directed toward the Romani that the album strives to combat. Laurent is a *gadjo*, long-haired, smart, and music-industry tough. He goes by the *nom de musique* of L'Ouïe Fine, a clever wordplay on his own name and French slang meaning "the fine sound." Laurent has a fatal flaw, however: He produces only bands he likes and believes in, which means he doesn't have a lot of bands in his roster. After first hearing Syntax, though, he came to believe in him and his message wholeheartedly. As Laurent explains to me, "I am one-hundred percent pure French, and my first image of the Gypsies was . . . *hmmm*." And he performs that great Gallic grimace that encompasses not only his whole body but his whole being. Then Laurent goes on, earnest now: "Yet it's not important what your background is; this music will speak to you."

The music didn't speak to the French government, however. Hearing that Laurent was organizing a gathering of Gypsies to be part of the filming of the "Gens du voyage" video, everyone from a representative of the gendarmerie to the French Minister of the Interior himself contacted him. The experience opened Laurent's eyes. "Finally, I personally had to tell the Minister of the Interior that I accepted full responsibility for whatever happened here." And with that, filming was allowed to proceed.

The video sums up Syntax's stance. Django's grandson, David Reinhardt, plays guitar, following Syntax and a group of Romani through an encampment. With nightfall, the Casta Cali duo sing their Catalan-Gitano flamenco refrain around a campfire. At times, Syntax wields *une serpette*, accenting his point with this traditional knife of the Manouche that is used for everything from trimming grape vines in seasonal labor to skinning illegally caught *niglos* for illicit Romani dinners. And throughout, he raps his message, moving with eloquence between logic and menace, pleading and defiance.

The short song video became the flashpoint for public knowledge of Gypsy jazz rap. And it had consequences that even Laurent was unprepared for: "After the video was first shown on French television, we had calls from all over France—women, both Gitans and *gadjé*—asking for Syntax's phone number. I had to tell them he was happily married with two children and *une caravane*."

Syntax's music both touched and broke hearts.

For his next album, Syntax has not lessened the political message, but he has relied even more on the Gypsy jazz medium. His rap has gone largely acoustic: Favino guitars, Balkan Tziganes accordion, and string bass, heavily boosted in Laurent's mix to give that quintessential rap bottom end. And Syntax's mainstream Gypsy jazz friends have joined in with vigor. Ninine Garcia reinvents the rhythm figure from his own composition "Cecel Swing" to back Syntax's 1960s-style lounge scat on "C'est des . . ." Sansévérino duets on "L'Orange," a sardonic parody of L'Academie Française and French propriety. On other tunes, Syntax is joined by Tchavolo Schmitt, Thomas Dutronic, Philippe Cuillerier's Doudou Swing ensemble, Titi Demeter, guitarist Eddie Bockomne, and the Pivala Quartet from Nancy. Where Syntax's first CD was rap mixed with Gypsy jazz, his second is Gypsy jazz with rap.

Throughout, there remains the inspiration and influence of Django. As Syntax explains to me, speaking in his passionate rapping lilt, "Music is essential. It's a history, it's a tradition. Music is like a voyage. It's our past, our present, our future, our destiny. We might not have written texts of our history, but it's all in the music. *C'est un patrimoine.*"

EIGHTEEN

The Most Dangerous Guitar Lesson
♪ *Jamming with David Reinhardt*

WHEN I FIRST MEET DAVID REINHARDT, I'm struck by the eerie sensation that I am looking back through the decades into the eyes of his grandfather, Django. For a moment, I am speechless. Like Django, David has dark eyes shaped almost like almonds with a soft, expressive light to them, his eyelids heavy, oriental. And in David's face I see an uncanny likeness of his ancestor. David is the son of Babik Reinhardt, Django's second son following Lousson Baumgartner, his first son with his legal wife, Naguine. Yet David resembles his grandfather more than his father or mother, Nadine. He too has Django's handsome visage, that supremely royal countenance. And the similitude doesn't end with physical appearances. As compared with contemporaries' descriptions of Django's demeanor, David shares Django's expressionless manner, his slowness to smile, reserved speech, reluctance to laugh—it's like a mask held up before us *gadjé*. All of these quick impressions blur my thoughts, leaving me to stutter over my *"Enchanté."*

Born December 23, 1986, David is nineteen years old. And he's been playing guitar for thirteen of those years. Babik first tutored him when he was just six, and together that same year they performed at Paris's Théâtre de Boulogne Billancourt for the Django d'Or Trophées Internationaux du Jazz, an annual French jazz award spectacular. But it was not until he was seventeen that David considered a musical career. Babik's untimely death in 2001 may have spurred him, and since then he has played numerous club gigs and festivals, including appearing as a special guest at Biréli Lagrène's Festival de Jazz à Vienne show and many others, culminating with a concert at the Festival Django Reinhardt in Samois-sur-Seine. Like his grandfather before him, David's now a veteran of the minstrel's life on the road.

Catching up to him on the road was another matter. France has untold kilometers of roads, and deciphering which one David was traveling down or parked alongside was a mystery for a crystal ball. In this matter, he also proves himself a true grandson of Django. And like many Romani today, his only reliable address is a cell phone number. And these, of course, are unlisted and thus for the most part, unknowable unless you are in contact already. So, for quite some time, David remained elusive.

I finally catch up with him by pure chance. A Romani friend of a friend told me David's band was about to kick off a gig at the Paris cabaret Le Baiser Salé—the Salty Kiss. And so, on a lustrous night in March 2005, I hurry across town.

Le Baiser Salé is located in one of the spider's web of backstreets ensnarling the ancient Les Halles markets. This is a *quartier* where you can find a prostitute on a street corner any time of night—or day. Most seem dressed in some local neighborhood fashion sense, mixing 1970s tartan skirts, decades-old fur coats, decrepit high heels like tottering stilts, and a vintage circus-clown's allotment of makeup. These are the old-fashioned whores fondly celebrated in Paris as *les traditionelles*, beloved less for their sex appeal than simply for being quintessentially Parisian. Just around the corner from the bar is one of the most glorious of the few surviving Art Deco Guimard arches, here at one of the many portals to the Châtelet *métro* stop. Next door is an exterminator's shop, Destruction des Animaux Nuisables Julien Aurouze, founded in 1872. The store front is complete with those beautiful Belle Époque windows, although these are full of proof of the powers of Monsieur Aurouze's wares: dozens of monstrous, tan Parisian rats (actually, a truly pretty pelt coloration), their necks broken in gigantic snap traps. These trophies are proudly displayed amid a collection of other stuffed vermin, hopefully rare, from tarantulas to unidentifiable mammals as large as your typical domestic cat. Just down the street is an obscure little shop specializing only in carnivorous plants, Venus fly traps lurking in the window looking insidious—and hungry. Nearby, the sign for Duluc's Detective Agency blinks on and off in red and green neon; Paris is the city of cheating spouses and so also a city with busy, fervent shamuses. From somewhere in the far distance, the sweeping beam atop the Tour d'Eiffel shines momentarily overhead. It all combines to create a perfect stage for Gypsy jazz.

Now, on the cabaret *terrasse* after introductions are made, David and I are talking music—although it's his guitarist cousin and fellow band member Noë Reinhardt doing most of the talking. David's mostly mum, answering just "*quay*" or "*non*," and I'm still recovering from my overblown sense of historical déjà vû. Then someone rings a bell, announcing the show's about to begin, David and Noë appearing as surprised by the timeliness as the rest of us.

Within the cabaret, the audience unconsciously settles into two quadrants—the *gadjé* jazz fans on one side and a cabal of the Reinhardts' fellow Romani on the other. Us *gadjé* are of all types. Men and women, young and old, a collision of fashion styles, and drinking everything from beer to wine to *pastis* to those evil-looking, too brightly colored Parisian cocktails, *diablos*. The Gypsies, though, are all older men, most with moustaches and near uniform in their dress of dark clothes, all drinking bourbon on ice. Yet among the Romani, one man stands out. An elderly gent, he sits like a king, regal within his entourage. He must be in his eighties—the same age Django himself would have been—his hair and clipped circumflex of a moustache perfectly silver against his tanned skin. His eyes are brilliant and clear, not bothering to ever look over at us *gadjé*, which seems only right. Around his neck is a scarf tied in the same manner Django often affected. Upon his head rests the most magnificent fedora imaginable, sharp creased and jauntily tilted just so, the perfect Romani crown.

With no introductions and no fuss, the music begins. David is joined by his bandmates: Noë and *gadjo* Samy Daussat, a young veteran of playing rock-steady rhythm behind most every Gypsy guitarist in Paris, from Raphaël Faÿs to Moréno Winterstein. The band's groove is tight yet loose with just the right swinging lilt, all sped along by bassist Théo Girard with Costel Nitescu's violin adding counterpoint to the guitar trio.

And with the music, David too comes alive. His reticence fades, and he loses himself to the swing. He turns up the volume on his Gibson ES-175DN and trades solos with Noë and the violinist, bobbing his head in time much the way Django did in the few films of him performing. David's face too bears a similar beaming expression to the many images of Django playing his guitar. It's as though he's surprised by the magic of his own music as his fingers fly over the fretboard.

Almost six months later to the day, I'm on a train south from Paris to rendezvous with David for clues to playing jazz *à la* Manouche. Considering his lineage, there are probably few others in the world better to study this music with. And in David's hands—as well as others of his young generation—lies the future of Gypsy jazz.

Over the phone, David gave me cursory directions to his *caravane*, and my quickly scribbled notes serve now as my map. Out in one of the countless old villages that have been leached up by the city of Paris, I find a bus, which wanders through featureless town after town. I fear I must long ago have missed my stop and am hopelessly lost. But at last we arrive in the main roundabout that signals the center of the *ville* of Paray-Vieille-Poste.

As I look around, I have an uneasy feeling: Perhaps I took the wrong bus or have my directions mistaken. Or maybe I was given a false address, a bum steer to get rid of me. This town is the picture of suburbia, and I can't begin to image David living here. It's as though I walked into a Jacques Tati film set. It's noontime, and *Paraysiens* wait patiently in the *boulangerie* to buy their midday baguettes. A *tricoleur* that appears freshly laundered and starched hangs in front of the *mairie*; the *poste* is closing for lunch; and a merry-go-round is bundled up in tarpaulins, awaiting the return of spring. Everything is so neat and orderly it's almost scary. After the chaos of Paris, I'm a stranger in a strange land.

I consult my directions again, spot the inevitable avenue Victor Hugo—a feature of every French city or town—then set off down the sidewalk. The avenue, like all the other streets I can see, stretches away from the roundabout in geometric precision; each is straight and true, lined by perfectly spaced beech trees bobbed like candelabra. There's none of Paris's blood-curdling traffic, the perfumes of ripe garbage, or—miracle of miracles—minefields of dog droppings. The lack of assaulting city noise is unnerving; I swear I even hear birds chirping. One after another, I pass well-to-do houses resting contentedly behind well-washed entry gates and fronted by gardens, each with their own ration of pruned and tended landscaping plants, a suitably French Peugeot or Renault or Citroën resting in the driveway. I count out the house numbers, but as far as I can see, the street continues on in carbon-copy fashion to the horizon. Something must be wrong here. I begin to believe I'm on a fool's errand.

Continuing my confused search, I come to the penultimate house number before what should be David's. And then I see it. A waist-high concrete wall girds the property of a nondescript house, set back and smaller in size than the uniform specifications of all the others. But it's not the house that catches my eye. Within the gravel courtyard are four Gypsy caravans, packed into the limited space with true genius.

Each *campine* is new, sparkling white, and capped by a satellite dish. Their windows are all open, featherbeds hanging out for a daily airing, Romani women scurrying about with mops and vacuums. A Gypsy's caravan is his or her castle.

I ask for David, and am pointed to *une campine*. A petite, smiling women leans out from the doorway: this turns out to be David's mother, Nadine, who never stops cleaning as she directs me to the house. Yet this house is not a home. It's merely another temporary camping spot, a seasonal retreat of convenience, where

David and his mother stay through the winter months. The rest of the year, their caravan is packed up, hitched to a car, and the family is on the go.

Befitting this, the house inside is largely empty. A long table haphazardly surrounded by chairs fills the dining room, which is a meeting point for meals as well as jam sessions. In the living room are a couch, chair, rug, and a monstrously large television. Nothing else—no lamps but an overhead fixture, no pictures on the walls, no books or magazines about, no knickknacks, and certainly no clutter. David's true home is the road.

Fresh from the shower at noon, David ushers me up a metal circular stairway to a second-story loft where he has a makeshift room. A mattress pallet and clothes dresser fill one half; a portable CD player and TV/DVD player are in a corner, surrounded by action movies, from Van Damme's latest heroics to *The Blues Brothers*. A photo of Django and another of Babik are pinned to the walls. David's guitars take up the most space here. In its case near the stairs, his Gibson awaits. A well-traveled *grande bouche* DiMauro hangs on a wall. An open case beneath holds his main guitar, a *petite bouche* Selmer copy made by Jean-Baptiste Castelluccia, son of Jacques Castelluccia, one of the first-generation Italian luthiers in Paris. On the headstock is emblazoned David's name; this is Castelluccia's Signature David Reinhardt Model, similar to the Modèle Django Reinhardt guitar made by Selmer in the final years. And like Django's own guitars, David's too is well-traveled—the fretboard shows the wear of his fingers' passages, the bottom bout is sanded through the finish, a victim of thousands of swipes by David's strumming arm.

David rounds up two chairs from other parts of the house and we sit down to play. He takes the DiMauro from the wall and hands it to me, casually informing me, "This was Baro Ferret's."

I almost drop the guitar, then grip it so tight as a reaction that I fear I might break the neck.

"Baro Ferret's guitar?" I ask.

David nods, nonplused.

I look the guitar over, at once terrified to be holding it, at the same time fascinated. It's a mid 1950s or early 1960s D-hole with the neck joining the body at the old-fashioned twelfth-fret mark. The soundboard is finished in a dark stain, which itself is stained even darker by time. Turning it over, the back of the headstock bears the luthier's heat-branded *marque*—J. DiMauro. My hands are shaky. Working up the audacity to strum this guitar of Baro's, I notice the frets are ground almost to nonexistence while the neck is bowed fit to fire arrows. The fretboard's sticky with sweat and dirt and who knows what else, whereas the steel strings are so oxidized my fingers will barely slide on them. They could easily be Baro's original strings.

This should be interesting, I tell myself. And I need all the help I can get.

As I now confess to David, I first taught myself to play a smattering of Gypsy jazz from listening to Django's recordings. Back in the late 1980s, I knew no one who could teach me even a lick of Gypsy jazz. Rockabilly or rock, sure; blues or American jazz from Charlie Christian forward, yes. But Django, no. People I asked just shook their heads and warned me I was crazy to even think about trying. And so I spun Django's LPs, lifting the needle arm after each line, whistling the melody to myself to keep it fresh in my head, and then trying to replay the music on my guitar. I had to guess where on the fretboard Django might have fingered the melody—it could have been played in a score of fingerings—to match his disability and the facility of then launching into his solo. Naturally, I was filtering Django's style through my own American style of playing guitar. I play Django approximately like T-Bone Walker might have played Gypsy jazz (or at least in my dreams): stiff wrist, broad swipes, and grandiloquent bluesy drama. That's surely not how Django played Django. And so the version of a simple tune such as "Minor Swing" that I deduced from a recording could be somewhat similar—or an ocean away from the way Django played it. I was about to find out firsthand.

And I find out right away. From the first notes I play.

"*Non!*" is David's succinct response. And like a morgue coroner performing an autopsy of a particularly brutal murder, he plunges in to dissect my playing.

Contrary to the American form of resting my right hand palm lazily on the bridge or using my little finger as a support on the soundboard, David orders me to keep my hand clear of the guitar top at all times. My extra fingers—those not holding the pick—are to be curled tightly into my palm, out of harm's way. Some players palm an extra pick under those fingers, just in case their main plectrum takes to the air. As David explains to me, my American style dulls the guitar's voice and dampens its volume. But perhaps more essentially, it slows down my hand, which becomes all-important for the velocity of playing. I can be lazy or lucky in some things, but neither will get me anywhere with Gypsy jazz.

David then shakes out his wrist, directing me to keep mine supple, as if I'm shaking out a lit matchstick. He orders me to keep it loose as much of the rhythm enhancements to the four-on-the-floor beat come from a quick flick of the wrist. This runs counter to American playing, which is more mechanical, the wrist usually locked in position and the elbow pivoting up and down in automaton fashion. Combined, these elements of playing *à la* Manouche come from the flamenco style, simply adding a pick instead of fingernails to increase volume. And instead of the famous flamenco *rasquedo*—the stylish fanning open of the fingers to create the signature strumming sound—with Gypsy jazz, that flourish is all in the wrist.

When David picks out melody and leads lines, he moves his whole arm forward on the guitar, picking over the sound hole for greater volume and a richer tone. Strumming the rhythm, he moves well back near the bridge, for a crisp sound. *"Leger et sec,"* he emphasizes—"light and dry." He looks me straight in the eye as if these are his final, dying words and I'm to remember them forever.

He picks primarily with a downward motion, which increases the volume and adds emphasis. This is one place where Gypsy jazz playing is absolutely, dead-on counter-intuitive to the classic American guitar picking of uniform up-down motion for speed and consistency. This music was incubated in the *bals musette* and Pigalle cabarets before the creation of microphones, never mind amplifiers. In those days, loudness was next to godliness, and these picking and strumming styles were equal to the task. While not all notes are struck downward—it's a personal choice in playing a melody line—the downward picking is elemental to the sound. David switches to up-down picking—*"aller et retour"*—only when essential for triplets and sixteenth notes. But for me, it goes against years of rigorous practice striving for that perfectly even up-down motion. Try as I might, I can't seem to shed it.

With my right hand's style now completely reconstructed, David moves to my left, fretting hand. There are fewer big secrets here—except sure and simple speed, which I'm obviously lacking. In fact, my playing coughs and sputters along like a Citroën 2CV while David accelerates away like a Ferrari, leaving me panting in his wake. But then again, many Gypsies spent their childhood playing guitar rather than going to school, giving them a head start.

Yet when we dive into arpeggios, David often plays different fingerings from the ones I know. This too dates from Django. During his eighteen-month convalescence following the caravan fire of 1928 that scorched and almost destroyed his fretting hand, Django taught himself not only to play guitar again but to finger the fretboard anew. The tendons and nerves in his two little fingers were ruined, leaving them a claw that he could barely control; they were now no use for fretting and he could only force them into action to finger the odd chord. He was left with his index and middle digits to play the guitar, and instead of playing most scales and arpeggios across the fretboard in the usual "box" fashion, he recreated his playing, moving up and down the fretboard, an easier and quicker reach for him. Thus, to play many of Django's melodies and solos, musicians today almost have to mimic Django's disability and recreate his longitudinal fingerings. And yet with his two fingers, Django was able to play what most of the rest of the world still can't play with all four.

Two fingers *and* a thumb, David reminds me now as we fret rhythm chords. As an aspiring garage-rock hero, I struggled through my teens to play those almighty power chords—barre chords fingered by barring the index fingers all the way across the fretboard. In the beginning, this required near-superhero strength in the index finger, or at least so it seemed to myself and every proto-rocker. Calluses came naturally, but building those inner and under finger muscles could only be done the hard way. Now, when I play barre chords effortlessly as the rhythm behind David's soloing, he stops the song and again says, *"Non."* Once more, he shows me all-new fingering for my heard-learned chords, again copying Django's disability. The glories of my index-finger barre are dispatched with a simple shake of the head. Instead, David consistently fingers these chords by wrapping his thumb around the neck onto the bass sixth, and even fifth, string. Again, like Django, David has long, thin, even graceful fingers, and his hand easily reaches around the neck to grasp these chords. My hands are less auspicious and the old DiMauro's neck is as thick as *une baguette*. I can't seem even in my mind to grasp these new fingerings. But as David warns me with that serious deep-into-my-soul look, "You must always finger the chords like this—*pour jouer comme les manouches."*

And so now that we are ready, we count off "Minor Swing" afresh. With a lifetime of practicing suddenly and instantly cast aside, my revamped playing is naturally all shot to hell. Here I am, attempting to speak in French while rock'n'roll truly walks and talks only English. I have to think not in the American musical A, B, Cs but translate everything into European *solfège* of *do, ré, mi*. I'm struggling to play solely in my newly acquired style *à la* Manouche and trying to think like Django with two fingers instead of four. And all the while, I'm picking Baro Ferret's ancient guitar, the burden of *that* history and the age of the instrument weighing upon me. I feel like a Gypsy circus performer, walking a tightrope in the heavens of the big top while trying to juggle flaming torches—all for the first time. But I muddle through the tune and receive a satisfied *"Bien"* from David.

I'm a little doubtful of the absolute veracity of that praise, but we charge on.

David's style of teaching guitar follows that of generations of Romani. The teacher plays a melody or strums a chord; the student listens, and then plays it back, the teacher patiently and painstakingly displaying the fingerings and playing the song over until the student knows it by heart. "Proper" musicians study *solfège*—ear-training—in France's Conservatoire Supérieur de Musique et Danse. But around campfires and in *roulottes* or today's high-rise slums, Gypsy children have learned this music in this same fashion for generations now. Call it *la conservatoire des caravanes*.

Django likely learned this way, as well. He first played violin, taught him by his father, Jean-Eugène Weiss. They probably practiced together in summer evenings around the fire or in the winter huddled in their *roulotte*, learning melodies by call and response.

David too studied this down-home style of *solfège* with Babik. But David also learned to read music, something Django and most of his generation of Gypsy jazz musicians never mastered. Yet this never held them back. There's a famous tale the Romani love to tell and retell time and again of Django playing with Duke Ellington during their tour of the United States in autumn 1946. Launching into a jam together, Duke asked Django, "What key do you want to play in?" Confused by the English term "key" yet not wanting to lose face, Django replied, "No key." Ellington was now the puzzled one: "But there has to be a key?" he said. Django simply told Duke, "You start. I follow." And, famed for his musical ear, Django immediately hit the right key.

Yet it's one thing to learn to comp jazz melodies by ear. It's quite another to improvise, and then further, create the chord and scale substitutions with which Django colored his music. His father may have taught him a minor scale, but it was likely Django who discovered for himself the intricacies of a diminished run. This was the result of his phenomenal ear and his vagabond musical spirit, always moving on and exploring new musical paths.

Still, Django's dominance over the genre he created could be the greatest limitation to the music's growth as so many players struggle simply to copy him, let alone use his inspiration as a jumping-off point to create their own music. But even today, Django's own music is being taken down new roads by the best of his Romani followers. Playing "Minor Swing," David shakes his head when I play the usual riff of root, minor third, and fifth. "Don't play it like that," he says, "try this..." He reorders the phrase as befitting his ear, picking out the fifth first, then root, and ending on that minor third. It's not the way Django played it on the rollicking 1937 side with his Quintette du Hot Club de France, but suddenly the old song sounds new and dynamic again.

The Gypsies never tire of telling another legend of Django and his prowess. I've heard this story told and retold with so many variations—various musical venues, differing songs, et cetera—that it's impossible to know where the original comes from. The stories surrounding Django have become legend, and then have gone a step further and become mythology. In one version, Django's on that same U.S. tour with Duke. He's listening to Ellington's big band rehearse when he hears one saxophone that's off key. The musically illiterate Django tells Duke the sax should be playing a B♭ and not a C. Duke says no, a C is correct. Then Duke scans his musical score and discovers Django is right.

Now as David and I jam together, when I hit one wrong note, David absolutely cringes. His shoulders shudder and his face involuntarily puckers. It's as if, expecting to bite into the glories of *un éclair au chocolat*, he's instead mistakenly tasted *une tarte au citron*.

I now improvise a solo as David and I jam on "Minor Swing." The burden of playing Baro Ferret's guitar—let alone mastering those rickety frets, rusty strings, and bowed neck—is trial enough. Yet leaving behind the need to translate French to English and notes from A, B, C to *do, ré, mi*, I can now focus, even lose myself, in just the music. My chorus is only a farrago of notes, a riffraff of riffs. But I am beginning to feel the spirit.

Now David takes the lead, playing one of Django's solos from the freewheeling 1947 "Surprise-Partie" live radio sessions. David's fingers prance up the fretboard, pirouetting perilously before the abyss of the sound hole, taunting and daring at the extreme edge of the guitar, before casually stepping back to safety. From quoting Django's solo, David moves into his own music. As on his trio's eponymous 2004 album, he plays with assurance and grace. While he can play Django, he rarely does. And while he can also play like Babik—floating off into rubato seances—he again prefers his own way. His style and voice may not be as virtuosic as Django's or as mellow as his father's, but it is his own.

With a subtle lift of his eyebrow, David signals to me that his chorus is coming to an end. In unison, we dive into the outro of the tune. We run through it once, pausing suspended in a stoptime break. Then we hit it again. Like Django, David ends the song with a flourish of a chromatic run leading back to the root.

We say our goodbyes out on the street, that avenue Victor Hugo. David proudly hands me a copy of his CD. I leave him there, smoking a cigarette under the plane trees on that strange suburban sidewalk, David tall and thin, the startling image of his grandfather.

I fall asleep on the train back into Paris, exhausted by this most dangerous of all guitar lessons. I certainly have yet to master the music, but with this brief visit to *la conservatoire des caravanes*, I now have some more tricks up my sleeve and more confidence in my fingers. After several more decades of practice back home, that is.

EPILOGUE ♩ Latcho Drom—*The Long Road*

THE STORY OF GYPSY JAZZ begins in *les marchés aux puces* of Paris. And it continues there today.

It's another lazy Sunday afternoon at La Chope des Puces in the heart of the flea market at Porte de Clignancourt. Outside, *les puces* is in full swing. I've negotiated safely around the Gypsy women promising to tell my fortune, around the pickpockets and streetsellers, past a sidewalk shell game set up on a cardboard box, through the haze of hookah smoke and marvelous aroma of Arab stalls with their dripping gyros. The venerable door handle at La Chope des Puces feels familiar as I twist it open, the lace curtains again dancing in the breeze as I enter. I lean against the bar and order yet another *noisette*. Ninine Garcia greets me with warmth; Mondine, the reigning elder sovereign of Gypsy jazz, nods. Guitarist Patrick Saussois rode in from Montrouge and parked his *moto* out front. He's now at the bar chatting with René Mailhes. Romane's standing next to me, explaining his next band project. Romani gentlemen group on one side of the bar, tourists from Sweden and Germany and England and the United States sit in the back. The waitress brings another batch of steaming *moules-frites* from the kitchen while the bartender pours more beer. Time may pass outside, but here, inside La Chope, the music goes on as usual through an eternal weekend afternoon.

The old glass door opens. A young Gypsy boy of maybe fifteen enters. On his face is a tentative mien as he looks around at the crowd of *gadjé* before he's hailed by Ninine. Handshakes ensue with Mondine and the other Romani, and he lights up a cigarette. I've not seen him before, nor, it appears, have the other *gadjé* as they pay him no mind. He moves with shy steps to a back corner of the bar.

Finally, Mondine tires of playing and thirsts for a *café*. The *gadjé* guitarists are obviously hungry to take his place, but Mondine calls out instead to the young Gypsy boy. He holds out his battered Favino Enrico Macias guitar as enticement. The boy shyly shakes his head. But the Romani man laugh and push him forward.

He's tall and slender, his hair combed neatly to the side, the first hints of a moustache on his upper lip. He'll look only at Ninine, not even raising his head to the crowd around the bar. In undertones, he and Ninine debate what song to play. His fingers on the steel strings are incredibly long, impossibly graceful. And then they begin.

Just when I think I know something about this music, just when I think I understand something of its history, just when I think I can play the music decently myself, along comes another Romani boy out of some encampment somewhere on the fringes of Paris, the secret *conservatoire des caravanes*. He might not have all the emotion of Django, the imagination of the Ferret brothers, the ferocity of Bousquet, or the spirit of Tchan Tchou. He may still falter a bit around the fretboard. But he plays and swings the music with more eloquence and elegance than I could ever dream.

NOTES

Prologue. Music in the Shadows

4 like a lowly banana: Sartre outraged the overly serious French jazz sophisticates by commenting in his essay "New York City": "*Le jazz, c'est comme les bananes, ça se consomme sur place.*"

Chapter 1. The Guitar with a Human Voice

8 "My friend bought some records": King, *Blues All Around Me*, 104. Also, Sawyer, *The Arrival of B. B. King*, 156–57.

8 "Django was a new world": King, *Blues All Around Me*, 104–5; and Obrecht, *Blues Guitar*, 127. Also, B. B. King interview by Wheeler and Obrecht.

12 *jazz tsigane*: Francis-Alfred Moerman, interview with author, Paris, 2001.

Chapter 2. The Boy with the Banjo

17 Edith Piaf: Piaf was known at this time by her real name of Edith Gassion. At age five, she was singing "La Marseillaise" in the *marchés* and living with her father in a caravan at the Porte de Montreuil. Crosland, *Piaf*, 20.

18 Vaugirard galleries: Paris's *marché aux cheveaux*—the horse-trading market—was originally located at the crossroads of the boulevards Saint-Marcel and de l'Hôpital in the 13th Arrondissement. In 1908, it was moved to the Vaugirard *galéries* on the rue Brancion in the 15th Arrondissement.

18 "*La Zone* is a zigzag paradise": Serge, *La grande histoire des bohémiens*, 140–65.

19 Flache ôs Coûrbôs: This is the Wallon spelling; in French it is "Flach aux Corbias." A derivative of the Latin "flaccus," "flache" is variously translated as "pond" or "depression," as in a valley. The area has long been a stopping spot for migrating birds. Pont-à-Celles Maire Christian Dupont correspondence with author, 2002.

22 The Romani's journey: Ian Hancock, correspondence with author, 2003–2005. Hancock, *We Are the Romani People*, 15–25. Also Hancock, *The Roads of the Roma*, 9–21.

23 Four, not three, nails: Danny Fender, interview with author, East Los Angeles, May 2007.

23 Upon visiting the Pope: Hussey, *Paris*, 98–99.

23 "Almost all of them": *Journal d'un bourgeois*, 234–38.

24 "They excite the *hatred*": McKenzie, *The Letters of George Sand and Gustave Flaubert*, 309.

24 The earliest traces: Asséo, *Les Tsiganes*, 44–45; and de Foletier, *Les Tsiganes*, 210.

28 their father's repertoire: Sara Reinhardt interview with Alain Antonietto, "Valses pour Django" in Billard and Antonietto, *Django Reinhardt*, 20.

28 Django's sister remembered: Reinhardt family interview with Alain Antonietto; correspondence with author, 2002.

29 Django learned to play: Salgues, "La légende de Django Reinhardt." *Jazz Magazine* N. 33, 21. Also Delaunay, *Django mon frère*, 36–37.

29 *Le Grand Gitan*: Boulou and Elios Ferré, interview with author, Paris, 2001; René Mailhes, interview with author, Paris, 2003; and Antonietto, "Django, la valse et le banjo..." in Billard, *Django Reinhardt*, 24–25.

30 "Valse Poulette": Tony Baldwin, correspondence with author, 2004. Along with "Valse Poulette," Castro is believed to have recorded two other 78s for Sonnabel, one of which has been found, the other remaining missing. Dominique Cravic, interview with author, Paris, 2005; and Alain Antonietto, interview with author, Paris, 2007.

31 ten *francs* a night: Delaunay, *Django mon frère*, 37–38.

Chapter 3. Bals Musette

Background on the *bals musette* and playing musette comes from a series of interviews and walks through Paris as well as correspondence with Francis-Alfred Moerman from 1999 to 2007.

34 Panam: Carco, *Panam*, 45.

34 "Of all the pleasures": Carco, *Nostalgie de Paris*, 75.

34 "like a ball": Carco, *Panam*, 51.

35 "The *bals musette*": Brassaï, *Le Paris secret*, no folios (74–80).

36 "*Ici, la danse n'est pas un art*": Carco, *Panam*, 48.

38 "The days of my *cabrette*": Péguri and Mag, *Du bouge*, 50. Péguri's recorded conversation was perhaps fictionalized, but likely true in spirit. In 1910, Bouscatel sold his famous *bal musette* to a Monsieur Corniault and retired from rue de la Lappe, although he continued to play his beloved *cabrette*. In 1919, the family Carcanague bought the *bal*, renamed it Bousca-Bal, and operated it until shutting the doors forever in 1963.

39 "Death to these foreign squeezeboxes": Noted in the newspaper *Le Courrier français*; quoted in Dubois, *La Bastoche*, 54.

39 "*Ça tourne!*": Péguri and Mag, *Du bouge*, 50.

41 "six fingers on each hand": Bazin interview with Cravic, "Charley Bazin," 44; and René Mailhes, interview with author, Paris, 2003.

41 "Les Frères Gusti banjoïstes": Alain Antonietto, interview with author, Paris, 2007.

42 *la toupie*: Francis-Alfred Moerman interview with author, Paris, 2002.

43 "Already everyone admired him": Delaunay, *Django Reinhardt*, 41.

44 visited Django's widow: Francis-Alfred Moerman, intervew with author, Paris, 2002.

46 They parked alongside: It's long been believed the caravan fire took place outside the Porte de Choisy, as recorded by Delaunay, but according to both Bella and Django's Hôpital Lariboisière admittance records, they gave their address as 136 rue Jules Vallès in Saint-Ouen, just outside the Porte de Clignancourt surrounding the *marché aux puces*.

47 Each afternoon, he made a pilgrimage: Sophie Ziegler interview with Delaunay, Fonds Charles Delaunay; Roger Chaput interview, quoted in Gumplowicz, "Django Guitare," 90–91; Delaunay, *Django Reinhardt*, 40–41. There's some debate over the date: Delaunay stated 1924; Chaput claimed it was 1926.

47 This bizarre concept of swing: As French trombonist Leo Vauchant remembered, "when the French would play, there was no sense of beat. They were playing things with rubato—there was no dance beat. It didn't swing. It didn't move." Quoted in Goddard, *Jazz Away from Home*, 17.

47 He learned by listening: Delaunay, *Django Reinhardt*, 41.

48 Beware this new music: Salgues, "La légende de Django Reinhardt," *Jazz Magazine* N. 34, 30–31.

48 Django was accompanying: There have long been doubts about the date of Hylton's visit to La Java and Django's subsequent burns in the caravan fire. Delaunay's biography gives the date as November 2, 1928, but Hylton was playing a month-long engagement then at Berlin's Scala-Theater, so it is doubtful he was in Paris at the time. The Hôpital Lariboisière's records state that Django and Bella were admitted on October 26, 1928, with burns from the fire. This date would fit the known facts of Hylton's schedule as well, as Hylton was then in transit from England to Germany to begin a concert tour on October 28, 1928, in Köln and could have ventured to Paris en route seeking Django. Archives de l'Assistance Publique-Hôpitaux de Paris, numéros d'enregistrement 18762 et 18763.

48 He had a beautiful woman: Salgues, "La légende de Django Reinhardt," *Jazz Magazine* N. 34, 30.

48 October 26, 1928: As noted previously, the Hôpital Lariboisière's records state that Django and Bella were admitted on October 26, 1928, with burns from the fire. Delaunay stated the fire took place on November 2, likely based on someone's memory that the celluloid flowers were for All Soul's Day. Archives de l'Assistance Publique-Hôpitaux de Paris.

49 Then they rushed: At the registration, Django was signed onto the docket as patient number 18763, his admittance to the Ward Nélaton underlined in red as *une affaire judiciare*, requiring gendarmes to check into the suspicious circumstances. Django was logged into the Hôpital Lariboisière as "Jean Reinloardt," age eighteen. His profession was listed as *musicien* and he and Bella were denoted as unmarried, French law not recognizing Gypsy marriages. Archives de l'Assistance Publique-Hôpitaux de Paris.

50 *l'Ourson*: Salgues, "La légende de Django Reinhardt." *Jazz Magazine* N. 35, 27.

50 He fashioned new chord forms: Grappelli, "Stephane Grappelly Tells," *Melody Maker*.

51 *"Tiens!"*: Salgues, "La légende de Django Reinhardt," *Jazz Magazine* N. 34, 32.

51 *"Ach moune!"*: Django quoted in Delaunay, *Django mon frère*, 45.

Chapter 4. Jazz Modernistique

This chapter is largely based on interviews with Hot Club founders Jacques Bureau in 2001 and Elwyn Dirats in 2002; and Quintette members Emmanuel Soudieux in 2003 and Beryl Davis in 2004.

53 Stéphane Grappelli: Grappelli's name through much of this era was spelled as "Grappelly." He changed the orthography of his name during the early 1920s while he was one of the Grégoriens. There are at least two versions of why. Stéphane told it this way: His Italian family name was constantly mispronounced as "Grappell-eye," particularly by the British. English words such as Piccadilly, however, received the correct Italianate pronunciation, so he became Grappelly. Others remember it differently: With Mussolini taking power in Italy and building his military might, Stéphane feared being drafted as his father before. With the change in spelling, he sought to hide his identity from the Italian army. Either way, he retained the orthography "Grappelly" for some four decades, reverting to "Grappelli" around 1969. Fred Sharp, interview with Delaunay, 1967.

53 "This young man": Grappelli, *Mon violon*, 79–80; Smith, *Stéphane Grappelli*, 43–44. Grappelli had crossed paths with Django several times earlier. Grappelli remembered first spotting Django and Joseph while they were busking in a Pigalle café. He also remembered seeing Django play his banjo in a *bal* on the avenue de Clichy and later, his guitar at La Boîte à Matelots in Paris with Louis Vola's *orchestre*.

54 "changed my destiny": Smith, *Stéphane Grappelli*, 31.

55 "My life started": Anick, "Reminiscing with Stéphane Grappelli," 10–12.

55 Hot Club de France: The original orthography was "Hot-Club" in *Jazz-Tango-Dancing* notices. Only later was the hyphen lost. *Jazz-Tango-Dancing*, November 1932, 9; Jacques Bureau, interview with author, Paris, 2001; Elwyn Dirats, interview with author, 2002.

56 "jazz propaganda": *Jazz-Tango-Dancing*, November 1932, 9.

56 "At the Claridge": Delaunay, *Delaunay's Dilemma*, 101–2.

57 "I could see": Grappelli, *Mon violon*, 80–82; Delaunay, *Django mon frère*, 66.

57 "Nobody had confidence": Louis Vola, interview with Fred Sharp, Paris, 1967.

57 *Négromanie*: The term was coined by Stéphane Grappelli's former bandmate, jazz pianist Stéphane Mougin, "Négromanie," *Jazz-Tango-Dancing*, October 1933, 9.

57 blackface: Frenchman Alain Romans, who played piano with Benny Peyton in the 1920s, was forced to perform in blackface: "One day, the little daughter of the owner of the Casino de la Forêt came over and touched my face. When she saw she had black on her fingers, she started to scream. Her father appeared, and when she told him what had happened, he got an ice-bucket and a napkin—this is the funny part—and wiped every face except mine. Then he spanked the little girl for telling a lie, and we played on." Quoted in Goddard, *Jazz Away from Home*, 19.

57 10 percent of the French musicians: *Chicago Defender*, June 10, 1922. *Chicago Defender*, July 22, 1922. Shack, *Harlem in Montmartre*, 77–83.

58 Frank "Big Boy" Goodie: Goodie is also variously known as "Goudie" on Hot Club concert posters and recordings.

58 "the lightness and freshness": *Jazz-Tango-Dancing*, February 1934.

58 "I was hesitant": Jacques Bureau, interview with author, Paris, 2001.

58 "At that time": Elwyn Dirats, interview with author, 2002.

59 "Once in the studio": Delaunay, *Django mon frère*, 67–68. The band for these Odéon auditions was later known as "Delaunay's Jazz," a misnomer that Delaunay explained in his memoir: When the auditions arranged by Nourry were finished, a recording engineer, not knowing what to call the band and knowing Delaunay from the past, simply scrawled across the blank label "Delaunay's Jazz." Delaunay later recovered these recordings before Odéon threw them away and released them years later on his Vogue label.

59 "No recording label": Grappelli, *Mon violon*, 81

59 "We did not yet know": Delaunay, *Delaunay's Dilemma*, 103.

60 "It was a grand success": Panassié, *Douze Années*, 141.

60 "The Hot Club": Delaunay, "French Jazz," 123. As early as March 1932, *Jazz-Tango-Dancing* editor Léon Fiot wrote, "Our idea is to form an *orchestre* of hot jazz composed only of the best French musicians, and of course they will be devoted to hot music, or to help its formation." The Hot Club even gave its name to sponsor an earlier band, the Hot Club Orchestre composed of Freddy Johnson, Big Boy Goodie, Arthur Briggs, and others who played a club concert. Léon Fiot, "En faveur du 'jazz hot,'" *Jazz-Tango-Dancing*, March 1933.

60 "I was a little dubious": Delaunay, *Django mon frère*, 68–69.

61 "*leger et sec*": This description of *la pompe* comes from Paul "Tchan Tchou" Vidal via Alain Cola; Tchan Tchou admonished Cola and his other rhythm players to keep their playing always "light and dry."

62 "For Django": Spautz, *Django Reinhardt*, 80.

62 "The recording sessions": Grappelli, *Mon violon*, 81.

62 "After several wax tests": Panassié, *Douze Années*, 142–43.

63 American fedora: Delaunay, *Django mon frère*, 69.

64 "What troubles": Goddard, *Jazz Away from Home*, 245.

64 "It was never possible": Panassié, *Douze Années*, 262–63.

65 He illustrated: Adams, "I Meet Reinhardt."

67 punched him in the nose: Roger Chaput, interview with Dominique Cravic.

67 "What are you doing": Battestini, "Emmanuel Soudieux."

70 "palm-pelting": "Reinhardt, Grappelly and Co. Here Again."

70 "For us": Sophie Ziegler, interview with Charles Delaunay, Fonds Charles Delaunay.

71 "Whenever Django had money": Emmanuel Soudieux, interview with author, Paris, 2003.

71 "I would rather": Sophie Ziegler, interview with Charles Delaunay, Fonds Charles Delaunay.

71 "With my guitar": Emmanuel Soudieux, interview with author, Paris, 2003.

73 Le Clown Bar is all clown: If all this adds up to an atmosphere too scary to dine in, fear not. The food makes you forget the strange clowns leering at you, smiling their too-happy smiles: fine *steak au poivre*, excellent fresh goat cheese with a wildberry sauce, a Minervois *rouge*, and perfect *moelleux au chocolat*.

73 circus music: Emmanuel Soudieux, interview with author, Paris, 2003; Delaunay, *Django Mon Frère*, 126–27.

75 "After the sun": Bricktop, *Bricktop*, 76.

76 "a brownskin princess": Hughes, *The Big Sea*, 172, 181.

76 Berthe Saint-Marie: Delaunay, *Delaunay's Dilemma*, 133–34.

76 throw their knives: Delaunay, *Django mon frère*, 103–4.

Chapter 5. Songs of One Thousand and One Nights

Much of this chapter is based on interviews with Jacques Bureau. The passage on Schnuckenack Reinhardt is thanks to Andreas Öhler's documentary film, *Die Ballade von Schnuckenack Reinhardt*, which I viewed in the French version, *La ballade de Schnuckenack Reinhardt*.

79 Ghetto Swingers: Schumann, *Coco Schumann, der Ghetto-Swinger*, 66; Fackler, "Music in Concentration Camps."

79 In the end: Hancock, "Jewish Responses to the Porrajmos."

79 "Whole families": Öhler, *Die Ballade von Schnuckenack Reinhardt*.

80 *Reichsmusikprüfstelle*: Levi, *Music in the Third Reich*, 120 and 127.

80 Under Goebbels's command: Kater, *Different Drummers*, 31.

81 Like all French entertainers: Heller, *Un allemand a Paris*, 27–28.

81 Le Shéhérazade: Kazansky, *Cabaret russe*, 164.

82 "I was witnessing": Delaunay, *Delaunay's Dilemma*, 150.

82 "Zazouzazouzazouhé": Panassié, *Monsieur Jazz*, 185; Loiseau, *Les Zazous*, 48. Although they looked down their collective noses at *les zazous*, the French jazz critics even argued over where the term "zazou" came from. Some said it was based on Calloway, others— such as Panassié—said it came from Freddy Taylor's scatting.

82 Swing-Heinis: Kater, *Different Drummers*, 102–10.

82 "Anything that starts": Kater, *Different Drummers*, 194.

84 "I viewed jazz": Legrand, "Jacques Bureau," 8.

85 Armand Stenegry: Kenrick, *The Destiny of Europe's Gypsies*, 107.

85 "Benny": Loiseau, *Les Zazous*, 41.

85 But by 1943: Gottlieb, "Delaunay Escapades with Gestapo Related."

86 At Fresnes: Jacques Bureau, interview with author, Paris, October 2001; Bureau, "Champagne!"

88 He dreamed: Emmanuel Soudieux, interview with author, Paris, 2003.

89 Django had vowed: There were unsubstantiated rumors that Django performed in Berlin in 1942 or 1943. Several Italian jazz musicians stated they saw him play at the Femina Bar on the city's Hohenstaufenstrasse; see Mazzoletti's *Il Jazz in Italia*. But like the other "Django" in the prison camp, this could have been one of Django's cousins in disguise. Either way, none of his French musical coterie remembered him playing in Germany during the war nor are there German accounts of him in Berlin.

89 "*Mon vieux* Reinhardt": Delaunay, *Django mon frère*, 114–15.

89 "I want to speak": Delaunay, *Django mon frère*, 106.

90 One such story: djangoreinhardt.free.fr/ninine.htm.

90 "played himself free": quotes throughout this passage come from the French-language version of Öhler, *Die Ballade von Schnuckenack Reinhardt*.

93 "When *les américains* arrived": Sophie Ziegler, interview with Charles Delaunay, Fonds Charles Delaunay.

93 the jazz played on: Beevor, *The Fall of Berlin 1945*, 358–60; Fest, *Inside Hitler's Bunker*, 115; Payne, *The Life and Death of Adolf Hitler*, 565.

94 "Panzer Swing": Delaunay journals, Fonds Charles Delaunay.

Chapter 6. Gypsy Bebop

Much of this chapter comes from interviews with René Mailhes in Paris in 2003 and 2007; with Boulou and Elios Ferré in Paris in 2001; and with Christian Escoudé in Paris in 2007.

98 "Salt Peanuts": Delaunay, in Gillespie, *to BE, or not . . . to BOP*, 330–31.

98 "inscribed the future": Hodeir, "Vers un renouveau de la musique de jazz?"

98 "He plays so well": Elios Ferré, interview with author, Paris, 2001.

101 Various versions: Ruppli, *Discographies Vol. 2: Vogue Productions*, 185. Alternative takes of several of these *valses bebop* have never been issued.

101 "revolution": Delaunay, liner notes to *Swing valses d'hier et d'aujourd'hui*, 1966.

101 Django's everlasting admiration: Francis-Alfred Moerman, interview with author, Paris, 2000; Elios Ferré, interview with author, Paris, 2001.

104 "I was performing": Les Paul, interviews with author, 2000 and 2001.

105 "Django was in ecstasy": Pierre Michelot, liner notes to *Pêche à la Mouche: The Great Blue Star Sessions 1947–1953*.

105 "There's money here": Pierre Michelot, liner notes to *Pêche à la Mouche: The Great Blue Star Sessions 1947–1953*.

106 "In Samois": Sophie Ziegler, interview with Charles Delaunay, Fonds Charles Delaunay.

107 She piled Django's things: Madame Ipsaïenne (daughter of Fernand Loisy) in Spautz, *Django Reinhardt*, 134.

107 *casseurs*: Sophie Ziegler, interview with Charles Delaunay, Fonds Charles Delaunay.

108 "I don't want to copy": André, "Les Lundis du jazz: Joseph Reinhardt."

110 "The U.S. Army": Christian Escoudé, interview with author, Paris, 2007.

112 "Laro had a great influence": Antonietto, "Adieu manouche"; and Antonietto, "Laro Sollero."

Chapter 7. Les Guitares à Moustache

It should be no surprise that this chapter is made up of many obsessive conversations about guitars with a variety of Gyspy jazz fans, including François Charle, Jean-Pierre Favino, Luc Degeorges, Scot Wise, Ted Gottsegen, Michael Simmons, and more.

119 *"Mon frère"*: Delaunay, *Django mon frere*, 140; Delaunay, *Delaunay's Dilemma*, 108.

122 the old *atelier*: Luc Degeorges has since moved his shop to 31 rue de Reuilly in the 12th Arrondissement.

122 J-P tells: Portions of this section also come from letters from J-P Favino in 1998 and 2000 as well as a 1994 interview with Jacques Favino by Patrice Veillon published on www.favino.com (accessed April 16, 2007).

128 *"C'est la guerre"*: Django's guitar was described in detail in three magazine articles of the time: Adams, "I Meet Reinhardt"; Henshaw, "Swing Guitars"; and Hodgkiss, "Django's Guitar."

Chapter 8. Crossroads

133 The roots: Hari, *L'Église des Saintes-Maries-de-la-Mer*, 2–25; Vaudoyer, *Les Saintes-Maries-de-la-Mer*, 10–27.

134 Veneration of Sainte Sarah: Mistral, *Memoirs*, 185–200.

134 goddess of fate: Hancock, *We Are the Romani People*, 72–73.

135 He founded La Mission: Le Cossec, *Mon aventure*, 6, 11, 20–35, and 42.

137 Indian goddess Kâli: Hancock, *We Are the Romani People*, 72–73. Hancock notes that in parts of India, Kâli has also been known, or perhaps syncretized, as the goddesses Parvati, Durgā, Umā, Bhadrakāli, and Sāti-Sara.

142 "In Stes-Maries they would meet": Clergue, *Roots*, no folios (6). "Those wonderful Gypsies from Lyon" were most likely Tchan Tchou and his band, the Hot Club de Jazz de Lyon.

144 Django sought: Delaunay, *Django Reinhardt*, 124–26.

144 "My people": Corbier, "A Thonon-les-Bains."

145 he hoped to revive: Even though Django did not finish the mass at this time, he remained committed to it. While traveling to Rome in 1950, he shared a train cabin with a curate who was knowledgeable about masses and Django queried him extensively on their structure. Evidently, he still wished to complete his work even then, years later, as his accompanying drummer Roger Paraboschi remembered. Paraboschi, correspondence with author, 2004; Bedin, "Django à Rome."

145 After Django's death: Antonietto, *Gipsy Jazz School*, 21–22.

Chapter 9. Dynasty

The basis for this chapter is of course several interviews with Boulou and Élios Ferré in 1999, 2000, and 2001, as well as correspondence with Élios over the years. Interviews with Francis-Alfred Moerman in 2001 and René Mailhes in 2003 also informed the chapter.

147 Jean-Jacques "Boulou" Ferré: The family name would be variously spelt as "Ferret" and "Ferré." As Élios explained, "Our family name, through many years, has been 'Ferré,' but there was a time when no one in my family knew how to write and it was for this reason that my ancestors accepted the orthography of 'Ferret' that was written down by the French bureaucrats in the municipal registers of the city of Rouen." Tuzet, *Jazz manouche*, 36.

148 Charles-Allain "Challain": Challain's Christian name appears in different forms over the years. On recordings with Django's Quintette, he was listed as "René" and "Auguste," while in later years he was more often known as "Charles-Allain."

148 Maurice "Gros Chien": Like Baro Ferret before him, Gros Chien Ferret changed his name from "Michel" to "Maurice" as he didn't like his given name.

150 "Baro" meant "Big One": The Romany nickname of "Baro" often appeared spelled phonetically in French as "Barreau" or "Barreault."

150 Using the privilege: Over the years there would thus be confusion between the names Pierre Baro, Pierre Matelo, and Jean Matelo. "Matelo" would also be phonetically spelled in myriad fashions including Matlo, Matelow, and Matelot.

150 83 rue Damrémont: Francis-Alfred Moerman, interview with author, Paris, 2001; Antonietto, "Matelo Ferret . . ." *Études tsiganes*.

152 The band recorded at least four sides: The four sides found to date include "Brise napolitaine" backed by "Gallito," and "Vito" backed by "Ne sois pas jalouse." It's quite possible other 78s were cut and released at the time but have yet to be rediscovered.

153 Maurice Alexander, had warned him long ago: Salgues, "La légende de Django Reinhardt." *Jazz Magazine* No. 34, 30–31.

153 quick recording session: This session was likely an offshoot of a Gus Viseur session, as Le Trio Ferret and bassist Speilleux formed Viseur's backing band. On October 20, 1938, a similar offshoot recording from a Viseur session for Charles Delaunay's Swing label resulted in the fascinating unissued tune "Andalousie" co-authored by Baro and played by Viseur's backing band comprising Le Trio Ferret, Speilleux, and Albert Ferreri on tenor sax. Ruppli, *Discographies Vol. 1: Swing*, 10.

154 "Gin Gin": The name "Gin Gin" was given to the song in later years and believed by Francis Moerman to have come from a nickname for Django's second son, Babik.

156 "There was nothing more execrable": Delaunay, *Delaunay's Dilemma*, 124. Delaunay made a similar statement at the time in his review, "Gus Viseur's Music."

156 "I have no hesitation in saying": Delaunay, "Gus Viseur's Music."

157 "There were 'No Swing Dancing' signs": Bergerot, *Paris Musette*.

158 "Panique . . . !": The title of "Panique . . . !" appears in various forms in various places. On the first Odéon label, it's simply "Panique." On what I believe is the first published sheet music, the title is noted as "Panique . . . !," which I chose to go by.

159 "La folle": Privat would soon re-record "La folle" (backed by "Ballade nocturne") with his own ensemble, playing it at a more relaxed tempo and without the intensity Baro brought to their co-composition. Privat's *orchestre Balajo* band on the recording included guitarists René "Didi" Duprat and Gaston Durand.

160 And he also procured women: Francis-Alfred Moerman, interview with author, Paris, 2001.

160 "raise an army by daybreak": Jean-Marie Pallen, interview with Scot Wise; correspondence with author.

160 *Swing valses d'hier et d'aujourd'hui*: Ruppli, *Discographies Vol. 2: Vogue*, 185. Alternative takes of several of these *valses bebop* have never been issued.

161 "Technically, Django did not scare me": René Mailhes interview with author, Paris, 2003.

162 Emmanuel Soudieux remembered: interview with author, March 2003.

162 None of the other Gypsy guitarists: Francis-Alfred Moerman interview with author, relating conversations with Baro, Sarane, and Matelo, Paris, 2003.

164 "Matelo carried the melodies": Francis-Alfred Moerman interview with author, Paris, 2001.

165 some 60,000 Russians: Kazansky, *Cabaret russe*, 164.

165 Le Château Caucasien: Kazansky, *Cabaret russe*, 155–56.

165 And waiting on the wealthy: Mez Mezzrow, quoted in Kazansky, *Cabaret russe*, 197.

166 René Duchossoir: Matelo shared sideman duties with the *gadjo* Duchossoir behind accordionists many times in the past. He was known affectionately as "Goudasse"—Old Shoes—a moniker bestowed him by Matelo as Duchossoir also worked for the postal service where he had a fine pair of shoes that he kept proudly polished to a brilliant sheen.

166 "Les Inédits" of Django: Ruppli, *Discographies Vol. 2: Vogue*, 171 and 173.

167 "When you stroll into Django Reinhardt's jernt": Caen, "An Evening in Paris Has Some Solid Kicks."

169 "I fell head over heels in love": Privat, *Jo Privat partitions*, 2–3.

171 "As to the violinist": Jo Privat, interview with Didier Roussin, undated (likely 1991), *Manouche Partie*. Privat stated, "As to the violinist, I believe Matelo has taken this secret to his grave; no one remembers his name. . . . He was Hungarian, a guy who played in a Gypsy *boîte du nuit*; it was Matelo who brought him along. . . . His name, I never knew."

172 "I moved to Paris": Francis-Alfred Moerman was born on May 13, 1937, in Gand (Ghent), Belgium, but would live most of his life in France.

173 "During his breaks": Francis-Alfred Moerman interview with author, Paris, 2001.

173 honorary "fourth brother"—Challain (Challain Ferret): René Mailhes, interview with author, Paris, 2003. Challain's sister Marie Ferret was René's mother.

Chapter 10. *La Dernière Valse des Niglos*

178 a special kinship with the *niglo*: Not to get too egg-headed here, but pessimistic Prussian philosopher Arthur Schopenhauer would likely have found all of this of great fascination. Schopenhauer's analogy of "The Hedgehog's Dilemma" could sum up this relationship between the Romani and *gadjo* cultures quite well. Based on the hedgehog's protective behavior of rolling itself into a spiny ball when attacked, Schopenhauer prophesized that the closer two people come together, the more likely they are to injure each other—and yet if they remain apart, they will each suffer the pain of loneliness. Schopenhauer, *Parerga and Paralipomena*, Volume II, Chapter XXXI, Section 396.

178 *niglos*: There are two plural forms of *niglo* that appear to be commonly used—*niglos* and *niglé*. In conversation, I most often heard *niglos* and so use that here.

179 Django caught *niglos*: Juliette Lasserre, interview with Anne Legrand; correspondence with author, 2004.

179 "Before cooking the *niglo*": Serge, *La grande histoire des bohémiens*, 93–43. Romani Joseph "Coucou" Doerr also recommends the benefits of moonglow in his memoir, *Où vas-tu manouche?* 19–20.

179 The classic recipe: Francis-Alfred Moerman, interview with author, Paris, 2001. See also Poueyto, *Latcho rhaben*. Hedgehog hunting and cuisine is described by Williams, *Nous, on n'en parle pas*, 37–44; and Yoors, *The Gypsies*, 15–16.

185 *un petit animal sauvage*: Léo Slabiak, correspondence with author, 2002.

186 "In the markets": Fandosa, *Un Gitano con madera de Santo*.

190 "detention, transportation, and keeping": http://ec.europa.eu/environment/nature/conservation/species/ema/about.htm and http://ec.europa.eu/environment/nature/home.htm (accessed June 30, 2007).

Chapter 11. Au Son des Guitares

Much of the information for this chapter comes from conversations and correspondence with Patotte Bousquet's longtime accompanist, Gérard Cardi, in Marseille in 2006–2007.

195 "If you are interested in how the other side of the world lives": Woon, *From Deauville to Monte Carlo*, 242.

198 Patotte Bousquet: Gérard Cardi spells Bousquet's nickname "Petôtte," perhaps better capturing the nuance of the local pronunciation. Gérard Cardi, correspondence with author, 2007.

199 He was born in 1925: Gérard Cardi, correspondence with author, 2007.

199 At fifteen, he and accordionist Émile Decotty: Antonietto, *Gipsy Jazz School* booklet, 16.

199 they played *every* night: Gérard Cardi, correspondence with author, 2007.

200 Marcel Bianchi: Charle, "Marcel Bianchi," 32–35.

201 Paul Pata: Francis-Alfred Moerman, interview with author, Paris, 2001.

202 The release of *Hommage à Django*: Gérard Cardi, correspondence with author, 2007.

203 "Now there was *un guitariste*": Christian Escoudé, interview with author, Paris, 2007.

203 Bousquet passed away: Gérard Cardi, correspondence with author, 2007; Alain Cola, correspondence with author, 1999.

Chapter 12. The Unsung Master of the Gypsy Waltz

Information in this chapter comes from several conversations with Moréno Winterstein in Paris, 1999–2006.

206 "All I ever thought about": Moréno Winterstein, *Moréno Boléro*.

206 Moréno was born in 1963: Moréno Winterstein, interview with author, Paris, 1999.

208 According to legend: Moréno Winterstein, interview with author, Paris, 1999.

209 Tony "Tieno" Fallone: Billard and Roussin, *Histoires de l'Accordéon*, 387. Fallone wouldn't record again until he was seventy-nine and released his beautiful 2003 CD *Accordéon mon ami*.

209 *Swinging Guitars* and *Nomades . . .* : Ruppli, *Discographies Vol. 2: Vogue*, 201.

210 "La gitane": On *Nomades . . .*, "La gitane" was incorrectly labeled as "Les yeux de Dolorès."

210 "The first time I heard Tchan Tchou": Moréno Winterstein, interview with author, Paris, 1999.

211 "I decided to stay in Toulon": Moréno Winterstein, *Moréno Boléro*.

211 *Yochka*: On *Yochka*, Moréno was backed by a talented young Manosque guitarist named Potzi, who has gone on to play in the French pop group Paris Combo, blending Gypsy jazz, Edith Piaf-style torch songs, and what might be termed "grunge musette."

Chapter 13. The Lost

This chapter is based on interviews with Dallas Baumgartner and Tchocolo Winterstein in Paris and Montmagny, 2007. Thanks are due as well to Madame Marie-Thérèse "Minou" Garcia and Augustine "Poupée" Renaud for a fine dinner. Background information comes thanks to Francis-Alfred Moerman.

217 Florine Mayer: Florine Mayer's given name also appears at times as "Fleurine."

217 136 rue Jules Vallès: Delaunay stated that they set up home outside the Porte de Choisy, but according to both Bella and Django's Hôpital Lariboisière admittance records, they

gave their address as 136 rue Jules Vallès in Saint-Ouen, just outside the Porte de Clignancourt surrounding the *marché aux puces*.

217 *l'Ourson*: Salgues, "La légende de Django Reinhardt," *Jazz Magazine* N. 35, 27.

218 Lousson's historical path is next seen in a photo: These photographs are reprinted in Dregni, *Django Reinhardt and the Illustrated History of Gypsy Jazz*, 135 and 129.

218 Django and Naguine's formal marriage: In his memoir, Delaunay stated that Django and Naguine's official marriage took place on July 22, but the wedding certificate states June 21. Balen, *Django Reinhardt*, 157.

218 Babik hired French attorney André Schmidt: André Schmidt, July 28, 1982, letter to Babik Reinhardt. Charles Delaunay letter to court (n.d.). Fonds Charles Delaunay, Bibliothéque Nationale de France. There have long been rumors that Lousson and Babik were not Django's only surviving sons. Several Romani told me that Django also had a son by one of Bella's sisters. Others are more expansive and yet vague, stating he had dozens of children by various Gypsy women.

Chapter 14. Minstrel

My thanks to Bamboula Ferret for our several conversations that made up this chapter. This chapter includes as well background from Hervé Legeay and M. C. Gayffier's interview in "La valse à Bamboula" from *French Guitare*. Thanks are also due to Koen and Waso De Kauter for their letters telling their history. Stochelo Rosenberg's story comes from his musical autobiography, *Stochelo Rosenberg*.

Chapter 15. Resurrection

Conversations with the four musicians here formed the basis of this chapter. I spoke with Biréli Lagrène several times in 2005 while he was on tour in Paris, Southern California, Moscow, and at his home outside Strasbourg. Romane was kind enough to come into Paris from his home in Samois-sur-Seine to meet with me at his record label's offices in 2000. Ninine Garcia took time out from playing at La Chope des Puces to talk numerous times, 1999–2007.

234 a minor miracle for Gypsies: Williams, "Un héritage sans transmission."

241 "Forget about Stochelo Rosenberg": www.stochelorosenberg.com (accessed April 6, 2007).

244 *"le p'tit café mythique"*: Thomas Dutronic, *My Dream of Love* liner notes.

Chapter 16. The Music Thieves

Naturally, much of this chapter comes from numerous conversations with Danny Fender, in San Francisco and East Los Angeles, 2006–2007. In piecing together Julio Bella's journey, my thanks to John Bajo; Bill Margitza, Randy, Ross Michael, and Arlene Margitza; as well as Anthony Barnett and Kevin Coffey. Background information on Romani music in the United States and elsewhere around the globe also came from several conversations with Bill Duna over the years, 1995–2007.

250 their population is estimated at one million: Hancock, "The Schooling of Romani Americans."

254 Romani began migrating to North America: Hancock, "The Schooling of Romani Americans."

255 "Hava Nagila": Loeffler, "Hava Nagila's Long, Strange Trip."

259 real name of William Margitza (Ziggy Bela): William Margitza was born on June 14, 1910, and died in August 1989.

260 *The Hot Jazz Violin of Julio Bella and his Quartette*: Edwards and Callahan, "Fortune Album Discography." The tracks making up this LP were recorded sometime in the late 1950s, according to Julius's brother, Bill Margitza, who played piano on the sessions, but they were not released by Fortune Records until about 1964. This likely explains the LP's crude equalization and monoaural recording. Others state the sessions indeed took place in 1963–1964.

260 Ziggy disowned Julio: John Bajo, interview with author, 2000.

260 Ziggy's "disappointment" was deep: Bill Margitza, interview with author, 2007.

261 "I grew up hearing my grandfather": Rick Margitza, correspondence with author, 2007; and Jung, "A Fireside Chat with Rick Margitza."

261 "The story behind this record": Rick Margitza, correspondence with author, 2007; and Rick Margitza interview, www.palmetto-records.net/artist.php?id=40&album=61 (accessed April 18, 2007).

Chapter 17. Gypsy Jazz Rap

My thanks to Syntax and Laurent Soullier for our conversations in Paris in 2007, which make up the basis of this chapter.

270 *voyageurs* were hit with a new law: "La taxe d'habitation pour les gens du voyage pourrait n'être appliquée qu'à compter de 2007," Association des Maries de France, December 12, 2005: www.maire-info.com/article.asp?param=6426&PARAM2=PLUS (accessed April 5, 2007); "Les gens du voyage manifestent contre la taxe d'habitation sur les caravanes," *Le Monde*, December 7, 2005: www.lemonde.fr/cgi-bin/ACHATS/acheter.cgi?offre=ARCHIVES&type_item=ART_ARCH_30J&objet_id=925807 (accessed April 5, 2007); Jacqueline Charlemagne, "Le droit au logement des gens du voyage: Un droit en trompe l'œil ?" *Les Etudes Tsiganes*: www.etudestsiganes.asso.fr/tablesrevue/jcvol15.html (accessed April 5, 2007).

276 "Syntax has literally invented *rap manouche*": Karim Madani, "Chtar Aacademy," *Groove*, December 2004.

276 "*Gens du voyage* is a debut": Jean-Eric Perrin, "Nomade's Land," *Rolling Stone* (France), January 2005.

Chapter 18. The Most Dangerous Guitar Lesson

This chapter is of course thanks to David Reinhardt and our meetings in 2005 and 2006. Background information also comes thanks to Noë Reinhardt, Pierre "Kamlo" Barré, and Samy Daussat.

286 "What key do you want to play in?": Django and Ellington quoted in "Jazz by Django."

RECOMMENDED LISTENING

THIS IS A PERSONAL list of some of my favorite recordings, organized by chapter. Today, many of these albums are easily available in the United States, thanks to Internet sellers. Some have even been licensed to American labels; when this is the case, I provide both the original and U.S. labels.

Chapter 2 *The Boy with the Banjo*

Gypsy jazz may begin with Django Reinhardt, but Django's own inspirations wander back in time to earlier Romani music. An invaluable collection of historic recordings of early Tziganes music from Django's era was assembled by France's premier Gypsy jazz historian, Alain Antonietto, on *Tziganes: Paris–Berlin–Budapest 1910–1935* (Frémeaux & Associés). This two-CD set is a wondrous venture into another time and world, and includes impossibly rare recordings of Georges Boulanger's "Les yeux noirs" and "Sombre dimanche." For Gitanos flamenco music of the same era, I recommend tracking down early recordings by Ramón Montoya or better yet, his follower and Django's contemporary, Sabicas.

At the time of this writing, Poulette Castro's recordings have yet to be reissued.

Chapter 3 Bals Musette

There are numerous collections of both old and current musette available. Above all others, I recommend *Accordéon Musette Swing 1913–1941* (Frémeaux & Associés), a two-CD set that includes classics by Émile Vacher as well as later swing musette pieces by Gus Viseur, Jo Privat, Tony Muréna, and more. This set also features Django backing Jean Vaissade on "Ma régulière," arguably Django's best musette playing, as well as Guérino's "Brise napolitaine" with Baro Ferret and Django.

For modern musette, there's the beautiful series of three CDs entitled *Paris Musette* (Just a Memory/La Lichère) with classic tunes recreated by Privat along with guitarists Didi Duprat, Didier Roussin, and others.

Chapter 4 Jazz Modernistique

There are available around 700 tracks featuring Django and often numerous recordings of the same song with different bands from different periods. Thus, deciphering which version of which song you're getting is not for the faint of heart. On the other hand, almost all of his recordings are good, if not great, so it's a fine problem to have.

There are many one-CD "greatest hits" collections of Django, and while they're all usually good, they often include only licensed songs from one period. And collecting even a sample of Django's various forays into swing, bebop, and modern jazz is not easy.

For the classic Quintette du Hot Club de France sides, I recommend *Django Reinhardt: The Classic Early Recordings in Chronological Order* (JSP Records). This four-CD boxed set is inexpensive yet has perhaps the best sound quality of any re-release of these sides.

If you want (most) every song Django every played on, you're in luck. France's Frémeaux & Associés has launched *Intégrale Django Reinhardt/The Complete Django Reinhardt*, twenty two-CD sets featuring all known tracks by Django's bands as well as any session he played on by other artists. Sound quality's good, liner notes and discography are excellent.

Chapter 5 Songs of One Thousand and One Nights

Django's swing sides with his clarinet-driven Nouveau Quintette are notoriously difficult to find. And what a shame, as this is some of his sweetest music. I recommend *Django Reinhardt Volume 2: Paris and London 1937–1948* (JSP Records), the companion to the early sides noted above.

Schnuckenack Reinhardt's recordings have been faithfully kept in print by his label all these years. I suggest his *Musik Deutscher Zigeuner 1* (RBM), the first in a six-series set.

Chapter 6 Gypsy Bebop

If Django's swing sides are rarities, his bebop is almost impossible to track down. In fact, many diehard jazz fans are even surprised to hear he recorded bebop. Happily, there's a single CD that includes the best of Django's bebop as well as his last modern jazz sessions, *Django Reinhardt & The Hot Club of France Quintet* [sic] *Brussels 1947, Paris 1951, 1952, 1953* (DRG Records). Never mind the long title or the fact that many of these sides were not with the Quintette; the music remains some of my favorite.

At this time, Baro Ferret's original 1940s–1950s *valses bebop* have not been reissued, which is a crime. His 1965 LP has been, however: *Swing valses d'hier et d'aujourd'hui* (Hot Club Records).

Most of Joseph Reinhardt's recordings have never been re-released—and are deserving. Among Django's other cohorts, I particularly love Oscar Alemán's *Swing Guitar Masterpieces 1938–1957* (Acoustic Disc), Henri Crolla's *Begin the Beguine* (Gitanes) collecting his early Vega sides, and the recent Léo Slab Quintet album, *La Roulotte* (self-produced) with guitarist Philippe Guignier.

Any CD by René Mailhes is a wonder. If I had to pick just one, I recommend *Gitrane* (Iris Musique).

Chapter 8 Crossroads

Numerous live "field" recordings of Gypsy religious music from Les Saintes-Maries-de-la-Mer have been issued over the years on French labels, but I don't know of any including Django's music recreated as hymns.

Chapter 9 Dynasty

Baro, Sarane, and Matelo Ferret have sadly been neglected by record labels in reissuing a comprehensive collection of their recordings. Hopefully, this will change. For now, the best one-CD collection is *Jazz Gitan 1939–1943* (EPM Musique), No. 144 in the label's Jazz Archives Series. This includes rare sides by the Trio Ferret as well as Sarane and Matelo's wartime jazz ensembles.

Gipsy Jazz School: Django's Legacy (Iris Music) is a two-CD set with rare songs by Django's followers, including everyone from the Ferret brothers to Tchan Tchou, Bousquet, Jacques Montagne, Lousson Baumgartner, Henri Crolla, Eugene Vées with Léo Slab, and more. It also features Django's mass, and a 101-page booklet of history and photos by Alain Antonietto. Required listening.

Matelo Ferret's *Tziganskaïa and Other Rare Recordings 1960–1978* (Hot Club Records) includes versions of Django's musette waltzes and most (but not all) of Matelo's masterpiece double-LP. The recording of Matelo Ferret's sessions with Jo Privat, *Manouche Partie* (Disques Nocturne), is an essential.

My favorite recording by Boulou and Élios Ferré is *Pour Django* (Steeplechase), one of the most adventurous Gypsy bebop albums ever.

Selecting just one album by Francis-Alfred Moerman is a sin. I love his *Gitan & Tsigane: Magie de la guitare* (Griffe), but his recent *The Best of Francis-Alfred Moerman* (Djaz Records) is easier to find and a fine place to start.

Chapter 10 La Dernière Valse des Niglos

For all of the Malha clan's influence on Gypsy jazz, there are sadly few surviving recordings. "La valse des niglos" by the Trio Ferret is on *Jazz Gitan 1939–1943* noted above; it's also recreated on the *Paris Musette* series.

Chapter 11 Au Son des Guitares

None of Bousquet's influential EPs or LPs are currently in print, another crime. Two powerful tracks by Bousquet are included on *Gipsy Jazz School*.

Chapter 12 The Unsung Master of the Gypsy Waltz

Happily, Tchan Tchou's first EP and LP have recently been reissued on one CD, *La Gitane* (Iris Music). My favorite album by Moréno is the recent *Le fils du vent* (Nord Sud), which includes samples of his Gypsy jazz, Balkan Tziganes music, some *valses manouche*, and a tribute to his mentor in "Sheik of Araby."

Chapter 13 The Lost

There is only a handful of known recordings by Lousson Baumgartner, and one appears on *Gipsy Jazz School*. Dallas Baumgartner's CD *Dallas Trio* (self-released) is pure old-time *puces* energy. It's also part of the Gypsy jazz tradition of homemade albums and is nearly impossible to find.

Chapter 14 Minstrel

Bamboula Ferret's *Oe Djoevia* (self-released) is one of the masterpieces of Gypsy jazz. And, sadly, it's one of the most difficult albums to track down. Produced by Bamboula's nephew, Fapy Lafertin, it was only ever for sale at gigs and religious pilgrimages. It's worth spending the rest of your life trying to find, however.

All of the albums by the original Waso lineup were only released as LPs and are out of print. Later Waso releases, orchestrated by Koen De Cauter, are equally hard to track down but well worth the hunt. The band's recent CD, *Ombre et lumiere* (Munich Records), is a fine overview of the band. Waso's *La ronde des jurons* (Map records) with bandoneonista Dick Van Der Harst is fascinating. Koen's side project, *Romani* (Map Records), and his musette recordings with the band Les P'tit Belges (Map Records) are all phenomenal. In fact, anything including Koen is soulful music.

Stochelo Rosenberg's debut, *Seresta* (Hot Club Records), and *Caravan* (Polygram) are both excellent, but my favorite is his recent *Roots* (Iris Music). Stochelo's cousin, Jimmy Rosenberg, released the pyrotechnical wonder, *Sinti* (Columbia).

Chapter 15 Resurrection

Biréli Lagrène is prolific in many genres of jazz. My favorite Gypsy jazz recordings are his first and one of his most recent—*Routes to Django* (Chante du Monde) and *Gipsy Project* (Dreyfus). His concert DVD, *Live Jazz à Vienne*, is also astonishing.

Angelo Debarre's first CD, *Gypsy Guitars* (Hot Club Records), with Serge Camps and bassist Frank Anastasio, remains a classic.

Ninine Garcia is more difficult. He has released a fine CD of smooth electric jazz, *My Dream of Love* (Djaz Records), but it doesn't capture the charm of a weekend afternoon at La Chope des Puces. You've just got to go there, hear Ninine and his father live, and give them a large donation in their tips basket for a copy of their homemade cassette, which is full of beautiful Gypsy jazz. In the same vein, one of my other favorite Gypsy jazz CDs is *Pouro Sinto*, now out of print, capturing a raucous campfire jam session by little-known Manouche musicians.

The Titi Winterstein Quintett's *Djinee tu kowa ziro* (Boulevard) remains one of my favorite CDs of hard-driving Alsatian Gypsy jazz. With three stellar solo guitarists, one of the best Gypsy violinists, and an excellent *gadjo* accordionist, it's tough and tight music.

Among other modern players, I recommend Romane's *Swing for Ninine* (Kardum), Patrick Saussois's *Alma Sinti* (Djaz Records), Rodolphe Raffalli's *À Georges Brassens* (Frémeaux & Associés), Jean-Yves Dubanton and Jean-Claude Laudat's *Mon pote le Gitan* (self-produced), Pierre "Kamlo" Barré's *Salammbô* (self-produced), and Tchavolo Schmitt's stellar soundtrack for the film *Swing* (Warner Music) featuring the glorious "Hasta la vista."

Chapter 16 The Music Thieves

At this writing, none of the music of Danny Fender, Johnny Guitar, John Adomono, or Julio Bella is easily available. Keep searching the Internet for news of one of Danny's concerts, go there yourself, and buy a copy of his homemade CD, *A Band of Gypsy's Past Present & Future*.

Among my favorite American Gypsy jazz bands is the Clearwater Hot Club from the northwoods of Minnesota. The band's debut, *Sammo* (self-produced), features then-nineteen-year-old bandleader Sam Miltich.

Chapter 17 Gypsy Jazz Rap

Syntax's landmark CD *Gens du voyage* (Desh Musique/L'Ouïe Fine/Night & Day) is sadly out of print, but copies turn up on eBay.

Among the modern avant-garde, I love Les Primitifs du Futur's *World Musette* (Paris Jazz Corner), Paris Combo's eponymous debut (Tinder Records in the US), and 8½ Souvenirs' *Happy Feet* (Continental).

Chapter 18 The Most Dangerous Guitar Lesson

David Reinhardt's album *David Reinhardt Trio* (RDC Records), with Nöe Reinhardt and Samy Daussat, is a fine collection of smooth modern Gypsy jazz.

RECOMMENDED READING

OR MORE ON DJANGO, I recommend Charles Delaunay's classic memoir *Django Reinhardt* for its first-person account as well as its undeniable charm, even though Delaunay often embroiders the history into hagiography. My friend Alain Antonietto, along with François Billard, authored the excellent study of Django's music, *Django Reinhardt: Rythmes futurs* (text in French only). I also humbly suggest my own biography, *Django: The Life and Music of a Gypsy Legend*.

There are few other books available on the history of Gypsy jazz. I recommend Alain Antonietto's liner booklet to the indispensable CD collection, *Gipsy Jazz School: Django's Legacy*. And again, I also humbly suggest my book with Alain and Anne Legrand, *Django Reinhardt and the Illustrated History of Gypsy Jazz*.

If you are interested in more on French Gypsy life—and read French—Romani author Matéo Maximoff's numerous novels and memoirs are astonishing. I especially recommend his autobiography, *Dites-le avec des pleurs*, now reprinted by his daughter, Nouka, and available through the offices of *Études Tsiganes* in Paris. Also, look into anthropologist Patrick Williams's several studies: "Un héritage sans transmission," *Mariage Tsigane*, and especially, *Nous, on n'en parle pas*. Jan Yoors's classic memoir about living with Gypsies in Belgium, *The Gypsies*, is also fascinating and inspiring.

For more on Balkan Gypsy music, Garth Cartwright's amazing travelogue *Princes amongst Thieves* is fine history, excellent writing, and a great read. And Isabel Fonseca's *Bury Me Standing: The Gypsies and Their Journey* is essential.

Last but far from least, *Gypsy Jazz* is also an homage to Paris, and if you're looking for more on the secret history of the city, I can't recommend enough Thirza Vallois's three-volume guide, *Around and About Paris*, leading you through the streets and alleyways.

BIBLIOGRAPHY

Adams, Sam. "I Meet Reinhardt." *BMG*, March 1946.

André, Jacques. "Les Lundis du jazz: Joseph Reinhardt." *Combat*, January 21, 1967.

Anick, Peter. "Reminiscing with Stéphane Grappelli." *Fiddler Magazine*, Summer 2002.

Antonietto, Alain. "Adieu manouche." *Jazz Notes*, July 2002.

———. "Discographie du jazz Tsiganes." *Études tsiganes*, No. 4, 1987; No. 1, 1988; No. 2, 1988; No. 3, 1988; No. 4, 1988.

———. "Histoire de la musique tsigane instrumentale d'Europe centrale." *Études tsiganes*, No.1, 1994.

———. "Joseph Reinhardt: Le Dernier voyage . . ." *Études tsiganes*, No. 2, 1982.

———. "Laro Sollero." *L'Echo des Cuilleres*, June 2002.

———. "Matelo Ferret de la csardas au jazz . . ." *Études tsiganes*, No. 4, 1982.

———. "Nomadismes, musique et nationalisme." *Études tsiganes,* No. 3, 1987.

———. Liner notes to *Gipsy Jazz School: Django's Legacy*. Paris: Iris Music, 2002.

Antonietto, Alain, and François Billard. *Django Reinhardt: Rythmes futurs*. Paris: Éditions Fayard, 2004.

Antonietto, Alain, and Dominique Cravic. "Roger Chaput: le premier compagnon . . ." *Jazz Magazine*, No. 448, May 1995.

Asséo, Henriette. *Les Tsiganes: Une destinée européenne*. Paris: Gallimard, 1994.

Balen, Noël. *Django Reinhardt: Le génie vagabond*. Monaco: Éditions du Rocher, 2003.

Battestini, Jean-Pierre. "Emmanuel Soudieux: Django, Stéphane . . ." *Jazz Dixie/ Swing,* No. 36.

Bedin, Michel. "Django à Rome: Alf 'Totol' Masselier et Roger Paraboschi." *Jazz Hot,* No. 600, May 2003.

Beevor, Antony. *The Fall of Berlin 1945*. New York: Viking, 2002.

Bergerot, Franck. Liner notes to *Paris Musette Volume 2: Swing et manouche*. Paris: Éditions La Lichère, 1993.

Billard, François, and Alain Antonietto. *Django Reinhardt: Un géant sur son nuage*. Paris: Lien Commun, 1993.

Billard, François, and Didier Roussin. *Histoires de l'accordéon*. Castelnau-le-Lez, France: Éditions Climats, 1991.

Brassaï. *Le Paris secret des années 30*. Paris: Éditions Gallimard, 1976.

Bricktop, with James Haskins. *Bricktop*. New York: Atheneum, 1983.

Bureau, Jacques. "Champagne!" *So What*, No. 27, October 1998.

———. *Un soldat menteur*. Paris: Robert Laffont, 1992.

Caen, Herb. "An Evening in Paris Has Some Solid Kicks." *Down Beat*, March 1, 1945.

Carco, Francis. *Nostalgie de Paris*. Geneva: Éditions du Milieu de Monde, 1941.

———. *Panam*. Paris: Librarie Stock, 1922.

Cartwright, Garth. *Princes amongst Men: Journeys with Gypsy Musicians*. London: Serpent's Tail, 2005.

Charle, François. "Marcel Bianchi: Premier guitariste électrique français." *Trad Magazine*, No. 44, January–February 1996.

———. *The Story of Selmer Maccaferri Guitars*. Paris: Self-published, 1999.

Charle, François, with Paul Hostetter. "Selmer Guitars." *Vintage Gallery*, April 1994.

"Chez Bouscatel, un soir." *La Haute Loire*, September 17, 1906.

Clergue, Lucien. *Roots: The Gipsy Kings and Their Journey*. New York: Onstage Presentation, 2004.

Corbier, Robert. "A Thonon-les-Bains: Django Reinhardt; premier guitariste du monde, veut composer une messe pour les 'romanis.'" Reprinted in Jean-Claude Rey, "Folie à Amphion: Django Reinhardt en Haute-Savoie au cours de l'année 1943," Société d'Histoire Locale La Salévienne/*Échos Seléviens*, No. 9, 2000.

Cravic, Dominique. "Charley Bazin, l'épopée de l'accordéon." *Accordéon Magazine*, No. 40, February 1999, and No. 41, March 1999.

———. Unpublished interview with Roger Chaput. 1995.

Crosland, Margaret. *Piaf*. New York: Fromm International, 1987.

de Foletier, François de Vaux. *Les Tsiganes dans l'ancienne France*. Paris: Connaissance du Monde, 1961.

Delaunay, Charles. *. . . de la vie et du jazz*. Paris: Éditions Hot Jazz, 1939.

———. *Delaunay's dilemma: De la peinture au jazz*. Mâcon: Éditions W, 1985.

———. *Django mon frère*. Paris: Eric Losfeld Editeur/Le Terrain Vague, 1968.

———. *Django Reinhardt*. London: Cassell & Company, 1961.

———. *Django Reinhardt souvenirs*. Paris: Éditions Jazz Hot, 1954.

———. "French Jazz." *The PL Yearbook of Jazz 1946*. London: Editions Poetry, 1946.

———. "Gus Viseur's Music." *Jazz Hot*, February/March 1939.

———. "Interview de Mme. Reinhardt." Fonds Charles Delaunay, boîte 25, Bibliothéque Nationale de France, Département de l'audiovisuel, no date but likely from 1953–1954.

———. "L'arrivée du BeBop en France." *Jazz Hot*, No. 328, June 1976.

———. "L'histoire du Hot Club de France." *Jazz Hot*, No. 19, January 1948; No. 20, February 1948; No. 21, March 1948.

———. "Le creation de la Marque Swing." Original manuscript, Fonds Charles Delaunay, Bibliothéque Nationale de France, Département de l'audiovisuel, no date [circa October 1947].

———. "Le jazz en France (1932–1944)." *Jazz Hot*, No. 250, 1969.

———. "Les debuts du jazz en France: Souvenirs par André Ekyan, Stéphane Grappelly, Alain Romans, Ray Ventura." *Jazz Hot*, No. 248, March 1969.

———. "The History of the Hot Club de France." *Coda*, November 1974, April 1976, and August 1977.

———. Untitled synopsis of Django's life submitted as planned film biography starring Robert De Niro to producer Louis C. Smith. Fonds Charles Delaunay, Bibliothéque Nationale de France, Département de l'audiovisuel, 1964.

Doerr, Joseph "Coucou." *Où vas-tu, manouche? U Manush djiren le an u kamlepen un frai*. Bourdeaux, France: Éditions Wallada, 1982.

Dregni, Michael. "Boulou and Elios Ferré: In the Footsteps of Django." *Vintage Guitar*, February 1998.

———. *Django: The Life and Music of a Gypsy Legend*. New York: Oxford University Press, 2004.

———. "Moréno: Keeping the Gypsy Fire Burning." *Vintage Guitar*, June 2000.

———. *Django in America*. Minneapolis: Éditions Noir et Blanc, 2001.

Dregni, Michael, with Alain Antonietto and Anne Legrand. *Django Reinhardt and the Illustrated History of Gypsy Jazz*. Denver: Speck Press, 2006.

Dubois, Claude. *Apaches, voyous et gonzes poilus: Le milieu parisien du début du siècle aux années soixante*. Paris: Éditions Parigramme, 1996.

———. *La Bastoche: Bal-musette, plaisir et crime 1750–1939*. Paris: Éditions du Félin, 1997.

Duna, William A. *Gypsies: A Persecuted Race*. Minneapolis, MN: Duna Studios, 1985.

Dutronic, Thomas. Liner notes to Ninine Garcia's *My Dream of Love*. Paris: Djaz Records, 2004.

Edwards, David, and Mike Callahan. "Fortune Album Discography." Last updated 1999. www.bsnpubs.com/fortune.html (accessed April 18, 2007).

Fackler, Guido. Music in Concentration Camps 1933–1945. *Music & Politics*. www.music.ucsb.edu/projects/musicandpolitics/fackler.html (accessed March 23, 2007).

Fandosa, Ángel M. *Un Gitano con madera de Santo*. Barcelona: N.p., 1973.

Fest, Joachim. *Inside Hitler's Bunker: The Last Days of the Third Reich*. New York: Farrar, Straus & Giroux, 2004.

Gillespie, Dizzy, with Al Fraser. *to BE, or not . . . to BOP: Memoirs*. Garden City, NY: Doubleday, 1979.

Goddard, Chris. *Jazz Away from Home*. New York: Paddington Press, 1979.

Gottlieb, Bill. "Delaunay Escapades with Gestapo Related." *Down Beat*, September 9, 1946.

Grappelli, Stéphane. "Django Reinhardt and the Bright Red Socks." *Melody Maker*, March 13, 1954.

———. "Stephane Grappelly Continues the Story of Django: The Early Days of the Quintet." *Melody Maker*, March 6, 1954.

———. "Stephane Grappelly Tells of Django's First Letter." *Melody Maker*, March 27, 1954.

———. "Stephane Grappelly Tells the Tale of Jazzdom's Magic Fingers." *Melody Maker*, March 20, 1954.

———. "Stephane Grappelly Tells—For the First Time—the True Story of Django Reinhardt." *Melody Maker*, February 20, 1954.

Grappelli, Stéphane, with Joseph Oldenhove and Jean-Marc Bramy. *Mon violon pour tout bagage*. Paris: Calmann-Lévy, 1992.

Gumplowicz, Philippe. "Django Guitare." *Le Monde de la Musique*, No. 82, October 1985.

Haederli, Freddy. *Django Reinhardt: The Discography*. Geneva: Self-published, August 2001 edition.

———. *Gus Viseur: The Discography*. Geneva: Self-published, March 1995 edition.

Hancock, Ian. "Jewish Responses to the Porrajmos (The Romani Holocaust)." Minneapolis: Center for Holocaust and Genocide Studies, University of Minnesota. www.chgs.umn.edu/Histories_Narratives_Documn/Roma_Sinti_Gypsies/Jewish_Responses_to_the_Porraj (accessed March 24, 2007).

———. "The Schooling of Romani Americans: An Overview." 1999. Posted at www.geocities.com/~Patrin/schooling.htm (accessed April 20, 2007).

———. *The Pariah Syndrome: An Account of Gypsy Slavery and Persecution*. Ann Arbor, MI: Karoma Publishers, 1987.

———. *We Are the Romani People/Ame sam e Rromane džene*. Hatfield, Hertfordshire: University of Hertfordshire Press, 2003.

Hancock, Ian, Siobhan Dowd, and Rajko Djuric, eds. *The Roads of the Roma*. Hatfield, Hertfordshire: University of Hertfordshire Press, 1998.

Hari, Albert. *L'Église des Saintes-Maries-de-la-Mer*. Strasbourg: Éditions du Signe, 2002.

Heller, Gerhard. *Un allemand a Paris 1940–1944*. Paris: Éditions du Seuil, 1981.

Henshaw, Laurie. "Swing Guitars" column. *Melody Maker*, May 1948.

Hodeir, André. "Vers un renouveau de la musique de jazz?" *Jazz Hot*, May–June 1946.

Hodgkiss, Allan. "Django's Guitar." *BMG*, December 1958.

Hughes, Langston. *The Big Sea: An Autobiography*. New York: Rinehart, 1940.

Hussey, Andrew. *Paris: The Secret History*. New York: Bloomsbury, 2006.

"Jazz by Django." *Newsweek*, November 18, 1946.

Journal d'un bourgeois de Paris, 1405 à 1449. Paris: Livre de Poche, 1990.

Jung, Fred. "A Fireside Chat with Rick Margitza," www.jazzweekly.com/interviews/
margitza.htm (accessed April 18, 2007).

Kater, Michael H. *Different Drummers: Jazz in the Culture of Nazi Germany*. New
York: Oxford University Press, 1992.

Kazansky, Konstantin. *Cabaret russe*. Paris: Éditions Olivier Orban, 1978.

Kenrick, Donald, and Grattan Puxon. *The Destiny of Europe's Gypsies*. New York:
Basic Books, 1972.

King, B. B., with David Ritz. *Blues All Around Me: The Autobiography of B. B. King*.
New York: Avon Books, 1996.

Le Cossec, Clément. *Mon aventure chez les Tziganes*. N.p.: Self-published, 1991.

Legeay, Hervé, and M. C. Gayffier. "La valse à Bamboula." *French Guitare*, N.d.

Legrand, Anne. "Jacques Bureau: Pionnier du jazz." *So What,* No. 22, February
1998, and No. 24, May 1998.

Legrand, Anne. Unpublished interview with Emmanuel Soudieux. Paris, November
1999.

Levi, Erik. *Music in the Third Reich*. New York: St. Martin's Press, 1994.

Loeffler, James. "Hava Nagila's Long, Strange Trip: The Unlikely History of a
Hasidic Melody." hillel.myjewishlearning.com/culture/Music/IsraeliMusicTO/
IsraeliFolkMusic/Hava.htm (accessed April 20, 2007).

Loiseau, Jean-Claude. *Les Zazous*. Paris: Le Sagittaire, 1977.

Maximoff, Matéo. *Dites-le avec des pleurs*. Romainville, France: Self-published,
1990.

Mazzoletti, Adriano. *Il Jazz in Italia: dalle origine al dopoguerra*. Rome: Laterza, 1983.

McKenzie, Aimee L., trans. *The Letters of George Sand and Gustave Flaubert*. New
York: Boni & Liveright, 1921.

Mistral, Frédéric. *The Memoirs of Frédéric Mistral*. Trans. George Wickes. New York:
New Directions, 1986.

Obrecht, Jas, ed. *Blues Guitar: The Men Who Made the Music*. San Francisco: Miller
Freeman Books, 1993.

Öhler, Andreas. *Die Ballade von Schnuckenack Reinhardt* (German television documentary). Berlin: Carsten Krüger Filmproduktion, 2000. (French version *La
ballade de Schnuckenack Reinhardt*. Paris: ZDF, 2000.)

Panassié, Hugues. *Douze années de jazz (1927–1938): Souvenirs*. Paris: Corrêa, 1946.

———. *Monsieur jazz: Entretiens avec Pierre Casalta*. Paris: Éditions Stock, 1975.

Payne, Robert. *The Life and Death of Adolf Hitler*. New York: Barnes & Noble Books,
1973.

Péguri, Louis, and Jean Mag. *Du bouge... au conservatoire*. Paris: World Press, 1950.

Poueyto, Jean-Luc, ed. *Latcho rhaben: Cuisine Tsigane*. Pau, France: L'Instep Formation, 1994.

Privat, Jo. *Jo Privat partitions*. Paris: Paul Beuscher, 1985.

"Reinhardt, Grappelly and Co. Here Again." *Melody Maker*, August 26, 1939.

Rosenberg, Stochelo, Leo Eimers, and Harry Klunder. *Stochelo Rosenberg*. N.p. (The Netherlands): Cento Productions bv, 2005.

Roussin, Didier. Liner notes to *Manouche Partie*. Paris: Disques Nocturne, 1991.

Ruppli, Michel, avec le concours de Charles Delaunay. *Discographies Vol. 1: Swing.* Paris: Association Française des Détenteurs de Documents Audioviseuls et Sonores, 1989.

Ruppli, Michel, avec le concours de Charles Delaunay. *Discographies Vol. 2: Vogue Productions*. Paris: Association Française des Détenteurs de Documents Audioviseuls et Sonores, 1992.

Salgues, Yves. "La légende de Django Reinhardt." *Jazz Magazine,* No. 33, January 1958; No. 34, February 1958; No. 35, March 1958; No. 36, April 1958; No. 37, May 1958; No. 38, June 1958; No. 39, July 1958; No. 40, August 1958; No. 41, September 1958.

Sartre, Jean-Paul. "New York City" in Seghers, Pierre, et al. *Jazz 47*. Paris: Revue America et le Hot-Club de France, 1947.

Sawyer, Charles. *The Arrival of B. B. King: The Authorized Biography*. Garden City, NY: Doubleday, 1980.

Schmann, Coco. *Coco Schumann, der Ghetto-Swinger: Eine Jazzlegende erzählt*. Munich: Deutscher Taschenbuch Verlag, 1999.

Serge. *La grande histoire des bohémiens*. Paris: Éditions Karolus, 1963.

Shack, William A. *Harlem in Montmartre: A Paris Jazz Story between the Great Wars*. Berkeley: University of California Press, 2001.

Sharp, Fred. Unpublished interview with Charles Delaunay, Louis Vola, and Gérard Lévêque. 1967.

Smith, Geoffrey. *Stéphane Grappelli*. London: Pavillion Books, 1987.

Spautz, Roger. *Django Reinhardt: Mythe et réalité*. Luxembourg: RTL Édition, 1983.

Tuzet, Jean-Baptiste. *Jazz manouche: La grande aventure du swing gitan de Django Reinhardt à Tchavolo Schmitt*... Paris: Éditions Didier Carpentier, 2007.

Vaudoyer, Jean-Louis. *Les Saintes-Maries-de-la-Mer*. Paris: Éditions Émile Paul Frères, 1927.

Vernon, Paul. *Jean 'Django' Reinhardt: A Contextual Bio-Discography 1910–1953*. Aldershot, Hampshire: Ashgate, 2003.

Wheeler, Tom, and Jas Obrecht. "B. B. King Interview." *Guitar Player*, September 1980.

Williams, Patrick. "Un héritage sans transmission: le jazz manouche." *Ethnologie française*, No. 3, 2000.

———. *Django Reinhardt*. Marseille: Éditions Parenthèses, 1998.

———. *Mariage Tsigane une cérémonie de fiançailles chez les Rom de Paris*. Paris: L'Harmattan, 2000.

———. *Nous, on n'en parle pas: Les vivants et les morts chez les Manouches*. Paris: Éditions de la Maison des sciences de l'homme, 1993.

Winterstein, Moréno. Liner notes to *Moréno Boléro*. Paris: al sur, 1996.

Woon, Basil. *From Deauville to Monte Carlo: A Guide to the Gay World of France*. New York: Horace Liveright, 1929.

Yoors, Jan. *The Gypsies*. Prospect Heights, IL: Waveland Press, 1967.

Zavatta, Achille. *Viva Zavatta*. Paris: Éditions Robert Laffont, 1976.

ACKNOWLEDGMENTS

T EN YEARS AGO, WE could not even have spoken to you about our
music," Danny Fender is telling me. "And we never could have invited
you into our home. Other Gypsies would have been on the phone, saying
'What are you doing?' We would have been ostracized from our people for
months. But times change."

And happily so, for all of us. I'm sitting in Danny and his wife Janet's dining
room in East Los Angeles. Around the table are Romani musicians Johnny
Guitar, George Fat Joes, and Lonnie Fender as well as Danny's mother and
father and a cabal of children eagerly listening in on our conversation. Everyone's
telling stories about the history of American Gypsy music—Singing Sam Stevens, John "Peeky" Adomono, Johnny himself and his band The Fantastics.
Wild times, good and bad. And they're playing songs on their guitars, from old-
time Yugoslavian Gypsy tunes to Chet Atkins country songs, Ventures surf
romps to their own compositions. Here is history alive and being shared—and
not just with me, the sole *gadjo*, but also with the future generations. And during
a break in the music, the teenagers borrow the guitars and start playing.

I was fortunate enough to be invited into many people's homes and caravans
and be part of scenes such as this. From Danny to David Reinhardt, René Mailhes
to Dallas Baumgartner, Paris to Les Saintes-Maries to East L.A. and beyond.
I truly can't find suitable words to express my gratitude for all of your sharing
and friendship.

This book began as a quest for a guitar lesson, but I learned so much more
along the way.

Among the Manouches and Gitans of France, my thanks to *la famille* Reinhardt and especially David Reinhardt; the family of Florine "Bella" Mayer—

Augustine "Poupée" Renaud, Mare-Thérèse "Minou" Garcia, Jeannot Garcia, and Michel Heil; the family of Lousson Baumgartner—Madame Rose and Dallas Baumgartner; Boulou and Élios Ferré; René Mailhes; Ninine and Mondine Garcia; Moréno Winterstein; Bamboula Ferret; Tchocolo Winterstein; Jeannot Malla; Christian Escoudé; Biréli Lagrène; Angelo Debarre; and Syntax.

In the American Gypsy world, I thank Danny and Janet Fender; Johnny Guitar; George Fat Joes; Bill Duna; Ian Hancock; Johnny Ugly; Paul Stevens; Robert Adams; Kevin Adams; Rick Margitza and others of the Margitza clan— Bill, Randy, Ross Michael, and Arlene Margitza.

Among Django's fellow musicians and the Hot Club de France founders, I was fortunate to spend thoroughly enjoyable and uproarious times with Jacques Bureau in Meudon-sur-Seine reminiscing about the history of jazz, surrealism, and politics in France. I thank Elwyn Dirats for evoking Paris in the 1920s and Django. For sharing memories, my thanks to Frank Ténot of *Jazz Magazine* and André Clergeat, Disques Vogue artistic director. I cannot thank enough Emmanuel Soudieux. At a mere eighty-five years of age, Monsieur Soudieux not only regaled me with phenomenal stories of Django but also acted most of them out in his Montparnasse apartment. He passed away in 2006. I also thank Beryl Davis, Franco Cerri, Roger Paraboschi, Coleridge Goode, Colette Crolla, and Léo Slabiak for his spirited correspondence.

I offer my thanks to Gypsy jazz musicians Dominique Cravic; Gérard Cardi and Jeanne Pénavaire; Pierre Barré; Patrick Saussois; Sam Miltich and all the members of the Clearwater Hot Club; Samy Daussat; John Jorgenson; Koen and Waso De Cauter; Romane; Jean-Claude Beneteau; Jon Larsen; Rodolphe Raffalli; and Fere Scheidegger.

Anyone who writes history owes a debt to the researchers and historians who came before, and I offer my thanks above all to Alain Antonietto, the master historian of *jazz tsigane*.

I owe a great debt to Francis-Alfred Moerman for his long reminiscences, tours of his old haunts in Paris, and musette guitar lessons.

I thank as well Anne Legrand for all of her time, assistance, and friendship during several visits to the Fonds Charles Delaunay at the Bibliothèque Nationale de France; François Charle; Laurent Soullier; Jean-Pierre Favino; Luc Degeorges; Sophie Riché and Agnès Masson at Archives de l'Assistance Publique–Hôpitaux de Paris; Christian Gauffre at *Jazz Magazine*; Alexis Blanchart at Iris Music; Evelyne Pommeret at *Études tsiganes*; Christian Dupont, Mayor of Pont-à-Celles; Freddy Haederli; Charlie Byrd; Les Paul; Chet Atkins; Oscar Peterson and Joanne Bain; Alain Cola; John Reeves; François Rousseau; Jacques Mazzoleni; Paul Vernon; John Bajo; Michael Horowitz; Ando Monta; Louis Clark Smith; Patrick Williams; Tony Baldwin; and Garth Cartwright.

I owe special thanks to a handful of fellow historians—Scot Wise and Ted Gottsegen—both of whom reviewed this book in early stages and helped immensely all along the way.

My thanks to Valérie Ferment, Pierre-François van de Moortele, and Jean-Christophe Germain for their assistance, good food, and good times.

At Oxford University Press, I cannot thank enough my editor, Suzanne Ryan, for her wisdom, guidance, and, especially, patience as I dropped everything to set off to follow a new lead. Thanks as well to everyone else at Oxford, including Norm Hirschy, Joellyn Ausanka, Darren Shannon, and Kim Craven.

Last but not least, a thanks to my family—Sigrid, Nico, and Marco—for the time they've allowed me and the adventures they've shared in search of the music.

INDEX